THE PEN AND THE SWORD

Michael Foot

THE PEN
AND THE SWORD

Jonathan Swift
and the power of the Press

'These were not days when public men
could afford to disdain the Press.'

WINSTON CHURCHILL, *Marlborough; His
Life and Times*

COLLINS
8 Grafton Street London W1
1984

William Collins Sons & Co Ltd
London · Glasgow · Sydney · Auckland
Toronto · Johannesburg

Foot, Michael
The pen and the sword.
1. Swift, Jonathan–Political and social
views 2. Great Britain–Politics and
government–1702-1714

First published 1957
Second edition 1966
Third edition 1984
© MacGibbon & Kee 1957

ISBN 0 00 217357 3

First printed by Compton Printing Works
(London) Ltd, London N1

Reprinted by
Robert Hartnoll Ltd., Bodmin

To my father and Jill

Contents

Acknowledgements

A LIST of the authorities consulted for this book is given on page 377. In particular, I must acknowledge my debt to Sir Winston Churchill's *Marlborough; His Life and Times*, published by George G. Harrap & Co. Ltd., and to the editions of the *Journal to Stella* and *The Poems of Jonathan Swift*, edited by Harold Williams and published by Oxford University Press.

My father encouraged me to write this book and he has supplied me with much information, his own notes on the subject and many volumes from his library.

Mr. Richard Findlater was kind enough to read the typescript and offer much valuable advice.

Special thanks are due to Elizabeth Thomas. Without her skill and endurance the task would have been impossible.

Illustrations

The illustrations are reproduced by kind permission of the National Portrait Gallery – Jonathan Swift, Duke of Marlborough, Duchess of Marlborough, Daniel Defoe, Duke of Somerset, Duchess of Somerset, Henry St John, Viscount Bolingbroke, Robert Harley, Earl of Oxford, Thomas, Earl of Wharton, and Queen Anne; Hulton Picture Library – Stella, Esther Johnson.

All the captions to the illustrations are quotations from the writings of Jonathan Swift.

CHAPTER ONE

The Vicar of Laracor

'The person I mean is Dr. Swift, a dignified clergyman, but one who, by his own confession, has composed more libels than sermons. If it be true, what I have heard often affirmed by innocent people, "that too much wit is dangerous to salvation", this unfortunate gentleman must certainly be damned to all eternity.'

—ALEXANDER POPE

AT THE AGE OF FORTY-ONE, in the year 1709, Jonathan Swift, Vicar of Laracor, sat for his portrait to Charles Jervas, a fellow-countryman from Ireland just starting to win fame in the great world of Queen Anne's London. The artist was eight years younger than the clergyman; but few intruders at the sittings could have guessed that the name of one would be well-nigh forgotten while that of the other was destined for immortality. Jervas was the pupil of Sir Godfrey Kneller, and when his master died he succeeded him as the most fashionable portrait-painter of the age. Alexander Pope prophesied that the ladies he flattered so lavishly would retain their bloom on his canvas for a thousand years, and no inclination to dissent from the judgement was noticeable in Mr. Jervas. He had recently returned from Italy where he had dropped the hint that a new Titian had appeared on the European scene. In London duchesses eagerly dispatched their daughters to his studio; his gallantry was celebrated no less than his genius; and when he escaped for brief spells to his native land a queue of court beauties sighed for his return. It is safe to assume that he was not in the habit of wasting his talents on visiting country parsons from the outskirts of Dublin. Swift, then, was already a figure in London society. His conversational prowess was established in the coffee-houses; over a number of years he had 'grown domestic' with a few of the leading Whig Lords; William Congreve and Richard Steele were among his drinking companions and Joseph Addison he claimed as his 'most intimate friend'; he was, moreover, the suspected author of a few political and religious pamphlets and one outstanding satire, *The Tale of a Tub*.

And yet it is not easy to measure Swift's reputation among his contemporaries at the time when Jervas paid him the compliment of painting his portrait. Nothing except one forgotten poem and a painstaking edition of the works of Sir William Temple had been published under his own name. When his pamphlets had appeared the buzz of rumour occasionally included him among the possible authors; only in one or two cases did a rare burst of vanity or the hope of preferment persuade him to divulge the truth, and even then the revelation was made only with the utmost circumspection. Journalists in that age risked the pillory just as statesmen risked impeachment; their ears, if not their heads, were at stake. Swift had a special reason for disowning his chief claim to eminence. A few prominent persons, headed by one or two peers of the realm, were smarting under the savage or indecent assaults which his pen had unloosed upon them, which may have had a considerable circulation in manuscript, and which, if the anonymous assailant had been unmasked, might have been expiated only by a duel. As for *The Tale of a Tub*, many years after Swift's death Dr. Johnson was still able to contest Swift's authorship; in his lifetime some doubts remained among those with the most solid reasons for exposing 'the impious buffoon' responsible. True, Addison had acclaimed him the most agreeable of companions, the truest of friends and the greatest genius of the age. Swift had responded in the same ecstatic terms. But the exchange of compliments proves little. 'The reciprocal civility of authors,' said Dr. Johnson, 'is the most risible scene in the whole farce of life'; so Addison's flattery would be dismissed if posterity had to pass final judgement on the Swift of 1709. Addison probably knew Swift's secrets as well as any man. He may have discerned before the rest how formidable this 'mad parson' really was. But to London society he appeared as a somewhat bizarre, if captivating, clergyman who dabbled in high politics and low lampoons, rubbed shoulders with the great, was occasionally to be seen at their dining-tables and who yet lived quietly in his own garret on an outlay of no more than £30 from one quarter day to another.

The truth is that Swift's leading ambitions were not literary at all. He had schooled himself to be a poet and then almost abandoned the enterprise in despair. Thereafter his literary efforts were usually undertaken to serve a well-defined purpose in some controversy of the hour. A Bishopric, with all its attendant influence in world affairs, was his real aim, and the failure of his rich friends to bestow that reward hurt him much more than the violence of the critics who were too furiously assaulted to appreciate his prose. He wanted 'a great title and fortune that I might be treated like a lord'; and yet after ten years' pursuit of that dream in Dublin and London he was still no more than Vicar of Laracor. Certainly in the England of 1709 he had not achieved enduring fame and greatness; he was a minor star in that spacious firmament. 'A nation of five and a half millions', wrote G. M. Trevelyan, 'that had Wren for its architect, Newton for its scientist, Locke for its philosopher, Bentley for its scholar, Pope for its satirst, Addison for its essayist, Bolingbroke for its orator, Swift for its pamphleteer and Marlborough to win its battles, had the recipe for genius'. Swift had not yet found his place in that gallery. In June 1709 he returned to Ireland where he feared he would be condemned to a life 'wholly useless'. The ships that sailed from Holyhead to Dublin Bay were often in danger of being captured by French privateers. If Jonathan Swift had been taken as part of the loot, no great loss would have been felt in the establishment of Church and State on either side of the Irish Sea.

It is necessary to look at the records more closely to discover why when he made that journey the Vicar of Laracor, despite the mark he had made, still counted himself a failure.

*　　*　　*

The face that appears in Jervas's portrait is worldly, self-confident, almost good-humoured, with a general air which may best be described as imperious. If Swift was the prince of misanthropes, as later generations were seemingly so eager to believe, if he had been soured and frustrated by his upbringing, no trace of that temper is evident here. Macaulay pictured the arrival on the political scene of a dark, fierce spirit, 'the perjured lover, a heart burning with hatred against the whole human race, a mind richly stored with images from the dunghill and the lazar house.' If such a monster ever lived, he was, according to Jervas's testimony, brilliantly disguised. A high dome-like forehead, black bushy eyebrows; the eyes themselves piercing, well set apart and, in Pope's phrase, 'quite azure as the heavens'; the nose almost pointed; the lips, the nostrils and the chin all delicately, even tenderly, curved; the cheeks rosy and full; such is the head, held erect beneath a flowing white wig.

Pope pronounced it 'very like', but the compliment may have been designed to gratify both the artist and his subject. Others did not share the same fulsome opinion of Jervas's ability. 'You are a practical believer,' said Dr. Arbuthnot to the painter when he had occasion to taunt him for his blasphemous Whig extremism; 'you strictly observe the second commandment, for, in your pictures, you make not the likeness of anything in heaven above, or in earth below, or in the waters under the earth.' However true the charge, Jervas certainly suffered from other failings; he was not for nothing the pupil of Sir Godfrey Kneller. Sir Godfrey bestowed a pink complexion, dimples and a double chin on almost all his heroes; probably Jervas was eager to prove that he could attain the same ideal. Yet, taking into account the likelihood that Jervas gave to Swift the same benefit of all the doubts which he accorded to the duchesses, it is impossible to dismiss this evidence that here was a man of commanding presence, a man of action and authority. No one surely could forget that face; all Mr. Jervas's conventional tastes could not obscure the indelible sign of mastery. He might have been not a needy clergyman, recently cheated of a Deanery, but the Lord Chancellor of England, one capable of holding his own with the great landowner barons of the time who exercised the right to make and unmake Kings. In such a manner indeed did he rule his own little Irish empire across the sea.

Laracor itself was not much more than a hamlet, one day's journey out of Dublin. The church at the crossroads was a low slated building without any claims to architectural merit, the Vicar's house a mere cottage surrounded by what Swift sometimes contemptuously dismissed as 'half an acre of Irish bog'. When first appointed to the post in the winter of the year 1700 he was shocked at the spectacle of his dilapidated prize. He quickly went to work with his usual fastidious energy, repairing the church, planting cherry trees, apple trees and ranks of willows in double rows, strengthening the river bank to make easier his pastime of catching trout. He grew to love Laracor, despite the fact that it always symbolized for him his failure in the pursuit of Church preferment. After all, it gave him the independence which he treasured with the same miserly care he showed towards all worldly goods. Together with the neighbouring Vicarage of Rathbeggan and Rectory of Agher which made up his domain it brought him an income of between £200 and £300 a year. Forty pounds out of that total went to pay the salary of his curate; another £20 or £30 at least each year was disposed of in charity. Swift was prudent almost to the point of avarice and for him the £200 was enough; enough to enable him to make the journey to London every few years and conduct his political forays with the assurance of a free man.

How diligently he performed his role as Vicar has long been a matter of dispute. But, whatever the verdict, it is hard to believe that he got much satisfaction from ministering to his score of parishioners. He was a Protestant priest in a Catholic countryside; an alien in the land of his birth. Just after the battle of the Boyne in 1690, when Catholic armies were being driven into the sea, he had shaken the dirt of Ireland off his feet as he doubtless hoped for ever. Pride and disappointment had made him return ten years later, but it must often have driven him to fury to constrict his restless nature within the compass offered by his clerical duties; only after many years did he acquire a kinship with the poverty around him and assume the unexpected mantle of an Irish patriot. 'I am this minute', he wrote to one of his friends at a time when he seemed to be immovably stationed at Laracor, 'very busy, being to preach today before an audience of at least fifteen people, most of them gentle and all of them simple. I can send you no news; only the employment of my parishioners may, for memory sake, be reduced under these heads: Mr. Percival is ditching; Mrs. Percival in her kitchen; Mr. Wesley switching; Mrs. Wesley stitching; Sir Arthur Langford riching, which is a new word for heaping up riches. I know no other rhyme but bitching and that I hope we are all past.' This was the shepherd of Laracor's report on his flock to the Reverend Dr. John Stearne, Dean of St. Patrick's Cathedral in Dublin. Incidentally, Sir Arthur Langford, head of one of the three wealthy families in the parish, was infected by Presbyterianism and the outbreak of the plague on his own doorstep caused Swift some distress. For the most part, however, he showed no dedicated concern for the immortal souls committed to his care.

Laracor had come to him in the first place as a poor, galling consolation. As a young man of thirty, he had aspired to a Royal Prebend at Canterbury or Westminster and, when that failed, to a Deanery in Ireland. He had settled his hopes on two peers of the realm, first the Earl of Romney and next the Earl of Berkeley. Both were guilty in his eyes of betraying his legitimate prospects and each today has the recompense of retaining a niche in literature as a first target of Swift's invective. Lord Romney was described by Bishop Burnet as 'of a sweet and caressing temper with no malice in his heart', although admittedly 'he did not follow business with a due application'. Swift's business, it seems, he did not follow with any application at all. He was by common consent the handsomest man of his age and won a reputation over thirty years as 'the terror of husbands' and the most shameless of profligates. Swift called him 'an old, vicious, illiterate rake, without any sense of truth or honour'. But that was the kindly, reminiscent reproof of later years. At the time the young disillusioned parson heaped upon 'the universal lover' a flow of coarse venom which still turns the stomach.

By comparison Lord Berkeley was gently treated. On his appointment as Lord Chief Justice of Ireland he took Swift with him to Dublin Castle as chaplain and secretary. Much to Swift's annoyance another secretary was soon taken on in his place; much to his mortification a vacant Deanery went to someone else. His temper was not improved by his belief that the newly appointed Dean had given a bribe to the newly appointed secretary and that his own youth was held to be the fatal bar against him. Swift is said to have taken his leave of Lord Berkeley and of Berkeley's new favourite with the words: 'God confound you both for a pair of scoundrels!' A poem followed so decorous in its satire by Swift's standards that it is clear the breach was not severe. Berkeley may have been 'intolerably lazy and indolent and somewhat covetous', but he was the father of Lady Betty Germaine whose vivacity and companionship Swift cherished all his life. Despite his relegation to Laracor, he was for ten years a frequent visitor to the Castle. There he dazzled the ladies with his charm, ingratiated himself with successive Lord Lieutenants and mimicked the part which he longed to play on the wider political stage in London.

But neither Dublin nor Laracor could hold him for long. Almost every hint of a change in the London climate of opinion beckoned him back, and if he retained his anchorage in Ireland at all the credit was due, not to the convivial nature of the Lords and Bishops who were sent to rule Ireland, but to 'the truest, most virtuous and valuable friend that I, or perhaps any other person ever was blessed with'; in other words, to Esther Johnson, to Stella. He first met her as a child of eight in the household of Sir William Temple; he was then in his early twenties. Thereafter he moulded her whole

life to suit his whim and temper. When he found himself settled at
Laracor, Stella 'was looked upon as one of the most beautiful,
graceful and agreeable young women in London'. Yet a word from
her guide and philosopher was sufficient to entice her to Ireland
along with her 'dear friend and companion', Rebecca Dingley.
While he was at Laracor the two ladies lodged at the neighbouring
village of Trim; when he departed for London they moved into the
Vicarage. Esther Johnson had judgement, wit, kindness, understanding; she had (as Swift claimed) 'gracefulness, somewhat more
than human, in every motion, word and action. Never was so
happy a conjunction of civility, freedom, easiness and sincerity'.
Rebecca Dingley was a mere shadow; her biography almost begins
and ends with the record that she loved animals, wore spectacles,
chewed large quantities of tobacco, and tripped over her petticoats
when she walked. Yet somehow these three became bound together
in the strangest intimacy in English literature. The proud, ambitious Swift prattled to his 'two monkeys', his 'naughty rogues', in
baby-talk; they repaid him with a lifetime of devotion. Stella was
'among all persons on earth' the one Swift would have chosen as
his wife 'if my fortunes and humour served me to think of that
state'; yet they were never known to be present alone in the same
room together. No one has ever unravelled the mystery of their
relationship. Probably Virginia Woolf has come nearest to explaining Stella's secret understanding of the man she loved. 'None knew
better than she that Swift loved power and the company of men;
that though he had moods of tenderness and his fierce spasms of
disgust at society, still for the most part he infinitely preferred the
dust and bustle of London to all the trout streams and cherry trees
in the world. Above all, he hated interference. If anyone laid a
finger upon his liberty or hinted the least threat to his independence, were they men or women, queens or kitchen maids, he turned
upon them with a ferocity which made a savage of him on the
spot.'

Yes, Swift loved power, and the key to power in the world he
had learned to know rested in the Cockpit in Whitehall, the seat of
authority of the English aristocracy. If a man could lay his hand on
the levers there, all else—wealth, preferments, influence and more
power—would be added to him. Yet how could this poor Irish
Vicar dream these dreams of a Caesar? He had one chief weapon in
his armoury, but so far his writings had made more enemies than

friends. For, if Swift loved power, he also hated lies and shams and every form of pomposity and imposture. He unsheathed his pen to rescue a friend, to savage an opponent, to serve an immediate cause. But soon the temptation to belabour every sign of pretension in sight became well-nigh irresistible. On some occasions, before the deadly instrument was back in its scabbard, enemy and friend had been smitten to the ground. Such a man equipped with such a weapon would have needed to walk delicately in any age. In the reign of Queen Anne unprecedented opportunities opened to those who were masters of the printed word, but the peril to a man's liberty was hardly less great. So, despite the urge to deal with the fools and knaves around him in the grand manner they deserved, despite a few soaring flights into the mood of irony which suited him best, Swift had so far been wary in his political dealings, showing the same cautious precision he applied to his personal affairs. He made excuses to himself, cursing the eternal screechings of Whig and Tory cats on the rooftops, disavowing the call of partisanship, mocking the whole tribe of scribblers and critics who let loose such a deluge of news-sheets, saving his finest wrath for the vulgar tradesmen of Grub Street. Swift in 1709 had not yet turned his hand to the same craft; at least, he had not done so with any settled design and allegiance. He was an unemployed condottiere, a trained soldier without a flag to follow.

*   *   *

Charles Jervas has left us with one portrait of him at that date. But his political ambitions and frustrations can be defined only by a brief review of the writings which had brought him to the fringe of great affairs. The apprenticeship he had served lasted twenty years. Ten of those twenty years (from 1689 to 1699), with a few short intervals, were spent at Moor Park in the household of the retired Whig statesman, Sir William Temple. Sir William disliked the rough hazards of politics; he preferred a life of graciousness and moderation. For a while he succeeded in instilling at least a pretension to the same tastes into his secretary. Swift adopted the temperate Whig opinions of his master. He feasted for hours in Sir William's library. But his education was much more than formal. At Moor Park he made his acquaintance with statecraft and statesmen, including King William himself, and acquired some understanding of the men who ruled the state. On one occasion he was sent to Kensington Palace as an emissary to urge Temple's views on the King and his chief adviser, the Earl of Portland. The mission was a failure. This was the first time he had 'any converse with courts' and he later told his friends 'it was the first incident that helped to cure him of vanity'. Thereafter for the rest of his life the spectacle of high politics and the labyrinthine means employed by politicians kept him both fascinated and repelled. He longed to play a part on that stage himself; yet he perfectly understood the aphorism of a famous statesman of the time that 'a man who would rise at court must start by crawling on all fours'. There at Moor Park, too, he made his first painful essays into authorship and saw his first poem printed in a paper called the *Athenian Mercury*. It was a lumbering Pindaric ode and is said to have provoked Dryden's sharp verdict: 'Cousin Swift, you will never be a poet.' Cousin Swift half took the hint, but rarely missed an opportunity of revenge on his great critic. He turned to write the prose which was to make him famous, but for several years still none of his writings saw the light of day.

Sir William died in 1699. Swift crossed to Ireland and established his base at Laracor. Then, at the turn of the century, he paid a visit to London and made his timorous entry into the active world of politics. The Tories had just increased their strength in the House of Commons, and their success prompted them to demand the impeachment of four of the leading Whig lords. The Whig majority in the House of Lords came to their defence. Swift wrote his first pamphlet in the same interest, 'sent it very privately to the Press, with the strictest injunctions to conceal the author; and returned immediately to my residence in Ireland.' It was a plea for temperance in politics, an exposure of the rancour which can lead to arbitrary government, a lofty discourse in which the arraigned Whig peers—Somers, Halifax, Orford and Portland—were compared with the heroic statesmen of Greece and Rome. Its most distinctive note was a denunciation of the embryonic party system. 'Man is so apt to imitate, so much of a sheep that whoever is so bold to give the first great leap over the heads of those about him (though he be the worst of the flock) shall quickly be followed by the rest. Besides, when parties are once formed, the struggles look so ridiculous and become so insignificant, that they have no other way but to run into the herd, which at least will hide and protect them; and where to be much considered, requires only to be very violent.' Not for the first or the last time in British history the scorn of party politics was asserted by a man who was serving a party interest.

The pamphlet was 'greedily bought and read'. Among the suspected authors of it were counted the great Whig leader, Lord Somers, and the great Whig Bishop, Gilbert Burnet. Its fame spread to Dublin where Swift was rebuked as 'a very positive young man' for daring to doubt Burnet's authorship. When he returned to London vanity persuaded him to reveal the truth, at least to some of those with a special interest in knowing it. Swift had started his literary career as a favourite of the Whigs. Lord Somers, Lord Halifax, and Lord Sunderland, an acquaintance of Moor Park days, eagerly embraced the young publicist who so shrewdly assessed their own Greek and Roman virtues, promising him early preferment once they were restored to power in the state. Lord Halifax, in particular, a patron of literature, became his personal friend. Bishop Burnet told Swift (or so Swift claimed) that he had been forced to disown the authorship 'in a very public manner, for fear of an impeachment with which he was threatened'. Swift had tempered the force of his indictment, believing that to go further was 'perhaps not altogether safe'. But he had made his impact. So early a success must have persuaded him that advancement for himself was certain once the swing of the pendulum placed these proud Whig leaders in the position of dominance which they so readily believed was theirs by right. Were they not, at least in their own eyes, the architects of the Glorious Revolution which had given King William his English throne and which had ensured the succession of Queen Anne? And were they not the chief advocates of the war against King Louis XIV and the Jacobite Pretender on which the Queen had embarked? They were in their own estimation the indispensable bulwarks of English greatness and when they bestowed their favour the chosen underlings might be expected to display a suitable awe.

A few years later—in May 1704—one among their number was granted his meed of flattery. *The Tale of a Tub* was published and the dedication was made to the Right Honourable John Lord Somers as 'a wise piece of presumption' by the anonymous author. Nothing was lacking in the tribute; it was done with a superb raillery which heightened the effect. But the pages that followed must surely have made the most haughty of the Whig grandees less appreciative of the compliment. When sometime later it was suggested that Lord Somers might be the real author of the work he had a better right still to feel the joke had gone too far. For *The Tale of a Tub* was a stupendous satire on almost every established institution and custom of the age. The papists on the one hand and the dissenters on the other were the two principal victims, but almost everyone else fell beneath the lash. 'Satire is a sort of glass', said the writer, 'wherein beholders do generally discover everybody's face but their own'. Not many beholders could fail to discover their own features in this glass, and if the Whigs as such were granted immunity, lawyers and bishops, courtiers and statesmen, philosophers and kings were mocked with the same coarse exuberance lavished on hack writers and political toadies in every shape and posture. Even the English Church, the pallid hero of the piece, did not escape, and, even in the year of Blenheim, the love of military glory was included among the proofs of madness with which all mankind was possessed. 'Is any student tearing his straw in piece-meal, swearing and blaspheming, biting his grate, foaming at the mouth and emptying his piss-pot in the spectators' faces? Let the right worshipful the commissioners of inspection give him a regiment of dragoons, and send him into Flanders among the rest'. Nothing was sacred. The whole was a *tour-de-force* in which the author upheld the ideals of political moderation with ribald extravagance and launched his crusade for the one true Church of Christ in the language of blasphemy.

It is not surprising that the author of this treatise 'written for the Universal Improvement of Mankind' left the country within a few days of publication. Swift went to Ireland and stayed there for a full three and a half years. Laracor had its compensations; in Dublin he was beginning to make a name as a man of influence in the Church; and in London his Whig friends, being still out of office, were unable to fulfil their promise of preferment. It is possible also that to be branded openly as the author of *The Tale of a Tub* would damn him incurably with too many who wielded power in Church and State. Swift was content to watch from afar the commotion created by the monster-child to which he had given birth. A few weeks after publication two young wits from Oxford were talked of as the guilty authors and the rumour was that their disavowal had been incriminatingly vague. William King, a high

Church writer, was also suspected; he felt it necessary to write a pamphlet repudiating the charge in which he asserted that the book had 'a Tincture of such Filthiness' as made it 'unfit for the worst of Uses'. William Wotton, one of the scholars attacked in the *Tale*, agreed with him. He called it 'one of the Prophanest Banters upon the Religion of *Jesus Christ* as such, that ever yet appeared'. A rising Tory writer, Dr. Charles Davenant, was impressed. He told his son that the book 'has made as much noise and is as full of wit, as any book perhaps that has come out these last hundred years'. He also wrote to the Duke of Marlborough's secretary requesting a chaplaincy for Swift's cousin, Thomas Swift, and claiming that Thomas was the real author of the masterpiece. More significant for Swift's future, however, was the effect on leading churchmen. They had some reason for concern, apart from the possible effect on the nation's morals; for one of the targets in the book was that 'apt conjunction of lawn and black satin we entitle a Bishop'. True, Dr. Francis Atterbury, the Queen's chaplain and one of her chief advisers on eclesiastical affairs, parried the blow lightly. He thought the book very well-written and 'would do good service'. Doubtless it was agreeable to see dissenters so mercilessly castigated even if the Bishops too must feel a flick of the whip. Yet even his urbanity was disturbed by 'the profane-strokes'. He feared they would do the author's 'reputation and interest in the world more harm than the wit can do him good'. George Smalbridge, another divine rising rapidly in the Church hierarchy, had a good excuse for expressing himself more forcibly, for he, along with Lord Somers and Lord Shrewsbury, was accused of perpetrating the crime. He quickly made it clear that not all the temptations which Satan had offered Jesus could have hired him to commit such a sin.

At some point in the years that followed Swift was unmasked at least before a few. It is hard to fix the date. A year after publication when the book was running into its fourth edition Thomas Hearne, a scholar at Oxford, noted the name of Swift as the author in his diary, and Daniel Defoe, at roughly the same time, marked 'the strange stench' which the book left behind and which enabled many to 'smell the author' who had departed for Dublin. And yet for some years the controversy about the authorship of the famous satire continued. Swift himself was torn between irritation that others, particularly his cousin Thomas, should claim the credit, and fear that Dr. Atterbury's prophecy should prove all too true; a crown of thorns was not his idea of the proper Christian reward. Some years after the book first appeared he wrote an apology as a preface for a new edition—the most grudging ever penned and the sole essay in that style ever extorted from him in his whole long career of libel and vendetta. Needless to say that apology was not directed to the 'great majority among men of taste' who had fully appreciated the delicacy of the work. It was designed to appease those among the clergy who 'are not always very nice in distinguishing between their enemies and their friends'. The book, he claimed, was written to celebrate the perfection of the Church of England. He was ready to admit it included 'several youthful sallies, which from the grave and the wise, may deserve a rebuke', but he would 'forfeit his life' if there were any opinions in it 'contrary to Religion and Morality'. Lest this offer might prove too tempting, the apology ended with a further effort at mystification. 'The world, with all its wise conjectures', claimed the author— with how much truth we cannot tell—'is yet very much in the dark; which circumstance is no disagreeable amusement either to the public or himself'.

One passage in the book throws a gleam of light both on the methods he had so far employed and the conditions under which journalists and pamphleteers were then working. *The Tale of a Tub*, for all its extravagance and all the enmity it aroused, was not shaped to produce a direct political result. It was savage and joyous in its general invective; it was not aimed at any particular victim. It was not down to earth; rather, along with some sections of *Gulliver's Travels*, it was the nearest Swift ever got to a flight into the philosophic stratosphere. Yet Swift knew better probably than any writer before or since that policies are made by men and that specific political effects could be achieved only if the men (and women) responsible were assailed in a manner making it impossible for them to dodge the line of fire. He must have marked with envy mixed with the disdain the multitude of scribblers who were practising the new political journalism more boldly than himself. Many pages of *The Tale* were devoted to the derision of Grub Street and yet suddenly a classical defence of their craft blazed forth.

'In the Attic Commonwealth,' he wrote, 'it was the privilege and birthright of every citizen and poet to rail aloud, and in public, or to expose upon the stage, by name, any person they pleased, though of the greatest figure, whether a Creon, an Hyperbolus, an Alcibiades, or a Demosthenes; but, on the other side, the least reflecting word let fall against the people in general, was immediately caught up, and revenged upon the authors, however considerable for their quality or merits. Whereas in England it is just the reverse of all this. Here, you may securely display your utmost rhetoric against mankind, in the face of the world . . . And when you have done, the whole audience, far from being offended, shall return you thanks, as a deliverer of precious and useful truths. Nay, farther: it is but to venture your lungs, and you may preach in Covent Garden against foppery and fornication, and something else: against pride, and dissimulation, and bribery, at Whitehall: you may expose rapine and injustice in the Inns of Court Chapel: and in a city pulpit, be as fierce as you please against avarice, hypocrisy, and extortion. 'Tis but a ball bandied to and fro, and every man carries a racket about him, to strike it from himself, among the rest of the company. But, on the other side, whoever should mistake the nature of things so far, as to drop but a single hint in public, how such a one starved half the fleet, and half poisoned the rest: how such a one, from a true principle of love and honour, pays no debt but for wenches and play: how such a one has got a clap, and runs out of his estate: how Paris, bribed by Juno and Venus, loth to defend either party, slept out the whole cause on the bench: or, how such an author makes long speeches in the senate, with much thought, little sense, and to no purpose; whoever, I say, should venture to be this particular, must expect to be imprisoned for *scandalum magnatum*; to have challenges sent him; to be sued for defamation; and to be brought before the bar of the house.'

That surely was the herald of a new Swift, one who would make statesmen and even Bishops regret that he did not confine himself to harmless explorations into the lower regions of profanity. But that hour had not yet come.

When Swift returned to London in the winter of 1707 he had various reasons for believing that a new and more hopeful chapter in his life was about to open. In *The Tale of a Tub* he had proved to himself and a select few that he possessed literary genius. He was entrusted with a special mission from the Irish Church which gave him a fresh status and importance. Political changes in London could hardly fail to prove advantageous; at last power was slipping into the hands of his Whig patrons. Altogether, he felt a sense of liberation, and possessed a new air of authority. He was in high good humour with himself and the world; only rarely did he show a flash of cold steel. During the next year and a half poems and pamphlets poured from his pen. All of them were published anonymously, after the fashion of the day; but few were of such a character that the secret of the authorship needed to be rigorously preserved. Moreover, the coteries in which he moved were impressed by the trenchancy and originality of his talk and demeanour. He soon gained a rich company of admirers among statesmen, men of letters and beautiful women. One of these last was Mrs. Finch who under the more impressive title of Ardeliah was lauded for her prowess in outwitting Apollo.

> *The Nymph who oft had read in Books,*
> *Of that Bright God whom Bards invoke,*
> *Soon knew* Apollo *by his looks,*
> *And Guest his Business ere he Spoke.*

> *He in the old Celestial Cant,*
> *Confest his Flame, and swore by Styx,*
> *What e're she would desire, to Grant,*
> *But Wise* Ardeliah *knew his Tricks.*

> Ovid *had warn'd her to beware,*
> *Of Stroling Gods, whose usual Trade is,*
> *Under pretence of Taking Air,*
> *To pick up Sublunary Ladies.*

Apollo might be resistible, but not this irreverent Vicar in such a mood.

In the same spirit he applied his mind to woo others less susceptible than his array of lovely ladies. For better or worse he was wedded to the Church of England. She offered a cause which he was prepared to fight for without quarter or qualms against all comers, although often the weapons he employed did not commend themselves to other members of his calling. In his *Argument Against Abolishing Christianity* he delivered his counter-attack in such a rumbustious fashion that those he defended quivered beneath the assault hardly less than his victims. Of course he admitted at the outset to the candid reader that 'my discourse is intended only in defence of nominal Christianity; the other having been for some time wholly laid aside by general consent, as utterly inconsistent with our present schemes of wealth and power'. But for nominal religion surely a most persuasive case could be made.

'Great wits love to be free with the highest objects; and if they cannot be allowed a God to revile and renounce, they will speak evil of dignities, abuse the government, and reflect upon the ministry.' Then he turned gravely to deal with more serious objections. 'Another advantage proposed by the abolishing of Christianity, is the clear gain of one day in seven, which is now entirely lost, and consequently the Kingdom one seventh less considerable in trade, business and pleasure; besides the loss to the public of so many stately structures now in the hands of the Clergy, which might be converted into playhouses, exchanges, market-houses, common dormitories, and other public edifices. I hope I shall be forgiven a hard word, if I call this a perfect *cavil*. I readily own there has been an old custom time out of mind, for people to assemble in the churches every Sunday, and that shops are still frequently shut, in order as it is conceived, to preserve the memory of that ancient practice, but how this can prove a hindrance to business or pleasure, is hard to imagine. What if the men of pleasure are forced one day in the week, to game at home instead of at the chocolate-houses? Are not the taverns and coffeehouses open? Can there be a more convenient season for taking a dose of physic? Are fewer claps got upon Sundays than other days? Is not that the chief day for traders to sum up the accounts of the week and for lawyers to prepare their briefs? But I would fain know that it can be pretended that the churches are misapplied. Where are more appointments and rendez vouzes of gallantry? Where more care to appear in the foremost box with greater advantage of dress? Where more meetings for business? Where more bargains driven of all sorts? And where so many conveniences or enticements to sleep?' So the weighty argument was piled higher and higher. Was it not clear that 'the abolishment of the Christian religion will be the readiest course we can take to introduce popery'? That fear should be conclusive and yet in the last resort there were further arguments even more telling. 'Upon the whole, if it shall be thought for the benefit of Church and State, that Christianity be abolished; I conceive, however, it may be more convenient to defer the execution to a time of peace, and not venture in this conjuncture to disoblige our allies, who, as it falls out, are all Christians, and many of them, by the prejudice of their education, so bigoted, as to place a sort of pride in the appellation'. This should settle the matter; if not, there was one final word. 'To conclude: whatever some may think of the great advantages to trade by this favourite scheme, I do very much apprehend, that in six months time after the act is passed for the extirpation of the Gospel, the Bank, and East-India Stock, may fall at least one *per cent*. And since that is fifty times more than ever the wisdom of our age thought fit to venture for the preservation of Christianity, there is no reason we should be at so great a loss, merely for the sake of destroying it.'

Thus Swift asserted the cause to which he had pledged his allegiance. His fellow clergymen might wonder how profound was his piety when he chose such methods to vindicate their simple faith. Swift himself may have had the same doubts, for he soon took steps in another pamphlet to put the case more straightforwardly. *A Project for the Advancement of Religion and the Reformation of Manners* appeared in the same year (1707). It was signed by 'a Person of Quality' and the proceeds were intended for the benefit of the poor. Lord Berkeley entreated Swift to ensure that a copy might be presented by the Archbishop of York to the Queen, and Richard Steele agreed that the author 'writes much like a gentleman and goes to Heaven with a very good mien'. The pamphlet outlined a comprehensive series of restrictions and censorships which would undoubtedly have commended themselves to Queen Anne. She might not have been equally pleased with his strictures on the low breed of men who, in the author's reckoning, were customarily appointed to positions of trust in the Church and in politics. Would it not be a great reform for the court to make genuine faith a reason for advancement? So Swift argued with as much reverence for royalty as he could muster, and against the objection 'that making religion a necessary step to interest and favour might increase hypocrisy among us' he produced an argument worthy of *The Tale of a Tub*. 'If one in twenty should be brought over to true piety by this, or the like methods, and the other nineteen be only hypocrites, the advantage would still be great. Besides, hypocrisy is much more eligible than open infidelity and vice; it wears the livery of religion; it acknowledges her authority, and is cautious of giving scandal. Nay, a long continued disguise is too great a constraint upon human nature, especially an English disposition; men would leave off their vices out of mere weariness, rather than undergo the toil and hazard, and perhaps expense, of practising them perpetually in private. And I believe it is often with religion, as it is with love; which, by much dissembling, at last grows real.' This was as near as Swift ever came to a eulogy of Queen Anne's bench of Bishops, and the Archbishop of York cannot be blamed if he failed to share Lord Berkeley's enthusiasm for the piece.

Was the Vicar of Laracor a convinced Christian and a sound Churchman? A whole library has been produced to answer the question but that mystery, like the enigma of his relations with Stella, remains unsolved. Certainly he never wavered in fighting for the Church's temporal interests; never did he disavow the most rigid and formal of her tenets. He served her in any quarrel with an unfailing pugnacity. But, despite all claims that devotion to the Church was the one consistent strand running through his life, it is hard to believe that this was truly his ruling passion. Not for her was he able to exert his powers to the limit. When he wrote about the Church either his boisterous humour or his contempt for Bishops or his hatred of humbug or his zest for politics struggled to break through. In *The Tale of a Tub* he excoriated the enemies of the English Church with a zeal he never brought to her defence. He doubtless tried hard against his own nature to make himself the kind of man the Queen and the Archbishops would delight to honour. He longed for the Bishopric which, as he had so unwisely hinted, hypocrisy had secured for others. The flesh was willing, but the spirit was weak. Often he claimed that, although hating mankind in general, he loved Tom, Dick and Harry. A strange corollary was also true. He loved the Church and Christianity with a watery affection; he needed to see the face and handiwork of particular enemies if his full genius was to be unleashed in hatred or in laughter.

Certainly his energies were not exhausted by the urge to defend his Church. He turned aside to engage in a quite different form of controversy, one which was nothing more than a tremendous joke. By 1709 Isaac Bickerstaff was a name much better known than that of Jonathan Swift. Swift borrowed it from some locksmith's shop-sign in Long Acre and used it as the pseudonym under which he attacked John Partridge, a cobbler turned almanac-maker who had won European fame by combining astrological forecasts with advertisements of quack remedies for venereal disease. The double fraud attracted Swift's powers of ridicule. He produced his own predictions for the year 1708. They started with the prophecy that Partridge would 'infallibly die upon the 29th March next about eleven at night, of a raging fever'. Then it was foretold that death would come to the Cardinal of Noailles, Archbishop of Paris, and a whole series of other eminent persons including King Louis XIV and His Holiness the Pope. A strong hint was given that the magic powers of forecast could easily be applied nearer home; 'but those in power have wisely discouraged men from meddling in public concerns and I was resolved by no means to give the least offence.' Making full allowance for this reticence Bickerstaff's forecasts far outbid in precision and sensation anything which John Partridge had ever attempted.

Promptly on March 30th an *Elegy* was sold on the streets of London announcing that the prophecy was fulfilled.

> *Well, 'tis as Bickerstaff has guest*
> *Tho' we all took it for a* Jest.
> Patrige *is dead, nay more, he dy'd*
> *E're he could prove the good* Squire *ly'd.*
> *Strange, an Astrologer should Die,*
> *Without one Wonder in the Sky;*
> *Not one of all his* Crony Stars,
> *To pay their Duty at his Hearse!*
> *No Meteor, no Eclipse appear'd!*
> *No Comet with a Flaming Beard!*
> *The Sun has rose, and gone to Bed,*
> *Just as if* Patrige *were not Dead:*

A few days later a pamphlet appeared explaining with circumstantial detail the last scenes at the death-bed, coupled with an apology that Bickerstaff had miscalculated the moment of Partridge's decease by some four hours. The world at large was invited to await the fulfilment of his next prediction about the Cardinal de Noailles, and a host of others joined in the fun. In Portugal the Inquisition ordered that Bickerstaff's predictions should be burnt, and from Paris came a solemn assault on their validity. Someone, probably Bickerstaff himself, rushed to the rescue of poor Partridge in a pamphlet called *Squire Bickerstaff Detected*. It explained how Partridge had been dunned for his own funeral expenses, and the deception was so skilful that Partridge reprinted the protest himself. Then the poor victim went further. In his almanac for the following year he had the temerity to claim that he was still alive. Swift's reply was devastating. He proved conclusively that Partridge *must* be dead. As for the Frenchman 'who was pleased to publish to the world, "that the Cardinal de Noailles was still alive, notwithstanding the pretended prophecy of Monsieur Biquerstaffe"': he took leave to ask 'how far a Frenchman, a Papist, and an enemy, is to be believed in his own case, against an English Protestant, who is true to the government'. Partridge was finished, and there was more than bombast in Bickerstaff's claim that 'in this dispute, I am sensible the eyes, not only of England, but of all Europe, will be upon us'. The brilliant hoax had made a reputation which neither Whigs nor Tories need watch with a censorious eye, and when in the spring of 1709 Richard Steele founded *The Tatler* he was glad to borrow the name of Bickerstaff for his own use to ensure his magazine's success and to give generous thanks to the man who had created it.

Steele's choice of the name Swift had made famous is one sign of the friendship he had established among men who had so far won a more certain place in the literary world than himself. Steele had written successful plays and was the chief editor of the government *Gazette*. Joseph Addison had gained fame and advancement ever since he had written a poem to celebrate the victory of Blenheim. He was a Member of Parliament and an Under-Secretary of State with a sufficient fortune to be able to lend £1000 to the spendthrift Steele. Jonathan Swift liked to picture himself as the third of this triumvirate. He could not match the worldly success of the others, but he had acquired some of the same tastes. 'Wine is the liquor of the Gods and ale of the Goths', he wrote to another friend, and the discriminating palate, surely, had been gained in the company of Steele and Addison. 'Excellent companions for an evening,' it was said, 'the one at the beginning, the other towards the close, for by the time that Steele had drunk himself down, Addison had drunk himself up.' Swift treasured the intimacy, particularly with Addison. Yet it would be no more than natural if the affection was tinged with jealousy. Almost all Swift's literary friends at the time—William Congreve, then at the peak of his reputation, was another—were Whigs. An Irish Protestant was inevitably a Whig in his sympathies. Swift had lived all his adult life in Whig circles and his earliest political pamphlets were written in their interest. With Addison he became a frequent visitor at the houses of the great Whig patrons, headed by Lord Halifax. He had every right to expect his earthly reward. Had he not been promised as much by Lord Somers some seven years before? Yet, while

Addison moved from his Haymarket garret to more elegant quarters and had a coach and four to sustain his new status in society, Swift for some reason was kept waiting.

One cause of the hesitancy shown by the authorities may have been the invidious name he had acquired by his suspected authorship of *The Tale of a Tub.* His aggressive championship of Church interests also prevented him from establishing complete harmony with the Whigs. His personal friends were Whigs; but they, for political reasons, looked askance at his Anglican hatred of dissenters. This divergence in outlook was for long submerged, but it appeared more sharply when, on his visit to London in 1707 and 1708, he started to discharge the special duty entrusted to him by the Archbishop of Dublin. A few years earlier Queen Anne had assisted the English clergy by remitting a tax paid by them known as the First Fruits. Swift's task was to use his influence with the Whig statesmen to win from the Queen the same remission for the Irish clergy. Doubtless he also welcomed the opportunity to further more directly his personal ambitions. When the Bishopric of Waterford became vacant he felt his chances were excellent. Lord Somers and Lord Sunderland were enlisted to press his claims. But somehow, if it was ever made, the application for the Bishopric failed and Swift confessed himself 'stomach-sick' with disappointment.

Then in June 1708 he had an interview with Lord Godolphin, the most powerful of all the Queen's Ministers. Godolphin made an offer. The First Fruits would be remitted on condition 'due acknowledgments' were given in return by the Irish clergy. Swift understood exactly what those acknowledgements must be. Godolphin wanted the acquiescence of the Irish clergy in the removal of the Test Act. Under that Act all except Anglican communicants were excluded from public offices and this was a bitter source of grievance among the dissenters in Ireland whom Godolphin and his colleagues wished to recruit as their political allies. So Swift was confronted with a dilemma. To gain one advantage for his Church and the credit for achieving it he must sacrifice her interests in another direction and in a manner which both he and his Archbishop had vowed to oppose. And even more irritating was the proof that his talents were not so well appreciated in high circles as they ought to be. The gross, calculating attitude of Lord Godolphin left its scar on Swift.

But what could he do? In that October of 1708 the Whigs took another step towards complete mastery of the Queen's Ministry. Lord Somers became President of the Council; Lord Wharton, another of the Whig leaders, was appointed Lord Lieutenant of Ireland; Joseph Addison was to go with him as Irish Secretary, a post worth at least £2,000 a year. It was, said Swift, 'a new world', a world in which the power of the Whigs seemed more securely established than at any time since the Revolution. He wrote hopefully to Archbishop King in Dublin: 'although I care not to mingle public affairs with the interest of so private a person as myself, yet, upon such a revolution, not knowing how far my friends may endeavour to engage me in the service of the new government, I would beg your grace to have favourable thoughts of me on such an occasion'. If a Bishopric was not available, he had a promise of being appointed Queen's secretary to accompany the Earl of Berkeley to Vienna. But nothing happened. Characteristically, Swift turned to take revenge for his maltreatment with his pen.

In December 1708 appeared his *Letter Concerning the Sacramental Test*. The author pretended to write from Dublin, taking the disguise of an Irish Member of Parliament. A new note was struck in the Swiftian repertoire. This was no satire on human folly, playful or gruesome; this was Swift for the first time crossing swords with the Grub Street politicians. At first he almost apologized for deigning to quote 'those infamous weekly papers that infest your coffee-houses'. But had they not become powers in the land? Were they not the mouthpieces of men of wealth and influence, even of Ministers of the Queen? 'How insipid soever those papers are, they seem to be levelled to the understandings of a great number; they are grown a necessary part in coffeehouse furniture'. Swift went into action against 'that paltry rascal', John Tutchin, and Daniel Defoe, 'the fellow that was pilloried I have forgot his name'. But behind them he saw more serious opponents—the proud Godolphin himself, who had spurned the entreaties of a poor Irish parson, and the whole phalanx of English Whiggery, which was so perfectly content to make his Church turn somersaults to suit their party interest. The whole pamphlet was a defence of the well-nigh indefensible Test Act, and, of course, the men who were most likely to be angered by so skilful an incitement of Church prejudice were the very Whig Ministers whom Swift was meeting on friendly terms every week.

Knowing how dangerous was the game he played, he made special efforts to keep his secret. Archbishop King had an inkling of the truth. Swift did his best to put him off the scent and perhaps at the same time to deceive the government agents whom he suspected of opening his letters to Dublin. 'I am used', he said, 'like a sober man with a drunken face, have the scandal of the vice without the satisfaction'. But all these precautions were not able to kill the suspicions of one man with whom Swift's fortunes now became inextricably linked. Thomas, Earl of Wharton, the great party manager of the Whigs, was not likely to look kindly on the antics of an interfering parson; much too often, in his judgement, the whining prayers of the Anglican clergy were indistinguishable from the last gasp of the Tories. It was natural that he and Swift should meet. He was the associate of Somers and Halifax and Sunderland, whom Swift already knew well. Since his appointment as Viceroy of Ireland it had even been suggested that Swift might go to Dublin as his chaplain, just as Addison was to go as Secretary. The meeting with Wharton took place just before the Earl departed for Ireland. No preferment for Swift was forthcoming, nor did Wharton show the faintest concern for the tribulations of the Irish Church.

*   *   *

So, for all his triumphs among his literary friends, Swift prepared, in the spring of 1709, to return to Laracor as poor and powerless as he had left. He described his disillusion to Charles Forde, one of his closest associates in Ireland: 'I believe by this time you are satisfied that I am not grown great, nor like to do so very soon: for I am thought to want the Art of being thoruow paced in my Party, as all discreet Persons ought to be, and sometime this Summer you may not improbably see me alighting at your House in my way to Residence.' Ireland offered him no consolation. 'I must learn to make my Court to that Country and People better than I have done,' he said, adding: 'if you find I pass for a morose Man, find some Excuse or other to vindicate me'. That was a curious lament from the Isaac Bickerstaff who only a few months before had captivated the whole town with his humour. He left London in June before Charles Jervas had had time to finish his portrait, taking with him a book he had been given by Lord Halifax—'the only favour I ever received from him or his party'. By the time he

reached Leicester, where he visited his mother, his spirits and—
more strangely—his dignity were gone. He wrote to Lord Halifax
begging 'some share in your Lordship's memory', urging that he
would 'sometimes put Lord Somers in mind of me', protesting his
hatred of 'the place where I am banished' and pleading that 'I
might live to be some way useful and entertaining, if I were permitted to live in town, or, which is the highest punishment of
Papists, anywhere within ten miles around it'. The letter ended
with a plea that Lord Halifax should join him in prayer for the early
death of a Dr. South, Prebend of Westminster, coupled with an
earnest declaration of his own fitness for the post. No one could say
that the author of *The Tale of a Tub* had not recovered his faith in
heavenly intervention. On June 30th, 1709, he sailed into Dublin
bay and went straight to Laracor without seeing anybody.

From afar his friends tried to make amends. 'I am quite ashamed
for myself', wrote Lord Halifax in October, 'to see you left in a
place so incapable of tasting you.' He and Mr. Addison had determined to seek a remedy, but then came the blow: 'Dr. South holds
out still but he cannot be immortal!' Richard Steele added his
word of encouragement. 'No opportunity is omitted among powerful men, to upbraid them for your stay in Ireland.' But Swift was
not easily appeased. 'When you write any more poetry,' he said to
Ambrose Phillips, 'do me honour: mention me in it. It is the common request of Tully and Pliny to the great authors of their age;
and I will continue it so that Prince Posterity shall know I was
favoured by the men of wit in my time.' Jonathan Swift was to be
remembered through the centuries as a character in a poem by
Ambrose Phillips! And then he added, still more pathetically: 'I
reckon no man is thoroughly miserable unless he be condemned to
live in Ireland'. As the months passed the note of pleading became
ever more urgent, even if the humour could never be finally exor-
cised. 'If you think this gentle winter will not carry off Dr.
South', he once more entreated Lord Halifax, could he not be considered for Cork, 'if the incumbent dies of the spotted fever he is
now under?' But no satisfactory answer came. Lord Wharton and
Secretary Addison were now established at Dublin Castle; they
offered the only substitute for London available. Swift had to content himself with the pleasure of Addison's company and the humiliation of making his peace with the Erastian Earl.

The news from England added to the gloom. Swift had good

reason for moderating his love of the Whigs, but they were the only friends he had. When his correspondents in London told how the tide had turned once more and was flowing in favour of the Tories, how Lord Sunderland had been dismissed by the Queen, how other dismissals were expected, Swift was not comforted. 'I believe you had the displeasure of much ill news almost as soon as you landed', he wrote on August 10th, 1710, to Addison, who had just returned to England. 'Even the moderate Tories here are in pain at these revolutions, being what will certainly affect the Duke of Marlborough and consequently, the success of the war.' Swift shared their anxiety, though he had never shown much interest either in the war or the Duke of Marlborough. He knew his strength and longed to employ it in political combat. But he could see little prospect in returning to a London where all his old associates would soon be out of office and where, despite all the Vicar of Laracor's prayers, Dr. Robert South at the age of seventy-five was making such a splendid recovery that he was destined to survive another seven winters.

CHAPTER TWO

The Captain-General

> 'Over the confederacy, he (the Duke of Marlborough)
> a new, a private man acquired by merit and by manage-
> ment a more deciding influence than high birth, con-
> firmed authority and even the Crown of Great Britain
> had given to King William. . . . I take with pleasure this
> opportunity of doing justice to a great man whose faults
> I knew, whose virtues I admired; and whose memory
> as the greatest General and the greatest Minister that
> our country or perhaps any other has produced I
> honour.'—VISCOUNT BOLINGBROKE

SOME TIME IN THE MONTH OF OCTOBER, 1709, John
Churchill, Duke of Marlborough and Captain-General of the
Queen's forces in Flanders, wrote to Queen Anne requesting
her to appoint him Captain-General *for life*. Ever since May of that
year he had been inquiring about precedents. An emissary was sent
to London to make a search in the Privy Seal offices. When the
answer came that a 'commision during life is a new instance and
liable to malicious construction', he applied to the Lord Chancellor. Obedient and secret investigations brought the same verdict;
in the days of Henry VIII the post of 'Constable' had been known
but Lord Cowper quickly concluded he could not consider 'that
obsolete office to be any guide in the present question.' Thereupon
the Duke wrote direct to the Queen. Perhaps she had been forewarned; for the rumour ran that Marlborough had wished the
House of Commons to take the initiative in making the appointment and that the scheme was divulged to the Queen by another of
her Ministers, Lord Somers, 'who had no mind to be his grace's
subject'. When the Queen sent a refusal, Marlborough did not let
the matter rest. In another letter he expostulated against all the
hardships of which he felt himself the victim. He complained of
Anne's treatment of his wife, Sarah; strongly hinted that the bedchamber woman, Abigail Masham, after intrigues with the ex-
Minister, Robert Harley, had given the advice which led to the
refusal; and declared his resolve to retire from the Queen's

service at the end of the war. The Queen was unmoved. She would not hear a word against Abigail. All she wanted was that Sarah should 'leave off teasing and tormenting me, and behave herself with the decency she ought both to her friend and Queen, and this I hope you will make her do'. Very soon the news of this interchange between the most successful of soldiers and the Queen he had served so long became known in the court and the coffee-houses. Some mocked; others were genuinely alarmed. Where would his vaulting ambition lead him next? Was it really his aim to become another Cromwell or, at least, a General Monk? Or could he be safely and scornfully dismissed as 'King John II'?

No one knows for certain to this day the motives which made him do it. The two letters he wrote to the Queen are lost and their terms can be assumed only from the Queen's reply. Even if they were discovered it is improbable that any new revelation would be forthcoming. The innermost thoughts of the Duke of Marl-borough are mostly concealed from posterity just as they were masked by perfect calculation and manners from his contemporaries. But it is possible to guess.

Marlborough no doubt believed he had earned the right to make almost any demand of Queen Anne. Before she ever ascended the throne, he and Sarah had been her most intimate friends, sharing the indignities which King William had inflicted upon her. From the moment he was placed in command of her armies he had brought nothing but victory. When he took the field in 1702 the military forces of France outnumbered those of all the nations ranged against her by more than 30,000 trained soldiers. At their head stood the famous French Generals—Tallard, Villars and Vendôme; names worth whole regiments on any battlefield. Yet Marlborough defeated them all. Blenheim, Ramillies, Oudenarde and Malplaquet! No commander in British history before or since can show such a sequence of triumphs. It was truly said that he 'never sat before a town which he did not take nor ever fought a battle which he did not win', and it was hardly less true that his diplomacy matched his military skill. He was for long the cement of the Grand Alliance which King Louis' ambition and King William's tenacity had assembled together; without his alternate tact and boldness, without his constant journeyings between campaigns to Vienna, to Berlin, to The Hague, and back to

London to avert a political crisis, the whole structure would have fallen to pieces.

Despite all the tough decisions which a Commander-in-Chief is bound to enforce on confederate powers, despite all the devious manœuvres he thought it necessary to execute, despite occasional acts of downright duplicity towards his chief allies, the day came when Marlborough's standing with his Queen and her Ministers became the foremost topic of interest in all the allied capitals as it was assuredly at the Court of Versailles. The Dutch, for all their early suspicions, came to regard him as a saviour; the Austrian Emperor made him a Prince and had offered him the Governorship of the Netherlands with a salary of £60,000 a year. When these were the prospects dangled before him by other governments, had he not the right to require special favours from his own Queen? And in the autumn of 1709 there were other and more urgent excuses for his presumption no less convincing to the Captain-General.

Despite eight successful campaigns, or perhaps rather because such endless fighting had not brought final victory, the strains upon the alliance were growing severe. He had just fought the battle of Malplaquet, and when the guns had barely ceased firing he wrote to Sarah: 'God Almighty be praised, it is now in our power to have what peace we please, and I may be pretty well-assured of never being in another battle.' No one realized better than he how the hour of peacemaking may be the most deadly for an alliance. With the passing of the years he had grown more temporizing, less confident in his judgement and action. As Captain-General for life he would hold the power of an almost independent potentate, able to reassert his will and impose it, if need be, on friend and foe alike. A year before, peace had been within the grasp of the allies; King Louis was on his knees pleading for it. But the chance had been wantonly cast away. Now the French were displaying new vigour; if their recovery continued, the lordship over them secured by the eight campaigns could easily be forfeited. As Captain-General for life he could hold the balance between ultimatum and retreat, and make a good peace for Europe and himself. He was fifty-nine years old and he longed for rest. Often he felt sick and weary. He hated the sight of blood, and more of it had flowed at Malplaquet than at Blenheim, Ramillies and Oudenarde put together. It was in fact the most murderous battle of the century. Perhaps he believed that by a last supreme exertion he could establish the cause for which he had fought, and retire with his glory and his riches to the palace of Blenheim in Woodstock Park which Queen Anne and the nation were preparing for him.

Both before and after he made his vain request to the Queen these were some of the desires he expressed to his friends. But others were bound to see in the proposal more sinister aims. Why should a man possessing such immense powers already wish to be Captain-General for life—especially if the blessing of peace was soon to descend on war-weary Europe? A year earlier Marlborough like many others had believed that peace was almost certain; he had himself been busy preparing the homeward transport of the English troops. He had not insisted that more lenient terms should be offered to King Louis, and when the French King rejected the ultimatum he expressed his amazement. True, he made some last-minute efforts to prevent the renewal of the war, but he never sought to exercise his authority decisively. In any case, all his pleas for moderation were made in secret; only Sarah knew how earnestly he prayed for peace in his heart; only his soldiers could testify how tenderly he cared for the wounded, how genuine was the anguish provoked by the spectacle of butchery on his normally impassive countenance. To many far away from the battlefield and at home in England he appeared as the symbol of the war which dragged on from year to year. They heard of the acclaim paid to him in Parliament as the war hero, of the new armies being recruited, of the rewards showered upon him, of the monument to his glory which Sir John Vanbrugh was constructing. Small wonder that some assailed him as the advocate of war without end.

Marlborough writhed with anger as these reports from London reached him in his camp. But he could hardly complain too vociferously. Open diplomacy would not have suited the Duke. The first tentative step towards peace negotiations had been taken by himself in a surreptitious approach to his nephew, the Duke of Berwick, who was enlisted in the armies of King Louis. The move had been made before one word of consultation had been exchanged with the Ministers in the Government he was serving or with any of his allies, with the Queen or even with Sarah. Possibly the reason for his reticence was that he took the opportunity in this first approach to remind the Duke of Berwick of the *douceur* of two million livres (about £300,000) which he had previously been offered by the French King if ever he found it possible to smooth the way for a convenient settlement. No evidence exists that Marlborough was deflected from his duty by these temptations. But the mystery of his character which inspired him to play so many roles at the same time was bound to fascinate his own generation as it has so many since.

The truth about the tortuous contradictions in his career was, of course, not then known. But it was known that he had risen to favour while his sister was mistress of King James II, that he had ridden out of London at the head of King James's troops and returned the same week at the head of King William's, that King William in turn had come to distrust his brilliant supporter and had sent him to the Tower to learn a lesson in loyalty. The suspicion was that he had retained some connexions with the Jacobite court across the Channel; the fact was that, even while he acted as the arch-champion of the Grand Alliance, he cultivated these connexions, as a policy of reinsurance, over a quarter of a century. Marlborough never ceased to curse the ingratitude of the English, 'the villainous people' who failed to appreciate with sufficient unanimity the service he had performed for the nation. In his secret correspondence, although never in his outward demeanour, he revealed his fury at the lies they told about him. What would have been his defence if they had discovered the truth! Most of the charges, notably those in a book called *The New Atalantis* by a certain Mrs. Manley, published early in 1709, were too extreme to be credible. But it was natural enough that so ambivalent a Colossus should arouse envy, suspicion and ceaseless curiosity.

Since the beginning of the reign he had been called 'the Grand Vizier', and the term, it seems, was used respectfully and not only as a nickname by his enemies. After he had been appointed Prince of Mindelheim by the Austrian Emperor he assumed (according to Lord Dartmouth, one of his detractors) 'the title of highness abroad which was given him by all the officers in the army; and he affected eating alone, which the Duke of Montagu (who had married one of his daughters) was to countenance by standing at his meals. Nobody in England would allow of such distinctions; but everybody thought his aim was to bring us by degrees to something much higher'. No doubt this report was highly coloured. But the Churchill family, their relations, their friends and their sycophants appeared to surround the Queen, to command automatic majorities in Parliament, to direct the armies and, for makeweight, to dominate the City of London. The caricature bore enough resemblance to the real features of society in 1709 to make the attacks upon him plausible. And this was the moment chosen to demand the Generalcy for life!

After Malplaquet Marlborough received the thanks of Parliament for his services in language more glowing than had ever been used before. The Ministers in office were more unanimously dedicated to the cause of crushing the power of France than at any time since 1702, when Queen Anne had first declared the paramount aim of her policy. The great Whig Lords, backed by the bankers, were the most steadfast supporters of the war, and a year earlier they had swept back to power at the elections on a burst of national patriotism. For the first time since the Revolution of 1688 they had secured a settled majority in the Commons. Indeed it was a rare event for the two Houses to find themselves so readily at one; during most of the reign they had been at each other's throats, fighting a desperate battle for party supremacy. In the Lords the great Whig statesmen who had led the Revolution had retained their control and had often resorted to the device of appealing to the public over the heads of the Commons by publishing reports of their proceedings. In the Commons the Tories for the most part had commanded a majority; they were the 'Church of England party' and in the tiny electorates of those times exercised a special influence through the activity of the Tory squires and the lower ranks of the clergy. Through most of the period when Marlborough was winning battles in the company of Dutch Calvinists, German Lutherans and a Catholic Emperor, the English Parliament, on the initiative of the Tories in the Commons, was engaged in a ferocious struggle to discover the proper means of destroying the twin monsters of popery and dissent.

Marlborough might be excused for thinking that he had a big enough task in fighting the war. How comparatively simple to guide English, Scots, Irish, Danes, Prussians, Hanoverians, Hessians, Saxons, Palatines and Dutch in the same harness towards the battlefields! But he was always embroiled in domestic controversies, until he came to speak of Whig and Tory with more venom than he ever directed against the obstinate Dutch or the Austrian Emperor in his most capricious moments. Only at last in the elections of 1708, following an attempt by the Pretender to invade Scotland, was a Whig majority with a single-minded devotion to the war secured in the Commons, and by that time the possibility of peace presented the real challenge to English statesmanship. Any commander in the field with a comprehensive view of the world struggle would naturally be outraged by such perversity.

Despite all the favourable signs, therefore, Marlborough was discontented. He saw himself sinking in the bog of English party warfare. Probably that was the clue to his mysterious blunder in approaching the Queen. A Captain-General for life would no longer be answerable to Parliament. Whig and Tory could knife one another in a contemptible contest while he was left free to conduct successful war or make a reasonable peace. Perhaps that was too much to hope for. But often, like so many others, he had toyed with a variation on the same theme. Let the hot men on both sides abandon their futile aspirations and make way for a national administration whose policy he himself might shape. Since the very idea of parties in the state was novel and utterly disruptive of the prerogatives which not only Anne but every King and Queen before her had claimed, he had sounder grounds for this conceit than the many opponents of the party system who have shared it since those times.

In short, Marlborough had excellent reasons for seeking an exceptional authority above the party battle. And both parties in the state, with their memories of Stuart or Cromwellian despotism to guide them, had no less excellent reasons for denying it. No doubt the sharp rebuff from the Queen added to his misgivings. Instead of appreciating the unexampled position which was already his without the new appointment, he gave the impression in his private correspondence that he felt the ground trembling beneath his feet. To understand his presentiments it is necessary to explore the maze of English politics.

* * *

SARAH

The politician in London who stood closest to the Duke in everything but precise party affiliation was his wife, the Duchess.

Sarah at the age of forty-nine was a source of boundless vitality and intrigue, insatiable in influence and ambition, masterful, outspoken, restless, an aggressive Whig, and, with it all, a wonder of loveliness. Often she plagued Marlborough with pettifogging complaints or even challenged his constancy to her. But all her actions, however infuriating, were prompted by her abundant love towards him. One of the lampooners compared Marlborough to the Roman hero, Belisarius, and the mystified Sarah asked her friend Bishop Burnet to explain the comparison. The Bishop, who gloried in his readiness to speak the truth without flattery, gave the bravest retort of his life. 'Belisarius', he said, 'had a brimstone of a wife.'

The records of Sarah the Termagant have been carefully preserved, thanks to the memories of the multitude who felt the cut of her tongue. In December, 1708, one anonymous pamphleteer gave his impressions of the Duchess he saw as a vision in a dream. 'On the Right-Hand an oldish Woman, of a fair countenance, in youthful Dress; her Chin and Nose turning up, her Eyes glowing like Lightning; blasted all she had power over with strange Diseases. Out of her Nostrils came a Sulphurous Smoak, and out of her Mouth Flames of Fire. Her hair was grizled and adorn'd with Spoils of ruin'd People. Her Neck bare, with Chains about it of Dice, mixed with Pieces of Gold, which rattling, made a horrid noise; for her Motions were all fierce and violent. Her garment was all stained with Tears and Blood. There hung about her several Pieces of Parchment, with Bits of Wax at the end, with Figures engraved on them. She cast her Eyes often with Rage and Fury on that bright Appearance I have described (the Queen); over whom, having no force, she tossed her Head with disdain, and glared about on her Votaries, till we saw several possessed with her.'

But there is another side of the story which enabled Henry Fielding to compose his portrait of 'the Glorious Duchess'. By any test she was a tremendous figure, able to argue and conspire with the foremost statesmen of the time and exerting her influence far and wide throughout political society. At every vantage-point on the arena her daughters and dependants, her friends and admirers, were stationed like sentinels to watch the Marlborough interest. One daughter was married to the eldest son of Lord Godolphin, the chief Minister in the Government; the second to the Earl of Sunderland, another member of the Ministry whose devotion to the Whig cause was rigid enough to satisfy even Sarah's standards; the third to the Earl of Bridgwater and the fourth to the son of the Duke of Montagu. In time she quarrelled with them all, daughters, sons-in-law, grandsons and grand-daughters. But one cause at least of her fury was the perspicacity with which she viewed the political scene. Hating both by temperament and for sound reasons of expediency every form of shilly-shallying, she made her choice. She had no patience with those, her husband included, who hankered always for some uneasy accommodation above party. The facts could not be altered; the beginning of wisdom was to face them. From her earliest days of active politics she imbibed Whig principles, a hatred of 'the gibberish' of the Tories 'about non-resistance and passive obedience and hereditary right', a splendid contempt for 'the High Church nonsense of promoting religion by persecution'.

King William heaped hardship on the Marlborough family, but that could not drive Sarah into the opposite camp. 'As I was perfectly convinced that a Roman Catholic is not to be trusted with the liberties of England, I never once repined at the change of government, no, not in all the time of that long persecution I went through.' When William sent Marlborough to the Tower, she still did not waver. To a friend who offered bail she replied that 'one of his best friends was a paper that lay upon the table, which I had often kissed, the Act of Habeas Corpus'. Those surely were the words of one who recognized the bulwarks of the new freedom which some Englishmen were beginning to enjoy in a style still denied to the subjects of Continental monarchies. So too, when the struggle was transferred to the larger stage of European war, Sarah adhered to a simple proposition. If English and European liberties depended on victory, Marlborough would need to make terms with the men who truly believed in them, the party which had burnt its boats and staked its future on the Protestant succession. This was the gospel which she preached in season and out of season, to the Queen, to the Duke and to the whole of her entourage. And who can say that she was wrong? Terribly late and by *force majeure* Marlborough was brought to the same conclusion. By 1709 he too had realized his fate was interlocked with that of the great Whig Lords. But how much safer his base at home might have been if he had appreciated the fact earlier and pursued the aim of an alliance with the Whigs from the beginning of the reign with something of Sarah's rock-like determination. How often as she watched his infirmity of purpose in handling men whom she regarded as his mortal enemies must she have wished to remonstrate: 'Give *me* the daggers!'

The case for the Duchess and the political course she prescribed has been submerged beneath the records of the most famous court intrigue in English history. Was it not her primary duty to mollify Queen Anne, to keep her firmly devoted to Marlborough's aims, to ensure, whatever happened in Parliament and elsewhere, that the Marlborough interest remained undisputed at the court? Did she not instead dissipate her position of supremacy over Anne, provoke the Queen beyond endurance and surrender her power into the hands of her rival, Mrs. Masham? How could it happen that the radiant Sarah was outwitted by the menial, red-nosed Abigail? Certainly in 1709 a major cause of Marlborough's anxiety was the screeching feud which had grown between his wife and the Queen. The Captain-General understood courts better than Parliaments; he understood Parliaments better than the fever of controversy, pulpit oratory and pamphleteering outside. He was the arch-manipulator. Everything could be managed. No situation was too delicate not to be retrievable by a recipe of courtesy, suppleness and the proper dose of deceit. He wished his wife would employ the same arts, but she was a woman whose pride it was to speak the rudest truth in the face of her dearest friends. And yet it is doubtful whether Sarah's disposition was the only cause of the estrangement with the Queen.

For years before she ascended the throne Anne delighted in Sarah's dominance. No words could properly express how abject was her love of 'dear Mrs. Freeman'. But at that time they had shared a common hatred against King William and no political conflict arose to mar the purity of Anne's adoration. Under Sarah's tutelage Anne's rival court was manœuvred brilliantly; they waited for 'the sunshine day' when Anne would be Queen and Sarah the most powerful woman English politics had known since Queen Elizabeth. But when the day dawned, already a cloud appeared. Anne loved her Church, which doubtless offered a balm more soothing than Sarah's ministrations. She favoured the Tories whom she regarded as the only true protectors of the Church. Indeed the Tories 'she usually called by the agreeable

name of the Church Party'. Her uncle was the Earl of Rochester, a
leader of the high-flyers, the high churchmen for whom Toryism
was more a religion than a party creed. Every claim of family
piety, every twinge of conscience left by the memory of the way
she had deserted her father, King James II, must have driven Anne
in the same direction. For what cause but that of the Church had
she been justified in preferring the odious King William to the pull
of her own blood? And if ever she was tempted to believe that
others besides her faithful Tories would truly uphold the cause of
the Church, Sarah's deafening logic was there to convince her.
'For my part,' wrote the Duchess, 'I had not the same prepossessions. The *word* Church had never any charm for *me*, in the mouths
of those who made the most noise with it; for I could not perceive
that they gave any other distinguishing proof of their regard for
the *thing*, than a frequent use of the *word*, like a spell to enchant
weak minds; and a persecuting zeal against dissenters, and against
those real friends of the Church who could not admit that persecution was agreeable to its doctrine.' For Sarah, the Whig cause
was England's cause and Marlborough's cause. That much in
politics was clear as the noonday. The interest of the Church was,
in comparison, at best the merest trifle, at worst an excuse for
intolerance towards whose who were most forthright in their
support of the Protestant war. It is hard to believe that the clash
with the Queen would not have come on grounds of principle, even
if Sarah had had the patience and humility of a saint.

As the years passed, the familiarity between the two jarred at
every encounter until it changed to loathing. Each was driven to
desperation by the mere mention of the other's name. Poor Sarah!
What was she to do? When Marlborough heard of the importunate
letters and interviews complaining of misusage and demanding
proper respect for his services which Sarah was pressing on the
Queen, he shuddered at his wife's incapacity to understand elementary psychology, advised her to stay away from the court and
leave time to heal the wound which her nursing would only
enflame. Meanwhile, Lord Godolphin and several others were
complaining that her absence left the Queen free to accept all the
advice which Mrs. Masham whispered into her ear.

Abigail Masham had been introduced to the Queen's household
several years before by Sarah herself. She was a distant relative
and owed everything to Sarah's patronage. Gradually she estab-

lished an independent position with the Queen and helped to fill
the void which the withdrawal of Sarah's affection had left. She
was also the cousin of Robert Harley, the most skilful of the moderate Tories and for a period the most prominent among the
Queen's Ministers after Marlborough and Godolphin. Abigail
never achieved the ascendancy over the Queen which had once
been Sarah's, but in office or out of office Harley supplied the
political acumen which Abigail lacked. Thanks to the Abigail-
Harley intrigue, the Queen, sometimes exaggeratedly described as
'the stupidest woman in Europe', was gaining the security she
craved, a new master if not a new mistress. Sarah stumbled on the
truth suddenly. Abigail had married without letting her patron
know, and Sarah's attempt to upbraid both the Queen and the new
favourite for the deception only confirmed her fear.

Within a few weeks Marlborough understood that his position
at home had been weakened at the one place where he might have
expected it to be strongest. He could not court the Queen and win
battles at the same time. Month by month the tension grew between the two women. Marlborough could see no way of repairing
the damage. 'I would go upon all-four to make it easy between
you,' he wrote a week or two before the battle of Malplaquet,
'but for credit, I am satisfied that I have none; so that I would
willingly not expose myself, but meddle as little as possible.' A
month later he did expose himself with his request to become
General for life. It was a rough remedy for so delicate a disease.
He had learnt by then that the Queen's anger was such that she
even failed to congratulate the Duchess on the victory at Malplaquet. That was one good reason why he sensed danger for the
future. All the plaudits of the faithful Lords and Commons could
not remove from his mind the suspicion that some conspiracy was
afoot and that the Queen herself might be a party to it. But was
there really so much cause for alarm? If the Queen could not
tolerate the Duchess, she still behaved with perfect correctness
towards the Duke and gave plentiful indication that she recognized how indispensable he really was. In that same October of
1709 when Marlborough had made his request to the Queen,
Anne wrote to Sarah: 'It is impossible for you to recover my
former kindness, but I shall know how to behave myself to you as
the Duke of Marlborough's wife, and as my Groom of the Stole.'

*   *   *

GODOLPHIN

Alongside Sarah, at Marlborough's right hand, stood Sidney, Lord Godolphin, Lord Treasurer in the Queen's Council and already described on a few rare occasions as the Prime Minister. The friendship between the three was extremely close; it gave the excuse to the Tory pamphleteer, Mrs. Manley—as if she ever needed one!—for her libel that Sarah was Godolphin's mistress with Marlborough's complaisance. Certainly in political matters the two men looked on the world with the same eyes. Like Marlborough, Godolphin had served the Stuarts and then swum with the stream when King William landed at Torbay. Like Marlborough, he had had doubts about the permanency of the Revolution and had taken the same secret precautions to assure the Jacobite court that his loyalty could be relied upon in the event of a second Restoration. Few bonds are so strong as a common treachery and as the years passed they soon found worthier reasons for the consolidation of their partnership. At every twist in the intricate political game necessary to sustain their authority they kept in step.

At the beginning of the reign they were both regarded as Tories or, at least, as friends to the Tory interest. The Queen lost no time in informing her Lord Treasurer that she was determined to govern without respect to party, choosing the men who would serve her most faithfully and abjure the rage of faction—a theme she repeated tirelessly month after month and one which was heartily acceptable to Godolphin and Marlborough, since the Queen's ideal of government exactly conformed with their own— as long as they were both among the chosen. The Queen at once showed her curious idea of a contempt for party by appointing an administration in which all but a few, and those the most amenable, of the Whig Lords were excluded, while immense power was accorded to several of the most rigid of the high-flying Tories— her uncle, the Earl of Rochester, the Earl of Nottingham, Lord Jersey, Lord Normanby and a number of their dependants, men who believed that the great problem of the age was less the defeat of King Louis on the battlefields than the full establishment of the power of the Church against the dissenters, the free-thinkers and the republicans who took cover and perpetually plotted beneath the emblems of the Whigs. If independence of party meant a coalition Ministry in which even the mildest of the Whigs might find favour and dispense patronage, these men had other ideas.[1] They had their own theory, too, about the war; they advocated a maritime strategy designed to keep the country's commitments strictly limited. Now that William was gone, why should English blood and English land taxes be spent so profusely to capture fortresses for the Dutch?

The clash between Marlborough and Godolphin and men dedicated to these doctrines was bound to be sharp, and it came quickly. When Marlborough had finished his first campaign, the Tory leaders in the House of Commons effectively detracted from the thanks of Parliament by coupling his name with that of their own naval hero, Sir George Rooke, who had just returned from an unsuccessful expedition to Cadiz. The Queen, angered by their ingratitude, made Marlborough a Duke with a pension of £5,000 a year. The pension proposal would have to pass the Commons where the Tories threatened to fight it. Thus before he had won any of his great victories Marlborough and Godolphin were given a plain indication of how fierce was the opposition to the war in Flanders from a considerable section of the nation they sought to mobilize for the struggle. Soon the Queen was persuaded to shed the most inflexible of her Tory advisers. But never could the Captain-General and the Lord Treasurer remove finally from their reckoning the possibility that the Tories might regain control over the Queen and the Ministry and shatter the European alliance they were painfully constructing. At the very moment when Marlborough was leading his armies across Europe to the Danube on his most audacious enterprise, two of the ousted Tory leaders, Rochester and Seymour, were threatening to attempt his impeachment. They vowed they would run him down when he came back as a pack of hounds do a hare. When the news of victory reached London they could not share the general rejoicing, a thought which still gave comfort to the old Duchess in her eighties when she completed her memoirs. 'It happened', she wrote, 'that my Lord Marlborough in the summer before the Parliament met, gained the Battle of Blenheim. This was an unfortunate accident; and by the

---

[1] Much debate continues between modern historians about the sense in which the terms 'Whig' and 'Tory' can properly be used. This issue is discussed in an appendix, where the use of the anachronistic term 'coalition' is also discussed.

visible dissatisfaction of some people on the news of it, one would have imagined that instead of beating the French he had beat the Church.' Two years later, after Ramillies, while the rest of London was saluting the victor with rounds of cannon-fire and a cavalcade to the Guildhall, the Tories contrived a debate complaining about a supplementary estimate. After Oudenarde, the rumble of discontent grew louder. After Malplaquet, they were in full cry against 'the butcher's bill'. Party views on most topics could easily be changed for purposes of expediency and to assist the major aim of gaining office, but neither Godolphin nor Marlborough could doubt that hatred of the war among some of the Tories was hardly less deep-rooted than their love of the Church. Other combinations must be fostered and accepted.

★   ★   ★

THE JUNTO

At first the Queen's ideal of an administration at the mercy of no faction was secured by an alliance with Robert Harley, the Tory moderate, and his brilliant aide, Henry St. John. But Harley's intrigue with Mrs. Masham and the Queen and the growing determination of the Whigs to exact a political reward for the sustenance they had given to the Marlborough-Godolphin foreign policies forced another shift in party alignment. Reluctantly, Marlborough and Godolphin turned to make new allies, to accept the Whigs as their political base, to bring into the Cabinet Council as their companions and perhaps their masters the little group of Whig leaders known as the Lords of the Junto.

The manœuvre was painful for both Godolphin and Marlborough. At every step forward toward the goal they had to meet the complaints of the Queen. At every half-step back the Whigs suspected them of double-dealing and heightened their terms. No doubt the frayed tempers of the two men were not improved by their awareness that the political destination they now realized to be desirable was the same which Sarah had marked out for them with such blazing clarity years before. At each stage when a new member of the Whig clique had to be forced on the Queen the deed could only be done by a near-ultimatum. Godolphin had to enlist the pressure of Marlborough and, on some occasions, threaten that a refusal by the Queen to approve the appointment of some new candidate from the detested Whig hierarchy might involve the resignation of the indispensable General who commanded her armies or the indispensable Lord Treasurer who filled her coffers. These hectoring tactics in turn infuriated the Queen and gave colour to the charge, sedulously spread in the country, that the rights of the monarch were being invaded by a family cabal. If it was to come to this, might it not have been wiser to exert the power of ultimatum while the trophies of Blenheim and Ramillies were untarnished by the heavier bloodshed of Oudenarde and Malplaquet and before the Queen had gained Harley as her back-stairs adviser? That had been Sarah's prescription for success. She was in the thick of the correspondence which passed between Marlborough in Flanders and Godolphin at home. Perhaps unfortunately for her political reputation her letters have been destroyed, and Marlborough's biographers, notably Sir Winston Churchill, invite us to accept at every move the superior wisdom of the Duke as he edged so cautiously towards the final compact with the Whigs. As it happened, the agreement was made so grudgingly that the Whigs themselves, for all their dependence on Marlborough's generalship, never learnt to trust without reserve the two men who had preferred their lofty pre-eminence above the strife of factions.[1]

At last, however, a Whig Ministry was effectively thrust on the Queen. Whatever might have been the prospects if Sarah's bold

[1] A hostile but perceptive observer described the fragile bond between Marlborough and Godolphin on the one side and the Whig Lords on the other which each was compelled to turn into something more solid. 'Our Ministers', he said, 'declared openly for the Whigs, and this created a new thing called a Junto, a Ministry within a Ministry: Some of this Junto had formerly been eminent leaders of the unanimous Whigs in the House of Commons; but they made their bargain before they would engage in the work, if the Ministers would turn out and take in as they pleased, then their party in the Parliament should stand by the Ministers on all occasions; however, it was some years before they could work it up to an entire confidence in each other: Sometimes the Ministers promised to gratify them with such changes of hands as they required, and after Parliament was up, neglected the performance: The next session the Junto would be sure to thwart them by their friends in the House of Commons; then all was made up again by a new bargain, which yet was perhaps but half performed; then the Junto quarrelled again, upbraided them with breach of promise, sought out for faults to tax them with, and now and then gave them a pinch in the House of Commons, till they promised a full compliance: And thus it passed through several sessions, sometimes in league, sometimes at daggers drawing. . . .'

advice had been accepted, Marlborough in 1709 had good reason for wondering what scars had been left by the harsh treatment of Anne. Not only was his wife quarrelling with the Queen; his faithful Godolphin by whose hand so many of the objectionable decrees had been delivered had lost credit with her too. Only a few months before the Queen had cried out to the Duke in her distress: 'For God's sake save me from the five lords of the Junto! For God's sake, do but make it your own case, and consider then what you would do, and why a handful of men must awe their fellow-subjects. There is nobody more desirous than I to encourage those Whig friends that behave themselves well; but I do not care to have anything to do with those that have shown themselves to be of so tyrannising a temper; and not to run on farther on those subjects, to be short, I think things are come to, whether I shall submit to the five Tyrannising Lords, or they to me.' Marlborough had answered that appeal with a deed. On one side stood the Queen, Harley, Mrs. Masham, and not so far behind them the outraged Tories, bent on revenge and ready if they could to seek an end of the war. On the other side were ranged the heads of all the allied states who regarded him as their pillar of hope, the Whig Lords dedicated to the cause of total victory and commanding large majorities in both Houses of Parliament, the City men who provided so much of the sinews for the fight—and Sarah. At last he made his choice. Sarah had reached her hour of triumph and the Whigs had reason to toast her as the greatest of them all.

In that autumn of 1709 three out of five of the 'tyrannising Whig Lords'—Lord Somers, Lord Sunderland and Lord Wharton—were Ministers of the Queen; a fourth, Lord Halifax, held a position of immense authority; and in November a place was found for Lord Orford, who with the others made up the famous Junto. Most official positions of influence in the state were now assembled in the hands of persons whose policies were guided by these five. How close was the compact between them, how true the accusation of 'a Ministry within a Ministry', it is difficult to estimate; but if the fear and envy of their opponents can be taken as one accurate measure the new phenomenon was menacing in the extreme. These were the usurpers of her rights whom the Queen regarded as 'the merciless men'. Lord Godolphin, even when at last he sought political alliance with them, never ceased to rail against their 'inveteracy'. Marlborough shared the belief that their aim was a monopoly of power. All of them, with the exception of Lord Orford, were politicians of outstanding capacity. They were not cowed by Marlborough's European reputation despite their desire to make good use of it to suit their own purposes. They had faith in their own competence to govern. The strongest strain of arrogance ran through them all. It formed a link more impressive even than their party association and in one sense makes their partnership over a number of years the more remarkable; for each was a man capable of carving his own fortune and qualified to assume the highest office.

Apart from individual gifts, they certainly had good grounds for their self-assurance. After Malplaquet a mood of war-weariness had settled on the nation, but why should they be alarmed by these sudden gusts of opinion? Looking back over the previous quarter of a century, had they not the right to believe that the future was theirs, that they could ordain the general political climate? Were they not shaping English society and indeed the map of Europe to their own pattern? True, they had suffered setbacks. After King James was removed from the throne, King William ungratefully refused to accept their bidding and become 'King of the Whigs'. After the first impulse of the Revolution had waned, Tory and Church of England sentiment showed its resilience. At most of the elections since 1689 the Tory voting power when combined with the influence of the monarch had been sufficient to gain substantial majorities in the Commons. Queen Anne had been possessed from the start by (what Sarah called) 'her most real and invariable passion for that phantom which she called the Church; that darling phantom which the Tories were for ever presenting to her imagination, and employing as a will-o'-the-wisp'. Together these influences had often been able to confound the high expectations for their party which the Revolution had aroused among the Whigs. And yet the manner in which the Whig leaders had surmounted these obstacles was the clearest proof of how potent their doctrine was. It was no trifling coincidence that Isaac Newton and John Locke could be counted among their colleagues. The spirit of the age was in league with them. By the middle of the reign it appeared that this spirit was being translated into practical political advantage. Through their superior wisdom the Junto had gained victory after victory over both the Queen and most other of their opponents, until in 1708 and 1709 the men she had been willing to condemn to the political wilderness only six or seven years before were now commanding exclusive power in the land.

One example of their mastery was the defeat they inflicted at the very point where the Tories counted themselves most impregnable. 'The Church in danger' was always the most profitable Tory cry. No sooner was Anne on the throne and the Tories in office than the leaders of the Church Party resolved to seize their opportunity. They took steps to destroy the device whereby the growing body of dissenters sought escape from the rigour of the Test and Corporation Acts. These Acts, faithfully applied, would have excluded multitudes in the rising middle class from all branches of government by compelling them to take the Church sacrament. Many took the sacrament once in order to qualify formally, but for the rest of the year continued to attend their own chapels, a practice condemned by Daniel Defoe 'as a kind of playing Bo-peep with God Almighty'. Time and again with the Queen's eager approval an Occasional Conformity Bill was introduced by the Tories in the House of Commons to close this loophole in the law for 'tender consciences'. On one occasion the Queen's own husband, Prince George of Denmark, was sent to the House of Lords to vote for the Bill. Unwilling to offend the Queen, Marlborough and Godolphin voted for it too. But time and again the Whig Lords whipped up their strength to quash the proposal. The parliamentary manœuvres were conducted so adroitly that the Queen herself became angered by the too insistent charge from the Tories that under her beneficent reign the Church was still in danger. In the end Lord Wharton, the least pious of the impious Whig Lords, was able to parry a fresh demand from the Archbishops for a special guarantee for the Church. 'The Church is secure without it,' he said, ' since the scripture has declared that the gates of hell shall not prevail against it.' The brazen sneer could not have provoked more anger among Churchmen had it been spoken by Beelzebub himself.

Hardly less spectacular was the audacity with which the Whig statesmen drove through the Act of Union with Scotland, even before they had acquired full control of the Queen's Council. England, but not Scotland, was at war with France, and when Anne died no security was provided for the Protestant succession in Scotland. The Act of Union was necessary to complete the revolutionary settlement, but so fierce was the opposition among wide sections of Scottish opinion that only a bold threat devised by the Whig leaders made possible the final achievement. If the Scots did not submit, Scotsmen would be treated as aliens in England and their trade across the border consequently brought to a standstill. The Aliens Act, introduced by Lord Somers, clinched the issue. Once more the Tories were exposed as the champions of a lost cause and the Whigs meantime were assured of a considerable addition to their voting strength in the new British Parliament. A few days after the process of ratification was completed Lord Wharton who had played a chief part in the consummation had an Earldom conferred upon him. It was the custom then for draftsmen to produce elaborate citations extolling in detail the virtues of the newly-chosen. Lord Wharton instead craved simplicity. 'By the Queen's will and pleasure' were the only words he wanted. He had spent a lifetime mocking the cause which was dearest to the Queen's heart. Nothing for him could equal the relish of seeing her make obeisance before the rising star of the Whigs.

Effectively too and with seeming success the Whigs had enforced their will in the conduct of the war and foreign policy. They could rejoice without qualification over Marlborough's victories and were able to turn to their own benefit the sour attempts of the Tories to diminish the towering stature of the Captain-General. The war was being fought to secure three aims: to prevent a Jacobite restoration in England; to protect the Dutch from being placed at the mercy of the French in the Netherlands; and, finally, to ensure that King Louis' grandson, Philip of Anjou, was not established on the throne of Spain. In allegiance to their idea of a naval strategy, the Tories stressed the importance of the conquest of Spain as against the war in Flanders. They found in Lord Peterborough, who had fought two campaigns there before his dismissal by the Whigs, a flamboyant war hero to share some of Marlborough's laurels. On every major count the preference for Spain had little to commend it. Philip of Anjou was popular in the country and the attempt of the Grand Alliance to install in his place the Hapsburg claimant, the Archduke Charles, roused widespread opposition from Spaniards. The idea of an easy conquest in Spain was always a will-o'-the-wisp. Nevertheless, for a while, the Tories no less than the Whigs were committed to the formula of 'No peace without Spain'; in other words, no peace until Philip of Anjou had been finally expelled from Spanish territory. This Tory insistence on the supremacy of the Spanish theatre of war blunted their other claim to be the real champions of a reasonable peace. The more far-seeing among them, notably Henry St. John, recognized the peril. By the end of 1708, he understood that a coherent Tory campaign for peace must entail a readiness to cut losses in Spain. But it was not easy to persuade his factious companions.

Meantime, the Whigs suffered no such embarrassment from divided counsels. They were still hot for the war, so hot that in the spring of 1709 they wrecked the prospects of peace which their allies, the Dutch, were sorely tempted to seize. King Louis was pleading for an armistice on almost any terms. Famine had come to put the coping-stone on Marlborough's victories. France was ready to surrender the whole Spanish Empire, including Spain itself, Naples, Sicily, and Milan, as well as Strasbourg and Alsace. Thus the Hapsburg Emperor would be appeased, and to the Dutch France would yield an extensive group of fortresses. As for Philip of Anjou, if he refused to abandon his throne and evacuate all his forces from Spanish territory within two months, the allies, keeping all their gains, would be entitled to renew the war. But one clause in the proposed treaty King Louis would not swallow. If Philip, now in control of nine-tenths of Spain, would not obey the dictate of the peacemakers, the French King was required to join with his victorious enemies to remove his own grandson from Spanish soil. It was this final, fantastic demand which disrupted the negotiations, and the Whigs were in no mood to remove the obstacle. Either they suspected some new trick on the part of the French King whom they regarded as a monster of perfidy, or their appetites were whetted for fresh military victories. Whatever the excuse for their overbearing diplomacy, it is evident that they were not much alarmed by the Tory bid to step forward as the peace party.

In October of 1709 the Whigs made another move to strengthen, as they thought, the weak links in the alliance and ensure that the war was fought to the bitter end. The Dutch wanted to stop the fighting hardly less than King Louis. They had suffered casualties on an enormous scale. Their trade was sorely hit. They were more concerned about the war on their own door-step than about Spain. Might they not be tempted to sign a separate peace? The charge of treachery could not be too forcibly pressed against them, for two years earlier England had signed a secret treaty with the Austrian Emperor assigning to the English monopoly trading rights with the Spanish Empire at the expense of the Dutch. To guard against this threat to the alliance, real or imaginary, the Whig leaders once more acted boldly, if unwisely. They sent their own agent, Lord Townshend, to negotiate at The Hague. Brushing aside objections from Marlborough, they instructed Townshend to sign the Dutch Barrier Treaty. According to this treaty, the Dutch, when victory was won, would be entitled to garrison an extensive list of fortresses in the Spanish Netherlands and along the French border, while England sacrificed the trading advantages she had secured in the secret agreement with the Austrians. In return, the Dutch pledged armed support for the Hanoverian succession in England, a cause they would surely have been compelled to uphold in their own interest without any bond. The unwritten commitment was that they, too, should accept the war aim: 'No peace without Spain.' By this time Marlborough himself had become dubious about the proposition. He could 'see no good end to the taking of measures for the forcing of them out of Spain'. But at this stage in the diplomatic negotiations he occupied a status subordinate to the men whom he had unwillingly joined to rescue his strategy from Tory sabotage.

Thus it appeared that the authority of the Whigs was preeminent in every field at home and abroad. They were dizzy with success. In that year of 1709, too, 'an Act was passed that was much desired, and had been often attempted, but had been laid aside in so many former parliaments that there was scarce any hopes left to encourage a new attempt; it was for naturalizing all foreign Protestants upon their taking the oaths to the Government and their receiving the sacrament in any Protestant church'. In these words the Whig Bishop, Burnet, applauded another luminous vindication of the principles of toleration, another stroke against Catholic tyranny. Wage-earners might complain about the threat to their jobs; the clergy looked askance at these additions to dissenting congregations; but the Whigs could rejoice with Roundhead fervour that the great Protestant cause was marching on.

In one sense, then, the men who now guided the nation's destiny could be pictured like their forbears with a Bible in one hand and a sword in the other. They sustained the war in the name of the Protestant faith. But in truth they bore little resemblance to the soldiers who had swept across the field of Naseby. They fought with new weapons in a new kind of struggle. Seventy years later Edmund Burke saw them as 'the wise men' who 'were not afraid that they should be called an ambitious Junto; or that their resolution to stand or fall together should, by placemen, be interpreted into a scuffle for places'. In his eyes they were the originators of the party system without which parliamentary government could not survive.

No doubt the portrait he painted is absurdly romantic. The men he portrayed as the immaculate upholders of constitutional government bribed the electors, seized pensions and places for themselves and their friends, pursued family vendettas with a Corsican ferocity, and often betrayed their high liberal principles to grasp a new addition of power. But they kept their central aim steadily before them. They wanted to guard the achievements of their Revolution and assure the Protestant succession. Today the challenge to those achievements which the Junto had to meet may not look very real, and the self-seeking of each member of it which mingled with their public aims may help to sustain the charge of hypocrisy. But the Whig leaders of Queen Anne's reign had an excuse for their fears when, as they knew, such men as Marlborough and Godolphin had intrigued with the Jacobite Pretender and when one of their own number, Lord Orford, was guilty of the same offence. Had it not been for the novel means whereby they scuffled for places *in concert* none of their victories might have come within reach. It is churlish not to admire the daring with which they exploited the potentialities of the developing constitutional system. One by one they forced their way into the Queen's councils in a manner which had never been attempted before. They did not shrink from browbeating her to secure their ends. Both Marlborough and Godolphin sympathized with 'the poor Queen', but both were compelled to exert their own authority to help make the threats effective. In the last resort—so it was said—Godolphin was forced to yield through Lord Wharton's lucky discovery of the manuscript of one of Godolphin's treacherous letters to the Jacobite court. A man like Wharton who boasted 'I own driving out King James and I would do it again' was not likely to stop short at blackmail for the exalted purpose of bringing another Stuart monarch to heel. Nor did he and his friends have qualms in delivering an open attack on the Queen's husband, Prince George of Denmark, for his conduct of the Admiralty.

No wonder the Junto Lords gained a reputation for ruthlessness. But they had other attributes besides. Lord Somers, Lord Halifax and Lord Sunderland were men of culture; they amassed great libraries and were the patrons of literature. Somers, 'the head and oracle' of his party, was the first lawyer of the age and gained a name for spotless integrity both among his own contemporaries (only Sarah had doubts!) and for nearly two hundred years later until the archives were opened. Halifax had founded the Bank of England and reformed the currency; he laid the basis for the Whig alliance with the City. Sunderland at the age of thirty-five was not overawed by his older companions who had been serving previous monarchs in high office when he had hardly left school; he often seemed to provide the driving force for new political conquests and did not hesitate to pick a quarrel with Marlborough, his father-in-law, or—more greatly daring—with Sarah herself. As for Lord Wharton, he symbolized the attractive Whig compromise between Roundhead principles and Cavalier tastes. At the time of the Revolution he had not confined his activities strictly to politics. He wrote the famous song 'Lillibullero' which, according to his own boast, sang a king out of his kingdom. Ever afterwards Wharton conducted his political affairs with a lilting abandon. He drank hard, blasphemed, fought duels, fornicated on a notorious scale, combined his political intrigues with an endless round of race meetings, and still earned the name of 'Honest Tom' among the devout dissenters whom he shepherded towards the polling booths. He was the great electioneer and organizer, performing both his duties and his pleasures with the same boisterous efficiency. None of the others showed quite the same open contempt for the flimsy conventions of the time, but all were suspected of devising their own moral codes and atheistic philosophies as cheerfully as they had dethroned their King. The manner in which they flaunted their mistresses was just another sign that they cared neither for God nor man nor monarch. If pride was the deadly sin, none could doubt their guilt. They were rebels against the forms of authority which prevailed over most of Europe, and those who trembled to see the old landmarks and institutions of English society at their mercy could be pardoned for fearing how far the convulsion was likely to go.

Sarah expressed a part of their creed with characteristic scorn: 'As princes', she said, 'are not the best judges of right and wrong, from the flattery they are used to, not to say worse of them, I think the best thing for them and the whole nation is not to let them have power to hurt themselves or anyone else . . . This makes me think of the old Castile oath: "We that are as good as yourself and more powerful choose you to be our King upon such conditions ".'

When language which would have raised a cheer from Cromwell's Ironsides came from the lips of a Duchess with the ambition of a Lady Macbeth burning in her bosom it is not surprising that the men she selected as her political confederates were regarded with suspicion by a Queen whose father had lost his throne and whose grandfather had lost his head. Sunderland was said to preach his republicanism openly, to swear among his friends that the only name he wanted was Charles Spencer, and that he hoped to see the day when there should not be a peer left in England. Queen Anne protested that he 'always treated her with great rudeness and neglect, and chose to reflect in a very injurious manner upon all previous Princes as a proper entertainment for her'. Such outbursts, along with Sarah's Castilian oaths, might be dismissed as bombast. But the Queen knew well enough that the threats of the Junto were not to be taken lightly. As she looked around her Council table in the autumn of 1709 she might be excused if her distaste changed to terror and if she murmured to herself as she vainly pleaded to the Duke: 'For God's sake deliver me from the five tyrannising Lords!'

*   *   *

ST. JOHN

Others beside the Queen felt themselves enslaved by the powerful array of Marlborough, the Duchess, Godolphin and the Whigs. Among them was Henry St. John, who had ambition enough to challenge them all. He was only thirty-one years of age, but he was already acknowledged as the most brilliant orator of the day. Indeed, the impact on his audience was such that his fame lingered on throughout the century. No doubt the recollection was assisted by the polished marble of the prose in which his unspoken orations were handed down to posterity, but the verdict remains indisputable. As Secretary-at-war during the years of Blenheim and Ramillies he had proved that he possessed other gifts. Marlborough recognized them at once, learned to love him as a son and, so it is alleged, as the clinching proof of his affection, gave him money from the miser's store to pay his debts. The figure could not have been trifling for in spectacular profligacy St. John could match the Earl of Wharton. When he was appointed Minister, a woman of the streets was said to have cried, according to Voltaire: 'Seven thousand guineas a year, my girls, and all for us!' But in 1709 he was out of office and out of Parliament and, more remarkable, living agreeably with his wife in the country. He had left the Ministry when the Whigs made their final thrust for power and had failed to secure a parliamentary seat at the subsequent election.

He affected to be content with his rural life, but all the while he was busy inciting his friends to a programme of action. He firmly believed—and there were good grounds for the assumption—that the Tories commanded a natural majority of opinion and effective influence in the country. That no doubt was the reason why, despite his free-thinking philosophy, he had tended to choose the Tory side in politics. But now that Marlborough and Godolphin had made terms with the Whigs, now that he and his friends were excluded altogether from power by this alliance, he was bent on revenge. 'What can redeem us from more than Egyptian bondage?' he asked with a fervour equal to the Queen's. More clearly than most others he saw the answer. He was convinced that resolute exertions must be made to end the war. Every obstacle must be swept aside. And the pursuit of that purpose would itself assist in rallying the only force which could defeat the Whigs. 'There is no hope, I am fully convinced', he said, 'but in the Church of England party.'

Henry St. John placed no reliance in half-measures. At the moment when he could give orders to no one but his horses, his hounds and his wife, his objective was nothing less than the complete overthrow of the men in power. Where such a grandiose aim would lead him or the nation he hardly seemed to care. He would inspire a party on the same principle on which he had grasped the leadership of the House of Commons. 'You know the nature of that assembly,' he wrote; 'they grow, like hounds, fond of the man who shews them game and by whose halloo they are used to be encouraged.'

*　　*　　*

HARLEY

The leader to whom Henry St. John revealed at least part of these thoughts was a politician of a very different temperament. Robert Harley, the friend of Abigail Masham, formerly the obedient confidant of Marlborough and Godolphin, was in 1709, like St. John, out of office and seemingly without any strong party following at his back. Throughout the whole of Queen Anne's reign, he occupied the centre of the political stage; he was the great House of Commons middleman. He joined and, as his companions thought, betrayed every faction and group in turn. But he bore no rancour. Within a few months of a violent quarrel, his enemy might be put off his guard or secured to a new combination by a winning stroke of flattery. No feud was ever allowed to forbid an expedient reconciliation. Where anything was to be got, it was said, Harley always knew how to wriggle himself in; when any misfortune threatened, he knew how to wriggle himself out. 'He was a cunning and a dark man,' said another of his enemies. The portrait is painted by an unnamed friend of Sarah after she had confessed that words had failed her in giving a 'just character'. 'This mischievous darkness of his soul was written on his countenance and plainly legible in a very odd look, disagreeable to everybody at first sight, which being joined with a constant, awkward motion or agitation of his head and body, betrayed a turbulent dishonesty within, even in the midst of all those familiar airs, jocular bowing and smiling, which he always affected, to cover what could not be covered. He had long accustomed himself so much to dissemble his real intentions and to use the ambiguous and obscure way of speaking that he could hardly ever be understood when he designed it, or be believed when he never so much desired it.' A whole anthology of abuse could be compiled on the character of Robert Harley. 'If any man was ever born under a necessity of being a knave, he was', said Lord Cowper. Yet almost all the men who at one time or another attacked him so fiercely for his secrecy, his trickery or his procrastination had at other times fallen beneath his spell. In his letters he had a bent for the most nauseating sycophancy. In real life he must have exercised a wonderful charm. St. John called him his 'dear Master' and he was only one among the members of all parties and none from whom Harley invoked for a period at least the strongest strain of loyalty.

The manner of compromise was also with him a political philosophy. He had a puritan ancestry which provoked Tory jeers. That had not prevented him from wheedling his way into their counsels in the days when King William was, in Harley's view, leaning too much towards the Whigs. But Tory fanaticism revolted him no less and in the first years of the Queen's reign he broke away to join Marlborough and Godolphin in an attempt to build an administration beholden to no party. They met together two or three times a week when Marlborough was home from the battles and concerted every act of policy in the closest collaboration. At first Harley seemed quite content to play the role of Lepidus in the triumvirate, displaying towards his two great partners a grovelling humility and vowing that his single purpose was to run their errands and serve them faithfully. But the show was deceptive. All the while he was perfecting his mastery of the House of Commons and just occasionally, in his letters to Godolphin, formulating his creed. 'If the gentlemen of England are made sensible', he wrote, 'that the Queen is the Head, and not a Party, everything will be easy, and the Queen will be courted and not a Party: but if otherwise——' The alternative was left open. It was not Harley's way to prepare for distant contingencies.

One day he was given an urgent message from the Queen by a gardener at the palace. It was a cry for help, an invitation to conspiracy which appealed to everything in his nature. Sometime during the same summer of 1708 he made the convenient discovery that he was related to Abigail Masham who had taken Sarah's place at the side of the Queen. Within a few months Anne was writing to him as her 'very affectionate friend', Sarah had sensed the danger and Marlborough and Godolphin were persuaded that they had been nurturing a viper. How deeply he had plotted against them is not known. But certainly Marlborough and Godolphin were convinced of his perfidy. A clerk called Greg in Harley's office had been discovered selling secrets to the French. The occasion was used to demand his dismissal by the Queen: either Harley must go or she would lose the services of her Lord Treasurer and her Captain-General.

Just before or after this ultimatum was delivered, Harley, the procrastinator, resolved to play for the highest prize. He attempted with the Queen's backing to form a new Ministry under his complete control, to call Marlborough's bluff, if bluff it was, and to stake everything on his hold over the Queen and his power with the Commons. Only by a hairsbreadth did the scheme fail. Marlborough and Godolphin refused to appear at the Cabinet Council and one of the moderate Whig leaders, the Duke of Somerset, informed the Queen that the nation's business could not proceed without them. If she insisted on retaining Harley all her most prominent advisers would leave her and the government of the nation would be plunged into confusion. Even then Anne was minded not to budge. It was Harley, it seems, who realized that the odds against him were too heavy and advised her to yield. Along with Henry St. John and the few other remaining Tories he surrendered his seals of office. Doubtless he marked the lesson well. If he was ever to prevail against the Marlborough-Godolphin-Whig alliance, something more than the Queen's favour was needed. Sarah's outbursts and Abigail's intrigues were not sufficient to wreck Marlborough's power. Indeed, the expulsion of Harley from the government seemed for a while to make the war administration impregnable. Blow followed blow for the fallen favourites. Harley himself was lucky to escape a worse vengeance from the Whigs. They exploited the case of the traitor Greg for all they were worth. If only Harley could be implicated he could be impeached or attainted for high treason. Only the emphatic and repeated assertion of Greg that his master was innocent checked the most vindictive of Harley's enemies in their pursuit. Meantime, the anti-Jacobite feeling in the country had been roused by the Pretender's attempted invasion of Scotland. It was a dangerous moment for anyone whose loyalty to the Protestant cause was not above suspicion. The Whigs romped back at the elections in the autumn of 1708. The Queen was driven to despair, and not all the efforts of Abigail, with Harley's encouragement, could rouse her to action.

Harley's friends in London scratched around to find him crumbs of comfort. One of those friends was a Member of the House of Commons called Erasmus Lewis. He had served Harley as a Secretary in his department and he continued the service to his successors. But he, too, had been captured by Harley's charm and, since the Queen was content to intrigue with her ex-Minister against her official advisers, it was not surprising when others followed her example. Erasmus Lewis noted the growing hatred of the war, counting it the only blessing when affairs had reached 'so miserable a posture'. 'Misfortunes which usually obscure people's reason make men now more clear sighted,' he wrote, 'and you would be surprised to hear men say publicly, we have spent so many millions to find out this great secret, that our General does not understand the *métier de la guerre*, that he has indeed twice or thrice thrown a lucky main, but never knew how to play his game, and that he is but a little genius, of a size adapted to getting money by all sordid and dishonourable ways, which I think never was the vice of a warlike nor indeed of a great spirit of any sort.' At the time when Erasmus Lewis was thus revealing his detestation of the Marlborough régime he was no doubt preserving an irreproachable demeanour towards the Ministers who still employed him. He must have thought Harley would be gratified by the news, the same Harley who a year before had sworn eternal fealty to Lewis's 'little genius'. During those same months Henry St. John was saluting Marlborough on his latest victory—and urging Harley to prepare the plan for his overthrow. Such was the web of intrigue weaved by some of those the Captain-General left behind him in London while he was fighting the enemy at Oudenarde and Malplaquet.

Harley needed little incitement. He lost no time in seeking to piece together the plot which had been so dangerously exposed once before. He was wary about St. John's advice to place his full reliance on the Church of England party. That might make him once more the prisoner of a faction. Of course the Tory voting power would be needed and approaches were made along the lines St. John had suggested. But Harley had other plans. If the Queen could not be roused to action, she must be enticed. What could persuade her better than the knowledge that other great men besides Harley and the Tories were ready to come to her rescue, that she could if she would dispense one by one with the tyrannizing Whig Lords without losing the services of her victorious General? It was a delicate game to play and it called for highly secret preparation. Harley looked around among the Whig Lords who had never ranged themselves decisively with the Junto, men with whom, after his fashion, he had retained his contacts over the years with a studied flow of compliments and favours. One was the Duke of Newcastle, the richest man in the country whose word might determine numberless elections. He was a member of the Whig administration, but flattery could instil the thought that a higher destiny awaited him. Another was the Duke of Somerset, the very man who had played a foremost part in Harley's dismissal. That was no bar to an approach.

No man, even in that age of political genius, deserved the high opinion which the Duke of Somerset held of his own talents. He was known as 'the proud Duke' and bore himself with an arrogance which made the Lords of the Junto seem modest by comparison. When his daughter Charlotte presumed to sit down in his presence he took steps to exclude her from his will. When he travelled abroad, outriders drove ahead to scour the country roads and protect him from the intrusion of vulgar eyes. But many were unimpressed by the Duke's elaborate display of his own grandeur. When Sarah feared that her husband was contemplating promotion for him to a more responsible post than Master of the Queen's Horse, Marlborough hastened to reply that he would not employ so witless a person in any position of consequence. Possibly the slight left its mark. The Duke of Somerset grew testy with the men who failed to appreciate his merits. He began to see himself as a candidate for the task of ending the vicious quarrel between the Queen and her Ministers.

Harley was quite ready to feed the illusion. For, despite the Duke of Somerset's failings, he had one priceless possession—the Duchess of Somerset. She was gaining an influence at the Queen's Court more subtle than Mrs. Masham's. She was (in Sarah's jaundiced vision) 'near the Queen's person; she had her ear whenever she pleased; she was soft and complaisant, full of fine words and low curtseys; and could by art and insinuation (seemingly unaffected and free from malice and passion) make all such disadvantageous impressions sink deeper into her mistress's heart'. The victim of the 'disadvantageous impressions' was, of course, Sarah herself, who too often made the mistake of underrating her enemies. For the Duchess of Somerset supplied the intelligence which her husband lacked and, although the richest and noblest-born woman in the land, had led a life which had taught her the virtues of independence and courage. As Lady Elizabeth Percy, at the age of four after her father's death, she held in her own right six of the oldest baronies in the kingdom. Many men struggled for the prize of her hand in marriage. At the age of fourteen she was contracted

66

to the son of the Duke of Newcastle. On his death she was contracted again, this time against her will, to Thomas Thynne of
Longleat. She was helped to escape to The Hague where she
instituted proceedings for the dissolution of the marriage. At the
court of Hanover she met Count Charles Konigsmark who gal-
lantly contrived the murder of Thynne as he rode in his coach
down St. James's Street. Thereafter Lady Elizabeth returned to
London and at the age of fifteen was married to the Duke of
Somerset. She did not live happily ever after, for the Duke treated
her not much better than his domestic servants with whom he
insisted on conversing only by hand signals. But Anne became her
friend. After Sarah and Abigail, the woman Charles II described
as 'the sad little heiress' had established some hold over the
Queen. Harley, to be sure, was not likely to neglect so useful a
connexion. No one as yet, however, could guess what the encroach-
ment of the Duchess of Somerset into the Queen's favour might
portend.

More immediately significant was the greatest of all Harley's
captures. In the days of the Revolution and the years of King
William one leader among the Whigs had been the Duke of
Shrewsbury. Since then he had spent his time in retirement either
at his home or in Italy. He was 'the King of Hearts', handsome,
gracious, an elder statesman still in the prime of life whom no one
could dismiss as a secondary figure. Everyone from Marlborough
downwards paid court to him, but none with such sinuous skill as
Robert Harley knew how to employ. Shrewsbury had recently
returned from Italy, bringing with him, as Sarah said, 'a very old
woman for a wife, an Italian Papist'. The charge about her Cathol-
icism was false but the mere rumour was sufficient in those days
to cast doubts on the Duke's Protestant purity. Marlborough and
Godolphin, none the less, would have been eager to bring him into
their counsels but Harley's wooing had been more successful.

Shrewsbury was genuinely convinced that 'the generality of the
nation long for peace'. Unlike most others he knew the story of
how foolishly, as he thought, the opportunity of achieving it had
been thrown away, and he talked with Harley about the advisa-
bility of making the facts public. Sarah, with her customary
charity, believed that Shrewsbury's estrangement from his Whig
colleagues had been assisted by the refusal of a pension for which
his 'Roman Duchess' had asked. By the autumn of 1709 he was

deeply engaged with Harley. That did not prevent him from paying a visit to Sarah and putting on 'the guise of the greatest value and friendship for her'. He opened the subject of the misunderstanding with the Queen and expressed the hope that the damage could be repaired. Perhaps he was just feeling the ground for Harley. Perhaps the kernel of the plot was to detach the Marlboroughs from their Whig friends, keep the Captain-General at the head of the army and thus avoid the direct challenge to his authority which had sundered previous schemes for securing a change of power in the state. Or perhaps, finally, the Duke of Shrewsbury, like the Dukes of Newcastle and Somerset, was being deceived by Harley who fostered their ambitions while at the same time encouraging St. John and the Tories to dream of a much bolder stroke against both the Junto and Marlborough himself. Nobody knows the full truth today as nobody knew it then. For the truth was concealed in the heart and mind of Robert Harley, and it was his custom not to be 'very communicative where he can act by himself, being taught by Experience that a Secret is seldom safe in more than one Breast'.

Harley, it may be seen, was the best-informed politician of his day. For him Abigail kept her hand on the pulse of the Queen. Erasmus Lewis hastened to pass on the latest nuance of opinion in Whitehall. St. John still worshipped him and supplied the qualities of daring and imagination which Harley himself lacked. Those great Lords, Whig and Tory, who had never pledged themselves too deeply with the most fanatical of the factions, were flattered by his interest and poured out their secrets in return. Through them he was sometimes able to plant suspicions and jealousies and expectations in the minds of the Junto Lords themselves, to overhear the latest whisper of their rivalries and ambitions. And while he noted every shift of opinion and manœuvre at the court or on the country estates, he never despised the men who shaped public opinion in the coffee-houses and far and wide throughout the kingdom by their newsletters and pamphlets.

It was by Harley's inspiration years before that Daniel Defoe had been rescued from Newgate prison. He wrote to Godolphin and explained the advantages to be gained from 'some discreet writer on the government side, if it were only to state the facts right; for the Generality err for want of knowledge, and being imposed upon by the Storys raised by ill-designing men . . .'

Defoe responded with unbounded devotion. 'Of all the Examples in Sacred Story,' he told Harley, 'None moves my Indignation like That of the Ten Lepers who were healed by Our Saviour. I Sir Like the One Gratefull wretch am Come back to Pay the Tribute of thankfulness which this So Unexpected Goodness Commands from me.' He was horrified at Harley's fall from office in 1708 and wrote to comfort him in his breach with 'a tottering party', not forgetting to ask his saviour's permission to let him continue at work for the men still in power. Harley's acceptance of such an arrangement was typical of his calculating composure when others were so ready to lose their heads in hot party strife.

Perhaps Harley owed to Defoe almost as much as Defoe owed to him. Week by week Defoe's paper defended the good name of his employer among some of the very sections of society, the dissenters and Presbyterians, who might be most offended by his flirtations with the Tories. Perhaps he gave Harley the real key to his cunning. 'Intelligence', wrote Defoe, 'is the Soul of all Publick Business.' He showed an incredible assiduity in supplying it. 'If you'll allow the Vanity of the Expression, *If I were a Public Minister*, I would if Possible kno' what Every body said of me.' Harley, it seems, was the first politician who with Defoe's help kept a press-cutting agency. And Defoe was not afraid to offer more ambitious advice. His master's aim, he suggested, should be not only to secure or retain office but to establish himself as 'Prime Minister of State', dominating the few who would compose 'a Supreme Ministry'. Such language had scarcely been used before; no such title was known to the constitution. But Defoe had worked out his scheme in much detail—'Cabinets of Ten or fourteen are Monsters and useless'—and his words left their mark on Harley's mind. Thanks to Defoe, Harley was perhaps the first man who dreamed of becoming Prime Minister of Britain. Certainly Defoe gave the most astute hints of how the prize might be gained. 'In your Particular Post Sir you may so Govern, as That Every Party shall believe you Their Own.' And again: 'This is the Dissimulation I Recommend, which is Not Unlike what the Apostle Sayes of himself; becoming all Things to all Men, that he Might Gain Some. This Hypocrise is a Vertue, and by This Conduct you shall Make your Self Popular, you shall be Faithful and Useful to the Soveraign and beloved by the People.' So one apostate child of dissenting parents encouraged the wiles of another with a biblical blessing.

*   *   *

Yet in the autumn of 1709 Robin the Trickster, as Harley was both popularly and unpopularly known, must have realized how formidable was his task if he was to regain the power he had lost. The path ahead of him was surrounded with pitfalls. St. John's grand and simple remedy of an appeal to the Church of England party might merely confirm the Junto in power by alienating the moderate Whigs whom Harley had courted so carefully. True, he had established with the Queen an understanding closer than that of any other politician of the time; she was the linchpin of his whole scheme. But the Queen was near despair. Abigail bewailed her lack of 'courage and resolution' and even felt it necessary to warn Harley against writing to her direct for fear that the Queen's Ministers might challenge her resort to unofficial advisers.

The truth was that for all the libels and lampoons, for all the war-weariness and all the ceaseless intrigue among the men in and out of office, Marlborough's power and prestige were still immeasurable. The giant cast his shadow not only across England but across a whole continent. Whatever attempts were made to nibble away his reputation in London, no doubts about his greatness were tolerated across the Channel. The centre of the eighteenth-century world was at Versailles and King Louis XIV was the most resplendent monarch Europe had known since Charlemagne. Eight years before at the start of Queen Anne's reign he had affected to treat England as his footstool. Contemptuously he had declared his intention to place the king of his own choosing on the English throne. If he had failed to fulfil that aim and if instead he himself had been compelled to melt down his golden plate to save France from beggary and invasion, the Duke of Marlborough was the man above all others who had made him do it. It was Marlborough who had changed the face of the Western world. Queen Anne herself and most of the statesmen of her age, whatever else they misunderstood, felt in their bones the immensity of his achievement. They trembled to think how naked they would be before the still powerful Louis if Marlborough's sword was no longer there to guard them and to help impose the peace which so many prayed for. Apart from those who secretly hoped for a Jacobite restoration,

St. John alone perhaps was willing to put all to the test, but he would gamble with the throne and the succession as readily as he dissipated his father's fortune.

Marlborough himself might have qualms about the shifting sands of London politics on which he was called upon to construct his strategy. He protested in his petulance against those who dared mock from afar and question his purposes. One such was John Tutchin, editor of the *Observator*. Marlborough wrote home furiously demanding protection from the rogue. 'If I can't have justice done me,' he said, ' I must find some friend that will break his and the printer's bones which I hope will be approved of by all honest Englishmen, since I serve my Queen and country with all my heart.' Was it just a coincidence that a few months later poor Tutchin was waylaid and beaten so savagely that he never recovered? However, these occasional tantrums on the part of the Captain-General were not witnessed by the outside world. Only when he made his request to the Queen to become General for life was an indication given that he had momentarily lost his poise; but no one could believe that one false step could really be so dangerous. In the sight of all observers his temper was unruffled and his touch of mastery still sure. He returned to England in that winter of 1709, with the name of another great victory emblazoned on his banners, to face a Parliament more united than ever before in celebrating his exploits. When he took his seat in the House of Lords he had good enough reason for despising all that the Abigails, the Harleys and the Tutchins could contrive against him.

'My Lord Duke of Marlborough,' said the Lord Chancellor, ' I am commanded by the Lords (when you should first appear in your place) to give as I now do, the thanks of this House for your continued and eminent services to her majesty, and the public, during the last campaign; of which nothing can be said greater, than her majesty (who always speaks with the utmost certainty and exactness) has declared from the throne. "That it has been at least as glorious as any which have preceded it"—But this repetition of the Thanks of this august assembly has this advantage of the former, that it must be looked upon as added to, and standing on, the foundations already laid here, in the records of this House, for the preserving your memory precious for all future times; so that your grace has also the satisfaction of seeing this everlasting monument of your glory rise every year much higher—

May God continue in a wonderful manner to preserve so invaluable a life; that you may not only add to this structure, but finish all with the beauties and ornaments of an honourable and lasting peace.'

Lord Cowper was so overcome by the occasion that he is said to have added the words: 'I cannot conclude without acknowledging with all gratitude the providence of God in raising you up to be such an instrument of so much good, in so critical a juncture *when it was so much wanted*,' and there were some who scoffed that in the last phrase the Lord Chancellor was less concerned with the fate of the nation than with the fate of the Whigs.

Envy and faction—or was it a love of freedom and a longing for peace?—might mutter their fears about the overmighty General, but in November 1709 not a single voice dared question the honour done him in the British Parliament which had now wrested the power to speak the final word from Kings and Queens, court favourites and bedchamber women.

Grub Street

O, Grub Street! how do I bemoan thee,
Whose graceless Children scorn to own
thee!
Their filial piety forgot,
Deny their Country like a Scot:
Tho' by their Idiom and Grimace
They soon betray their native Place:
Yet *thou* hast greater Cause to be
Asham'd of them, than they of thee.
—SWIFT *On Poetry: A Rapsody*.

WHILE JONATHAN SWIFT was journeying back and
forth from London to Laracor in the first decade of
the eighteenth century and while the Duke of Marlborough was complaining so frequently about the villainy of 'the
public prints', a great change was taking place in the life and
custom of men of letters in every rank. Within the short space of
not much more than ten years the status of poets and pamphleteers, printers and publishers was transformed. The revolution
came so quickly that those who lived through it often failed to
appreciate the new world they had entered. Some commentators,
on the other hand, have written as if the fruits of the revolution
were already safely harvested; they portray an Augustan age for
literature largely freed from the strife and ignominy of earlier
times. It is not easy to imagine that a struggle for the elementary
right to print continued in the same London entranced by the
placid graces of a Joseph Addison. But such a struggle there certainly was. It is important to discover how it was conducted and
what were the stakes involved. The Duke of Marlborough, like
many others bred in the habits of the seventeenth century, despised
the new trade. But the men who practised it were called upon to
display courage of an order not entirely different from that required on the fields of Blenheim and Malplaquet.

Most statesmen of Queen Anne's reign could not altogether
exclude from their minds the earthshaking possibility that a
Catholic and Jacobite King might yet recover the English throne

and that the old persecutions provoked by deep disunity within the nation might be renewed; they took high risks and the most intricate precautions. In a barely credible series of intrigues they sought to establish some favour for themselves at the Jacobite Court of St. Germain's with which their country was at war but which might soon be dispensing favours and penalties once again from Whitehall. Others besides politicians were forced to combine furtive manœuvre with their flashes of daring, and among them were the journalists and poets who have not always been acclaimed as the boldest and least corruptible of mankind. They had some excuse.

Under previous Stuart rulers they had led a life of degradation when they were allowed to live at all. Four years before Swift was born, a London printer called John Twyn was brought before the King's Bench on the charge that he had undertaken to print a pamphlet calling in question the exact conformity between the laws of God and those enforced by human magistrates. Twyn 'thought it was good mettlesome stuff, but saw no hurt in it'. All his pleas for mercy were swept aside. He was sentenced to be hanged by the neck, cut down before he was dead, shamefully mutilated and his entrails taken out; 'and you still living, the same to be burnt before your eyes, your head to be cut off, and your head and quarters to be disposed of at the pleasure of the King's Majesty'. Most of the sentence was executed and the fragments of his body were exhibited on Ludgate, Aldersgate and the other gates of the city as an example to others who dabbled in the same black art.

With such memories to guide them and with the future so uncertain, those writers who were seriously engaged in the business of politics could not be blamed if they decided that their blows must be struck in the dark. They were not making reputations in polite society; they were at war. It is necessary, then, to distinguish between the new elegance which the great men of literary London enjoyed and the still dangerous profession which others followed in the changing climate. Swift moved between one little world and the other. He too could delight the readers of the *Tatler* with an essay on manners; overnight he could become 'Samson with a bone in his hand, rushing on his enemies and felling them', a Samson moreover who knew how cruelly the Philistines would use him if once he fell within their grasp.

The most dramatic change of the period was in the writer's dignity and his place in the social hierarchy. A few years before Queen Anne ascended the throne, John Dryden, the leading man of letters of the day, a Poet Laureate who had more than once come to the rescue of the King, had to beg for his salary from the First Lord of the Treasury, pleading 'my extreme wants, almost to arresting'. 'Be pleased to look on me with an eye of compassion. Some small employment would render my condition easy.' Such was the obeisance towards authority shown by one who had helped drive the foremost Whig statesman of the time into exile with his *Absalom and Achitophel*. That poem circulated all over the kingdom; the Poet Laureate became a most powerful engine of government propaganda. Yet, even when his influence was at its peak, he had to grind out prologues and epilogues to win bread for his family. He mourned the death of his patron in language which fittingly revealed how pitiful a creature a Stuart poet might be.

> *Tho little was their Hire, and light their Gain,*
> *Yet somewhat to their share he threw;*
> *Fed from his Hand, they sung and flew,*
> *Like Birds of Paradise, that liv'd on Morning Dew.*
> *Oh never let their Lays his Name forget!*
> *The Pension of a Prince's Praise is great.*

How different was the scene a quarter of a century later! A few years after Queen Anne's death, Alexander Pope, a declared Catholic in a Protestant era, the unabashed companion of 'chiefs out of war and statesmen out of place', scornfully explained that he would never accept a court pension even if one were offered, and when his friend, John Gay, revealed a similar contempt for royal displeasure he sent his congratulations in terms which underlined with what assurance the poets had risen from their knees. 'Princes indeed,' he said, 'and peers (the lackeys of princes) and ladies (the fools of peers) will smile on you the less; but men of worth and real friends will look on you the better. There is a thing, the only thing which kings and queens cannot give you—for they have it not to give—liberty, which is worth all they have, and which, as yet, I hope Englishmen need not ask from their hands. You will enjoy that, and your own integrity. While you are nobody's servant, you may be anyone's friend. . . .'

The change in posture from Dryden to Pope is one of the glories of Queen Anne's reign. Something may be due to the differing temperament of the two men and nothing can detract from the honour which the writing profession owes to the twisted, sickly, much-maligned linen-draper's son who symbolized the emancipation. In fact a host of comparisons among lesser men could be cited to prove the case. In the thirty years before the Revolution, it is hard to single out more than two or three active writers who failed to accommodate their opinions at least once and in the most shameless fashion to the prevailing political breeze of the moment; in the first thirty years of the eighteenth century apostasy on the grand scale had become something more than an everyday offence. The secret of the change is, of course, that the court had ceased to be the sole fountain of patronage. Even the statesmen of both parties assembled round the court no longer retained the absolute power to decide an author's fortune. He was able now to appeal over the heads of kings and noblemen direct to the public.

Writing a hundred years later William Hazlitt marked the change. 'What a hubbub it would create', he said 'if it were known that a particular person of fashion and title had taken a front-box in order to decide on the fate of a first play! . . . An author nowadays no longer hangs dangling on the frown of a lord, or the smile of a lady of quality (the one governed perhaps by his valet, and the other by her waiting maid), but throws himself boldly, making a lover's leap of it, into the broad lap of public opinion on which he falls like a featherbed; and which, like the great bed of Ware, is wide enough to hold us all very comfortably.' Hazlitt's tribute to his colleagues was doubtless tinged with irony. Many poets, good and bad, still starved after Pope had made a fortune. Many essayists, good and bad, behaved like flunkeys after Addison had survived a lifetime of political consistency. Swift had not dealt the death-blow to sycophancy. But never again, after the flowering of a more manly spirit in the days of Queen Anne, did the craft of writing suffer quite the same debasement as Dryden had endured.

One sign of the change was the simple matter of financial rewards. John Milton was paid £10 for *Paradise Lost*; Matthew Prior half a century later made 4,000 guineas with a collection of his poems. Samuel Butler died in poverty even though Charles II knew his *Hudibras* by heart; de Fonvive, a not very prominent newspaper editor of Queen Anne's time, made a steady income of

£600 a year. In other words, a spectacular growth must have occurred in the number of readers, and along with it went a no less significant change in the attitude of public men. Debates in Parliament were conducted behind closed doors; elections might be determined by the prior dispositions of the Queen and her favourites through the manipulation of the Lord-Lieutenancies in the counties; Ministerial changes were often settled up and down the backstairs of the Palace; but it was also true that a new public opinion did exist which could not easily be flouted. 'A Man Can Never be Great That is Not Popular, Especially in England,' wrote Daniel Defoe to Robert Harley. 'Tis Absolutely Necessary in the Very Nature of Our Constitution, where the People have So Great a Share in the Government. Besides, the People here, in Recovering their Just Rights, have Usurpt Some, That are Not Their Due, Vizt, Censuring Their Superiors, But the Government is bound to Submit to the Grievance because tis Incurable.' Of course, Defoe, with a sound vested interest to promote, over-stated the case; but the mechanics of the British political system were changing. The parliamentary orators had no audience beyond the palace of Westminster; by some means they must influence the coffee-house politicians and the idols of the populace outside. Peers and commoners who normally played little part in the life of Parliament could be sent bustling to London by a pamphlet which incited the clergy in their pulpits or the merchants in the City.

The printing press was the formidable new weapon in politics. Whig and Tory Ministers competed for the services of the men who were learning the trade. The literary courtiers who had once looked to an omnipotent King now found themselves courted. One day the Chancellor of the Exchequer climbed the staircase of Addison's lodgings in the Haymarket to beg him to write a poem celebrating the victory at Blenheim; within a couple of years the poet had a post in the Government even though he had never made a speech in the House of Commons. Such events showed that writers had gained something more substantial even than a new dignity. Immense power in the state might soon be theirs.

The distinction was important for Swift. He was not concerned about money for his writings; indeed (with the exception of *Gulliver's Travels*, published many years later), he was hardly paid a penny piece for any of them. Dignity without power he would probably have dismissed as cant. But the chance to shape policy and see Dukes and Archbishops dancing to his will—that was a prize worth striving for. If he had arrived in London thirty years earlier, he could never have dreamed such a role was possible unless he in turn was prepared to toady. But in the reign of Queen Anne he had the chance to achieve something new—to exercise the power he craved and still keep his immaculate independence.

Another event ushered in the new freedom. In 1695—two years after Swift had his first poem published—the law imposing a censorship on the press was allowed to lapse. For the previous thirty years, with one short interval, a Licensing Act had decreed that every legal work should be censored by the judges, every political and historical work by the Secretary of State, and every religious, scientific and philosophical work by the Archbishop of Canterbury or the Bishop of London. To make assurance double sure the number of printers, outside the universities, was limited to twenty in London and one in the city of York. If many succeeded in circumventing these edicts, it was not due to the conscious laxity of Roger L'Estrange who was appointed censor by the Secretary of State in 1663 and was knighted for his diligence by King James twenty-two years later. To stamp out the evil which had helped cause the Great Rebellion he demanded the severest measures, not only against authors and printers, but also against 'the letter founders, and the smiths and joiners that work upon presses, with the stitchers, binders, stationers, hawkers, mercury women, pedlars, ballad singers, poets, carriers, hackney coachmen, boatmen and mariners'. These measures should include 'death, mutilation, imprisonment, banishment, corporal pains, disgrace and pecuniary mulcts'; hawkers in the streets should be compelled to wear a special mark of shame and informers should be well bribed to bring the criminals to justice.

While suppressing every other sheet, L'Estrange was also charged with the task of producing the one official paper, *The Intelligencer*, which soon changed its name to *The London Gazette*. How much intelligence the public was likely to receive from this quarter was revealed by the editor's general views on newspapers stated in the first issue. 'Suppose the press in order, the people in their right wits, and news or no news to be the question,' he wrote, 'a public mercury should never have my vote, because I think it makes the multitude too familiar with the actions and counsels of their superiors, too pragmatical and censorious, and gives them not only a wish but a kind of colourable right and licence to be meddling with the government.' Right up till the Revolution of 1688 he continued to believe that liberty of conscience was 'a paradox against Law, Reason, Nature and Religion'. He did not succeed in his plan of total suppression; several journals led a fitful life for a few months and several more pamphlets and religious tracts broke through the government dykes. But in the twenty-five-year reign of Roger L'Estrange no great names adorn the records of English journalism; only *The London Gazette*, selling some six to eight thousand copies, survived from year to year. It was not until after 1688 and, more particularly, after 1695 that the flood came. *London Posts, Postboys, Flying Posts, Newsletters, Observators, Mercurys* poured out thick and fast, once, twice or three times a week. Political poems and pamphlets followed at a pace to match. Daniel Defoe claimed that his poem *The True-Born Englishman*, published at the turn of the century, ran into nine genuine and twelve pirated editions and sold 80,000 copies on the streets.

It had never been the intention of those who allowed the Licensing Law to lapse to inaugurate an era of freedom. No big change was desired or expected and year by year efforts were made in either the Lords or the Commons to re-establish some system of regulation. But, narrowly in some instances, all such efforts were defeated. When in 1703 a formal attempt was made 'to restrain the licentiousness of the press' and restore the censorship, workmen from London's seventy printing and publishing shops petitioned the House of Commons and successfully warded off the threat to their livelihood. A subtler means was required if ever this evil genie of freedom was to be conjured back into its bottle. At the end of her reign Queen Anne was urging her Ministers to find a method of dealing with 'the false and scandalous libels, such as are a reproach to any government'. One idea was to revive the Licensing Act, another to compel authors to put their names to their writings. Both were abandoned in favour of a Stamp Duty on newspapers included in an Act of Parliament primarily concerned with a tax on soaps, silks, calicoes, linens and such-like commodities. The cowardly device had considerable effect; many newspapers failed to survive the impost and a long battle had to be fought to recover the lost ground. But, in the seventeen years between the end of the Licensing Acts and the beginning of the

Stamp Duties, England had a taste of freedom which was never forgotten. Roger L'Estrange died a broken old man in the same year when Addison was celebrating Blenheim and Defoe starting his *Weekly Review* which he sustained single-handed for nine years. How horrified would Queen Anne have been to learn that her reign was to become famous as the first in which the printing press began to establish itself as the Fourth Estate of the realm!

Yet strong and decisive in the long run as were all these forces making for liberation, the path of the political journalist was still arduous. The foremost literary figures could bask in the new sunshine of wealth and prestige, but Grub Street felt the chains and the darkness. And it was by the new race of publisher-printers, by some of the men dismissed as hacks and among those compelled to work at least on the fringes of Grub Street, that the never-ending battles for the right to print were fought. Dr. Johnson gave this definition: 'Originally the name of a street in Moorfields in London, much inhabited by writers of small histories, dictionaries, and temporary poems; whence any mean production is called *grubstreet*.' The indictment is much too ungenerous. For prominent among those whom Alexander Pope also portrayed floundering in the nearby mud of Fleet-ditch and bespattering their betters with filth were the party-writers. Many of their productions may have been mean, but it was not beneath the majesty of Parliament and the Queen to take note of them. The law of libel, for example, was fantastically wide in its scope; general attacks on the government no less than personal attacks on particular Ministers were frequently made the grounds for prosecution. Licensing laws had gone, but the pillory, Newgate and the common hangman remained. If Ministers were reticent in invoking the law, either the House of Lords or the House of Commons could urge the Secretaries of State or the Attorney-General to take action or themselves summon the offenders to the bar and consign their outpourings to the flames. The Secretaries of State had the power to issue warrants for arrest, and they were often most unscrupulous in employing it. Sufficient evidence might not be available for a conviction, but printers could easily be ruined by frequent, harassing arrests which never led to a court action. A further hazard was provided by the powers granted to the men specially charged with smelling out libels. They had salaries to earn and justify. The most notorious among them, one Robert Stephens, nicknamed 'Robin Hog', knew the printing world intimately and wielded his authority with shameless favouritism and severity. Writers were liable to see not only their papers but large chunks of their personal property taken from them by the government agents; printers suffered even more severely from the seizure of their type.

The pillory was the most notorious mode of punishment for those who lived by the pen. Later in the century this ordeal seemed to lose something of its terror and the *Grub Street Journal* was able to claim that among printers this instrument 'is so universally esteemed that he who has the honour to mount the rostrum, is always looked upon amongst them, as a graduate in his profession'. But this judgement surely has more than a touch of bravado. Those condemned to the pillory were 'exposed in a high place, with their heads put thro two pieces of notched wood; the uppermost whereof being made to slide down, shuts the neck into the notch. The criminal's hands are confined on each side of his head in the same manner; and thus he stands in this ridiculous posture for more or less time, or with more or fewer repetitions, according to his sentence. If the people think there is nothing very odious in the action that raised him to this honour, they stand quietly by and only look at him; but if he has been guilty of some exploit disliked by the tribe of 'prentices, he must expect to be regaled with a hundred thousand handfuls of mud, and as many rotten eggs as can be got for money. It is not lawful to throw stones, but yet 'tis often done'. Stone-throwers, it seems, were not brought to justice. The law against licentious publications was equally nebulous, but more ruthlessly applied.

Among those who risked this fate for their political opinions are several who gained immortal ignominy in the *Dunciad*. When the poem first appeared a frontispiece showed the figure of an ass heavily laden with tomes and scattering news-sheets right and left; these were the works of Pope's enemies (did any man ever boast so many?) and no one could charge him with partiality in the judgements he inflicted. He flayed them all, heroes and hacks, Whigs and Tories.

> *Tis the same rope at different ends they twist*
> *To Dulness Ridpath is as dear as Mist.*

Yet both Ridpath and Mist deserve a worthier monument; both suffered imprisonment and exile for their faiths; both sustained over a period of years newspapers which the leading statesmen feared and courted; each through a lifetime of turmoil could plead that he had never wavered in service to his chosen cause.

George Ridpath was, in Swift's estimation, 'a Scotch rogue' from Edinburgh. There in his student days he was put in irons for burning the Pope in effigy, and the clash with authority persisted when he went to London to become what his enemies called 'a newsmonger'. Along with Daniel Defoe he shared the distinguished title of 'The British Libellers'. Others variously acclaimed him as 'one of the best pens in England' or even as 'a truly loyal and ingenious gentleman of great piety'. So substantial at any rate was his service to the Whigs that when the Tories decided to prosecute him, fellow-Whigs were called upon to subscribe two guineas for the defence as the price of membership of the party. But on this occasion Ridpath feared something worse than the pillory. He broke bail, fled to Scotland and thence to Holland with a price on his head. Since the Attorney-General had charged he 'outwent all his predecessors in scandal', his discretion was doubtless justified.

Nathaniel Mist gave an equally valiant service to the Tories and his career was even more spectacular. Every few years he suffered the pillory or imprisonment or both. His frequent arrests were not surprising; Daniel Defoe had joined *Mist's Journal* as a Government agent and was busy taming the Jacobite editorials and informing on his obstreperous colleague. On one occasion Mist was summoned from Newgate to the bar of the House of Commons to answer for some articles attacking the Duke of Marlborough. Recantation at the bar was not considered a disgrace, but Mist refused to divulge the names of his contributors and returned to Newgate in the company of a number of those who had been helping to sell his paper. Only after nearly two decades of successful defiance did he finally seek refuge in France. Even then he refused to make a truce with his enemies. The hovel where *Mist's Journal* was produced was ransacked and the printing press destroyed. Yet a few weeks later *Fog's Journal* was on the streets breathing the same Jacobite war-cries. By some mysterious means Nathaniel Mist or his spirit was still at work from his place of exile.

And there were many more of a similar breed. Ned Ward
described the low life of London in language that is anything but
deathless; but he stood twice in the pillory for 'writing reflecting
pamphlets on several ministers of state'. Charles Leslie started
The Rehearsal to combat the flood of Whig journals. When he was
prosecuted he pleaded pardon; but one narrow escape did not
prevent him six years later from delivering a general assault on the
Whig divines in a pamphlet called *The Good Old Cause or the
Lying Truth,* 'in which he expresst himself that no laws made for
twenty years past are good'. He absconded and was outlawed; a
year later he crept back under an alias and renewed the fight.
John Dyer, a few years earlier in King William's time, was imprisoned twice for seditious publications and then brought to the
bar of the House of Commons and reprimanded 'for his great
presumption' in daring to take note of the proceedings of Parliament. A resolution was passed insisting 'that no newsletter writers
do, in their letters or other papers that they dispense, presume to
intermeddle with the debates or any other proceedings of the
house'. The reproof did not succeed. Dyer and a multitude more
still did presume to intermeddle. 'Such a gentle rebuke', wrote
Dean Kennet, 'could not reform a fellow who wrote for two very
necessitous causes—for the Jacobite party and for bread.' Lord
Mohun was less gentle; he believed that insults to his peers and
more particularly to himself should be tackled by more direct
methods. He found Dyer in 'one of his factious coffeehouses' and
pointed out his own name in one of the newsletters. Dyer confessed
the authorship whereupon he was cudgelled and made to swear
that the offence would not be repeated. Edmund Curll, another of
Pope's victims, had an even more historic meeting with the House
of Lords. Swift called him 'a prostitute bookseller' and Defoe
agreed in denouncing him as a 'contemptible wretch in a thousand
ways'. He had his ears cut off for an obscene publication and was
enshrined as 'Dauntless Curll' in the most contemptuous passages
of the *Dunciad.* Literacy piracy was his stock-in-trade and authors
were naturally outraged, but he combined this main occupation
with an agreeable sideline. He had an urge to let the public know
how members of the aristocracy really lived. Not content with
being reprimanded for publishing the trial of one Earl he persisted
five years later in producing the 'works of the Duke of Buckingham'. Once more he found himself on his knees at the bar of the

Lords and a solemn resolution was passed making it a breach of privilege to print without permission 'the works, life or last will of any lord of this house'.

Lords and Commons in fact competed with one another in their vigilance over the press and, since for some two generations with rare intervals the one was predominantly Whig and the other predominantly Tory, writers on all sides had something to fear. And there were others besides with less august authority who presumed to impose their whims as unofficial censors of the newly liberated press. Abel Roper, editor of the *Postboy*, was no dare-devil; Swift called him 'my humble slave' and his enemies said he would write for any side which paid him. He was arrested following a complaint from the envoys extraordinary from the King of Portugal and the Duke of Savoy. They protested at his 'insolence' and 'demanded satisfaction'. He recanted, begged the pardon of the two envoys and escaped further punishment. No one in that age, it seems, was shocked that a foreign emissary should succeed in silencing an English journalist. Ambassadors were men with well-defined rights which is more than any Grub Street politician could claim. The chief surprise was that Roper was let off so lightly; it merely 'increased the suspicion of many that he was, underhand, favoured and countenanced by some Great Men'.

Altogether, not a single session of Parliament during Queen Anne's reign passed without some action being taken against the 'malicious and villainous libels' which individual writers were alleged to be perpetrating. At its very first meeting the House of Lords did 'humbly desire Her Majesty to order Mr. Attorney-General to prosecute, with the utmost severity of the law, the authors or publishers of such scandalous reports' and the Queen quickly replied that 'she was very ready to do any thing of this kind'. Dr. James Drake was ordered to be prosecuted for claiming that a plot had existed to exclude Queen Anne from the throne. He argued that he was doing no more than repeat the 'tittle-tattle of almost every coffeehouse and drawing room', but such excuses were not acceptable. Dr. Drake, it is true, could be suspected of Jacobitism, but at the same time a move was made against another writer who gave his reasons for 'attainting and adjuring the Pretended Prince of Wales'. He spoke of those who 'whispered horrible things of blind and clancular bargains' and was obviously alarmed at the underground intrigues which prominent statesmen might still be conducting with the royal exile across the Channel. Since the same House of Lords was demanding ruthless measures to forbid all intercourse by letters or by any means whatever between the subjects of the Queen and the subjects of France and Spain, this unknown criminal might have been forgiven for his brave exposure of the same peril. But clearly the Lords were on the watch to suppress not only open calls to treason but even insinuations, however cloaked, which might 'disturb the Peace and Quiet of the Kingdom'.

Irony was one of the most favoured styles of the day and the lordly censors had to have their wits about them. The law courts needed a fine power of literary discrimination for the same reason and they found it tempting to resolve most doubts against the defendants. When the Grand Jury of the City of London and Middlesex was confronted with a pamphlet called the *Memorial of the Church of England* which they construed despite all pretences as more of an attack on the Queen and the Duke of Marlborough than a defence of the Church, they felt moved to expostulate: 'We cannot therefore, without high Ingratitude to Heaven and to Her (the Queen), but with great Concern take notice of the many Popish, Factious and Seditious Books, Pamphlets, Papers, and Treasonable Libels, frequently Printed, Published and Dispens'd Abroad under various Titles, Denominations, Innuendoes, cunning Cyphers and Disguises (yet so as to be understood) boldly reflecting upon Her Majesty, our Established Church and Civil Constitution'. The Duke of Marlborough pressed for action. 'I think it,' he wrote to one of the Ministers at home, 'the most impudent and scurrilous thing I have ever read. If the author can be found, I do not doubt he will be punished; for if such liberties may be taken of writing scandalous lies without being punished, no Government can stand long.' In this particular instance both Houses of Parliament joined the Grand Jury in the pursuit of the offender and the Queen issued a proclamation offering a reward for his capture. Only the hapless printer, one David Edwards, could be found. He was taken into custody, cross-examined by the Secretary of State and promised a pardon if he revealed the name of the author. He first sought to implicate three members of Parliament; then he explained that the manuscript had been brought to him by two women, one of them masked, and that he had made a bargain to deliver 250 copies to four porters. The unmasked woman and the porters were discovered, but not the real author. He happened to be the same Dr. James Drake who had been denounced a few years before by the House of Lords. Dr. Drake, Fellow of the Royal Society and Member of the College of Physicians, acknowledged by one of his enemies for his 'Mastery of the English Tongue' and 'manly stile', had learned his lesson. He too must adopt the ways of Grub Street and even that precaution did not save him from appearing once more in the courts for his seditious writings. He had played his part in persuading the Queen and her Government to enforce the law more strictly.

'Several Persons, either prompted by their own ill Humour, or, which is more probable, aided and countenanced by some Great Men out of Place, having of late in their Publick Writings, stretched too far the Liberty of Englishmen, and presumed too much on the Mildness of her Majesty's Government; the Ministry thought fit to give a seasonable Check to their Licentious Pens.' Thus Abel Boyer, a Huguenot exile who had worked his way into the front rank of the new race of newspaper editors, marked the new severity against the press in the middle of Queen Anne's reign. He compounded for his hypocrisy in welcoming 'seasonable checks' by reprinting at length the outrageous opinions which caused him so much pain. Swift dismissed him as 'a little whiffling Frenchman' who would be better employed in teaching his language to children. But the attack was very wide of the mark. For some twenty years Boyer circumvented the old rule enforced against John Dyer prohibiting any report of parliamentary debates. This was a most considerable feat, for the law was no dead letter. Frequently either the Lords or the Commons reasserted their privileges, claiming even that to mention the name of a Member of Parliament in the press was an offence. Abel Boyer walked the tight-rope with a wonderful balance and only allowed himself the mildest show of sympathy for less skilful practitioners of the art.

Among these more clumsy victims was John Asgill who had the distinction of being expelled from both the Irish and the English House of Commons for pamphlets he had written. His crime was nearer blasphemy than sedition, but since the interests of Church and State were so closely interwoven the dividing line might be a fine one. Indeed, often the charge was stated in the vaguest terms when it was stated at all. Queen Anne's Inquisition was not argus-eyed. A rich spate of invective escaped the attention of grand juries, royal proclamations, resolutions of both Houses, Attorney-Generals and Secretaries of State. Yet the burning of books and newspapers must have been a common sight at Palace Yard, Charing Cross and the Royal Exchange, and for every author who paid the penalty at the pillory how many more spent their ingenuity or subdued their consciences in seeking not to 'stretch too far the Liberty of Englishmen'?

In the last months of Queen Anne's reign, indeed, a celebrated case occurred which marked a direct collision between the forces of the old suppression and the new freedom. After a great debate Sir Richard Steele was expelled from the House of Commons for writing his pamphlet, *The Crisis*. If such a hammer-weight could be used to brand the writing of so well-connected a citizen, what mercy could be expected for lesser men? Yet in the debate itself Sir Robert Walpole pronounced a new doctrine. 'Why', he asked, 'is the author answerable in parliament for the things which he wrote in his private capacity? And if he is punishable by law, why is he not left to the law? By this mode of proceeding, parliament which used to be the scourge only of evil ministers, is made by ministers the scourge of the subject. . . . The liberty of the press is unrestrained; how then shall a part of the legislature dare to punish that as a crime which is not declared to be so by any law passed by the whole? And why should this House be made an instrument of such a detestable purpose?' Dyer, Ridpath, Boyer, Roper, Drake and a hundred others could have smiled at Sir Robert's assumption about the unrestrained liberty of the press. But if the deed was not done, the word had been spoken. The martyrs of Grub Street had not been pilloried in vain.

One further contrast between two men shows how stifling the atmosphere could still be in the literary underworld. Neither Sir Robert Walpole as he moved between the great Whig country houses nor Alexander Pope in his comfortable grove at Twickenham was likely to have the sympathy or interest to understand.

> *Earless on high stood unabashed De Foe*
> *And Tutchin flagrant from the scourge below.*

Thus with a callous fling Pope placed these two among the dunces. But Daniel Defoe was no dunce; nor did he lose his ears; nor was he unabashed by the punishments he did suffer. John Tutchin was at least effective enough to provoke the combined animosity of the English Parliament, the Duke of Marlborough and Jonathan Swift.

Both of them, Defoe and Tutchin, were reared in the same school; they had dissenters' blood in their veins and at an early age their fight for religious freedom merged into treason. Both marched under 'King Monmouth's' banner to join the last great battle fought on English soil at Sedgemoor. Defoe escaped capture; Tutchin was less fortunate. He was brought before Judge Jeffreys, sentenced to prison for seven years and ordered to be whipped once a year through every market town in Dorsetshire. But the Glorious Revolution brought a dramatic change in their fortunes. Tutchin was able to visit Judge Jeffreys, now a prisoner in the Tower of London, and lambast in heroic poems every form of 'popery, Tyranny and Arbitrary Government' even to the point of criticizing King William himself.

Meantime, Defoe soared to the heavens. King William was his hero and soon became his patron and his friend. The butcher's son was a frequent visitor at the court where few Englishmen were admitted on favoured terms. And that was by no means the most spectacular of his triumphs. He seemed to have every talent—originality, daring, unquenchable zest and a splendid capacity to communicate it to others. How well he understood the mood of the more restless among his countrymen and how well equipped he was to lead them forward to new ventures! In him the rebellious spirit of the Levellers strove for new expression. He was gay and dashing too, eager to taste life to the full and live ever for new occasions. No grovelling note was detectable in his *Poor Man's Plea*, no respect for old custom in his protests against the subjection of women, against the barbaric treatment of prisoners, against the old cobweb laws which imprisoned the beggars and let the rich break loose. Parliament, like Kings, must be made to serve the people. 'Our name is Legion and we are many'—such was the ultimatum delivered by his own hand to the Speaker of the House of Commons. Both the old landed interest and the new stockjobbers from the City had better heed this vibrant new voice in their midst. In short, Defoe had all the makings of the first modern Radical—a Thomas Paine or a William Cobbett a century before their time. But then came Newgate and the pillory and one of the most significant apostasies in English history.

His pamphlet *The Shortest Way with Dissenters* was a wonderful essay in irony and gusto. So successfully did he mock the persecuting zeal of the high churchmen that parsons offered prayers for the Queen to act on his programme of annihilation. But within a month the Government had issued a warrant for the arrest of the anonymous author who dared make Earls and Archbishops look like fools. The House of Commons ordered that the book should be burnt. Defoe was tried, fined, condemned to stand three times in the pillory and sent to gaol during Her Majesty's pleasure. How great was his popularity at this time stood revealed when the moment came for him to be exhibited outside the Royal Exchange. Instead of pelting him with mud and eggs the crowds acclaimed their hero and distributed his new verses written specially for the occasion.

> *Tell them, The Men that placed him here,*
> *Are scandals to the Times!*
> *Are at a loss to find his guilt,*
> *And can't commit his crimes!*

But Defoe's *Hymn to the Pillory* was almost his last act of defiance. 'I agreed', he told William Penn, 'to give the Court No Trouble but to plead Guilty to the Indictment, Even to all the Adverbs, the Seditiously's, the Maliciously's, and a Long Rhapsody of the Lawyers et Ceteras; and all this upon promises of being us'd Tenderly.' The plea was heard. 'Nor is there any Thing so Mean (which I can Honestly Stoop to Do) That I would not Submitt to To Obtain her Majties Favour.' The favour was granted. Still in Newgate he was able to start his *Weekly Review* which he ran for nine years with incredible diligence and a careful regard for the susceptibilities of those in power. After a few months he was at large again—still bubbling with energy, still surveying the world with a journalist's quick eye, but no longer the ardent champion of popular reform.

Within a year or two he was urging the House of Commons to take action against other journalists who could not achieve his own judicious restraint. 'The nation groans', wrote the man who is sometimes described as the father of English journalism, 'under the load of this impertinence; eternal clamours are in every news-house, and every society, and every hour some new comet appears in the horizon of letters.' For the rest of his twenty-six years, almost without a break, he was ready to reach an accommodation with any Government which would help feed his eight children and stave off his endless queue of creditors. Whig and Tory, Tory and Whig, he would work for them all until in the end he was assigned to the newspaper office of Nathaniel Mist to pass himself off as a Jacobite and play the informer against him. 'Thus I bow in the House of Rimmon,' he acknowledged.

Yet he had his excuse; the fate of John Tutchin was there as an example. Soon after Queen Anne came to the throne Tutchin had started a paper called the *Observator* in which he upheld the same principles he once fought for at Sedgemoor. Unlike Defoe he felt that the right to print involved something more than questions of party or personal advantage. However, when it seemed probable that Parliament might reinstitute some form of press regulation, he was ready to compromise. The fact that Tutchin took this attitude is proof enough how fragile was the idea of freedom or how menacing were the means of persecution. 'How far', he wrote, 'a restraint of the press, as formerly, may be consistent with the liberties of Englishmen, is a question too hot for one to meddle with, that has burned his fingers already.' Eventually John Tutchin was tried at the Guildhall. 'It has been the great indulgence of the Government', said the Attorney-General, 'that he has not been prosecuted before. He has been taken notice of by the House of Commons, and been before the Secretary of State, where he has been admonished to take care of what he should write; but he would not take warning.' Somehow, after a tortuous and technical legal battle, he was acquitted. Tutchin was greatly impressed by the fairness of his trial. 'I have been allowed all the fair play that possibly could be allowed,' he wrote; 'I have made perhaps the longest defence that was made in such a cause, and more pleadings allow'd upon it, than in the trial, condemnation, and execution of many hundreds of men and the transportation of some thousands in the West in the reign of King James.' But that was not the end of his story. One night the man who had survived the Bloody Assizes and the Queen's Inquisition was waylaid by unknown assailants and beaten so cruelly that he died of the wounds. His child, the *Observator*, was left as a legacy to his wife; it lived on as the chief exponent of extreme Whiggery for the entire reign until in turn it was strangled by the Stamp Duty.

Defoe and Tutchin were dismissed by Swift as 'two stupid, illiterate scribblers'. He affected not to remember the name of the man who composed the hymn to the pillory and would readily have dispatched to the flames the Whigs' 'weekly inflamer', John Tutchin. Among the printers a spirit of loyalty to their craft was already in the making. They kept the confidence of authors and began to round on any of their number who betrayed secrets to the government informers. But as yet no common professional pride or sympathy bound together the journalistic warriors in different camps. No one took up the cudgels on behalf of an enemy. No one, least of all Swift, believed that the liberty of the press should be so grotesquely extended that it might protect the rights of his licentious competitors. The war was too fierce for such gallantries. For indeed the newspaper and pamphlet trade where men were besmirched in the dust of political strife was no business for gentlemen, and the gentlemanly writers never ceased to deplore the crude desperation of those who practised it. Swift expressed his contempt among the foremost. In the year 1709 he had not yet stepped down into that arena. Grub Street had still to feel the impact of a genius.

CHAPTER FOUR

The Great Debate

(November, 1709—September, 1710)

'If an Englishman considers the great ferment into
which our political world is thrown at present, and how
intensely it is heated in all its parts, he cannot suppose
it will cool again in less than three hundred years.'

—JOSEPH ADDISON

IN NOVEMBER OF 1709 an unforeseen event occurred which
soon stirred political excitement to the highest pitch. A spur to
act swiftly was given to those who plotted the disruption of the
Marlborough-Godolphin-Whig coalition. And while they conducted their manœuvres, the nation was plunged into a great
debate.

November 5th was 'Gunpowder-Treason' day. It was also the
day when William of Orange had disembarked at Torbay. Perhaps
the double anniversary, dear to Protestant hearts, gave a heightened significance to the sermon preached in St. Paul's Cathedral
before the Lord Mayor by one of the leading high church clergymen. Henry Sacheverell, Doctor of Divinity and Fellow of Mag-
dalen College, Oxford, had already gained a reputation as a rabble-
rousing parson; long since he had hung out 'the bloody flag of
defiance' to dissenters and those Whiggish low churchmen willing
to extend the toleration allowed to the dissenting sects. He was
'a Man of a large, strong Make, and good Symmetry of Parts; of a
lurid Complexion, and audacious Look, without Sprightliness:
The Result and Indication of an envious, ill-natured, proud, sullen
and ambitious Spirit'. This judgement of an enemy was shared by
a few of his backers, but the great congregations swayed by his
mob oratory were not worried by any defects of character. Reading
the sermon he delivered on 'The Perils of False Brethren, both
in Church and State', it is easy to imagine 'the Fiery Red that
overspread his Face', 'the Gogling Wildness of his Eyes', 'the
Hellish Fury' that issued from his mouth. A cataract of abusive
epithets against dissenters and all who espoused their cause

poured forth, skilfully mingled with the most militant of scriptural texts.

The spectre of a new Puritan despotism was paraded before Mayor and Aldermen: 'They are pleased now to soften their Lewd Principles and cover their Dangerous Tenets with the Name of Speculative Opinions; but what Fatal Practices they have created, and whether their Seditious Thoughts will not again Exemplify themselves in the same Bloody Actions, We shall be convinced, to our Sorrow, if We don't Apprehend. That the Old Leaven of their Fore-Fathers is still working in their Present Generation and that this Traditional Poyson still remains in this Brood of Vipers, to sting us to Death, is sufficiently Visible, from the Dangerous Encroachments They now make upon our Government and the Treasonable Reflections They have Publish'd on Her Majesty, God Bless Her! Whose Hereditary Right to the Throne, They have had the Impudence to Deny, and Cancel, to make Her a creature of their own Power; and that by the Same Principles They Placed a Crown upon Her, They tell Us, They (that is, the Mob) may Reassume at their Pleasure.' According to Sacheverell, both Church and State were in danger; one, the 'Pure Spouse of Christ' might soon be 'Prostituted to more Adulterers than the Scarlet Whore in the Revelations' while the other was at the mercy of the 'Crafty Insidiousness of wily Volpones'. These were the most fearsome of all the legion of all the False Brethren, for 'like Joab they pretend to speak Peaceably, and smite Us Mortally under the fifth Rib'. When in his peroration the Doctor invited his flock to put on the whole armour of God no one could suppose he was summoning them to the conquest of some heavenly Kingdom. The enemy was there in their midst. Anyone who dared question the Church doctrine of passive obedience and 'the utter Illegality of Resistance upon any Pretence whatsoever' was guilty; in other words, he was arraigning the men in power and among the foremost the Lord Treasurer, the ex-Tory Lord Godolphin, widely known by the nickname of Volpone.

Dr. Sacheverell knew that he had preached a provocative sermon. When the Lord Mayor took him home in his carriage, urging the publication of the masterpiece, the Doctor answered that 'he had spoken some bold Truths, which might displease some People'. But the flattery succeeded, the sermon was printed and within a short time had sold 40,000 copies. The Queen's

Ministers were not prepared to let the challenge pass. Godolphin, it was said, was piqued by the reference to himself; he had long been irritated by the failure of some of his fellow-Ministers to take more severe action against the Government's enemies in the pulpits and in Grub Street. Some feared the danger of making Sacheverell a martyr, but the majority were determined to stage a grand defence of their political faith. Daniel Defoe, who, for all his trimming, could never forget the part the high churchmen had played in sending him to Newgate, was at first overjoyed by the decision. Once he had recommended that 'you should let such People run on till they are *out of Breath*'. Now 'this modern Boanerges had waked the landlady and the whole house with his fiery zeal and his hard-mouth'd Rhetorick'. Certainly the doctrine of passive obedience struck at the roots of Whig doctrine and the Whiggish constitution; it denied the foundation on which William had been crowned as King and Anne had succeeded as Queen; it might imply the acceptance of the claims of the Jacobite Pretender. On earlier occasions the Tory cry that the Church was in danger had been countered by bold action from the Whigs; might not boldness succeed again? If a proper example could be made of Sacheverell, how many others could be silenced? 'A Man', wrote Defoe, 'who having sworn Allegiance to the present Government, yet believes the Doctrine of Non-Resistance and Hereditary Right, is guilty of Perjury: if he preaches it, he is guilty of Treachery—and if he does not believe it, and yet preaches it, he is guilty of Hypocrisie.'

The Whig Parliament was not content with the customary censures inflicted on pamphleteers and newsmongers. Arrangements were made for the impeachment of Dr. Sacheverell to be staged in Westminster Hall in the sight of the whole nation, before Queen and courtiers, Lords and Commons. Mr. Christopher Wren was required to build the scaffolding and decorations after the manner employed for the trial of Strafford half a century before. The delay caused by these elaborate preparations gave time for a fever of interest in the Doctor's case to rise throughout the country. The Tories realized that at last they had found a hero. Their leading lawyer, Sir Simon Harcourt, and one of their most prominent churchmen, Dr. Francis Atterbury, were assigned to help Sacheverell with his defence. Prayers for his deliverance were offered in many of the churches; for the case was now presented as a momentous clash between the Whig Ministers and the Church. If Sacheverell was not defended, the republicans and atheists who lorded it over the Queen would stop at nothing. Thus the Church and Tory propagadandists rebutted the Whiggish design to brand them as Papists and Jacobites. By the time all was ready for the trial to open, the prosecutors of the outrageous parson were themselves on the defensive. 'Well, Gentlemen, to speak a little Allegorically,' wrote Defoe on February 25th, 'on Monday the 27th Instant Madame *Revolution* is to be try'd for her Life—God send her a good Deliverance. If she is to be condemned we are all in a fine Pickle.'

During the next three weeks, while the trial continued, the eyes of London were centred on Westminster Hall. Sacheverell drove along the Strand and down Whitehall in a glass coach amid cheering crowds and protected by a menacing array of bludgeons and drawn swords. 'He had the unparallel'd Presumption', said one Whig observer, 'to pass through the Streets in State, like an Ambassador making his Entry, rather than like a Criminal conducted to his Tryal: What shouts and Huzzas were made all round about, by the Servants, Hirelings, and Dependants of the Party! What Indignities and Affronts were offered to Men of the First Quality, to Bishops, to the Managers, and to other Members of both Houses! What Execrations were uttered against all that would not declare for the *High Church* and *Sacheverell!* And what Blows were distributed among such Stiff neck'd Persons as refused pulling off their Hats to this Senseless Idol! Yet the Doctor, Good and Pious Soul, professes in his speech, to *abhor all such Disorders.*' At night the shouts and huzzas changed into riots. Dissenting chapels and meeting-places were broken up and the furniture piled on to bonfires. The houses of Whig leaders were threatened. Only the arrival of the dragoons saved the Bank of England. The trained bands, assisted by the Queen's bodyguard, were rushed from place to place to prevent riot from developing into something more violent. For a while the capital seemed gripped by an hysteria and the same mood affected the portentous gathering in Westminster Hall. Peers and peeresses were there in the early hours, scrambling for seats and determined not to miss a single moment of the enthralling drama. 'It is not to be expressed', wrote Richard Steele in the *Tatler*, 'how many cold chickens the fair ones have eaten since this day sevennight for the good of their country . . . A neighbour of mine was telling me, that it gave him a notion of the ancient grandeur of the English hospitality, to see Westminster Hall a *dining room*.'

Among the other great ladies fascinated by the proceedings were Queen Anne herself and her Groom of the Stole, the Duchess of Marlborough. As the Queen went through the streets to take her seat in the box specially constructed for her by Christopher Wren, her sedan was surrounded by multitudes of people crying: 'God Bless your Majesty, and the Church: We hope your Majesty is for Dr. Sacheverell.' Anne at first said the Doctor deserved to be punished, but the sight of her chaplains clustering round Sacheverell gave a hint that she might have changed her mind. Sarah's impatience as she sat at the Queen's side can be imagined. 'His (Sacheverell's) person', she wrote, 'was framed well for the purpose and he dressed well. A good assurance, clean gloves, white handkerchiefs well managed, with other suitable accomplishments, moved the hearts of many at his appearance, and the solemnity of his trial added much to a pity and concern which had nothing in reason or justice to support them. The weaker part of the ladies were more like mad or bewitched than like persons in their senses . . . Several eminent clergymen who despised the man in their hearts, were engaged to stand publicly by him in the face of the world, as if the poor Church of England were now tried in him.'

Against this sentiment the Whig leaders unleashed their massive eloquence. They restated the case for rebellion against princes who themselves broke the law; refurbished the theories of an original contract between rulers and their people; recited precedents from British, Roman and Biblical history, not omitting the example of the Maccabees, which proved how at moments of necessity all the great heroes of the past had set aside the sycophantic doctrine of passive obedience. How Sarah's blood must have tingled when she heard the pure milk of her gospel poured forth with such learned assurance! And how Anne must have squirmed to see her authority so rigidly constricted by her masterful servants! The last famous occasion when the right to resist had been invoked was at King William's accession; how else could the existing constitution, Queen Anne's title and the Hanoverian succession be justified? The toleration of dissenters was the law of the land, an inseparable part of the revolutionary settlement; those who strove to upset it could only do so to serve some more sinister aim. 'When Mercenary Scribblers are employed by a Party to vent their Malice,' said

Robert Walpole, 'it may fit to leave them to the course of Common
Justice; But when the trumpet is sounded in Sion; when the Pulpit
takes up the Cudgels and gives the Alarm,' the time for action had
come. General Stanhope was even more explicit. He dismissed
Sacheverell himself as 'the insignificant tool of a Party'; but when
'animosities were raised in the City of London, the Fountain Head
of the Supplies which the Nation so readily contributed towards
this necessary War, his Offence deserved the severest Animadver-
sion'. For if Sacheverell was right, 'the Queen was no more than
an Usurper; neither House of Parliament had an Authority to sit;
all their Proceedings were illegal; and all the Blood and Treasure
that has been spent since the Revolution were spent in an ill
Cause'. Bishop Burnet showed how radically he and his friends
had abandoned any mystical notions of monarchy; he recalled the
'memorable Expression' of the Emperor Trajan when he delivered
the sword to the governors of the Provinces as the emblem of their
authority: '*For me, but if I deserve it, against me.*'

So the Whigs sought to vindicate in one mighty prospectus the
actions of themselves and their fathers in expelling King James,
the war aims of Marlborough and the Queen's Ministers, the sole
infallible reasoning which could forbid the return of a Jacobite
king. On every item but one they proved their case with irrefragable logic and Sacheverell's defenders were driven to seek refuge
in a maze of sophistries. What the Whigs had failed to prove was
what it was proper or necessary to invoke the final powers of the
British Parliament in the panoply of Westminster Hall to shut the
mouth of one ranting parson. They could have learnt a lesson from
the captain of the Queen's guards. When instructed to restore
order on the first night of the impeachment, he asked the pertinent question whether he was required to preach a sermon or
fight a battle.

Against Sacheverell's doctrines the Whig case was indeed overwhelming. But against the deeply-rooted instincts and traditions
which he expressed with such violence they had no sufficient
retort. The Church was the most powerful institution in English
life; it instilled the old creed that not much distinction need be
drawn between the divinity of Christ and the divinity of Kings and
Queens. Every year anniversary sermons were preached on the
Blessed Martyr; the most precise parallels were drawn between the
persecution which drove Jesus to Calvary and Charles to the

scaffold. Queen Anne had revived the custom that the sovereign could cure the sick by her miraculous touch. When the suspicion spread that the sympathies of the same godlike Queen were on the side of Sacheverell, it is not surprising that the Church could raise a whirlwind of support. And, of course, there were other circumstances which helped to set alight the Sacheverell agitation. The never-ending war had produced serious hardship. A bad harvest had helped to double the price of bread in a few months. The press-gangs were at work. A flood of Protestant refugees from the Continent seemed to add to the distress of the poor. Whiggish and dissenting pamphleteers did not hesitate to assail the sacred Church and the sacred Queen. Was the picture painted by the Doctor in his sermon of a 'brood of vipers' plotting 'to sting us to death' really so fantastic when the merciless Whig Lords had forced their will on the Queen and when the Marlborough family, with their supposed vested interest in the continuance of the conflict, occupied a place in the eye of the nation such as no other had achieved for generations? In short, Sacheverell touched off an explosion of all these mounting resentments. If he had been left alone the explosion might still have come; it would have taken longer to mature. As it was (in the words of Henry St. John) the Whigs 'had a parson to roast' and 'they roasted him at so fierce a fire' that they 'scorched themselves'.

After long and grave debates the members of the predominantly Whiggish House of Lords gave their verdict: they voted Sacheverell guilty by 69 votes to 52. But the punishments were so slight that the Doctor impudently thanked his prosecutors for their clemency while the crowds outside lit bonfires to celebrate his victory. Defoe claimed that a new kind of mob had been recruited to back the high church campaign—'the vilest of the People, the Scum of the Earth, the Drunken, Swearing, Damning and most Hellishly debauched.' Nothing like it, he insisted, had ever been seen on the streets of London before, adding to drive home his charge: 'Walk from *St. Paul's* to *St. James's* and Pick up all the Whores you can find, and that will be 500 at least, in spite of all the Constables and Reformers—I wager what you please, Nineteen in Twenty of them, are for Sacheverell.' The Queen's Ministers were truly frightened. 'The Prosecution of Sacheverell which made so much noise both at home and abroad,' wrote another observer, 'ended in the Burning of Two of his

Sermons; yet these small Flames new Kindled old Animosities and set the Whole Nation in Combustion.'

Thereafter Sacheverell moved round the country on a tour of triumph. 'Everybody knows', wrote Sarah, 'that he was sent about several counties; where with his usual grace he received as his due the homage and adoration of multitudes; never thinking that respect enough was paid to his great merit, using some of his friends insolently, and raising mobs against his enemies, and giving ample proof of how great meanness the bulk of mankind is capable; putting the air of a saint upon a lewd, drunken, pampered man, dispensing his blessings to all his worshippers and his kisses to some, taking their good money as fast as it could be brought in, drinking their best wines, eating their best provisions, without reserve and without temperance. And, what completed the farce, complaining in the midst of this scene of luxury and triumph, as the old fat monks did over a hot venison pasty, in his barbarous Latin, "Heu, quanta patimus pro Ecclesia." Oh, what dreadful things do we undergo for the sake of the poor Church!'

Certainly there were grounds for Sarah's gorgeous spleen. The Doctor had driven his glass coach through her schemes for a stable Whig ascendancy. Every figure at the court was affected by the rage of controversy outside. The Queen felt a new sense of power as men and women rallied so enthusiastically to the cause of her dear Church. Robert Harley, who hated high church fanaticism hardly less than Defoe, was yet emboldened to proceed with his plot; some of his friends feared with good cause that the hysteria might go too far and that it would 'raise the Tories to their old madness'. But most insidious of all was the impact on the wavering Whig moderates whom Harley was working to enlist in his projects. The Duke of Shrewsbury voted *Not guilty*. The Duke of Argyll, the great chief of the Scottish Whigs, could not bring himself to vote for acquittal, but—now in league with Harley too—he helped to ensure that the punishment was nominal. The Duke of Somerset used the occasion to impress his talents and loyalty on the Queen. Even Lord Somers absented himself from the final vote on the absurd excuse (according to Sarah) that his mother had just died. Perhaps the promise of £1,000 he was soon to receive from secret funds on the orders of the Queen helped to smooth his compliance. Altogether, the Sacheverell episode rattled the nerves of the members of the Whig Junto. At this critical moment they lost the cohesion which had raised them to power and for a few desperate months two or three among their number played the fatal game of *sauve qui peut*.

*   *   *

While the nation's attention was concentrated on the Sacheverell affair, a series of incidents at the court showed that the Queen, on her own initiative or prompted by others, was no longer prepared to submit to the Whig mastery. The first move was made several weeks before the proposed impeachment had reached its inglorious climax. Marlborough was out-manœuvred on a matter which fell peculiarly within his province—the appointment to fill a vacancy as Lord-Lieutenant of the Tower. The post went to Lord Rivers, one of the disgruntled Whigs who had now joined forces with Harley. Encouraged by this success, the Queen tried to secure a military promotion for Abigail's brother, Colonel Hill.

Marlborough was outraged by the suggestion. He feared the effects of such an unwarranted appointment on his authority with the army and felt the moment had come for a showdown with the Queen over the persistent intrigues of Abigail and her friends. He exerted himself to the limit to rally Godolphin and the Whig Ministers. Let them confront the Queen with an ultimatum: either Anne must dismiss Abigail or she would lose the services of her Captain-General. It was a bold threat to make. Sarah eagerly supported the idea, urging her Whig friends to appreciate what victory could mean. Not only would the Queen fear to lose her great military chief; if she was compelled to retreat, the way would be open for 'an entire union, as I have ever wished, between Lord Marlborough and the Whigs'. At last their uneasy comradeship could be sealed by a joint triumph over the common enemy. Sarah's son-in-law, Sunderland, was equally ready for the challenge; he was prepared to ensure, if need be, that the issue of Abigail's illicit influence over the Queen should be brought out into the open and that addresses in Parliament should demand her dismissal. However, Godolphin and the other Whig leaders worked to modify these audacious counsels. Marlborough still wrote to the Queen begging her to 'reflect what your own people and the rest of the world must think who have been witnesses of the love and zeal and duty with which I have served you when they shall see, after all I have done, it is not able to protect me against the malice of a bedchamber woman'. But the ultimatum in its precise form was never delivered. Fear that Marlborough might indeed resign and the hint of Sunderland's plan were enough to make the Queen recoil and withdraw her insistence on Colonel Hill's promotion.

Sighs of relief came from the Whig leaders. Godolphin believed that a real victory had been won. The first blow, if such it was, of Harley and his fellow-plotters, had at least been parried. Amid grandiloquent applause from both Houses of Parliament, Marlborough was invited to resume his military command and full powers at any renewed peace discussions. Godolphin wanted to describe him in the official declaration of the Queen as 'God Almighty's chief instrument of my glory and my people's happiness'. Anne preferred to express 'a just sense' of Marlborough's 'eminent services'. The alteration in tone was one small sign of the Queen's suppressed anger. But even if Abigail remained at her bedside, the incident had shown once more how immensely powerful Marlborough's position really was and how panic-stricken everyone from the Queen downwards felt at the possibility of his retirement. Those who most earnestly wanted peace no less than those prepared for the continuance of the war could not imagine a world where the victor of Blenheim and Malplaquet was no longer at the head of the armies.

Within a few days of the ending of the Sacheverell trial, however, the struggle was renewed. Perhaps Sarah, along with Sacheverell, gave strength to the Queen's courage. Urged by her friends to reassert her influence at the court and hearing that Anne was provoked by calumnies against her which the Duchess was alleged to have uttered, Sarah resolved to force her way into the Queen's presence. She wanted to kill the rumours and perhaps rekindle her authority. But the interview ended with brutal charges and counter-charges. Anne was stony-hearted and stubborn. Tears, if it can be believed, came from the eyes of Sarah; it is not recorded how nearly they resembled drops of boiling oil. The Duchess 'left the Palace like a fury', and the clash between the two women reverberated around the chancelleries of Europe. The Queen had a fresh incentive to act. Abigail incited her with Harley's prompting. The Duchess of Somerset was now her constant companion, and the Duke of Somerset, heading a group of Whig moderates nicknamed the Juntilla, helped to foster the notion that the grip of the Junto could be first loosened and then broken altogether.

In the early days of April positive action was taken. Lord Godolphin was amazed to hear that, before he or Marlborough had even been consulted, the Queen had appointed the Duke of Shrewsbury to a place among her Ministers. Godolphin had no particular objection to the Duke. Indeed, like Marlborough, he had long hoped to secure Shrewsbury's assistance as a possible counterbalance to the more rigid Whigs comprising the Junto. Moreover, according to the constitutional ideas of the time, the Queen had every right to make any appointments she pleased without consulting anybody. But Shrewsbury had opposed the impeachment of Sacheverell. He had been, as Godolphin remonstrated to the Queen, 'in a publick open Conjunction in every Vote with the whole Body of the Tories, and in a private, Constant Correspondence and caballing with Mr. Harley in every Thing'. Obviously his elevation was aimed at the Junto and, as Godolphin believed, directly against himself. He feared that the Queen intended further changes and, when she repudiated the charge, he brushed aside her protestations with something near rudeness.

Meantime the appointment created a new bone of contention between Godolphin and the Junto Whigs. They suspected that he and Marlborough had connived at Shrewsbury's appointment to reduce their own influence. The fatal distrust among the leading members of the coalition was re-created at the very moment when unity between them was imperative. 'Of all things the Whigs must be sure to be of one mind,' wrote Marlborough to Sarah, 'and then all things, sooner or later, must come right.' At last he had acknowledged the core of her doctrine. But the realization had come perilously late, so late that the necessary alliance had never been securely soldered. Shrewsbury himself, either from a congenital desire to please everyone or through a deceit deeply planned with Harley, fed the old illusion. He claimed that he had never exchanged one word with Abigail in his life and made fulsome assertions of his regard for Marlborough and the Duchess to Godolphin who passed them on to the Captain-General. Both men were eager to believe that Shrewsbury might be their friend after all. Once more it was Sarah who discerned the truth and blurted it out at every opportunity; no gracious bows, no 'King of Hearts', could put her off her guard.

As the weeks passed it was evident that another blow was intended. Harley was at work wherever an opening appeared. He corresponded with the leaders of the peace party in Holland; he intrigued with officers serving directly under Marlborough's command, feeding them with the promise of future favours and receiving present intelligence in return. Shrewsbury's appointment had shown what could be achieved without any real risk. The Queen was no longer isolated. Shrewsbury, Somerset and Newcastle among her official advisers concerted the next step with Harley and he in turn kept in touch with St. John and the Tories. All the comings and goings up and down the backstairs of the palace bred the rumour that Sunderland was to be the next victim. He was the member of the Junto most detested by the Queen; his threat to humiliate Abigail in public had made her hatred of him uncontrollable. Marlborough had no special love for his aggressive son-in-law, but he understood the peril. 'If the Whigs suffer Lord Sunderland to be removed,' he said when the rumour reached him, 'I think in a very short time everything will be in confusion.'

The word 'everything' in that context had a particular meaning. The dismissal of Sunderland would reveal that the Queen had come near to accepting the ideas of those who desired a complete subversion of power in the state and that, in precise terms, meant a dissolution of the existing Parliament. This was the key to most of the intrigues at the court. It was the essential link between the manœuvres of the politicians and the public controversy stoked up by Sacheverell.

Under the Triennial Act the Parliament had another year to run. The Whigs commanded a majority in both Houses. Another year meant another winter session in which, through the exercise of their power to vote supplies, the Whigs would be able to dictate their will on other issues—as they had done for example in ordering the impeachment of Sacheverell. That weapon had proved a boomerang, but as long as the Whigs could direct affairs in Parliament there was always the chance of rescuing the situation. Such had long been Sunderland's view. It was necessary to put some stuffing into Godolphin and that, thought Sunderland, was a task for Sarah; her ardour could overcome his 'coldness and slowness'. It was necessary too for the Whigs to keep together. Given these conditions, 'I am sure our union and strength is too great to be hurt'. But, of course, there was one other condition—the Parliament must be made to last. An election held amid the Sacheverell fever might undermine the very basis of the power which the Whigs had exercised for the past two years. If on the other hand the Parliament survived, other prospects might soon open before them. Marlborough could win another victory on the battlefield. King Louis might submit to the terms of peace. Spain might be conquered by force of arms. Some hidden event might come to the aid of the Whigs as Sacheverell had come to the aid of the Tories. In short, as long as the Parliament lasted no loss was irreparable: the whole ship could still be saved from wreckage. A new push could be made against Abigail, appointments objectionable to the Whig Junto could be countered, the Queen could be shackled once more by the Whig power as she had been in 1709. The decision about an election rested with the Queen; she was not required to rely on any Ministerial advice. In April, soon after Shrewsbury's appointment, she prorogued Parliament. No hint of a dissolution had at that time been heard in any quarter. Indeed, this was the one point from which Daniel Defoe could derive any comfort when he pondered on the catastrophe of the Sacheverell impeachment. 'Patience, Gentlemen, do not run so fast,' he said to the Tory high-flyers. 'Tho' now you carry all away with a Torrent; and to talk to you now, would be to put One's Thumb in to stop the Tide at Gravesend—Yet have Patience, the Elections are not to Morrow, no *neither*, God be thank'd, *are They this Year*.'

In May and June, however, the idea of a dissolution before the Parliament had run its natural term became the talk of the town. It played a governing part in every calculation. The high Tories started clamouring for it; they saw it as the foundation on which all their rising hopes could be raised still higher. They in turn brought pressure on Harley, urging him to exert his influence with the Queen. Harley's real aims were, as usual, a secret he kept to himself. (Certainly he concealed them with astonishing success from his agent, Defoe, who called on him frequently for instructions; all through these months Defoe continued to attack Sacheverell and support the Whig Ministry without once suspecting the game his employer was playing.) If Harley staked all on a dissolution he had to be especially careful not to reveal his hand. For his design was dependent, temporarily at least, on the co-operation of men like the Duke of Somerset and the Duke of Newcastle. They were still Whigs even if they disliked the Junto. They wanted a gradual change of Ministers, not a complete overthrow of the Whig majority in the House of Commons. Moreover, for these indispensable agents in the Harley plot, elections were a very costly business. They were as much opposed to an election as Sunderland and Marlborough themselves and, if they had suspected Harley of working for this end, the Juntilla might easily have looked for means of thwarting him at other points. The Whigs of the Junto, of course, solidly opposed a dissolution. They wanted to hold what they had got. But the fear of a dissolution worked to loosen the bonds between them. Risks should be taken to prevent the Queen from resorting to this final weapon. If she could be appeased by their tolerance of a Shrewsbury or the removal of a Sunderland, might not the sacrifice be worth while? The Queen, too, had an interest in resisting the clamorous Tory demand. A dissolution might destroy her dream of at the same time removing the Junto, retaining Marlborough and gathering round her Ministers such as Shrewsbury, Somerset, Newcastle and Harley, tied to no faction and giving their sole allegiance to her. Certainly at midsummer the three wealthy Dukes were casting the weight of their influence strongly against a dissolution. Harley, in all probability, fostered the idea in the Queen's mind strongly enough to ensure that the weapon was available if the right moment came, but not so strongly or overtly that the Whig moderates could convict him of double-dealing.

There were indeed plenty of other good reasons why Harley must move cautiously in all his schemes. At every jolt against the Godolphin Ministry, the public credit dropped. The banking influence was securely in the hands of the Whigs and, if the change in Ministerial power was made too abruptly, Harley might find himself summoned back to the Queen's service amid a financial crash. He would not have the money available to keep the armies in the field while peace negotiations were started. Similarly, a collapse in the military prestige of the Grand Alliance, such as would follow the resignation of Marlborough, could easily destroy the chances of peace by reviving French hopes too sharply. A premature dissolution, even if the Queen's approval for it could be gained, might spell catastrophe in the City, at the court and at the peace table. Meantime the mere threat of a dissolution worked

THE PEN AND THE SWORD

wonders. It made the Whigs willing to tolerate other Harleyite moves. It even softened their displays of hatred for Abigail. With the assistance of some moneys from the secret service funds, it helped to entice Lord Somers, the most eminent of the Junto, to flirt with Harley behind the backs of his colleagues. Moreover, elections required preparation and one necessary preparation was the appointment of a sufficient number of Tory Lords-Lieutenant in the counties. Time was needed to let all these schemes develop. How closely Harley advised the Queen on a deliberate, well-conceived plan, how much the skilful avoidance of a precipitate decision was due to his procrastinating temper is impossible to gauge. He certainly succeeded in keeping his friends sufficiently united and his enemies sufficiently afraid to be able to strike the next blow with success and impunity.

Sarah saw it coming. She resolved to make an appeal to the Queen, invoking the memory of their ancient friendship. Some of her essays in that style were certainly not well designed to improve the Queen's mood. But the letter she addressed to Anne early in June was a masterly statement of Marlborough's case. Instead of criticizing the Queen's conduct in the past, Sarah now concentrated more on warnings for the future. Was Anne fully aware of the desperate course on which she had embarked? Changes in the Ministry could easily lead to a destruction of the Parliament. That in turn could mean a most serious catastrophe for the country. It was not solely a question of gratitude for Marlborough's past services. If Lord Godolphin's position was menaced, the finances of the state would be disrupted, since 'it is known to be true, that the whole interest and business of the city, is now in the hands of such men as will not trust my Lord Rochester or Mr. Harley with a shilling'. The Queen's armies would be starved; the French would have her at their mercy to demand what peace they wished. The removal of Lord Sunderland could not be regarded as an isolated event. It would mean a dramatic transfer of power to the newly appointed favourites and their aim, behind the Queen's back, was to enforce the dissolution of the Parliament which remained as the chief obstacle to the ambitions they had dared not reveal. An appeal, half pathetic, half remonstrative, on behalf of the Duke was not omitted; perhaps his life, at least his health, was at stake. But the main theme amounted to an invocation of the Queen's sense of statesmanship. 'Therefore, pray, Madam, con-

sider seriously what you are doing and what a precipice you are
going upon.'

However, Sarah's profound arguments, like her tears or her
fury, were in vain. On June 14th the news broke like a thunderclap.
Sunderland had been dismissed, and the storm was up.

All the rumours which had been circulating during previous
months suggesting that the Queen had resolved to carry through a
Ministerial revolution now appeared to be confirmed. The impact
of the blow was felt far and wide. 'The Whig day is gone,' wrote
Defoe, 'and the enemy is broke in like a Flood—And like a Flood
they will ravage all before them.' At Vienna and at The Hague,
England's allies feared either that the next attack would be aimed
directly at Marlborough himself or that he would abandon in disgust the task in which he seemed to secure such fitful backing from
his own Queen. They went down on their knees before him, pleading that he should retain his command, and straightway also made
the most emphatic representations to the English court about the
perils which must follow if the same course were pursued further.
The court at Versailles was correspondingly elated by the news
and the French envoys now engaged in fresh and abortive peace
discussions at Gertruydenberg assumed a new tone. They calculated that the English Ministry might be overthrown, that the
Parliament might be dissolved, that easier peace terms might soon
be available to them; they even hinted that the Captain-General
might be dismissed and disgraced. 'The French laugh,' wrote
Defoe; 'they talk high at Gertruydenberg, bid you send them
Home when you please; what is the matter? 'Tis evident 'tis from
no Disaster befallen your Army, no Blow, no Defeat, no Disappointment there; their view is at Home, where they see your credit
sinking and a Party prevailing that will Ruin the National Credit.'

No one anywhere could doubt that the dismissal of Sunderland
was a stupendous event. In London, and particularly in the City,
the consternation was immediate. On the very next day four
directors of the Bank of England secured an audience with the
Queen and informed her of the financial dangers she was courting
if further Ministerial changes were attempted. The Queen at once
gave the assurance for which they asked and the rumour ran that
her promise of no further change could be taken as a sign that she
opposed the dissolution of the Parliament. But no words from
Anne could now check the alarm for long; had she not made the

same promise after the appointment of Shrewsbury and then broken it? She herself wrote to Godolphin assuring him that she contemplated no further removals and explaining that if he or Marlborough deserted her service at so critical a juncture, they and they alone would be responsible for the resulting confusion. Was she really so unaware of the injury she had inflicted on her Captain-General and the whole Grand Alliance or was she so deeply engaged with Harley that she was now ready to practise any deception? It is impossible to know. But the public evidence remained, despite all assurances to bankers, ambassadors and Ministers alike, that the Queen's authority now seemed to be directed against the men who still commanded a majority in her Cabinet Council. They too feared—for reasons very different from those of the Queen or Harley—that Marlborough might resign. On the night of Sunderland's dismissal they met together at Devonshire House. Seven leading Whigs, along with Godolphin, sent an urgent message to the Duke in Flanders. They implored him to stay at his post. The survival of the alliance depended on it. And another reason underlined afresh the dominating thought in their calculation. To keep Marlborough at the head of the army was 'the most necessary step that can be taken to prevent the dissolution of this Parliament'.

Clearly the Whig leaders believed that the Queen's mind was not made up on that most delicate of all issues. If the election could be prevented, all might still be saved. Marlborough was persuaded by their entreaties, although he was in 'no ways convinced that my continuing will save the Parliament; for Mr. Harley and his friends know the whole depends on that. . . .' Thus he wrote home to Sarah, warning her of the dangers ahead and begging her to be careful, 'for you are in an country amongst tigers and wolves'. Marlborough knew now that he was engaged in the political fight of his life. Two days later his spirits showed signs of revival. The tigers and wolves could still be caged. 'Keep your temper,' he wrote, 'and *if Parliament continues,* we will make some of their hearts ache.'

The political forces ranged against one another were now most precariously balanced. For if the Whigs had lost ground at the court and in the country since the Sacheverell affair they still had great assets. All the Whig moderates, whose defection to Harley had shaken the authority of Marlborough and the Junto, were still rigidly opposed to a dissolution. Perhaps the strong reaction from the City and the allies to Sunderland's dismissal would have its effect on the Queen. Above all, at every crisis, the indispensable status of the Duke of Marlborough was acknowledged even by those who worked to discomfort his associates. He was still the presiding figure in the drama, and if the Whig Parliament met again in the autumn his old mastery could still be reasserted. A few of the Whigs indeed believed that even if an election was forced upon them it was by no means certain all would be lost. Throughout the whole of the Queen's reign the scene had been dominated by the Duke and his policies; was it really conceivable that all could be overturned and the fruit of so many exertions cast away in a few brief months of hysteria?

Thus the calculations of the men around the court swayed back and forth, and while they conducted their intrigues the nation was engaged in a great debate. Personal ambitions, corrupt motives, intricate political and family combinations played their part. But the issues involved were not trifling. The peace of Europe, the liberties of Protestant peoples, the meaning of monarchy, the succession, the honour of England—these were some of the stakes, and all were now intermingled with the controversies aroused by the Sacheverell impeachment. The citizens of Queen Anne's time discussed them all with a splendid fervour, exploiting on a scale never known before the new instrument of the printing press which made public opinion a truly potent force in the land. The politicians around the court, whether Whigs or Tories, were learning how idle it was to lament the old days of the Licensing Laws, and the Queen herself, when she prorogued Parliament after the Sacheverell debates, paid a striking tribute to those others who now presumed to intrude into the arguments of the courtiers and the Parliament men. 'The suppressing Immorality, and prophane and other wicked and malicious Libels'—so ran the speech from the throne—'is what I have always recommended; and shall be glad of the first Opportunity to give my Consent to any Laws, that might effectually conduce to that End . . . I could heartily wish, that Men would study to be quiet, and do their own Business, rather than busy themselves in reviving Questions and Disputes of a very high Nature; and which must be with an ill Intention, since they can only tend to foment, but not to heal our Divisions and Animosities.'

The response to this royal appeal was an explosion of the most rumbustious controversy which England had known since the Civil War.

* * *

One evidence of what Anne called 'the Heat and Ferment that is in this poor Nation' was a series of addresses presented to the Queen from cities and counties all over the country. Behind the professions of loyalty the political aims of the various parties were made abundantly plain. The high church party or the Tories directed their fervour for monarchy against the Queen's Whig advisers and backed the demand for the dissolution of Parliament. The low church party or the Whigs were no less skilful in identifying their allegiance to the Queen with their trust in the Ministers and the Captain-General. But from the way in which the different addresses were received the real sympathies of the Queen became increasingly obvious.

'Long may Your Majesty Live and Reign over us, as the Nursing-Mother of our Spotless Religion, the Delight and Darling of a happy People, and the Terrour and Scourge of Ambitious Tyrants,' said the County of Gloucester. The County of Cornwall was determined to make it known that Louis XIV was not the only tyrant suspected of ambition. Their address 'begged Leave, in all Humility, to beseech Almighty God, to inspire Your Majesty with a continued Courage, to assert the just Rights of Monarchy and the Church of England, with the succession to the Crown in the Protestant Line, as by Law establish'd, against all Opposers and Innovators, whatsoever . . . May your Majesty's Arms still gloriously Conquer Abroad, and Your Goodness prevail upon Your Enemies at Home, till there be no Power able to resist the one, or Malignant left to disturb the other'. The County of Oxford came nearer to the crux of controversy. Having noted that 'the most open Patrons of Resistance are equally Encouragers of Blasphemy and Profaneries; and that the poisonn'd Arrows, which have been shot as well against God as his Vice-Regent, have come out of the Same Quiver', they could not refrain from looking forward to the moment 'when Your Majesty to the extreme Joy of Your Loyal Subjects, shall in your Princely Wisdom, Judge it proper to call another Parliament'. A whole series of addresses were 'mainly levelled, like so many Batteries, against the Ministry and Parliament, and the whole Moderate Party'. The Whigs replied in kind. 'The Persons truly dangerous to Your Majesty and the Protestant Succession,' said the address of the Borough of Hereford, 'are those that traduce the Honour and Justice of the Revolution; those who seditiously suggest the Church to be in Danger under Your Majesty's Administration . . . We cannot therefore go so far as to concur with any Insinuation, which seems to be made use of to induce Your Majesty to dissolve the present Parliament, who deserve so well of Your Majesty and the British nation.'

These slogans of the competing parties were elaborated in a deluge of pamphlets which 'flew about like hail'. One of the most remarkable features of the controversy was how high a proportion of it was concerned with great constitutional issues. It might have been expected that the continuance of the war itself would dominate men's minds, that most other issues would occupy a subordinate position and that the performance of the leading party protagonists would be tested by their attitude to this supreme matter. True, the war and the conduct of the war leaders were occasionally mentioned. The Whigs began to suggest that the removal of Marlborough was a primary aim of the Tories, and the Tories often attacked Marlborough and, even more readily, his supporters in the Whig Junto. But the main debate turned on other questions. The Queen's title to the crown, the varying Whig and Tory doctrines about the nature of the Revolution of 1688 and its implications affecting the Queen's right to choose her own Ministers and govern as she pleased—these were the topics which stirred the most fervent eloquence. Interwoven with them were two kindred issues, one theoretical in a sense, the other severely practical and immediate. The Tory enthusiasm for the Queen was linked with their love of the English Church and their hatred of dissenters. And week by week their hopes were concentrated on the dissolution of the Parliament.

In short, Dr. Sacheverell himself and the commotions aroused by his trial retained their catalytic force for many months. During the year no less than seventy-five tracts relating directly or indirectly to his case were published. The Tories were naturally eager to profit from the occasion, but many were dubious about the Doctor's credentials and even more dubious about the riots and disturbances provoked in his name. Benjamin Hoadly, one of the most brilliant Whig pamphleteers, mocked the Tories for their readiness to accept such a champion, suggesting that soon a map of the new apostle's travels would be published, that his statue would be set up in all the market-places, and his picture in all parish churches. Where was the Doctor's campaign leading the nation? Moderate Tories, no less than confirmed Whigs, must face the reality.

'Is this the time for such a total alteration, as must shake the confidence of friends and inspire the enemy with hopes? Is this the season for an entire change of hands, when publick credit must be sunk into nothing, before the rest of Europe can have time to know whom they are to depend upon, and the people at home whom they are to trust? Is this a day for a new general, or to disgust the old, when he is happily in the favour of all abroad, and in the midst of the execution of glorious projects? Or is this a time for a new choice of a House of Commons, when such an opportunity is more likely than ever to be improved by our common enemies into a civil war amongst ourselves? . . . At home, such threatenings have been given out, and such insults made, that I dread to think lest the field of election should become a field of battle. . . . Alas! Whither are we running so hastily? And what is the spirit which we have been raising? We see the beginning of these things; but we see not the end.'

Benjamin Hoadly had indeed shown, not only that the Whigs had a powerful case, but that they were fighting back against the scares which Sacheverell had raised. The moderate Tories felt an answer was necessary. They produced a pamphlet: *Faults on both sides; or an Essay upon the original Cause, Progress, and mischievous consequences of the Factions of this Nation.* Some said that the author was Robert Harley himself or at least that the ideas in the pamphlet were largely dictated by him. *Faults on both sides* was certainly a powerful statement of the moderate Tory view; it revealed in the open how persuasive the case must have been which Harley was busy presenting to Shrewsbury, Somerset, Newcastle and the Queen.

The pamphlet begins by admitting that there were honest men in both parties, honest Whigs who were faithful to the Church and honest Tories who had no desire to persecute dissenters. The whole history of the previous twenty years was traced and in the apportionment of blame for the pursuit of factious party quarrels the Tories were indicted as much as the Whigs. Indeed, the author still claimed to uphold the Whig principles of the Revolution.

His protest was against the excessive allegiance to party which 'has proved to us like a whip-saw, whichsoever extreme is pulled, the nation is still miserably sawn between the two'. Formerly perhaps the high-flying Tories had been most guilty, but thanks to the dexterity of Robert Harley, the best men of that party had been restrained from persisting in extreme courses. Thereafter the real menace both for the nation and the Whigs came from the 'great men among their leaders that stick at nothing'. Had they not removed Harley for no other crime than that of 'faithfully discovering to the Queen some mismanagements of the ministers that would be of ill consequence if not redressed in time'? Had they not invaded the Queen's rights by proposing action against 'a modest, discreet, inoffensive, virtuous gentlewoman at the Queen's court'—in other words against Abigail? Had not 'a certain very great man [Marlborough], whose general behaviour had always been remarkably soft, easy, courteous and cool to all, presumed to dispute the disposal of a single regiment in the army with his sovereign and to such a degree of animosity, as to depart from her presence in disgust, without returning until the good Queen (may I say) submitted and yielded the point to him'? So, it was alleged, the Whig plan had unfolded stage by stage. 'I must yet tell you of another step larger than this, and even so high that it wanted but one of the top; in a word, they had projected to get the great man created general for life.' Faced with this challenge, 'it was necessary for the good Queen to look about her . . .', to put 'some speedy check to the formidable power of a few men, who have given indications too evident to be slighted, that they have entered into confederacies and taken resolution to govern both Queen and nation according to their own pleasure'. These were the reasons why other men had been willing 'to enter into healing and moderate measures'. Honest Whigs should have no fears. If they abandoned 'the ill designs of the Junto', employments would still be open to them and the nation could be saved. Meantime, no one should be incited by the Whig rumours that a complete change of Ministers, with all the Whigs out and all the Tories in, was intended; dissenters need not fear an attack on the principles of toleration; no plan was afoot to bring back the Pretender; the public credit would be protected; no one need be alarmed lest the allies would be shocked and the nation forced into a dishonourable peace; 'we need take no more pains to answer these calumnies than the parson did to confute the cardinal, and that was to tell him in short, Bellarmin, thou liest'.

Such was the creed of Harleyism presented to the outside world. A cool, composed St. George would come to the rescue of the maiden and save her from the dragon of the Junto. The deed could be done without bringing any of the catastrophic consequences prophesied by the Whigs. Marlborough could continue to direct the war, but as a servant of the Queen and not her master. The interests of the Church could be protected without unleashing a new persecution of dissenters. All the furious animosities of the past few years could be stilled, and eminent men from both parties or none could take their place among the Queen's Ministers. Was this not a programme to command wide appeal and had not the whole of Harley's life been dedicated to serve this same cause of moderation? The Whigs, of course, could paint a very different portrait. Often they mocked the clandestine capers in which Harley was thought to be engaged. Often the exaggerated deviousness of his conduct aroused more ridicule than alarm. But his enemies would have been wiser to understand why Sarah called him 'the grand master of the whole machine'. For in the months after the dismissal of Sunderland, while the great debate raged in the country and while Harley through his agents took steps to steer it along channels suitable to himself, he executed at the court a manœuvre more subtle than any even he had previously attempted.

*　　*　　*

With the departure of Sunderland, the Whig power had been no more than curbed. Another blow must follow. Harley's Tory supporters clamoured for action and above all thirsted for the dissolution of the Parliament which, as they believed, would deliver almighty power into their hands. Harley was now seeing the Queen almost every day. Perhaps if he urged the dissolution strongly enough she would bow to his judgement. But such a course might be perilous in the extreme. At once, if the project was revealed, the Whig moderates like Somerset and Newcastle, who had never been parties to the idea of an early election, would desert him. They might even join forces once more with Godolphin and confront the Queen with so powerful a demonstration of strength that she might waver in her resolve. Was it not possible that Harley would find himself thwarted again as he had been only two years before? Was it really wise to risk destroying the partnership with Shrewsbury, Somerset and Newcastle which he had taken such pains in consolidating? Moreover, despite all the high spirits of the Tories incited by the Sacheverell campaign, the result of the election itself could not be reckoned as a foregone conclusion. Elections were determined in a considerable degree by the attitudes of the Sheriffs and the Lords-Lieutenant in the counties. Thinking that the next election would not come until the following year the Whigs had neglected to oust several of the Tory Sheriffs. But the Lords-Lieutenant were still mostly Whigs. New appointments to the Lord-Lieutenancies were governed by the decisions of the Lord Treasurer, Lord Godolphin; no Tory appointment was likely to pass his vigilant eye. Thus, if the attempt to secure the dissolution came too speedily, either the Whigs might be rallied to support the Ministers or the election itself might be mismanaged.

The aim must be to isolate Godolphin as Sunderland had been isolated, and for that purpose Harley still required the aid of the men most opposed to the Tory dream of a dissolved Parliament. Somerset must be encouraged to believe that he was the right man to step into the Lord Treasurer's shoes. Shrewsbury must be invited to consider accepting the same honour. Newcastle must be kept in line. How adroitly the game was played is shown in the correspondence which passed between Harley, Newcastle and the other Whig leaders. In July Harley wrote to Newcastle complaining of a report which had been 'maliciously and industriously spread that the Parliament was dissolved'. The effect on stocks had been serious and Harley assailed the mischief-makers who dared indulge in such tactics. Newcastle could hardly believe that the man who wrote to him in these terms was himself plotting a dissolution. A few days later Lord Halifax who was now engaged in talks with Harley wrote to Newcastle describing how he had impressed on all whom it might concern 'that the preserving the public credit is necessary to enable them to hold the Government, that the dissolving this Parliament would give such a shock to the credit that no people could furnish them with the money to "subsist" the army'. Halifax was the foremost financier of his time; such a judgement could not easily be discounted. Newcastle needed no convincing; he exerted his influence with Harley to reinforce the same arguments. Sometimes the faint suspicion crossed the minds of other among Newcastle's Whig correspondents—Lord Somers, the Duke of Devonshire, Lord Cowper—that someone was playing a double game and that preparations were in fact being made to sell the vital pass. Newcastle expressed these fears to Harley, Harley took precautions to pacify him and Newcastle in turn encouraged his Whig friends to continue their parleys with Robin the Trickster. Early in August an official announcement bolstered their hopes. Parliament was prorogued until September 26th. That surely was a strange announcement to make if a dissolution was really intended. Might it not be that the faithless Harley was proving himself faithful on this one all-important test? If so, what folly it would be to forfeit everything by offending the Queen and pushing her, perhaps against her will, into a total surrender to the Tory demand for an early election?

By these well-directed plausibilities not only the Whig moderates but the members of the Junto themselves were lulled into the belief that the Parliament could be saved even if Godolphin fell. Two of their number, Somers and Halifax, were inveigled into a temporary compliance with Harley's schemes; they had some old scores to pay off against Godolphin and the acceptance of his removal was preferable to the irretrievable calamity which an election might entail. The rumours of all these confabulations did not fail to reach the Lord Treasurer's ears. But the Queen played her part to perfection. Right up till the night of August 6th Godolphin was reassured. That day he had quarrelled at the Cabinet Council with both the Queen and Shrewsbury, but when he confronted the Queen with the direct request whether she wished him to continue in her service she replied with an unhesitating 'Yes'. That night he wrote to Marlborough. 'I think', he said, 'the safety or destruction of the parliament remains still under a good deal of uncertainty.' Godolphin regarded the issue of the dissolution as the last card in his hand. If the Queen dropped a hint that she intended to dissolve, he still might have time to mobilize all the Ministers, both the Junto and the moderates, against it.

Next day the Lord Treasurer received a letter from the Queen abruptly dismissing him from his office, offering the consolation of a four thousand pounds a year pension, but adding the insult 'that, instead of bringing the [Lord Treasurer's] staff to me, you will break it, which, I believe, will be easier to us both'. The Queen's orders were obeyed. Godolphin broke his staff and threw the pieces in the fireplace. The Queen wrote to Marlborough, giving him the news and assuring him 'I will take care that the army shall want for nothing'. The Lord Treasurer's duties were put in commission; one of the commissioners was the newly-appointed Chancellor of the Exchequer, Robert Harley. The whole fabric of the state trembled at so mighty an event as the fall of the great Minister who, second to Marlborough alone, had borne the chief burden of the war. Daniel Defoe was torn between joy at seeing his patron restored to office and horror at the consequences which must follow for that 'poor, distress'd Lady, Public Credit', who had lost 'the best friend that ever she had in this Nation'. None of the Whig Ministers stirred themselves to protest. No counter-attack was planned. Godolphin himself wrote to Marlborough urging him not to resign. The whole political world held its breath for fear of shattering a prospect so tenderly poised. Godolphin had gone. But no order, not so much as a whisper, had come from the Queen affecting the dissolution of the Parliament. The old, last hope of the Whigs still showed a quiver of life.

One among their number was not prone to self-deception. During the past few months Lord Wharton had been absent from the scene of action. He had been occupied governing Ireland and using his position as Lord-Lieutenant to help make good the large fortunes dissipated in previous election campaigns. Along with Lord Sunderland he was the most resolute and buoyant of the members of the Junto. Attempts had been made by the usual circuitous Harleyite means to seduce him from his loyalty to his colleagues but no evidence exists that he—unlike Lord Somers and Lord Halifax—was ever tempted by the offers. His creed was that the only way to deal with enemies was to fight them. Even after the dismissal of Godolphin, Sunderland was convinced that all was not lost. 'If you, Lord Godolphin and the Whigs', he wrote to Marlborough, 'do act cordially and vigorously together, without suspicion of one another, which I am sure there is no reason for, it is impossible but everything must come right again.' Wharton shared the same opinion. But he was naturally alarmed by the news from London.

He talked the matter over with Jonathan Swift, who was now

quite a frequent visitor to Dublin Castle. The momentary uneasiness between the two men had given place, at least on Wharton's side, to a jovial tolerance. His grudges soon healed and he pleasantly inquired from his companion when next he intended to pay a visit to England. Swift replied that he had no business there since all his old friends would soon be out of office. That conversation occurred just before the news of Godolphin's dismissal had been confirmed in Dublin. A few days later both men changed their minds. Wharton, it seems, resolved to return and challenge the new dispensation at the court; a Ministry dominated by Robert Harley was no place for him and, if an election was to take place, it could hardly proceed without the expert assistance of 'Honest Tom'. Swift, too, could not resist the attraction of the new world in London; when the Irish bishops conveniently decided that the moment was opportune to renew their demands on behalf of the Irish Church and that Swift should again be dispatched as their emissary, he leapt at the chance. The decision was made overnight and the Vicar of Laracor had just enough time to request a free berth from the Lord-Lieutenant. At the end of August the vice-regal yacht sailed out of Dublin Bay, carrying on board the most explosive piece of cargo ever shipped across the Irish sea.

CHAPTER FIVE

Appointment with Mr. Harley

(September 7th—October 4th, 1710)

'The prejudices of his education prevailed so far, that he could not forbear taking me up in his right hand, and stroking me gently with the other, after an hearty fit of laughing, asked me, whether I were a Whig or a Tory.'—*Gulliver's Travels, Voyage to Brobdingnag.*

WHEN JONATHAN SWIFT arrived in London on September 7th, 1710, he stepped into a world where the political tension had come near to breaking-point. For the past month Robert Harley had assumed the position as the most influential of the Queen's Ministers. No longer need he rely solely on his access to the backstairs of the palace and already the proof of his authority with the Queen made him the centre of attraction for all those who expected favours in the future. But his most testing problems were far from solved. 'To be thus is nothing; but to be safely thus!' Would the Duke of Marlborough retain his command or would he, by a sudden resignation, force a crisis which might bring in its train calamitous consequences at home and abroad? Could the public credit be sustained or would the stocks continue to fall as they had done throughout the summer when each fresh attack was made on the Whig power? Sunderland and Godolphin had been removed, but what form of Ministry was now to take over? A few Tories, notably Harley himself, had received their reward, but the great bulk of the party was still excluded from the promised land. In particular, when was the signal to be given for the long-awaited dissolution of the Parliament? After the dismissal of Godolphin in August, most observers believed that the hour had come. But four weeks later the word had still not been spoken. Probably only three persons in England knew the answer to this last teasing, all-important question—the Queen, Mrs. Masham and Harley. Perhaps the ultimate choice rested with Harley and perhaps he had not been able to make up his mind.

The Tories did not fail to express their impatience. Dr. Sacheverell was touring the country and raising a tumult of support wherever he went. The Tory tide must be taken at the flood; for the party enthusiasts this was the single, exclusive point of concern. They waited on the news from London; instead of a call to battle came the whisper that Harley was engaged in another intricate contortion. 'This is the old Whiggish Game still,' wrote Defoe gleefully. He used the argument partly to explain why he, a supporter of the old Ministry, would not berate the new one with the same fury employed by the Whig extremists. But undoubtedly he was genuine in his belief that a middle-of-the-road policy was intended. Several of the Tories had long fretted against Harley's taste for moderation; was it not conceivable that he was contriving some counterplot to cheat them of their spoils? On one occasion the Tory churchman, Dr. Atterbury, vented their anger to Harley's face. 'Some of his particular friends' were determined to inform their procrastinating leader 'how very uneasy they were at his conduct, that the Parliament was not yet dissolved, nor so many of the Whigs turned out as was expected, and that they were wholly in the dark as to the measures he was taking'. Even the good-tempered Harley exploded at so ungrateful a rebuke. He was entitled to believe that all the gains of the previous few months had been due to the expert timing of his successive strokes. Now the high churchmen who could not appreciate his artistry seemed eager to jog his elbow and wreck the whole design. Possibly he was still unconvinced about the certainty of victory at the polls; he had barely had time to make the first changes in the County Lieutenancies. No doubt the electoral scene, so unmistakable in its contours in the country at large, looked a little different through the fetid political atmosphere of London. Or, possibly again, Harley *was* engaged in other schemes which could not conveniently be discussed with headstrong doctors of divinity.

Certainly the removal of Godolphin had 'stunned the Whigs'. At the moment when the blow came, none of them had expected it. They had no concerted policy to set against the unfolding plan, if such it was, of their rivals and so, as politicians will, they made a firm resolution to hope against hope. Lord Somers and Lord Halifax were still ready to believe that Harley's real aim was the maintenance of a coalition of 'moderates' in which they would be allowed to retain their influence. The chance remained that the dissolution could be avoided; was not that the half-promise which Harley still dangled before the Duke of Newcastle? Lord Godolphin, meantime, comforted himself and his friends with another prospect. He shared the lack of confidence with which Chancellors of the Exchequer usually observe the antics of their successors, wondered how the mounting financial dangers were to be dealt with, and dreamt 'he saw Mr. Harley in a sculler alone rowing against the wind and tide without any person to assist him'. How long could this one-man odyssey continue? Godolphin, moreover, was not willing to despair about the results of the election and he was not alone in his opinion. Most prophets foretold a Tory victory. But there were others—among them, for example, men with such various experience as Lord Sunderland, Arthur Maynwaring and Joseph Addison—who believed that the Whig cause, if asserted with sufficient vigour, could achieve a satisfactory resurgence.

The truth was that Harley and his associates had embarked on an enterprise of very considerable delicacy. For the noisy Tory propagandists who had set their hearts on routing the dissenters the sole objectives were to sweep every Whig from office and win a thumping electoral victory. But such a course of action, even if the electoral victory could be guaranteed, might involve a financial crash and the immediate resignation of Marlborough—two events which could hardly fail to make the conclusion of a reasonable peace infinitely more difficult. At once the French would heighten their terms. A protracted war or a bad peace, coupled with a violent orgy of high church fanaticism, could easily bring the Whigs back in strength. Harley knew better than anyone how swiftly the political kaleidoscope could change. The need was to soften the public alarm, to steady the stock market, to gain time; time in which peace negotiations might fructify, time in which the giant Captain-General could be cut down to normal size in the public imagination. Then his eventual departure from the scene could be borne with equanimity and indeed with enthusiasm.

That this was one of the considerations weighing on the minds of Harley and his associates is shown in the pages of a new weekly journal called the *Examiner* which made its appearance during August. Part of its purpose was to stoke the fires for the election when it came. But unlike the high Tory journals, which were content to back Sacheverell or were not afraid to appear openly

Jacobite in tone, the *Examiner* argued that the moderate Tories would prove themselves more effective opponents of the French King and more capable administrators either in war or peace than the Whigs. It was not an easy case to prove.

In its first issue the *Examiner* sought to dispel the notion that Marlborough's removal was either desired or unavoidable. 'Can anything be more absurd', it asked, 'than this suggestion, that upon a Change in the Ministry, or a Dissolution of the Parliament, the *English* General will be so mortified that he can serve no longer? It seems tho' they have been made sensible of his Military virtues, they are still unacquainted with his Civil. His actions are guided by a nobler Principle, than the little Interests of any Party. His Duty to her Majesty, and his Love to his Country, will never suffer him to forget that he has receiv'd all the Honours and Advantages which a gracious Queen and a generous People could heap upon a Subject. And without doubt he is of a Spirit to make all the returns that are in his Power. The Insinuation therefore of the Duke's Resentment could come from none but his Enemies; and if the *French* Ministers had this Intelligence from *England*, we can easily guess who are their Correspondents.'

Of course, the *Examiner*'s tribute to the Duke's sense of duty was partly ironic. The simultaneous attempt to retain Marlborough's services if he could be persuaded to stay, and to destroy his reputation lest he was resolved to go, called for some subtlety. The prickly fear and jealousy of the Tories towards the Duke could not be altogether concealed, but in the main they strove to exclude both the question of his command and the conduct of the war from the great debate. Only those at the centre of affairs knew how crucial these issues really were. Almost certainly the anonymous author of the article in the *Examiner* was Henry St. John. He had re-emerged from his country retirement and quickly made it clear to Harley that he expected a foremost place in the new Ministry. Doubtless in consultation with Harley, and with the assistance of Dr. Atterbury and Matthew Prior and a few others, he had started the *Examiner*. Nothing quite like it had been seen before in English journalism. Daniel Defoe had seized the opportunity of Harley's return to power to pay his respects to his old master and swing his *Weekly Review* more into line with the new trend. But Defoe, for all his self-conscious show of independence, was a paid hack. The men who launched the *Examiner* were leading politicians of the day, and one of them—Robert Harley—was the Queen's closest adviser who wanted a new weapon to use against his enemies—including those who sat cheek by jowl with him around the same Cabinet table.

Fearful of Marlborough's reaction to events and conscious of the huge risks they were running abroad as a result of domestic upheavals, Harley for a moment adopted a more daring scheme to minimize the perils with which he felt himself encompassed. He decided to make a secret approach to the Elector of Hanover, the man who would succeed Anne on the throne of England—assuming that all French efforts to secure a Jacobite restoration proved abortive. The Elector and his armies had given loyal support to the Grand Alliance. Was he not a possible candidate to succeed Marlborough as Commander-in-Chief? And might not Harley and his friends win favour by making the proposal? An attempt by the new Ministers to promote the authority of the Elector could help to kill the charge that they were Jacobite in sympathy. Here, at least, was a constructive initiative and one offering an escape from so many despairing arguments which merely underlined once more the indispensability of the Duke.

One of Harley's recruits from the Whigs, Lord Rivers, was chosen to undertake the mission to Hanover. Unfortunately for the Tories, the story that a plan was afoot to displace Marlborough from his command leaked out in the Dutch press. Alarm quickly spread from one allied capital to another and the consternation was fully shared by the Elector himself. Marlborough had courted him for years and Harley's stroke of cunning was not likely to count against such gracious and accomplished persistence. On September 8th the Elector wrote to Marlborough a letter of reassurance: 'I hope', he said, 'that nothing will be capable of inducing the Queen to take the command of her armies from a General who has acquitted himself with so much glory and so much success, and in whose hands I shall always see it with pleasure.' Lord Rivers received a cool reception at the Hanoverian court. Harley on this occasion had shown himself somewhat too clever. Once more, as so often before when a move was made against him, the pre-eminent stature of the Duke was established for all to see.

It was at this precise moment when the future King of England was restating so forcibly Europe's awe-struck opinion of the Captain-General that the Vicar of Laracor made his reappearance on the London scene. So far the paths of the two men had never crossed. Swift had never concerned himself with the European conflict and Marlborough's name had never figured in any of the controversies arousing his interest. Once, as we have seen,—in August of that year, 1710—he had condoled with Addison about the ill-effects which the disturbance of the Whig régime might have on the fortunes of the Duke and the war. But this was no more than a passing phrase. Apart from the pacifist sentiments hinted at in *The Tale of a Tub*, no evidence exists that he had ever applied his mind to the issues involved in the great Continental struggle. If he had never expressed an adulation for Marlborough in the ecstatic language of his two friends, Addison and Steele, he had also not been known to dissent from their verdict. He was a pugnacious Churchman and a mild, disgruntled Whig. Certainly he was fascinated by the political commotion which he found all around him on his arrival in London. But his immediate interest was either personal or connected with the prospects of securing the concession for the Irish Church which he was charged to press. A zest for politics was in his bones. But, as yet, no companion or no cause had captured completely his political imagination. Swift, at the age of forty-three, had not started on the career which was to make him famous. Marlborough, at the age of sixty, was entitled to believe, despite all his fears and mortifications, that his story of unblemished triumph might soon culminate in a blaze of glory.

*　　*　　*

At once the Vicar of Laracor plunged into a whirl of dinner-parties and coffee-house confabulations, calling on all his old friends and picking up the threads of his social and literary associations where he had left them. Two nights after his arrival he wrote with some glee to Stella: 'The Whigs were ravished to see me, and would lay hold on me as a twig while they are drowning, and the great men making me their clumsy apologies etc.' To Archbishop King who had given him his instructions on behalf of the Irish Bishops the boast was framed in slightly different terms. 'Upon my arrival here', he said, 'I found myself equally caressed by both parties, by one as a sort of bough for drowning men to lay hold of; and by the other as one discontented with the late men in power.'

No other evidence exists that the caresses from the Tories had started so promptly. More probably Swift was merely revealing to his correspondents his own mood of detachment. His discontent with the late men in power was quickly revived by an interview with Lord Godolphin. Godolphin had a contempt for journalists and no particular love for churchmen. In his treatment of Swift he was 'altogether short, dry and morose'. Doubtless he had graver matters on his mind than the remission of the First Fruits for the benefit of the Irish clergy. He sent Swift away empty-handed, enraged by his coldness and 'almost vowing revenge'. But the same complaint could not be made against his old Whig friends. Richard Steele and Joseph Addison were overjoyed to see him; for a week or two at least the old triumvirate was re-established. The St. James's Coffee-house, the resort of the Whigs, was still his chief port of call; the fervent Whig, Charles Jervas, was eager to retouch his portrait. For Swift himself—despite the mighty political convulsions which had intervened—the prospect looked not so different from that which he had disconsolately abandoned a year and a half before. 'Everything', he wrote, 'is turning upside down; every Whig in great office will, to a man, be infallibly put out; and we shall have such a winter as hath not been seen in England.' Swift could not repress his excitement at the thought, but no sign of an opening for himself had appeared. 'Everybody asks me, how I came to be so long in Ireland, as naturally as if here were my *Being*, but no soul offers to make it so: and I protest I shall return to Dublin and the Canal at Laracor with more satisfaction than ever I did in my life.' It is hard to believe that he was genuine in his intention of turning his back on 'such a winter', but the assurances to Stella were strong and repeated. A week after his arrival in London he saw Lord Somers who at least received him more courteously than Godolphin and who recommended he should apply once more to Lord Wharton. Swift had learnt to expect no response from that quarter. Wharton in any case was 'working like a horse for the elections'. Both Somers and Wharton expected at any moment to be turned out of office. 'I protest upon my life, I am heartily weary of this town, and wish I had never stirred,' wrote Swift.

In seven hectic days he had learnt enough to believe that all his old friends were doomed. When they had had the power they had done nothing for him. Now they were 'drowning men' themselves. Once or twice he found a kindred spirit with whom he could talk 'treason heartily against the Whigs' in a way which sent him home 'rolling resentments in my mind'. Thus for another two weeks he dined and gossiped, watched and waited until one night—the night of September 20th—he 'heard the report confirmed of removals; my lord-president Somers: the duke of Devonshire, lord steward; and Mr. Boyle, secretary of state, are all turned out today. I never remember such bold strokes taken by a Court; I am almost shocked at it, though I did not care if they were all hanged. We are astonished why the Parliament is not yet dissolved, and why they keep a matter of that importance to the last. We shall have a strange Winter here between the struggles of a cunning provoked discarded party, and the triumphs of one in power; of both which I shall be an indifferent spectator, and return very peaceably to Ireland, when I have done my part in the affair I am entrusted with, whether it succeeds or no'.

Harley had taken the plunge at last. How genuine had been his professed intention to preserve a coalition with the Whigs no one could tell. But a number of factors combined to make any further pursuit of this aim disadvantageous or impracticable. Some of the Whig leaders, in particular Lord Sunderland and Lord Wharton, viewed with horror the idea of an accommodation with their old enemy; their opinion influenced the waverers like Lord Somers. The old chief of the high church Tories, Lord Rochester, saw the Queen and impressed upon her how fierce was the Tory hostility to the sufferance allowed to the Whig leaders since the fall of Godolphin. News from Spain gave a spur to Tory boldness. The first messenger brought reports that a spectacular victory had been won by the allied armies; King Louis' grandson had been driven from Madrid and the chance of a victorious peace seemed suddenly to have come much closer. Perhaps this unexpected support for the old Tory thesis that Flanders was a secondary theatre compared with Spain gave the last screw to the nerve of Harley and the Queen. In any case they had incentive enough in the sheer momentum of rising Tory strength in the country. If Harley did not bow before it, he might easily be swept aside altogether to make way for a more audacious leader. The barely credible fact is that he played his double game right to the end. During the last few days before the Rubicon was crossed, many of the Whigs were approached to test how firm was their loyalty to their colleagues. Robert Walpole was urged to retain his post at the War Office with the flattering assurance that he was worth half his party. As late as September

18th the Lord Chancellor, Cowper, was visited by Harley and informed that 'all should be easy' and that 'a Whig game was intended at bottom'. Next day, as Swift had correctly learnt, Lord Somers, the Duke of Devonshire and Mr. Boyle felt forced to resign (no doubt they knew they were about to be dismissed) and their places were taken by the Earl of Rochester, the Duke of Buckingham and Henry St. John. When the Cabinet Council met to swear in the new Ministers, the Queen at once announced that she had decided to dissolve Parliament. Lord Cowper rose to protest and the other two members of the Whig Junto, Lord Orford and Lord Wharton, were ready to back him. But the decision was made and the Queen was not prepared to listen to any argument. Wharton and Orford handed in their resignations. A few hectic hours passed during which the Queen ordered the Lord Chancellor to affix his seal to the proclamation announcing the dissolution. Cowper refused on the grounds that the matter had never been discussed at the Council. And he refused to accept any proposals that he should continue in office after his colleagues had departed. His honourable stubbornness merely emphasized the failure of his friends to show that quality at an earlier date when it might have stopped the rot.

At last the overthrow of the Junto was complete. At last the Queen's prayer for release from the five tyrannizing Whig Lords had been fulfilled. The man who had worked the miracle had established a hold over the Queen such as no other courtier had ever secured. By his manipulation of Mrs. Masham, the Duke of Shrewsbury and a host of lesser figures, Harley had achieved a sensational transformation in the scene. The Whigs hardly knew how it had happened. Arthur Maynwaring, a close friend of the Duchess of Marlborough, expressed his amazement to her in colourful language. It had all been done, he exclaimed, 'by a stinking ugly chambermaid, that has betrayed her only friend to a papist (Shrewsbury) in masquerade, that went to Italy to marry a common strumpet, and to the most arrant tricky knave in all Britain, that no man alive believes any more than an Oates or a Fuller; to have all this plainly designed and actually transacting, is what I will defy the Bishop of Salisbury, or whoever is best read in history, to shew any parallel for'. Another observer struck by the wonder of the event was King Louis XIV. 'It is impossible', wrote a member of his court, 'for me to describe the transport of joy the King was in upon reading that part, (viz) the dissolving of Parliament; "Well", says the King, "if Monsieur Harley does that, I shall say he is *un habile homme*, and that he knows how to go through what he has undertaken".'

Two other men could not be expected to share the same enthusiasm: rather, they had every right to feel aggrieved at the deception practised upon them. One was the Duke of Newcastle who had retained his office in the hope that he could help to prevent the dissolution. Harley had taken the precaution of warning him a few days earlier of the Queen's decision, 'it being resolved', as he carefully insisted, 'in her own breast, and indeed it is impossible to carry on Parliament without intolerable heats'. Dazed by the explosion of anger from his Whig colleagues in London, the Duke of Newcastle turned to the task of saving his Whig candidates from annihilation. The other deluded Duke took his moment of awakening more bitterly. For the previous few weeks the Duke of Somerset had suspected that Harley had no intention of reserving for himself the high place he had earned by his treachery to his Whig friends. When the full revelation burst upon him he was outraged. On the night the dissolution was announced he flew out of the Cabinet Council in a passion, cursed and swore at his servants, and left London too angry even to eat his supper. A few days later he relieved his feelings in a letter to his fellow-dupe, the Duke of Newcastle. 'I came hither yesterday,' he wrote, 'to take care to keep out as many Tories and Jacobites in this new Parliament as I can. I am glad to find so true a spirit among the poor discarded Whigs as to unite and keep out the common enemy.'

Now that the battle was joined, indeed, the Whig dejection lifted. One of Marlborough's close friends in London, the Earl of Stair, informed him that 'the delay of dissolving Parliament has been a great disadvantage to the new party. The Whigs have recovered themselves and are united and bold'. Everything now hinged on the outcome of the election and that precept applied not only to great matters of state but also to Swift's business on behalf of the Irish Bishops. 'Things are in such a combustion here', he wrote to Stella on the day after the dissolution had been declared, 'that I am advised not to meddle yet in the affair I am upon.'

One part of the combustion was supplied by the printing press. 'Pamphlets and half sheets', wrote Swift, 'grow so upon our hands, it will very well employ a man every day from morning till night to read them, and so out of perfect despair I never read at all.' It is impossible to believe his self-denial was really so strict. One at least among the new publications was essential reading for anyone who dined with the great. Not content with the weekly outburst in the *Examiner*, St. John had written a pamphlet which provided an election manifesto for the Tory candidates. Once again no frontal attack was made on the Captain-General; other targets might prove easier and less dangerous to hit. Among the first—always the most popular victims of the rage of a war-weary nation—were England's allies. Blood and treasure had been poured out to save the Dutch and the Austrians. Towns had been taken and battles won in the very place where such victories injured the French King least. What was to be the final result of so tremendous an exertion in pursuit of so false a strategy? 'Britain may expect to remain exhausted of men and money, to see her trade divided amongst her neighbours, her revenues anticipated even to future generations, and to have this only glory left her, that she has proved a farm to the bank, a province to Holland, and a jest to the whole world.' Nearer home the selection of targets was simpler still. The aim was to exploit the popularity of the Queen and arraign all those who had invaded her prerogative to suit their own interest. 'Instead of the mild influences of a gracious Queen governing by law, we soon felt the miserable consequences of subjection to the will of an arbitrary Junto, and to the caprice of an insolent woman. Unhappy nation, which expected to be governed by the best, fell under the tyranny of the worst of her sex! But now, thanks be to God, that fury, who broke loose to execute the vengeance of heaven on a sinful people, is restrained, and the royal hand is reached out to chain up the plague.' The Duchess of Marlborough was fair game, even if the Duke had still to be spared, and she was only one member of the conspiracy. Had not this same arbitrary Junto attempted to ensure that the 'slavery' they wished to impose on the Queen should 'pursue her even into her bed chamber'—by the removal of Abigail? Had they not seized the occasion of the 'intemperate sermon' preached by Dr. Sacheverell 'to try the title of the Queen and to limit the allegiance of the subject'? Had they not called in as their confederates 'the members of the bank, the Dutch and the Court of Vienna' to offer to the crown 'such indignity, as no man, who has the honour of his country at heart, can with patience bear'? These, said St. John, 'are the topics you must insist upon, as the real causes which have prolonged the war, distracted the nation, and given France spirit enough at last to break off the peace'. Somehow or other it was necessary to steal from the Whigs their patriotic garb as the backers of the war and the supporters of the victorious General. St. John was not content to stay on the defensive. He stirred every xenophobic emotion, not against the enemy, but against the allies, and pictured the Whigs making war, not against King Louis, but against their own Queen.

Swift had never met St. John or any of the great personages associated with the *Examiner*. But certainly he must have become a reader of the paper. This was the authentic voice of the new men in power and every coffee-house gossip would need to know what it said. Moreover, Swift's closest friend, Addison, whom he was meeting almost every other day, had started the *Whig Examiner* to put the Whig case in reply. Obviously Swift became embroiled in the argument. If he did not quarrel directly with Addison himself, he was quite ready to do so with the more outspoken Steele. The news got around of his 'treason talk' against the Whigs. Someone picked up the information that the suspected author of *The Tale of a Tub*, the creator of the original Bickerstaff, was cursing the Whigs for the way they had misused him. Someone must have passed on the information to Harley. Probably that someone was the Tory M.P., Erasmus Lewis, who had kept Harley so well informed when he had been expelled from office two years before. Lewis no doubt told Swift how ready Harley would be to listen to his entreaties about the First Fruits. No doubt he told Harley that the curiosity of this Vicar from Laracor was not confined to spiritual mysteries. 'I am already', wrote Swift on the last day of September, 'represented to Harley as a discontented person, that was used ill for not being Whig enough; and I hope for good usage from him. The Tories dryly tell me, I may make my future, if I please; but I do not understand them, or rather, I do understand them.' Next day, however, he was laughing 'to see myself so disengaged in these revolutions' and gloating because his invitations to dinner had become so frequent that he had spent no more than three shillings in meat and drink from the moment of arrival in London three weeks before. Since he regarded the eight shillings a week he was required to pay for his new lodgings in Bury Street, as 'plaguy deep', the point was of some importance.

Certainly Swift must have been the most popular of guests. The peculiar charm had reasserted itself at once. Lords and ladies tumbled over one another to secure his presence at their dinner tables and among the most eager was his old friend and member of the Junto, Lord Halifax. Swift was royally received at his Lordship's home at Hampton Court, but he was not to be easily seduced from his new mood of political independence. 'Lord Halifax began a health to me today: it was the Resurrection of the Whigs, which I refused unless he would add their Reformation too: and I told him he was the only Whig in England I loved, or had any good opinion of.' Halifax was sufficiently flattered to press his guest to stay the night. But Swift declined. He had an urgent summons next day in London—another appointment with the engaging Mr. Lewis. So Swift returned to Bury Street to discover that all was at last fixed for his interview with Mr. Harley. As he put out the candle that night his landlady entered his room with one of Lord Halifax's servants who brought a message from his master. Would Swift not return to dine at Hampton Court the following evening? But the last-minute appeal had come too late. 'Business of great importance' made it impossible for the Vicar of Laracor to gratify the importunate Whig Lord.

Wednesday, October 4th, was the great day. Amid a financial crisis and an election campaign, the most powerful politician in England still had time to spare for the Irish clergyman whom Erasmus Lewis had recommended so assuredly. 'Today', wrote Swift to Stella, 'I was brought privately to Mr. Harley, who received me with the greatest respect and kindness imaginable: he has appointed me an hour on Saturday at four, afternoon, when I will open my business to him, which expression I would not use if I were a woman. I know you smoakt it; but I did not till I writ it.' Harley's charm was a match for Swift's and the two men at once felt a warm and exciting kinship. How far any other matters apart from Swift's old story about the First Fruits were discussed at this first encounter, no one knows. But the supposition is clear. A few hints from Harley had been enough to give a glimpse of an entire new horizon to his normally so circumspect visitor. The pleasures of Laracor faded; London was now to be his parish. And at once the bargain was sealed with a deed. Ever since Lord Godolphin had insulted him with his morose indifference Swift had been nurturing his revenge in a savage lampoon; he was a man who usually let the sun go down on his wrath, waiting for the morning to add the final touch of vitriol. After the interview with Harley he straightway took his first political poem to the printer and returned home pondering who next deserved a place among his victims. 'I have more mischief in my heart', he told Stella. Probably Stella understood well enough that she must now expect a lonely winter.

CHAPTER SIX

The First Shot

(October 5th—November 23rd, 1710)

'He then desired to know what arts were practised in
electing those whom I called commoners: whether a
stranger with a strong purse might not influence the
vulgar voters to choose him before their own landlord,
or the most considerable gentleman in the neighbour-
hood. How it came to pass that people were so violently
bent upon getting into this assembly, which I allowed
to be a great trouble and expense, often to the ruin of
their families, without any salary or pension; because
this appeared such an exalted strain of virtue and public
spirit, that his Majesty seemed to doubt it might possibly not always be sincere: and he desired to know
whether such zealous gentlemen could have any views
of refunding themselves for the charges and troubles
they were at. . . .'—*Gulliver's Travels, Voyage to Brobdingnag.*

WHILE THE EFFECTIVE PRIME MINISTER OF BRITAIN
pursued his courtship of the Vicar of Laracor and while
Swift marvelled to himself and to Stella how very well
his new acquaintance seemed to know his Christian name, the
country was engaged in the roughest and dirtiest election campaign
of the century. Every observer bore witness to the fury of the contest. Bishop Burnet denounced the 'unheard-of methods' employed by the Tories. 'The practice and violence used now in
elections', he wrote, 'went far beyond anything I had ever known
in England.' Popular demonstrations took place all over the
country. 'A vast concourse of rude multitudes', said the Bishop,
'behaved themselves in so boisterous a manner, that it was
not safe, and in many places not possible, for those who had a
right to vote, to come and give their votes for a Whig.' According
to the Duke of Beaufort's reports to Harley, the Whigs were not
backward in meting out the same treatment. 'There is no lie',
he wrote, 'that is possible to be invented that they don't use,
they are descended so low as to bully and threaten to stick people

by the wall, if they will not vote for them; and tell them they
are confident Robin the Trickster, which is the epithet they
give you, will be turned out, and his gang, in a few months,
and then they will hang and ruin all those that are not of their
side.' For Lord Godolphin 'the riddle' was how such 'arbitrary
proceedings' would long continue without wrecking the constitution.

'The Treatings, the Caballings, the Briberies, and Corruptions,
as well as the Heats and Animosities of Parties, against this
approaching Election', wrote Daniel Defoe, 'surmount all that
have ever gone before them; never so much Money spent,
nor so foolishly; never so much Drunkenness, Ravings, Feuds,
Raging of Parties, at least not in my Time, have been seen in
this Nation.' As he surveyed the scene of tumult and frenzy,
Defoe lost his customary optimism. The nation was tearing
itself to pieces; nothing like this had been witnessed since
the Civil War. Gone for a few weeks was his comforting
faith that both Whigs and Tories, once they assumed office,
would always be compelled to act as moderate men, upholding
the principles of the Revolution. The news which poured in
to him from every quarter told of 'a People so Miserably Divided
against themselves' that 'their Destruction cannot be far off'.
'We strive not like Men, but like Devils, like Furies,' he continued. 'We Fight not as if we would kill one another only,
but as if we would tear one another's souls out of our Bodies;
we Fight with all the Addition of Personal Envy, Revenge,
Hellish Rage, Irreconcilable, Implacable Malice . . . Nor do we
fight only with Clubs, as at *Marlow*, *Whit-Church* etc.; with
Swords and Staves, as at Coventry; with Stones and Brickbats, as
at . . . But we Fight with the Poison of the Tongue, with Words
that speak like the Piercing of a Sword, with the Gall of Envy, the
Venom of Slander, the Foam of Malice, and the Poison of Reproach, bitter Revilings, unsufferable Taunts, injurious Backbit-
ings, and unmannerly Railings.' Beer flowed in a richer flood
than had ever been known before. The Tories, said Defoe, 'first
made the poor freeholders drunk and then told them to vote
for the Church'. When the record number of election petitions
involving a hundred seats came to be examined, one elector
testified that he had drunk a 'new liquor . . . called Whistle-
Jacket . . . made up of brandy and treacle'; another accused the

mayor of making him 'so drunk with brandy that he did not know what he did'; everywhere it was evident that money, like the brandy and the hogsheads of ale and wine, had been poured out on a tremendous scale.

Yet, if this had been all, the Whigs might have held their own; other even more compelling tides were moving against them. Abel Boyer, the Whiggish journalist, whose sympathies were however sufficiently concealed to permit him to apply for the post of editor of the official *Gazette* following the removal of Richard Steele, assigned four reasons for the electoral decline of his friends. First, 'many of the Whig Gentlemen, who either could not be induc'd to believe that the Last Parliament should be dissolv'd, till the Blow was given; or who, in Case of a Dissolution, thought themselves secure of being rechosen, had supinely neglected making an Interest; while those who designed to oppose them, had early taken all the necessary Measures to carry their Point'. Secondly, the ferment raised by the Sacheverell trial had tended to increase rather than abate. Thirdly, 'All the Inferior Clergy, (a few excepted) thinking themselves attack'd thro' the Sides of Dr. Sacheverell, were more than ordinarily zealous and diligent'. Finally, 'the Mobility, whose tumultuous rising in favour of Dr. Sacheverell, seem'd, if not allow'd, at least conniv'd at, by the impunity of their Leaders; and whose Spirits had wonderfully been inflam'd by a Multitude of licentious Writings, in which the Whigs were represented as Atheists and Republicans: The Mob, I say, appeared now with unusual confidence, and, as it were, arm'd with Authority, at the Elections, on the Side of the Church and Monarchy; and, not only by reproachful Language, and odious Epithets, but even by Blows, deterred those who came to vote contrary to the Voice of the People: Insomuch that if the Whigs had not, on this Occasion, practis'd as well as profess'd Moderation, these New Elections might have ended in (what was by many apprehended) a Civil War'.

Again and again in the contemporary records that same spectre appears. Harley might claim that the old clash between Whig and Tory had lost its meaning. Swift, enraptured by the attentions of his new Tory friends, still dined on good terms with Addison and Steele. But the passions aroused in the country at large cut deep. If the modern Whig bore small resemblance to a Roundhead, it was still possible to scratch a Tory and find a

Cavalier. Many of them went to the polls with an oak-leaf stuck in their coats, the oak-leaf of Boscobel, symbol of Charles II's deliverance and the symbol too, perhaps, of another Jacobite restoration.

Nowhere was the battle more ferocious than in London. In the City of Westminster the number of voters was comparatively large, dissenting opinion was strong and vocal, and the Whigs had every reason to expect success. They had a formidable candidate in General Stanhope. During the election he was away at the wars and, as everyone thought, winning victories in Spain. His opponent was a well-known brewer and the Whig pamphleteers had an easy time contrasting the claims of the two contenders. Addison in the *Whig Examiner* purported to recall a story from Plutarch in which General Alcibiades had fought for a prize conferred by a vote with an Athenian brewer called Taureas, alias Toryas. 'Have I not born the dust and heat of the day,' the General was alleged to have said in his oration to the populace, 'while he has been sweating at the furnace? Behold these scars, behold this wound which still bleeds in your service; what can Taureas shew you of this nature? What are his marks of honour? Has he any other wound about him, except the accidental scaldings of his wort, or bruises from the tub and barrel. . . . O ye men of Athens; you know my actions, let my antagonist relate what he has done for you. Let him produce his vats and tubs, in opposition to the heaps of arms and standards which were employed against you, and which I have wrested out of the hands of your enemies. And when this is done, let him be brought into the field of election upon his dray-cart; and if I can finish my conquest sooner, I will not fail to meet him there in a triumphant chariot.' General Stanhope, it might have been thought, had a demagogic appeal of his own sufficient to prevail against the worst that the Sacheverellites might do. Swift found himself caught in the election tumult and thought that Stanhope was winning. 'We met the electors for parliament men,' he told Stella; 'and the rabble came about our coach, crying A Colt, a Stanhope, etc. We were afraid of a dead cat, our glasses broken, and so were always of their side.' But the high church Tories were not to be outdone either in physical violence or lavish invective. Several who showed their enthusiasm for Stanhope were knocked down in the streets and Stanhope himself was openly accused of every known vice, including sodomy. When the votes were counted Toryas the

Brewer had easily carried the day. Similar scenes—with a similar result—took place in the neighbouring City of London. When the high church candidates were elected bonfires were lit, unlighted windows were broken and Whig merchants walked in fear of their lives. 'Some days before,' reported Boyer, 'the Mob committed a more barefac'd, and audacious Piece of Outragiousness: For, as Sir Gilbert Heathcote, one of the Whig candidates, was going out of Guildhall, they not only insulted him by reviling Language, but one of them spit in his Face; an Affront which perhaps was never offer'd before, in any Civiliz'd Nation, to a Person of his Character; He being at that Time, the Lord Mayor of London Elect, and, as such, one of the most eminent Civil Magistrates in Christendom.'

Sir Gilbert was not the only eminent Whig leader to suffer indignities at the hands of the electors. Lord Wharton, the Duke of Somerset and most of the other Whig grandees who controlled— or thought they controlled—several seats in Parliament saw their candidates go down like ninepins. Altogether, the Whigs had not merely lost their majority in the Commons; they had been beaten by more than two to one in a Tory landslide. Some 320 Tory Members confronted 150 Whigs with 40 'doubtfuls'. At previous elections the 'doubtfuls'—fertile soil for Harley's sowing—had usually numbered more than a hundred. Now they were being squeezed out by the two contending parties. In particular, the high Tories, including among their number several avowed Jacobites, had gained a victory beyond their most ambitious expectations.

Perhaps the more subtle reason to which Henry St. John ascribed their success must be added to those adduced by Abel Boyer. St. John had long believed that the heart of the nation was overwhelmingly Tory. Only by bold presumption and artifice were the Whigs able to wrest the advantage temporarily to their side. 'How much time, how many lucky incidents, how many strains of power, how much money must go to create a majority (for the Whigs),' he wrote; 'on the other hand, take but off the opinion that the Crown is another way inclined, and the church interest rises with re-doubled force, and by its natural genuine strength. I believe there is not any instance to be produced of so many, nor such prodigious majorities, as all the elections were carried by.' St. John had good grounds to congratulate himself on his own foresight. This was the deliverance he had prophesied two years before when he and his friends were enduring Egyptian bondage. Now, second only to the Duke of Marlborough and his 'dear Master', Harley, he was the most powerful man in the Kingdom. He had no reason for qualms at the scale of the triumph. If the Church of England Party needed a leader with an adventurous spirit to match the audacity they had shown in the election campaign he had every qualification to groom himself for the role.

*   *   *

Robert Harley could not view the sweeping Tory victory with the same unalloyed approval. Before the election he had refused to favour the wholesale expulsion of Whigs from office. During the election he made elaborate gestures towards the dissenters in the attempt to assure them that no attack on religious toleration was intended. Before the election his refusal to accede to the Tory demand for the dissolution might be attributed to superior wisdom or cunning. How superfluous all his precautions now appeared in the light of the actual election results! Swift very soon learnt with what a cautious eye the chief architect of the Tory success watched the progress of his handiwork. 'I have been told', he wrote on the day after their first meeting, 'that Mr. Harley himself would not let the Tories be too numerous for fear they should be insolent and kick against him; and for that reason they have kept several Whigs in employment, who expected to be turned out every day.' Harley's desires in this sense had been shattered at the polls. Even so he did his best to withstand the high Tory pressure. The few remaining Whigs who held Ministerial posts, including the Duke of Newcastle and even the Duke of Somerset, were persuaded or allowed to retain their offices. Some of the leading Tories, notably the Earl of Nottingham, were still kept out. Nottingham advocated drastic measures to crush the Whigs for ever; for example, he proposed the impeachment or prosecution of the Whig leaders, starting with Lord Sunderland. Harley's influence was still strong enough to forbid such excesses. And, indeed, he had the most powerful of reasons for appeasing the Whigs, even though their parliamentary power was now crippled.

All the signs were that the financial crash which he had so long feared had come. Soon after Harley first assumed office the situation looked bad enough. Annual expenditure had risen from three

million pounds in the last year of peace to the colossal total of
thirteen million; the unsecured national debt stood at a figure of
nine and a half million. A quarter of a million soldiers and multitudes of sailors were waiting for their pay; the Civil List was heavily
in debt; public securities were still falling. When the full measure
of the Tory victory was realized stocks fell by 30 per cent and the
Bank of England refused to discount foreign bills. At the end of
October Lord Halifax gave the Duke of Newcastle his expert
opinion on the crisis. 'The publick credit', he said, 'is fallen past
retrieve, though I must do Mr. Harley the Justice he does what he
can to support it. But till men's minds are better satisfied of the
new ministers, nothing can raise it.' Swift had never concerned
himself with questions of public finance, but he could not fail to
sense the alarm. 'I am afraid the new Ministry is at a terrible loss
about money,' he wrote to Stella on October 28th; 'the Whigs talk
so, it would give me the spleen; and I am afraid of meeting Mr.
Harley out of humour. They think he will never carry through this
undertaking. God knows what will come of it. I should be terribly
vexed to see things come round again: it will ruin the church and
clergy, but I hope for better.' Swift did indeed express his hopes in
some stockjobbing on his own account. During that October he
invested the large total of £300 from his puny fortune in the calculation that the stocks could fall no lower. So great was the faith
inspired by his new friends.

The most attractive characteristic about Mr. Harley was in fact
how well he preserved his good humour in the face of all these
pressing anxieties. The high-flying Tories muttered their disap-
proval and wondered what better they could expect from 'the
spawn of a Presbyterian'. But Harley faced his new problems with
all his old imperturbability. Somehow the engines of propaganda
which had brought electoral victory must be put in reverse. The
allies must be reassured. The utmost secrecy was required in
initiating discussions for peace. The powerful Whig financiers
must, if possible, be mollified. Only thus could the financial crisis
be prevented from developing into anarchy. Certainly Harley had
his hands full during that hectic October. Yet he still had time to
spare to cultivate his new protégé. He told Swift to come and see
him often, listened patiently to his case about the First Fruits and
made haste to introduce him to his famous colleagues. One night
Swift was invited to dine with the newly-appointed Attorney-

General, Sir Simon Harcourt. On another occasion his companions were Lord Peterborough, the favourite Tory General, and Matthew Prior, the poet, diplomat and journalist who was now contributing to the *Examiner*. Together they licked their lips over Swift's lampoon on Lord Godolphin which had quickly become the talk of the coffee-houses. Probably Harley guessed the author, and the elaborate compliments which he helped to extract from the other two must have impressed Swift more than ever with the superior taste of his new friends compared with the treatment he had received from the old. He was 'forty times more caressed'. Within a fortnight he was asking Stella: 'Do they know anything in Ireland of my greatness among the Tories?' A day or two later the 'excessively obliging' Harley was able to tell him that the Queen was ready to grant his request about the First Fruits. Only four short weeks had passed since the two men had met and the conquest was complete. Harley had found his way direct to Swift's heart. And now he enlisted his services in an enterprise too secret even for Stella's ears. A few cryptic sentences were the only reference to the matter allowed to appear in that most intimate of all journals which passed between Bury Street and Laracor. 'I came home early and must go write,' he told her. In fact the *Examiner* had discovered a new writer and the first contribution from the new hand appeared on November 2nd. 'It is a practice I have generally followed,' ran the opening sentence, 'to converse in equal freedom with the deserving men of both parties; and it was never without some contempt, that I have observed persons wholly out of employment, affect to do otherwise.' The aside was no doubt aimed at Steele who had been producing 'scurvy *Tatlers* of late' and whose party animosity had also helped to injure Swift's friendship with Addison.

The great issue of the hour was the financial crisis. Swift was so meticulously careful in dealing with his own financial affairs that he often balanced the gain of a free dinner against the coach fare home or the tip he would eventually have to pay his host's servants. Now he applied the same simple rules to the nation's business; the result was a startling exposure of the whole sad state of affairs which the Harley Ministry had been called into being to remedy. Others before Swift had attacked the new race of stockjobbers and the politicians who served their interests. But he managed to fit all these hated figures into a coherent pattern and to turn the tables against the very persons who were blaming the new Ministers for the collapse of the public credit. Could it really be true that some people had an interest in prolonging the war? Swift's first answer was merely to invite his readers to open their eyes. 'There is no great mystery in the matter,' he wrote in his best plain matter-of-fact tone. 'Let any man observe the equipages in this town; he shall find the greater number who make a figure, to be a species of men quite different from any that were ever known before the Revolution, consisting either of generals and colonels, or of such whose whole fortunes lie in funds and stocks: so that power, which according to the old maxim, was used to follow land, is now gone over to money.' Thus the enemy was established; he was real and his features could be defined. And how had he been able to fix his grip on the whole nation? 'In order to fasten wealthy people to the new government, they'—that is, 'the new dexterous men'—'proposed those pernicious expedients of borrowing money by vast *premiums*, and at exorbitant interest: a practice as old as Eumenes, one of Alexander's captains, who setting up for himself after the death of his master, persuaded his principal officers to lend him great sums, after which they were forced to follow him for their own security.' By financing the war through borrowing rather than taxation, the power of the financiers had been exalted. 'By this means the wealth of the nation, that used to be reckoned by the value of land, is now computed by the rise and fall of stocks: and although the foundation of credit be still the same, and upon a bottom that can never be shaken; and though all interest be duly paid by the public, yet through the contrivance and cunning of stockjobbers, there has been brought in such a complication of knavery and cozenage, such a mystery of iniquity, and such an unintelligible jargon of terms to involve it in, as were never known in any other age or country of the world.' Thus the counter-attack was carried into the enemy's camp. If the nation suffered by the fall in the stocks the guilty men were those who had constructed the whole rickety edifice in the first place. The removal of these men was the first step in restoring confidence. Of course it had been right, therefore, for the Queen to 'extricate herself, as soon as possible, out of the pupillage of those who found their accounts only in perpetuating the war. Neither have we the least reason to doubt, but the ensuing Parliament will assist her Majesty with the utmost rigour, till her enemies *again* be brought to sue for peace, and *again* offer such terms as will make it both honourable and lasting; only with this difference that the Ministry perhaps will not *again* refuse them'.

Such was Swift's first essay in weekly political journalism. Its quality may be appreciated by comparing Swift's *Examiner* No. 14 with its thirteen predecessors. St. John, Matthew Prior and Dr. Atterbury were no mean controversialists. But none of them could strike the hot iron with the deftness of Swift. Not only had he shown the way whereby the new Ministers could secure a propagandist advantage for themselves from their financial embarrassments. More deliberately than most others had attempted before, he stated the supreme objective—the making of a good and speedy peace. Most of the Tory leaders were secretly ashamed of the support they had received from the raucous Sacheverell. Such aid in the election battle could not be scorned. But now they wanted an argumentative statement of their case and an indictment of their predecessors which would stand the test among the keen wits of the coffee-houses who played such a big part in forcing the sudden changes in political currents. Swift revealed in his early contributions to the *Examiner* how quick was his appreciation of a political mood. Defoe could plead and cajole and disseminate news which showed which way the wind was blowing. Steele and Addison trifled with politics and eagerly relapsed into more congenial topics. Addison was one of the Whigs who had survived at the elections but after a few weeks his *Whig Examiner* was allowed to die. Such dilettantism was not for Swift. For all the cynical gaiety of his reports to Stella, he was a serious politician, and he showed it at this, his first real opportunity. He could persuade, mock, instil passion or excite to action, and whichever faculty he chose to employ for particular occasions he spoke always as one having authority.

Second only to the urgent need to restore some faith in the public finances two further interlocked questions presented themselves to the new Ministers for immediate attention. How was their desire for peace to be realized? And what in the meantime was to be done with the Duke of Marlborough, the man who represented the last counterpoise of the old power which Harley had overthrown and yet one whose authority in Europe was so prodigious that he constituted by himself something like a High Contracting Party? This was the old dilemma which had often restrained Harley and the Queen from acting more precipitately earlier in the year. Time and again they had to temporize in the pursuit of their designs for fear that the Captain-General would throw in his hand. Now that the election was over, the high Tories could see little reason why Marlborough should not be given the same treatment accorded to Sunderland and Godolphin. Perhaps a direct order dismissing him from his post would cause too violent a convulsion. But could he not at least be goaded into resignation so that all the far-ranging consequences of the act could be laid at the door of his own arrogance and spleen?

These were the reckonings of men whose horizons were limited to the apportionment of places and pensions in Whitehall. Even Henry St. John toyed with the same idea. Years later he recalled the atmosphere of that November in 1710 when the triumphant Tories were trooping back to London. 'I am afraid', he said, 'that we came to court in the same dispositions as all parties have done; that the principal spring of our actions was to have the government of the state in our hands; that our principal views were the conservation of this power, great employments to ourselves and great opportunities of rewarding those who had helped to raise us and of hurting those who stood in opposition to us. . . .' So, if a major aim was to hurt the opposition, why not Marlborough among the foremost? On party grounds the case was clear. Had he not increasingly thrown his influence on to the side of the Whigs until at last the Junto had been enabled to exercise its brief spell of absolute power? Personal motives pushed in the same direction. Harley, St. John, Mrs. Masham, the Queen, all of them glowered with envy in the shadow of the great man. For all of them ancient obligations to the Marlborough family grated on the memory; all of them could count more recent offences committed by the Duke or the Duchess which cried out for revenge. Considering how powerful were all these incentives for satisfying the high Tory hatred of him, considering how fierce was the rage of party feeling in that aftermath of the election, why was the step not taken? No stronger testimony could be found to the power still wielded by the Duke of Marlborough. Fear was the sole motive which could restrain such deep-seated enmity and malice. And the fear was well founded. If a Tory victory could knock down the stocks by 30 per cent, what would be the financial consequences of Marlborough's removal? If the dissolution of Parliament could bring tears of joy to the eyes of King

Louis, what jubilations would be ordered at Versailles if the Captain-General was disgraced? The peace, no less than the last shred of public credit, depended on him. That was the reason why Harley and St. John were afraid to strike.

Before the full measure of the election victory was known Henry St. John, as Secretary of State, urged his agent at The Hague to help kill the rumours which might injure the new Ministers' power to pursue any settled policy. 'You may venture to assure every body', he wrote, 'that credit will be supported, the war prosecuted, the confederacy improved, and the principle in which we engaged pursued as far possible. Our friends and enemies both will learn the same lesson that, however we differ about things purely domestic, yet we are unanimous in those great points which concern the present and future happiness of Europe.'

That was the façade presented to the world by St. John. Another line of policy was initiated in private by Harley. Throughout the war King Louis's Minister, the Marquis of Torcy, had kept a secret agent in England, a Jesuit priest called the Abbé Gaultier. Gaultier was a friend of Lord Jersey, a high Tory suspected of Jacobitism. Jersey had kept in touch with Harley and possibly one or two other Tory leaders. How faithfully Gaultier's reports of Jersey's soundings represented the true mind of Harley no one can tell. But certainly from midsummer onwards the French were led to believe that Harley and his friends adopted towards the prospect of peace an attitude very different from that of the Whigs. In September Jersey passed on the word that the Queen was resolved on 'a prompt peace'. Early in October the suggestion was made that the return of the Pretender was not excluded and that several of the new Ministers had a 'particular fondness' for him. Some complication was introduced by the progress of the war in Spain. After General Stanhope's victory at Saragossa in August—the same victory news of which had persuaded Harley and the Queen to take the final step in ordering the dissolution of the Parliament —Jersey had urged that any attempt to open negotiations must wait. But by November the fortunes of battle had changed once more. Stanhope had been compelled to evacuate Madrid and was facing retreat and disaster. Very soon the whole objective of conquering Spain would have to be written off; Jersey's hopes of starting negotiations rose as the chance of military victory in Spain faded.

Such were the first tentative beginnings of an approach towards a separate peace. One common interest at least was shared by King Louis and Harley. If possible terms were to be discovered in advance, if the path was to be smoothed, the deed must be done in the dark; for the essence of the new plan, as opposed to previous negotiations, was that England wished to act behind the backs of her allies. And if that was the aim, might not the whole project be disrupted if Marlborough suddenly departed from the scene? If the mask were torn aside the allies themselves might make their own bids for a separate peace and Marlborough and the Whigs would be enabled to raise a new storm in England against the seemingly all-powerful Tories. Already the Elector of Hanover was threatening to withdraw his troops from the battle-fronts if Marlborough were removed from his command. Marlborough and the Whigs were informing the Elector that the real intention of the new Ministers was to restore the Pretender. How disastrously these tendencies might develop if Marlborough was no longer there as a proof of their good faith and a cover for their intrigues! It was an awkward, hateful paradox that Harley and St. John had to acknowledge. How could they themselves survive without the sword of Marlborough?

Necessity did not improve the manners of Her Majesty's Ministers towards their indispensable colleague. The old game of girding at him by interference with military appointments was renewed. Intrigues with some of his disgruntled subordinate officers were conducted more insultingly than ever. St. John in particular was riled by the grudging respect he must still offer to the Duke and in a letter to John Drummond, his agent at The Hague, he assumed a tone of mastery which he was afraid to translate into deeds. 'I must take the liberty to say', he wrote early in November, 'that the situation of the great man here will chiefly depend on his own conduct; things are gone so far, that there can be no thoughts of returning now to Egyptian bondage; and if he should engage, though never so artfully and covertly, in the measures of those people to whom of late he has so closely linked himself, it is impossible to say how high the ferment would rise, and into what dangers he would run himself.' This was St. John, the scourge of the Whigs, the new director of the nation's affairs. A sentence later he may have been asking himself what he proposed to *do* about 'the great man' who now more than ever represented the last remaining hope of the Whigs he was sworn to destroy. 'For my own part,' he added, 'I protest and solemnly tell you I wish him sincerely well.'

Harley was even more explicit, thanks partly to the blunt warnings he received from John Drummond. Drummond was as eager as anyone to end 'this bloody, pernicious, expensive and destructive war'. But living at the focal point of the Grand Alliance in the Dutch capital he could not see how the end could be consummated without Marlborough. Daily he received the reports from France; all the calculations of the enemy were based on the hope that Marlborough might be removed. A new peace conference was the British Government's aim; the only way to secure it was to make the French see 'plentiful provision made for the war, the Alliance entire, and the same Generals to deal with who have always baffled them'. Reports from the allies reinforced the same demand. Never had their faith in Marlborough stood so high; never had the unanimity been so widespread in insisting that neither war nor peace could be successfully prosecuted without him. 'Pensionary Buys', continued Drummond, 'came to me two days ago after Lord Rivers left this place almost with tears in his eyes, saying "Lord! What shall become of us, Lord Rivers would give me no satisfaction that the Duke shall return, for God's sake write to all your friends, let him but return for one campaign till the French but once make new proposals, let the Queen afterwards do with him what she pleases, but must the safety of us all be put in the balance with a personal pique which perhaps may be reconciled if rightly gone about"?' Drummond was convinced that the pique *could* be overcome. A reconciliation between Harley and Marlborough was 'in no wise impracticable'; it was imperative. If any doubt remained about Marlborough's return to the command, the whole cause for which he and Harley and St. John had conspired for months would be lost. Harley was obviously impressed. 'I do strongly assure you', he replied, 'I have not the least resentment towards him (the Duke) or anyone else. I thank God my mind puts me above that. I never did revenge injuries and never will sacrifice the public quiet to my own resentment. . . . In one word I do assure you, I can live and act with the Duke now in the same manner and with the same easiness as the first day that ever I saw him.'

One special Harleyite touch was applied to clinch the case. Since the departure of Godolphin, Harley was responsible for the monies provided by the state for the building of Blenheim palace in Woodstock Park. Marlborough was fascinated by the project and wrote home constantly urging that the architect and builders should be encouraged to complete their task with the utmost speed. He seemed to care more for this mammoth monument than for anything else, next to Sarah, and she in turn regarded the obsession as his greatest weakness. Harley now pleaded as a proof of his goodwill to the Captain-General that he had given orders for the work to continue. These protestations, to be sure, were not intended for Drummond's ear alone. Drummond was in constant touch with the Duke and the obvious intention was that soft words would help to heal the manifold wounds which Harley had inflicted upon Marlborough and his friends. Always the argument was brought back to the same stumbling-block. There were still too many risks in challenging Marlborough directly. Samson, if he wished, could bring the whole temple crashing to the ground. But was there not some other device? Could not Samson be shorn of his locks?

During the first three weeks of November Swift had frequent meetings with these two self-styled 'well-wishers' of the Duke of Marlborough. 'Mr. Harley speaks all the kind things to me in the world; and I believe would serve me, if I were to stay here.' Many joyful nights they spent together cursing the Whigs. Swift was now suspected for the company he was keeping and momentarily felt the need to defend himself even to Stella. 'Why should the Whigs think I came to England to leave them?' He could truly claim that no such sinister aim had prompted him. Without the accident of falling beneath Harley's spell he might soon have been on his way back to Laracor. 'Who the Devil cares what they think?' he said to himself and to Stella. 'Am I under obligations in the least to any of them at all? Rot 'em, for ungrateful dogs; I'll make them repent their usage before I leave this place.' Soon Harley introduced him to St. John and the meeting was hardly less successful than his first encounter with Harley. 'The Secretary used me with all the kindness in the world.' Not only was the Vicar of Laracor elaborately flattered for his skill as a versifier. Much more telling was the assurance that he was fast becoming a man of political influence. Swift was not wholly deceived but even his shield of independence and cynicism was not proof against such skilful wooing. 'He

(St. John) told me, among other things,' wrote Swift, 'that Mr. Harley complained he could keep nothing from me, I had the way so much of getting into him. I knew that was a refinement; and so I told him, and it was so: indeed it is hard to see these great men use me like one who was their better, and the puppies with you in Ireland hardly regarding me; but there are some reasons for this which I will tell you when we meet.'

That was no doubt another reference to the work he was doing on the *Examiner*. Obviously he was itching to tell Stella the truth. But the risk was too dangerous. The mails to Ireland might be opened and Swift was now the repository of some of the closest secrets of Harley and St. John. While they were writing in one sense to John Drummond at The Hague, their talks with Swift must have followed a different scent. With him at least some of the disguises could be dropped and their conversation must have turned to the baffling issue of the Duke of Marlborough's future. In his first contribution to the *Examiner* Swift had made a passing reference to the 'uneasiness' of 'a general who has been so long successful abroad; and might think himself injured if the entire ministry were not of his own nomination'. That was the first mild stroke from Swift's pen besmirching the great man's reputation. The problem called for more extensive treatment and in the *Examiner* No. 17, published on November 23rd, the battle was opened in earnest. Two days later Parliament was to meet. Few topics of conversation among the M.P.s can have surpassed in interest that aroused by the latest issue of the *Examiner*. Only two or three persons in the world knew the secret of the author. But the inspiration was thought to come from near the throne itself. This is what he wrote:

'I will employ this present Paper upon a Subject which of late hath very much affected me, which I have considered with a good deal of Application, and made several Enquiries about, among those Persons who I thought were best able to inform me; and if I deliver my Sentiments with some Freedom, I hope it will be forgiven, while I accompany it with that Tenderness which so nice a Point requires.

'I SAID in a former Paper (Numb. 14) that one specious Objection to the late Removals at Court, was the Fear of giving Uneasiness to a General, who hath been long successful abroad: And accordingly, the common Clamour of Tongues and Pens for some Months past, hath run against the Baseness, the Inconstancy and Ingratitude of the whole

Kingdom to the Duke of *Marlborough*, in return of the most eminent Services that ever were performed by a Subject to his Country; not to be equalled in History. And then to be sure some bitter Stroak of Detraction against *Alexander* and *Caesar*, who never did us the least Injury. Besides, the People who read *Plutarch* come upon us with Parallels drawn from the *Greeks* and *Romans*, who ungratefully dealt with I know not how many of their most deserving Generals: While the profounder Politicians, have seen Pamphlets, where *Tacitus* and *Machiavel* have been quoted to shew the Danger of too resplendent a Merit. If a Stranger should hear these furious Out-cries of Ingratitude against our General, without knowing the Particulars, he would be apt to enquire where was his Tomb, or whether he were allowed Christian Burial? Not doubting but we had put him to some ignominious Death. Or, hath he been tried for his Life, and very narrowly escaped? Hath he been accused of high Crimes and Misdemeanours? Has the Prince seized on his Estate, and left him to starve? Hath he been hooted at as he passed the Streets, by an ungrateful Rabble? Have neither Honours, Offices nor Grants, been conferred on him or his Family? Have not he and they been barbarously stript of them all? Have not he and his Forces been ill payed abroad? And doth not the Prince, by a scanty, limited Commission, hinder him from pursuing his own Methods in the Conduct of the War? Hath he no Power at all of disposing Commissions as he pleaseth? Is he not severely used by the Ministry or Parliament, who yearly call him to a strict Account? Has the Senate ever thanked him for good Success; and have they not always publickly censured him for the least Miscarriage? Will the Accusers of the Nation join Issue upon any of these Particulars; or, tell us in what Point our damnable sin of Ingratitude lies? Why, it is plain and clear; for while he is commanding abroad, the Queen dissolveth her Parliament, and changeth her Ministry at home: In which *universal Calamity*, no less than *two Persons* allied by Marriage to the General, have lost their Places. Whence came this wonderful Sympathy between the Civil and Military Powers? Will the Troops in *Flanders* refuse to fight, unless they can have *their own* Lord Keeper; *their own* Lord President of the Council; *their own* chief Governor of *Ireland*; and *their own* Parliament? In a Kingdom where the People are free, how came they to be so fond of having their Counsels under the Influence of their Army, or those that lead it? Who in all well-instituted States, had no Commerce with the Civil Power; further than to receive their Orders, and obey them without Reserve.

'WHEN a General is not so Popular, either in his Army, or at home, as one might expect from a long Course of Success; it may perhaps be ascribed to his *Wisdom*, or perhaps to his Complection. The Possession of some one *Quality*, or a Defect in *some other*, will extremely damp the Peoples Favour, as well as the Love of the Soldiers. Besides, this is not an Age to produce Favourites of the People, while we live under a Queen who engrosseth all our Love, and all our Veneration; and where, the only Way for a great General or Minister, to acquire any Degree of subordinate Affection from the Publick, must be by all Marks of the most *entire Submission and Respect* to her sacred Person and Commands; otherwise, no pretence of great Services, either in the Field or the Cabinet, will be able to skreen them from universal Hatred.

'BUT the late Ministry was closely joined to the General, by Friendship, Interest, Alliance, Inclination and Opinion; which cannot be affirmed of the present; and the Ingratitude of the Nation lieth in the People's *joining as one Man*, to wish, that such a Ministry should be changed. Is it not at the same Time notorious to the whole Kingdom, that nothing but a tender Regard to the General, was able to preserve that Ministry so long, until neither God nor Man could suffer their Continuance? Yet in the highest Ferment of Things, we heard few or no Reflections upon this great Commander; but all seemed unanimous in wishing he might still be at the Head of the Confederate Forces; only at the same Time, in Case he were resolved to resign, they chose rather to turn their Thoughts somewhere else, than throw up all in Despair. And this I cannot but add, in Defence of the People, with Regard to the Person we are speaking of; that in the high Station he hath been for many Years past, his *real Defects* (as nothing Human is without them) have in a detracting Age been very sparingly mentioned, either in Libels or Conversations; and all his *Successes* very freely and universally applauded.

'THERE is an active and a passive Ingratitude: Applying both to this Occasion; We may say, the first is, when Prince or People returns good Services with Cruelty or ill Usage: The other is, when good Services are not at all, or very meanly rewarded. We have already spoke of the former; let us therefore in the second Place, examine how the Services of our General have been rewarded; and whether upon that Article, either Prince or People have been guilty of Ingratitude?

'THOSE are the most valuable Rewards which are given to us from the certain Knowledge of the Donor, that they *fit our Temper best*: I shall therefore say nothing of the Title of *Duke*, or the *Garter*, which the

Queen bestowed the General in the beginning of her Reign: But I shall come to *more substantial* Instances, and mention nothing which hath not been given in the Face of the World. The Lands of *Woodstock*, may, I believe, be reckoned worth 40,000 *l.* On the building of *Blenheim Castle* 200,000 *l.* have already been expended, although it be not yet near finished. The Grant of 5000 *l. per Annum*, on the Post Office is richly worth 100,000 *l.* His Principality in *Germany* may be computed at 30,000 *l.* Pictures, Jewels, and other Gifts from Foreign Princes 60,000 *l.* The Grant at the *Pall-Mall*, the Rangership, &c. for want of more certain Knowledge, may be called 10,000 *l.* His own, and his Dutchess's Employments at five Years Value, reckoning only the known and avowed Salaries, are very low rated at 100,000 *l.* Here is a good deal above half a Million of Money; and I dare say, those who are loudest with the Clamour of Ingratitude, will readily own, that all this is but a Trifle, in Comparison of what is *untold*.

THE reason of my stating this Account is only to convince the World, that we are not quite so ungrateful either as the *Greeks* or the *Romans*. And in order to adjust this Matter with all Fairness, I shall confine myself to the latter, who were much the more generous of the two. A Victorious General of *Rome* in the height of that Empire, having *entirely subdued his Enemies*, was rewarded with the larger Triumph; and perhaps a Statue in the *Forum*; a Bull for a Sacrifice; an embroidered Garment to appear in; a Crown of Laurel; a Monumental Trophy with Inscriptions; sometimes five hundred or a thousand Copper Coins were struck on Occasion of the Victory; which, doing Honour to the General, we will place to his Account: and lastly, sometimes, although not very frequently, a Triumphal Arch. These are all the Rewards that I can call to Mind, which a victorious General received after his return from the most glorious Expedition; conquered some great Kingdom; brought the King himself, his Family and Nobles to adorn the Triumph in Chains; and made the Kingdom either a *Roman* Province, or at best, a poor depending State, in humble Alliance to that Empire. Now, of all these Rewards, I find but two which were of real profit to the General: The *Laurel Crown*, made and sent him at the charge of the Publick; and the *embroidered Garment*; but I cannot find whether this last were paid for by the Senate or the General: However, we will take the more favourable Opinion; and in all the rest, admit the whole Expence, as if it were ready Money in the General's Pocket. Now according to these Computations on both Sides, we will draw up two fair Accounts: the one of *Roman* Gratitude, and the other of *British* Ingratitude; and set them together in Ballance.

A Bill of ROMAN Gratitude.				A Bill of BRITISH Ingratitude.			
Imprim.	*l.*	*s.*	*d.*	*Imprim.*	*l.*	*s.*	*d.*
For Frankincense and Earthen Pots to Burn it in	4	10	0	*Woodstock*	40000	0	0
A Bull for Sacrifice	8	0	0	*Blenheim*	200000	0	0
				Post-Office Grant.	100000	0	0
An embroidered Garment	50	0	0	*Mildenheim*	30000	0	0
A Crown of Laurel			2	Pictures, Jewels &c.	60000	0	0
A Statue	100	0	0	*Pall Mall*	10000	0	0
A Trophy	80	0	0	*Grant &c.*			
A thousand Copper Medals, Value halfpence a Piece	2	1	8	Employments.	100000	0	0
A Triumphal Arch	500	0	0		540000	0	0
A Triumphal Carr, valued as a Modern Coach	100	0	0				
Casual Charges at the Triumph	150	0	0				
	994	11	10				

'THIS is an Account of the visible Profits on both Sides; and if the *Roman* General had any *private Perquisites*, they may be easily discounted, and by more probable Computations; and differ yet more upon the Ballance; if we consider, that all the Gold and Silver for *Safeguards* and *Contributions*; and all *valuable Prizes* taken in the War, were openly exposed in the Triumph; and then lodged in the Capital for the Publick Service.

'So that upon the Whole, we are not yet quite so bad at *worst*, as the *Romans* were at *best*. And I doubt, those who raise this hideous Cry of Ingratitude, may be mightily mistaken in the Consequences they propose from such Complaints. I remember a Saying of *Seneca, Multos ingratos invenimus, plures facimus*: We find many ungrateful Persons in the World, but we *make* more, by setting too high a Rate upon our Pretensions, and under valuing the Rewards we receive. When unreasonable Bills are brought in, they ought to be taxed, or cut off in the Middle.

Where there have been long Accounts between two Persons, I have known one of them perpetually making large Demands, and pressing for Payments; who when the Accounts were cast up on both Sides, was found to be Debtor for some Hundreds. I am thinking, if a Proclamation were issued out for every Man to send in his *Bill of Merits*, and the lowest Price he set them at, what a pretty Sum it would amount to, and how many such Islands as this must be Sold to pay them. I form my Judgment from the Practice of those who sometimes happen to *pay themselves*; and I dare affirm, would not be so unjust to take a Farthing more than they think is due to their Deserts. I will Instance only in one Article. A Lady of my Acquaintaince, appropriated twenty-six Pounds a Year out of her own Allowance, for certain Uses, which her Woman received, and was to pay to the Lady or her Order, as it was called for. But after eight Years, it appeared upon the strictest Calculation, that the Woman had paid but four Pounds a Year, and sunk two and twenty for her own Pocket; It is but supposing instead of twenty six Pounds, twenty six thousand; and by that you may judge what the Pretensions of *Modern Merit* are, where it happens to be its own Paymaster.'

*   *   *

A rival newspaper, the Whig *Medley*, described this outburst as 'the falsest, as well as the most impudent paper that ever was printed'. But the *Medley* was an intelligent paper; Arthur Maynwaring, Sarah's friend and adviser, was one of its chief contributors. It is scarcely possible that he did not appreciate the subtlety of the diatribe. Its most spectacular feature, of course, was the directness of the attack on the Duke. Some of the mud would stick, however busy the Duke's partisans might be in scraping it off. But there was much more to the piece than this old Grub Street device. After such a grand mockery of the charge of ingratitude, who would so readily again believe the tale that the nation or the new Ministers had treated Marlborough unfairly? Ingratitude! At a single blow the favourite Whig word had been robbed of its usefulness even if it was not actually expunged from their vocabulary. Whenever it was mentioned again in any company no one could fail to recall the *Examiner*'s accountancy; indeed, most of the facts about Marlborough's wealth could not be disputed. Hitherto on balance the Whigs had had the best of the pamphlet and newspaper war. They had more journals written in their interest and several excellent writers. Within a few issues the new voice on the *Examiner* had changed the terms of the conflict.

Swift was well aware that he had caused a sensation. In the following issue of the *Examiner* he blandly acknowledged his achievement. 'When I first undertook this paper,' he wrote, 'I was resolved to concern myself only with things, and not with persons. Whether I have kept or broken this resolution, I cannot recollect; and I will not be at the pains to examine, but leave the matter to those little antagonists who may want a topic for criticism.'

CHAPTER SEVEN

The Duke's Return

(November 23rd—December 31st, 1710)

'I could not forbear shaking my head, and smiling a little at his ignorance. And being no stranger to the art of war, I gave him a description of cannons, culverins, muskets, carabines, pistols, bullets, powder, swords, bayonets, battles, sieges, retreats, attacks, undermines, countermines, bombardments, sea-fights; ships sunk with a thousand men, twenty thousand killed on each side; dying groans, limbs flying in the air, smoke, noise, confusion, trampling to death under horses' feet; flight. pursuit, victory; fields strewed with carcases left for food to dogs, and wolves, and birds of prey; plundering, stripping, ravishing, burning and destroying. And to set forth the valour of my own dear countrymen, I assured him, that I had seen them blow up a hundred enemies at once in a siege, and as many in a ship, and beheld the dead bodies come down in pieces from the clouds, to the great diversion of the spectators.'

—*Gulliver's Travels, Voyage to the Houyhnhnms.*

THE *Examiner* quickly became a power in the land. Its circulation can only be guessed; probably it sold some four or five thousand copies. But no other political journal in that age gained so great a reputation in so short a time. Not only was it recognized in the London coffee-houses as the most authentic voice of the Queen's most favoured Ministers. Soon its influence extended to other parts of the country where the enthusiasts of the Church party eagerly awaited their 'weekly antidote' to the 'weekly poison' dispensed by the Whigs. An 'honest parson' of Thirsk had his copy posted from London every Thursday and received it on Sunday in time for use after the evening service. He 'usually invites a good number of his friends to his house, where he first reads over the paper, and then comments upon the text; and all the week after carries it about with him to read to such of his parishioners as are weak in the faith, and have not yet the eyes of their understanding opened; so that it is not doubted but that he will in time make as many converts to the true interest of the State, as ever he did to the Church'. John Gay contrasted its effect with that produced by some of its rivals and underlined the chief reason for its appeal. 'I presume I need not tell you', he said, 'that the *Examiner* carries much the more sail, as 'tis supposed to be writ by the direction, and under the eye of some great persons who sit at the helm of affairs and is consequently look'd on as a sort of public notice which way they are steering us.' Swift was conscious of his new-found influence. 'It would be happy for me . . . not to be forced to hear my own work railed at and commended fifty times a day, affecting all the while a countenance wholly unconcerned. . . .' How much of this sudden leap to success was due to the famous *Examiner* No. 17 it is impossible to gauge. But one fact is known. One sentence in that article drew blood, and the protests of his victim, if they ever reached his ears, must have gratified the Vicar of Laracor hardly less than his triumphs in secular conversion.

A copy of the 'infamous print', as she called it, was carefully studied by the Duchess of Marlborough. Little or nothing could be done about the general satire against her husband, although the Whig journals attempted a ponderous reply. But the last paragraph was a direct attack on the Duchess and the manner in which she had discharged her duties over a period of eight years as Mistress of the Robes. The charge was that she had stolen £22,000 a year. Sarah prided herself on her careful housekeeping and her anger at such an accusation would have been violent enough even if it had been made by some obscure scribbler. She could not have known that Swift was the author, although she afterwards claimed that she suspected him. She did know that the *Examiner* was inspired by Robert Harley; she believed that he concerted most moves with the Queen; she knew, further, that both Harley and the Queen were well aware of her honesty in financial dealings. The attack in the *Examiner* came as the last straw in the campaign of calumny against her. How dare they assail her as a common pickpocket! Her reply was to draw up one of her formidable documents for the Queen, setting forth, complete with balance sheets and statistical evidence, the record of her faithfulness and frugality. This was dispatched to the Queen along with the offending copy of the *Examiner*. For the last time Anne showed a twinge of sympathy for the idol of her youth. 'Everybody', she said, 'knows cheating is not the Duchess of Marlborough's crime.' Sarah was not satisfied. So severe was the provocation from many quarters, so widespread the rumour that further action was soon to be taken against her, that she contemplated the revenge of publishing her earlier correspondence with the Queen. Anne demanded the return of her letters. Sarah refused. The news of this exchange became known and the political world trembled at the thought that at any moment one or other of the two women might erupt with volcanic fury.

A whiff of this sulphurous atmosphere was detectable in the House of Lords when the new Parliament met in the last days of November. After a resolution had been passed offering an address of thanks to the Queen, Lord Scarborough, a friend of Marlborough, suggested that the time was also proper to thank his Grace. The Duke of Argyll demanded an explanation: who was meant by 'his Grace'? When Scarborough laboriously explained that he meant 'his Grace, the Duke of Marlborough who had made such a Glorious Campaign', Argyll led a counter-offensive backed by some of the most vocal of Marlborough's enemies. Four towns had been captured during the campaign, but only one was any use, the other three having cost more blood than they were worth. Before any thanks were offered to Marlborough an account should be rendered concerning the chief business he was charged to transact. He had been sent to Holland earlier in the year as a plenipotentiary to make a peace, but no report had been received. So distraught were Marlborough's supporters at the reception given to the proposal that they were unable to devise any sufficient riposte. They gladly accepted a compromise suggesting that any resolution of thanks to the Duke should be postponed until his return.

Henry St. John remarked on the scene: 'One would imagine that Scarborough had been hired by somebody that wishes Lord Marlborough ill to take so unconcerted and ridiculous a measure.' And yet a year earlier both Houses of Parliament had expressed their thanks to his Grace without a dissenting voice. Six months earlier he had been appointed plenipotentiary with the unanimous support of the Whig and Tory chiefs. Every autumn for years past the tribute to his services had been made so regularly that Lord Scarborough had good reason for feeling amazed at the controversy he had stirred. The House of Lords was still regarded as the stronghold of the Whigs. None the less, the result of the elections and the clear evidence of the change in court favour had caused a sudden alteration in the attitude of a large number of peers. Marlborough's enemies were emboldened, the waverers had grown in number and his friends had become timorous and apologetic; even Lord Wharton was reported to have lost his 'usual briskness'. That the great Whig grandees had so swiftly seen their grip on the House of Lords loosened was an event little less startling than the result of the election itself. Swift's assault in the *Examiner*, produced on the very eve of the reassembly of Parliament, may have played its part in working the transformation. He revealed the readiness of the court to humiliate the enemy they knew not how to destroy. St. John showed the same temper in the letter which he wrote on November 28th to Drummond at The Hague. 'If he (the Duke) comes home, and disengages himself from the Whigs,' he wrote, 'if he puts a stop to the rage and fury of his wife; in short, if he abandons all his new, and takes up with his old friends; by the Queen's favour, and by the remains of regard for him which are preserved in the breasts of several people, he may not only stand his ground; but, in my humble opinion, establish himself in as lofty a situation as it becomes a subject to aspire to: but if he imagines that people will any more be caught with general and elusive discourse; if he thinks that people will any more engage to him whilst he is under no engagement, nor gives any security to them; depend upon me, for once, he will find himself deceived.' St. John could afford to parade his newly gained sense of superiority in his private correspondence. But no settled policy for deciding the future of the Duke was evident amid the sneers and the venom. The Duke of Argyll and others who had served in the army gazed half-enviously and half-fearfully on the authority still wielded by the Captain-General. They were ready to inflict pinpricks; but they too possessed no coherent plan for his overthrow. Swift had attacked more savagely than anyone else in the confidence of the Queen's Ministers. But his purpose had been strictly limited and he was still most insistent on the absolute necessity of concealment. 'I am at present', he told Stella at the end of November, 'a little involved with the present Ministry in some certain things (which I tell you as a secret) . . . To say the truth, the present ministry have a difficult task, and want me . . . For God's sake, not a word of this to anyone alive.' Stella was given a minute daily account of most of Swift's doings. She had not yet been introduced either to the *Examiner* or to the Captain-General.

The fate of Marlborough was not the only dilemma confronting the new Ministry, although it cast its shadow across the rest of the scene. Once the spectacular electoral victory had been won, only three levers of power remained available to the Whigs—the House of Lords, the City and Marlborough's prestige. The Tories, as we have seen, had already started to break up the solid phalanx of strength which the Whigs had hitherto commanded in the Lords. Harley's political cunning and financial skill had started to mitigate the hostility of the City towards the new administration. But the reaction to other events of both Harley and St. John showed how well they understood the greater delicacy of their task in dealing with the Duke. Both after their different styles offered alternate blandishments and insults to the Duke, and meantime demanded patience of their followers while feeding their angry temper in the columns of the *Examiner*. Considerable political risks were involved in this policy of deferring, however ungraciously, to the European reputation of the Captain-General. In the aftermath of the election the current of high Tory fanaticism was so strong that both Ministers had some difficulty in retaining their foothold. If the advice of the most rabid of the Tories had been followed— so St. John believed—the Ministry would have been blown up in twenty-four hours.

It is easy to imagine the mood in which the new House of Commons assembled. A huge change had taken place in its membership. More than a third of the total were new men who felt that having routed the Whigs and the enemies of the Church in the country they now had the right to see their triumph repeated on the political stage in London. They cared nothing for the susceptibilities of the City or the Duke which Harley was so eager not to offend too roughly; these subtleties had figured not at all in the countrywide campaign. They at once elected the high Tory member for the University of Oxford, William Bromley, as Speaker, and trusted that the Queen's Speech would at least give some hint of the measures whereby the last traces of the Whig power were to be exterminated. To their dismay they discovered that Harley and even St. John spoke a language very different from their own. Both must take responsibility for the words put into the Queen's mouth, words which contrasted sharply with the strident slogans of the election.

'The carrying on the War in all its Parts, but particularly in *Spain*, with the utmost Vigour', said the Queen, 'is the likeliest

Means, with God's Blessing, to produce a safe and honourable Peace for us, and all our Allies, whose Support and Interest I have truly at Heart. For this Purpose, I must ask from you, *Gentlemen of the House of Commons*, the necessary Supplies for the next Year's Service: And let me put you in Mind, that nothing will add so much to the Efficacy, as Unanimity and Despatch.' Thus it appeared that one of the first acts of the men who had railed so successfully against the iniquity of heavy taxation to sustain a standing army and an endless war would be to persist in evil-doing with Whiggish docility. Nor were the Tories given much comfort on the issues affecting the Church which had stirred the fiercest passions. 'As we are Fellow-Christians and Fellow-Subjects with those Protestant Dissenters, who are so unhappy to entertain Scruples against Conformity with our Church,' said the Commons in response to the Queen's address, 'we are desirous and determined to let them quietly enjoy that Indulgence which the Law hath allowed them.' The Whigs objected to the substitution of the word 'Indulgence' for the stronger term 'Toleration'; they felt it presaged the attack on the dissenters which the high-flyers wanted, and when that particular item of news reached the City stocks fell by more than 2 per cent. So swift a reaction to so slender a provocation was clear enough evidence of the tight-rope which Harley still had to walk. But, in truth, if anyone had a cause for complaint on grounds of deception it was not the Whigs. In the light of the Sacheverellite oratory which had helped to win so many Tory seats, the readiness of the Queen's most prominent Ministers, who devised the Commons' reply, to embrace Protestant dissenters among their fellow-Christians sounded almost like sacrilege. Clearly no change in the law of toleration was intended and such an omission amounted to little less than a betrayal of the Tory creed. 'We shall always steadily adhere to the Protestant Succession in the House of Hanover, and be most watchful to prevent any Danger which may threaten that settlement,' said the same Commons' reply. The Whig opposition—'showing their teeth before they can bite', according to the Tory gibe—sought to improve the occasion with a specific motion excluding the Pretender. Harley neatly diverted the debate by showing himself more Hanoverian than the Whigs. No doubt the parliamentary novices who crowded the Tory benches marvelled at the soft answer which turned away Whig wrath and won a debating victory. But, for all Harley's virtuosity, how dispiriting these tones must have sounded in ears attuned to the thunder outside!

Some older hands among the Tories were eager enough to mobilize the discontent of those who expected a more daring leadership. The rumour ran that Harley had quarrelled with the high Tory spokesman, Lord Rochester. Then came the counter-rumour that Rochester had been convinced by Harley's persuasive moderation. One observer of the first parliamentary skirmishes quickly concluded that both would be deceived 'if either of them thinks they can govern this House of Commons by these policies, there being a great many country Gentlemen that are resolved to proceed with methods of their own'. The sustained roar which greeted any open avowal of these intentions by a high Tory spokesman in the Commons left no doubt in Harley's mind that he had a serious problem on his hands arising from the prevalent temper on his own back benches. He did not quail before the threat, believing it could be mastered by the same arts which had served him well before. He told his obstreperous supporters 'that the Whigs were a daring inveterate sett of men, and must not be exasperated too much at one time; that the administration was not thoroughly settled, and a peace was necessary, and if the Whigs should break out during the war, it would ruin all; and on these and the like pretences was very earnest that gentlemen wou'd have a little patience'. These arguments by themselves might not have proved sufficient, but Harley had another which for a while settled the issue. He had been 'the chief agent in bringing about the late change'; he had 'the absolute disposal of all affairs under the Queen'; he had the ear of the Queen herself. A breach between him and the Tory majority in the Commons would wreck the whole enterprise. With this threat, in the first days of his administration, Harley, the opponent of party alignments, posed the issue of confidence to his followers in a fashion not so different from that employed by a modern Prime Minister. He won from them a surly obedience. But many sought by other means an escape from frustration and a guarantee of more adventurous action in the future.

Ever since the days of King William a body of members—high Tories or near Jacobites—had met together in the October Club, a name derived from the October ale which they consumed to assist their plottings. Before the election of 1710 the number involved was so small that the Club exerted no perceptible influence.

But in the new Parliament the Bell Tavern in King Street where the Club dined soon became the place where as many as one hundred and fifty members met to shape the business of the Commons. 'These gentlemen resolv'd and engaged to stand firm with one another, and to meet weekly in order to concert measures, in which the minority should yield to the majority.' At first their victories were confined to comparatively trivial matters. Election petitions were watched to ensure that the Whig interest was defeated, even in such cases where Harley's friend, the Duke of Newcastle, had a stake. Pressure was applied to get the Ministers to prepare legislative measures which would assist the Church and protect the landowners. General support for the time being was pledged to the Harley régime. But there was no doubt about the further aims—to 'drive things to extreams against the Whigs, to call the old ministry to account, and get off five or six heads'. Once this programme was fulfilled, the way might be open for other more ambitious projects which could now only be darkly hinted at. Was the issue of the succession really settled? Was there still not a chance that 'the lawful King'—as many Tories still regarded the Pretender—could succeed Anne instead of the upstart Elector of Hanover? The October Club—so ran the sneer—was Hanoverian when sober and Jacobite when drunk.

These long-range speculations about a Jacobite restoration were never formulated in precise terms, but no one could deny the rough logic which inspired the October Club's demand for action against the Whigs. Harley and St. John—with the *Examiner* giving the lead on the same theme—had assured the country that crimes of matchless enormity had been committed by the former Whig Ministers. Why then was their punishment delayed? How could the wrathful Tory army in the country be answered if this simplest of all the electoral war cries was not to be satisfied? Impeachment was the accepted means of enforcing party revenge. Lord Godolphin, it seems, was the first most favoured victim. Harley must have been horrified by the mere suggestion. He understood how disastrous such action would be in deepening the antagonism of the City. Moreover, was there really any case against him apart from that inspired by mere partisan spite? And might not the impeachment of Godolphin prove a boomerang in the hands of the Tories as the impeachment of Sacheverell had dealt a death-blow to the Whigs? Godolphin was reprieved. But as the days passed the claims of another candidate for butchery were canvassed. What a Tory holiday could be provided by the impeachment of Lord Wharton! Harley must still have opposed so direct a challenge to the most dynamic of the Whigs. But if he objected to risking another grand trial in Westminster Hall much could be said for Wharton's arraignment before another tribunal. While Harley held tight the reins of government, no reason existed why the *Examiner* should not be let loose. Swift had some old scores of his own to pay off against Wharton. He gladly undertook the role of unofficial prosecutor on behalf of the Government, and discharged the duty with such relish that for a while even the bloodthirsty appetites of the Bell Tavern had their fill.

The crimes of the Earl of Wharton—in the eyes of the Tories—defied satire. Some blunter instrument was needed for the work of demolition. A hundred years later another master of English invective, William Cobbett, explained the distinction. 'Swift has told us', he said, 'not to chop *blocks* with *razors*. Any *edge*-tool is too fine for work like this: a pick-axe, that perforates with one end and drags about with the other, is the tool for this sort of business.' Wharton was, in the mature opinion of Swift expressed when he looked back on a long career of ferocious controversy, 'the most universal villain I ever knew'. He was the epitome of a loose-living, arrogant, dissenter-loving, church-hating Whig. He had been sent to Ireland to bully the clergy and recoup his own fortune. His private life had been notorious ever since, in some wild orgy of his youth, he had invaded a Gloucestershire church and disburdened himself on the altar. More pertinent still, he was the foremost Whig—next only perhaps to Sarah and Sunderland—whose nerve had not wavered amid the Ministerial revolution which had thrown him and his friends out of office. Wharton was still scheming for revenge. No wonder the October Club bayed for his blood. Moreover he was no distant and awe-inspiring god like the Duke of Marlborough; Swift had seen him often face to face. He knew this victim better than any other.

The first mild essay on the topic had appeared in No. 15 of the *Examiner* which purported to discuss in an academic manner the Art of Political Lying. Wharton was easily identifiable as the hero of the piece. 'The superiority of his genius consists in nothing else but an inexhaustible fund of political lies, which he plentifully distributes every minute he speaks, and by an unparalleled generosity forgets, and consequently contradicts the next half-hour.' But lying was only one count in the catalogue. In the week when Parliament reassembled, the *Examiner* went to work on Wharton more boldly. Addison had compared the Whig General, Stanhope, with Alcibiades; Swift now portrayed Wharton as Verres, the Roman Governor of Sicily.

'I have brought a man here before you, my lords, who is a robber of the public treasure, an overturner of law and justice, and the disgrace, as well as the destruction, of the Sicilian province . . . To pass over the foul stains and ignominy of his youth, his corrupt management in all employments he has borne, his treachery and irreligion, his injustice and oppression, he has left of late such monuments of his villainies in Sicily, made such havoc and confusion there, during his government, that the province cannot by any means be restored to its former state, and hardly recover itself at all under many years, and by a long succession of good governors. While this man governed in that island, the Sicilians had neither the benefit of our laws, nor their own, nor even of common right. In Sicily, no man now possesses more than what the Governor's lust and avarice have overlooked, or what he was forced to neglect out of mere weariness and satiety of oppression. Everything where he presided, was determined by his arbitrary will, and the best subjects he treated as enemies. To recount his abominable debaucheries, would offend any modest ear, since so many could not preserve their daughters and wives from his lust. I believe there is no man who ever heard his name, that cannot relate his enormities.'

Lord Wharton considered that he had been 'damnably mauled'; otherwise, it seems, his natural geniality was undisturbed. The attack must be pressed home. Not many days later what Swift described to Stella as 'a damned libellous pamphlet' on the same subject was distributed privately. It was entitled: *A Short Character of His Ex. T.E. of W. L.L. of I—. With an Account of some smaller Facts, during his Government, which will not be put into the Articles of Impeachment.* Nobody, according to Swift, knew the author or the printer, but when 'some bold cur' ventured to publish the pamphlet publicly he was rewarded by a sale of two thousand within two days. 'I must here declare', said the unknown author at the outset, 'that I have not the least view to his person in any part of it: I have had the honour of much conversation with his lordship, and am thoroughly convinced how indifferent he is to applause, and how insensible to reproach. . . . He is without the sense of shame or glory, as some men are without the sense of smelling; and therefore a good name to him is no more than a precious ointment would be to those. Whoever were to describe the nature of a serpent, a wolf, a crocodile, or a fox, must be understood to do it for the sake of others, without any love or hatred for the animals themselves.' Thereafter Swift filled out the portrait and the wonder is that, despite all the infamies attributed to him, the ribald, swaggering, tyrannical Whig Lord still emerges as a real man. How impossible to believe that an enemy, however diabolically clever and consumed with hate, could have invented such a monster from his own imagination!

'Thomas, Earl of Wharton, Lord-Lieutenant of Ireland, by the force of a wonderful constitution, hath some years passed his grand climacteric without any visible effects of old age, either on his body or his mind, and in spite of a continual prostitution to those vices which usually wear out both. His behaviour is in all forms of a young man of five-and-twenty. Whether he walks, or whistles, or swears, or talks bawdy, or calls names, he acquits himself in each beyond a templar of three years standing . . . He swears solemnly he loves you and will serve you, and your back is no sooner turned, but he tells those about him, you are a dog and a rascal. He goes constantly to prayers in the forms of his place, and will talk bawdy and blasphemy at the chapel door. He is a Presbyterian in politics, and an atheist in religion; but he chooses at present to whore with a Papist . . . He will openly take away your employment today, because you are not of his party; tomorrow he will meet or send for you, as if nothing at all had passed, lay his hands with much friendliness on your shoulders, and with the greatest ease and familiarity in the world, tell you that the faction are driving at something in the House: that you must be sure to attend, and to speak to all your friends to be there, though he knows at the same time that you and your friends are against him in that very point he mentions: And however absurd, ridiculous, and gross, this may appear, he has often found it successful; some men having such an awkward bashfulness, they know not how to refuse upon a sudden, and every man having something to fear or hope, which often hinders them from driving things to extremes with persons of power, whatever provocations they may have received. He hath sunk his fortunes by endeavouring to ruin one kingdom, and hath raised them by going far in the ruin of another. With a good natural understanding, a great fluency in speaking, and no ill taste of wit, he is generally the worst companion in the world; his thoughts being wholly taken up between vice and politics, so that bawdy, prophaness, and business fill up his whole conversation . . . He bears the gallantries of his lady with the indifference of a Stoic, and thinks them well recompensed by a return of children to support his family, without the fatigues of being a father.'

It is not recorded what Lord Wharton thought of this further 'mauling', although months later when he bumped into Swift accidentally he greeted him with all his old jovial good temper. The pamphlet reached Dublin, and Archbishop King, possibly suspecting the true author, wrote a letter to Swift protesting against 'this wounding in the dark'. Stella also sent a mocking reproof, claiming that newsboys had cried beneath her window that Swift was the culprit. 'Fie child!' he replied, 'you must not mind what every idle body tells you. I believe you lie; and that the dogs were not crying it when you said so! Come, tell the truth!' Possibly this was one of the occasions when he was content for the mask to drop. The impeachment of Wharton, despite Harley's reticence, was a real possibility. A growing reputation with the October Club men was a prize worth having both in his own interest and in Harley's. By his assaults on the Whigs Swift was establishing himself as a chief bulwark of the new Ministry. During that December fresh attacks were made on Somers, Cowper, Sunderland and the Duchess. The special note of savagery was reserved for Wharton. But week by week Swift was becoming fascinated by the much more intractable problem confronting the new Ministers: *What was to be done with the Duke?*

While the Ministers and their new servant searched for a solution, an incident happened in Marlborough's camp which enabled them to show something of their mettle. Three of his officers—Lieutenant-General Meredith, Major-General Macartney and Brigadier Honywood—were alleged to have joined in a drunken toast demanding 'Damnation and confusion to the new Ministry, and to those who had any Hand in turning out the Old'. It was further alleged that they had dressed up a hat on a stick, labelled it Harley and fired their pistols into the scarecrow. At least this was the report conveyed to the Queen by some unknown informer. Orders were promptly sent to the Duke to be delivered unopened to the three offending officers. They were summarily cashiered. Their own claim was that they had done no more than drink a health to the Duke of Marlborough and confusion to his enemies. Two of them were Members of Parliament; all three were brilliant officers and personal friends of Marlborough. The move against them was clearly a calculated insult to the Captain-General. But it was also an indication of the genuine fears which some sections of opinion in London felt about his power and status. That anxiety, feigned or real, had been fed by some of Marlborough's dissident officers. 'Some restraint', Lord Orrery had written to Harley, 'should be put to that exorbitant power Lord Marlborough has in the army. I am every day more convinced of that necessity, for he plainly disposes of preferments here with no other view but to create a faction sufficient to support him against the Queen and her friends in case every other prop should fail.' Ever since his application for the post of Captain-General for life his enemies had hinted that no limit could be set to his ambition. Richard Steele, one of his most ardent admirers, had once imprudently portrayed him in the *Tatler* like Caesar before the Rubicon:

> *Great Jove, attend, and thou my native soil,*
> *Safe in my triumphs, glutted in my spoil:*
> *Witness with what reluctance I oppose*
> *My arms to thine, secure of other foes.*
> *What passive breast can bear disgrace like mine:*

The fears that the Whigs might, under Marlborough's leadership, seek an armed deliverance from their new thraldom were always fanciful; not a scrap of evidence exists that any serious plotting was ever started. But such fears were at least a tribute to the awe in which Marlborough was held, and the theme suited Swift perfectly. He hated war and despised soldiers. He firmly believed that part of Harley's mission was to restore the authority of the civil power. In No. 21 of the *Examiner*, published in the middle of December, he singled out the ambition of the Captain-General for attack as he had previously rubbed home the charge against his avarice.

'No private man', he wrote, 'should have a commission to be general for life, let his merit and services be never so great. Or, if a prince be unadvisedly brought to offer such a commission in one hand, let him (to save time and blood) deliver up his crown with the other. . . . Caesar indeed (between whom and a certain general some of late with much discretion have made a parallel) had his command in Gaul continued to him for five years, and was afterwards made perpetual Dictator, that is to say, general for life,

which gave him the power and the will of utterly destroying the
Roman liberty. . . . The request in its own nature is highly criminal,
and ought to be entered so upon record, to terrify others in time to
come from venturing to make it.' Marlborough's great blunder had
given Swift his opening. One of his deepest instincts was a loathing
of the futility of war and his detestation was easily transferred to
those who gloried in it. Years before in *The Tale of a Tub* he had
started his lifelong campaign against the pretensions of military
men; now he could give it a particular application.

'Another maxim', he continued, 'to be observed by a free state engaged in war, is to keep the military power in absolute subjection to the
civil, nor ever to suffer the former to influence or interfere with the
latter. . . . The whole system by which armies are governed, is quite
alien from the peaceful institutions of a state at home. . . . I know not
any sort of men so apt as soldiers are to reprimand those who presume
to interfere in what relates with their trade. When they hear any of us
in a coffeehouse, wondering that such a victory was not pursued, complaining that such a town cost more men and money than it was worth
to take it; or such an opportunity was lost of fighting the enemy; they
presently reprove us, and often with justice enough, for meddling in
matters out of our sphere, and clearly convince us of our mistakes in
terms of art that none of us understand. Nor do we escape so; for they
reflect with the utmost contempt of our ignorance, that we, who sit at
home in ease and security, never stirring from our firesides, should
pretend from books, and general reason, to argue upon military affairs;
which, after all, if we may judge from the share of intellectuals in some,
who are said to excel that way, is not so very profound or difficult a
science. But if there be any weight in what they offer, as perhaps there
may be a great deal; surely these gentlemen have a much weaker pretence to concern themselves in matters of the cabinet, which are always
either far above, or much beside their capacities. Soldiers may as well
pretend to prescribe rules for trade, to determine points in philosophy,
to be moderators in an assembly of divines, or direct in a court of justice,
as to misplace their talent in examining affairs of state, especially in
what relates to the choice of ministers, who are never so likely to be ill
chosen as when approved by them. . . . To say the truth, such formidable sticklers can have but two reasons for desiring to interfere in the
administration; the first is that of Cæsar and Cromwell, of which, God
forbid, I should accuse or suspect any body; since the second is pernicious enough, and that is, to preserve those in power who are for
perpetuating war, rather than see others advanced who, they are sure,
will use all proper means to promote a safe and honourable peace.'

Lest these references might be considered insufficiently apposite, Swift then referred directly to the toasts drunk by the offending officers and the danger lest 'inflamed by youth and wine' they might scatter 'madness and sedition throughout a whole camp'. Of course, 'these orgies' were abhorred by the general, but consider the danger.

'If men of such principles were able to propagate them in the camp, and were sure of a general for life, who had any tincture of ambition, we might soon bid farewell to ministers and parliaments, whether new or old. . . . The fortune of war hath raised several persons up to swelling titles, and great commands over numbers of men, which they are too apt to transfer along with them into civil life, and appear in all companies as if it were at the head of their regiments, with a sort of deportment that ought to have been dropt behind, in that short passage to Harwich. It puts me in mind of a dialogue in Lucian where Charon wafting one of their predecessors over Styx, ordered him to strip off his armour and fine clothes, yet still thought him too heavy: "But" (said he) "put off likewise that pride and presumption, those high-swelling words and that vain-glory"; because they were of no use on the other side of the water. Thus if all that array of military grandeur were confined to the proper scene, it would be much more for the interest of the owners, and less offensive to their fellow subjects.'

The sermon was personal and direct, and what pleasure it must have given the Vicar of Laracor to preach it! It was known that the Captain-General would soon return to London. That autumn Swift himself had arrived in London, a political nonentity with the most modest expectations. Now, on the eve of Christmas, he was not only presenting to the nation the great issues of the age, but also advising the Duke and his lieutenants on their proper deportment, with a fair assurance that every word he wrote would leave its sting where he intended.

* * *

The Captain-General who landed at Sole Bay on December 26 amid the storms of winter bore little enough resemblance to a Caesar or a Cromwell. He was made sick and despondent by the dramatic change in his fortunes. The campaign itself had been unsatisfactory. At its commencement he had hoped for a final battle which might at the same time ensure peace and reverse the decline in his influence at home. But either the risks were too great or his military nerve had been weakened. 'I can't say I have the same sanguine spirit I used to have,' he had lamented. On one occasion the French generals had seemed to invite him to fight a second Malplaquet. The temptation or opportunity was rejected. A repetition of that murderous victory, no less than an outright defeat, might easily have destroyed the leverage of political power which he still retained. Yet, despite the absence of spectacular fighting, casualties had been heavy. Typhus had struck harder than ever before. 'It is impossible, without seeing it,' he had written to Godolphin, 'to be sensible of the misery of this country; at least one half of the people of the villages, since the beginning of last winter, are dead, and the rest look as if they had come out of their graves. It is so mortifying that no Christian can see it but must with all his heart wish for a speedy peace.'

That Marlborough's humanity was genuine is testified by plentiful evidence; all the more infuriating, therefore, must have been the constant charge that he perpetuated the war to please his own vanity and fill his own pockets. Some responsibility for failing to conclude the peace talks with King Louis's emissaries did rest on his shoulders; at the critical moment he had not exerted his power to the limit, allowing himself to be overborne by the obstinate Whig Junto. But, almost certainly, he was not conscious of his own error. First the Whigs and now the Tories had failed to recognize and make obeisance before his genius. At every turn he felt himself betrayed and insulted by 'these new vipers' who controlled the state. He was the servant of a 'villainous people', the victim of a plot contrived by a bedchamber woman. His self-pity was prodigious. If his correspondence with Godolphin and Sarah is a true guide, he must have been sorely tempted to lay down his command. Certainly he had good grounds for his wrath. During the previous few months he had been forced to bear one mortification after another. His nephew, Sunderland, had been made the chief target of the Queen's anger and unceremoniously expelled from office. His closest friend, Godolphin, had suffered the same fate and had even been denied the pension which the Queen had promised. Tory spokesmen in the Commons had never ceased to rail against the payments required to sustain 'the golden mine of Blenheim' until Godolphin had been driven to the contemptuous cry: 'Let them keep their heap of stones!' Harley and St. John with greater subtlety had been busy undermining his authority in his own army. He had left England before the verdict had been passed on

Sacheverell and before the Whig supremacy had been challenged; now he returned to face a London where so much power had been stripped from his friends and where he himself had become the butt of gibe and slander in every coffee-house. Finally, he must have known from the court intelligence reaching him in the previous few weeks that a more abject humiliation awaited him. A plan was in the making to disgrace his beloved Sarah. Weeks before he had told her that there was 'no barbarity that you and I must not expect'; now the prophecy was about to be fulfilled. The Duke must have pondered what vestige of his own dignity would be left after the final clash between the Duchess and the Queen.

Yet Marlborough did not flinch. The reasons why he resolved to submit to the ordeal so meekly cannot be deciphered with certainty. Perhaps the motive was a genuinely noble understanding of how decisively his demeanour might settle the future of England and Europe. No doubt he was encouraged by the manner in which his own soldiers and his European allies had reacted against the successive hardships thrust upon him with fresh displays of faith in his leadership. Perhaps the love of power had become so deeply embedded in his character that he could not consider willingly surrendering a single particle of it. 'I detest Mr. Harley,' he had told Sarah weeks before, but when she hinted that he might retaliate on his traducers by refusing to take their orders he resisted the temptation. 'We are', he had written, 'in circumstances that require great temper, by which I hope that we may at last overcome our enemies.' Marlborough's mastery of his own temper on all public occasions and in all public transactions was consummate and unfailing. All the irritations which fill his private correspondence were concealed from other eyes. Whenever he stepped out on to the public stage he became at once the unruffled courtier and diplomat. And never was his poise more needed, never was it displayed in such shining perfection, as in the last days of December, 1710, when he returned to London with such bitterness in his heart.

An unexpected welcome awaited him. 'Upon his Entrance into the City, about Five O'clock in the Evening, his coach was attended by Multitudes of People, with Links and Flambeaux; who, by their loud Acclamations, expressed their joy at his Grace's happy Return.' The passage of a famous man through the streets was normally the occasion for celebrations. But when the doors and windows were flung open the cries which came forth were pointed and Whiggish. 'God Bless the Duke of Marlborough!' 'No wooden shoes!' 'No Popery!' With a leader at their head the Whigs could still raise a stir to match the clamour Sacheverell had excited six months before. If Marlborough had wished he could have driven straight to St. James's Palace with the City crowd as his bodyguard and given a hint to the Queen how mighty was the power still commanded by her great servant. How such an entry would have fed the rumours that he returned as a Cromwell! Instead he went first through the side streets to the house of his son-in-law, the Duke of Montagu, and waited for the crowd to disperse. Then he hired a hackney-coach to take him to the palace. The Queen was graciousness itself. For half an hour she and her Captain-General discussed the weather and the state of the roads until he begged leave to be excused. He had been five nights without sleep; his handsome face had grown thin and careworn; everyone who saw him marked the change. At this first encounter nothing was exchanged but the courtesies.

But Harley and Mrs. Masham had doubtless primed the Queen that a new relationship must be established at the earliest possible moment and everyone around the court waited excitedly to hear how the Duke would respond to the rude reception prepared for him. At the next audience the Queen took the initiative. 'I am desirous you should continue to serve me,' she said, 'and I will answer for the conduct of all my ministers towards you. . . . I must request that you would not suffer any vote of thanks to you to be moved in parliament this year because my ministers will certainly oppose it.' Even Marlborough's equanimity might have been disturbed by such a welcome. But he was not to be provoked. 'I shall always be ready to serve your Majesty, if what has recently passed should not incapacitate me,' he replied. During the next day or two all the Ministers—all except Harley—visited him to pay their respects. Many of them were eager to report that he had shown a grovelling obeisance. Perhaps they were merely revealing their spleen; perhaps they knew how uncertainty about the Duke's future 'had cast a fresh Damp on the Publick Credit'. Harley made his report to the Duke of Newcastle. 'The Duke', he wrote, 'had a very cold reception last night. This day he had by appointment an audience for an hour and a half. He made great professions of compliance. That was told him which you advised. How long he will keep his temper I cannot tell. Certainly he has advisers who will ruin him, and while we are keeping all things in temper, they will drive it to extremity.' Harley, it seems, was nettled by the deliberate pose of humility which the Captain-General had assumed on his home-coming. Ambition should be made of sterner stuff. To at least one of the Ministers indeed he appeared almost carefree, for Lord Dartmouth reported that 'he did not despair of laughing heartily with me one day at all these hurly-burlies'.

Christmas, 1710, was no less memorable in the career of Jonathan Swift. Day by day, hour by hour almost, he found himself caught up in the rush of great events. His friend Harley had worked wonders in establishing the first beginnings of confidence among the City men and two days before Christmas Swift was able to boast that his own modest investment, made in the darkest hour of the financial crisis, was already a good bargain if he chose to sell. But Christmas Eve brought news of a disaster. General Stanhope's army had suffered a shattering defeat in Spain 'and it was odd to see the whole countenances of the Court changed so in two hours'. Harley's work was undone. 'Bank stock will fall like stock-fish by this bad news'; but Swift, loyal to his new masters, would not consider selling. Every night he was dining with one or other of the foremost men in the state, with Sir Thomas Hanmer, with Bishop Smallbridge, with Lord Peterborough, with Harley, with St. John. 'I wonder I never write politics to you,' he told Stella on December 30th. 'I could make you the profoundest politician in all the lane.'

Next day he could restrain himself no longer and Stella was introduced for the first time to the Captain-General. Swift had received from St. John a report of the great man's temper. 'He told me he had been with the Duke of Marlborough, who was lamenting his former wrong steps in joining with the Whigs, and said he was worn out with age, fatigues, and misfortunes. I swear it pitied me; and I really think they will not do well in too much mortifying that man, although indeed it is his own fault. He is covetous as Hell, and ambitious as the Prince of it: he would fain have been general for life, and has broken all endeavours for Peace, to keep his greatness and get money. He told the queen, he was neither covetous nor ambitious. She said, if she could have conveniently turned about, she would have laughed, and could hardly forbear it in his face. He fell in with all the abominable measures of the late ministry, because they gratified him for their own designs. Yet he has been a successful general and I hope he will continue his command.'

173

What Swift reported to Stella of what St. John had claimed to
have heard that the Queen said to Marlborough is not evidence.
No doubt Harley and St. John liked to flatter themselves with the
thought that Marlborough had become compliant to their will. It
seems much more probable that he had made a steady resolution,
in the face of all provocation, to comport himself with impeccable
good manners, never to risk the loss of his office and to wait for
his hour of recovery and revenge. That was his mood when he
talked with his friends among the Whigs. When he talked with
the Tories the accent changed and a new hope was encouraged in
their breasts—that the Duke might once again change his allegiance
and serve them as he had served their enemies. Both Harley and
St. John were puzzled. Partly persuaded by Swift perhaps, they
attempted to restrain their animosity towards him even if in
public they must still pander to the hungry ambitions of the
October Club. Swift believed that he was informed about every
nuance in the political scene and he had some excuse for this
belief. Night after night he sat up drinking with the Queen's
two chief Ministers, finding them 'as easy and disengaged as
schoolboys on a holiday'. Yet sometime during that Christmas
Harley set in train a secret enterprise which was not divulged to
Swift or to St. John and which at all costs must be concealed from
the Duke. In a note from the Abbé Gaultier to the French Minister, the Marquis of Torcy, dated December 28th, the first definite
news was conveyed that the Government in London was ready to
make large concessions to secure a peace. The stealth with which
the manœuvre was set on foot was one sign of the sense of guilt
felt by Swift's companion.

If the case for Harley's conduct through these months had been
left to be stated by himself, or even by his most agile disciple,
Daniel Defoe, it would have seemed to the outside world what it
so often was, a squalid tussle for office and power. It was Swift's
genius which elevated the argument to a higher plane. He loved
intrigue and his new-found intimacy with the great men in the
state. He prided himself—falsely as we know today—on being
informed about all their most secret schemes. But more powerful
than any of these inspirations in making him so brilliant a champion of the cause he had adopted was his blazing hatred of war
and all its accompaniments—a hatred which still scorched when
some twelve years later he wrote the *Voyage to the Houyhnhnms*.

CHAPTER EIGHT

Revolt in the Commons

(January 1st—March 7th, 1711)

'It is allowed, that senates and great councils are often troubled with redundant, ebullient, and other peccant humours, with many diseases of the head, and more of the heart; with strong convulsions, with grievous contractions of the nerves and sinews in both hands, but especially the right; with spleen, flatus, vertigos, and deliriums; with scrofulous tumours full of foetid, purulent matter; with sour frothy ructations, with canine appetites and crudeness of digestion, besides many others needless to mention. This doctor, therefore, proposed, that upon the meeting of a senate, certain physicians should attend at the three first days of the sitting, and at the close of each day's debate, feel the pulses of every senator; after which, having maturely considered, and consulted upon the nature of the several maladies, and the methods of cure, they should on the fourth day return to the senate house, attended by their apothecaries stored with proper medicines; and before the members sat, administer to each of them lenitives, aperitives, abstersives, corrosives, restringents, palliatives, laxatives, cephalalgics, icterics, apophlegmatics, acoustics, as their several cases required; and according as these medicines should operate, repeat, alter, or omit them at the next meeting.'
—*Gulliver's Travels, A Voyage to Laputa.*

'GET THE *Examiner*s AND READ THEM; the last nine or ten are full of the reasons for the late change, and of the abuses of the last ministry; and the great men assure me they are all true. They are written by their encouragement and direction.' Thus Swift half-revealed his new identity to Stella on the first day of January; from the exultant note struck in those early *Examiner*s, she must have believed that her 'Presto' was riding on the crest of success with his new companions. Assuredly there was nothing uncertain in the sound of this Tory trumpet. The merciless assault on Wharton, the rollicking mockery of Marlborough, the exposure of the stockjobbers, the attack on the military men—all these were indications surely that the new administration was built on a rock. But these confident tones represented little more than Swift's skill in capturing the brief, exhilarating mood after the election. At the beginning of the New Year the accent changed both in his private correspondence and in his weekly article. He was perpetually amazed—and sometimes aghast—at how 'easy and merry' both Harley and St. John were ready to be on their convivial occasions. Swift saw trouble ahead and he saw it coming soon. 'It is often in people's mouths', he wrote, 'that February will be a warm month.'

The bad news from Spain had caused a fresh revulsion in the City, and Swift feared 'people will think that nothing thrives under this Ministry'. Defeat had made the Whigs 'the most malicious toads in the world'. They were watching for their chance and no quarter could be expected if the tables were turned once more. More serious and overt was the ungovernable temper of 'the young men in Parliament', the country members, the violent Tories who clamoured for dramatic action against the Whigs. Little enough had been attempted to satisfy them; no move had been made even against Wharton. The rumour was that the Queen favoured his impeachment; but still nothing was done. Swift felt he understood better than the Ministers this frustration of the men who had won the sweeping electoral victory which Harley himself had never thought possible. He wondered how long they could be kept on the leash, although he appreciated perfectly the grounds for Harley's moderation. Indeed a chief cause of his doubts was the excessive toughness which he thought they were showing towards the Duke. The risks were appalling. 'We have nothing to save us but a Peace,' he wrote to Stella. That was the grand objective. But to gain it Marlborough's services were still required, and yet many besides Swift believed that he would not stay at his post. In the first days of January, Robert Walpole, one of the Whigs who still retained an official position, was dismissed following his defiance of a threat that he would be charged with corruption if he failed to work with the new Tory Ministers. Cardonnel, Marlborough's friend at the War Office, concluded that Marlborough's dismissal could not be long delayed. Swift had been learning quickly during his short stay in London. He no longer relied on the momentary expressions of malice or anger against the Duke which fell from the lips of his Tory friends. He had reached the same estimate of the international situation and of Marlborough's crucial place in it which Harley and St. John also appreciated in their more sober reflections. The battle-fronts must be kept in being if peace was to be secured. No opening for peace (so far as Swift knew) had yet appeared. Yet that must be the great aim if both the Whigs and the rebellious Tories were to be thwarted. 'I tell the ministry this as much as I dare,' he wrote; 'and shall venture to say a little more to them, especially about the Duke of Marlborough, who, as the Whigs give out will lay down his command; and I question whether ever any wise state laid aside a general who had been successful nine years together, whom the enemy so much dread; and his own soldiers cannot but believe must always conquer; and you know that in war opinion is nine parts in ten.'

The way these warnings were received prompted his greatest misgivings. Neither Harley nor St. John could conceal his fierce personal hatred of Marlborough. They envied him, admired him, feared him and needed him. The consequence of this galling combination was that their moods and policies towards him changed without discernible provocation. At one moment St. John, at another Harley, was the pacemaker in showering insults upon him. Then by turn each would grudgingly seek to repair the damage. In November and December Harley's agent at The Hague, John Drummond, had pleaded with the new Ministers that the Duke should be appeased. In January he too had become infected by the rancour of the Duke's enemies in London. 'As for the great man,' he wrote, 'deal with him as he deserves. I have nothing more to say for him. I believe his wife may advise him sooner to curse God and die than be reconciled to you. If he let such a wife and such a son-in-law manage him may he fall in the pit they have digged for him.' That surely was a response to some outburst of spleen against the Duke from Harley—an event all the more remarkable since he so rarely permitted himself to express his true feelings in writing. A day or two earlier St. John had been at pains to impress upon Drummond that the Dutch must be reassured, that the armies would be supplied; in short, that Marlborough's strategy would be sustained. Yes, Marlborough was still indispensable, although St. John himself never used the hateful word. He was eager, however, to kill the rumours which had reached Holland of the Duke's triumphal reception in the London streets. 'As to the great man . . .' he told Drummond, 'he was not received with the

acclamations you heard of; and they are much mistaken who imagine that he can be upon any other bottom than what the Queen
pleases to put him. I dare say he is convinced by this time that he
cannot lead either his mistress, or anyone else, as he used to do. We
shall send him over a subject, take care you do not put royalty into
his head again.'

This was the brand of venom which had helped to paint the
first portrait of Marlborough in Swift's mind and which had inspired his *Examiner* No. 17. Harley and St. John were, after all, the
two chief sources from which he formed his opinion. But, for all
the love and admiration which he felt towards them, Swift was not
dazzled by their judgements. Often it has been suggested that he
became nothing more than the obedient servant of Harley and St.
John, reflecting in all he did their political will and their personal
whims. He himself has fostered the half-truth by the boasts of his
intimacy with 'the great men'. But the charge is refuted both by
the doubts which he confessed to Stella and even more by the case
he presented in the *Examiner*. He quickly understood the difference
between routing a defeated enemy and fighting an evenly-contested
battle. By January, 1711, he had recognized that the enemy was
far from defeated. The gibes, the flouts, the invective were all
needed still to rally the Tory squires and enrich the sermons of the
clergy. But gradually he addressed himself—as only supreme controversialists will do—less to the weakness of his opponent's case than
to its strength. He gave a creditable coherence to the Tory argument
at the very moment when week by week he was struggling to
reconcile the erratic, often contradictory advice he received from
his two masters. Harley was contemptuous of his hot-headed
followers who so little understood how the gains of previous
months had been won. Moreover, he had other business to transact
which he concealed from almost all his friends and fellow-Ministers,
including Swift and St. John; on his orders the Abbé Gaultier
was in the first days of January smuggled through the lines to
Paris with instructions to test the chances of starting peace discussions. St. John had immediate interests to absorb him. The Grand
Alliance must be held together while a fresh policy was devised.
The new members of the House of Commons must be assured that
the Ministers were aware of their discontents even if as yet little
could be done to allay them. Swift's task could no longer be limited
to the simple one of celebrating the overthrow of the Whigs,

placating the passions of the October Club, and lambasting the ambition and the avarice of the Captain-General. He appreciated the force of the case made by the Whig journals and soon realized that his treatment of the Duke called for greater discrimination. At moments he was truly nervous; neither Harley nor St. John seemed to recognize to the full how strong was the Tory whirlwind and how easily it might wreck their too casual manœuvres or give to the Whigs the opportunity for which they waited.

The most telling cry of the Whigs was their appeal to the patriotic spirit of the nation. King Louis XIV was the ancient enemy of England, her allies, her traders and her religion. Yet how he must rejoice at the political convulsion which had taken place in London! A pamphlet entitled *The French King's Thanks to the Tories of Great Britain* put the point with ironic emphasis. 'If I should endeavour to recount all the numerous obligations I have to you,' King Louis was imagined to write, 'I should not know where to begin, nor where to make an end. . . . To you and your predecessors I owe the supineness and negligence of the English court, which gave me opportunity and ability to form and prosecute my designs.' In particular, his thanks were due to the Tories for their treatment of Marlborough and their slogans at the election. 'It is with pleasure I have observed, that every victory he hath obtained abroad, hath been retrieved by your management at home. . . . What a figure have your tumults, your addresses, and the progresses of your Doctor, made in my Gazettes? What comfort have I received from them?' King Louis's 'Brother of England'—in other words the Jacobite Pretender—was allegedly no less grateful. The Whig charge was that Harley and his friends were little better than Jacobites themselves or at least that their policies were serving the interests of France.

A smell of treason filled the air. This particular pamphlet had been published before the election and the fact that Swift still felt it necessary to reply in the first week of January shows that it had had some influence. He hotly repudiated the indictment. The French King had 'left off reading my papers, and by what he has found in them, dislikes our proceedings more than ever and intends either to make great additions to his armies, or propose new terms of peace: so false is that which is commonly reported, of his mighty satisfaction in our change of ministry'. And how dare the Whigs prate of their patriotism! The Ministerial change had been decreed

by the Queen and the Whig refusal to approve it amounted to a
barefaced aspersion upon her. Equally beside the mark were their
glorification of the General and the army, and their pretence that
the *Examiner*'s criticisms of them amounted to a betrayal of the
national cause. So far was the *Examiner* from wishing to deny due
praise to the victorious troops that 'I could wish every officer and
private soldier had their full share of honour in proportion to their
deserts; being thus far of the Athenians' mind, who, when it was
proposed that the statue of Miltiades should be set up alone in
some public place of the city, said they would agree to it, whenever
he conquered alone, but not before'. All that the *Examiner* had
claimed was that the army and particularly the General must be
kept in a subordinate status; 'otherwise, one of these two incon-
veniences must arise, either to be perpetually in war, or to turn the
civil institution into a military.' The talk of serving the interests of
the French or the Pretender was nothing more than a scare. It had
been used to swell the military power until it threatened to enslave
the Queen and overturn the constitution. 'Instead of aiming at
peace, while we had the advantage of the war, which has been the
perpetual maxim of all wise states, it has been reckoned facetious
and malignant even to express our wishes for it.'

By these assertions, in the early weeks of January, Swift rebutted
the charge that his friends were lacking in patriotism. But his
general tone had noticeably altered. Some credence was being
given to the rumours that the new Ministry could not last. Perhaps
the presence of the Duke in their midst helped to revive the droop-
ing spirits of the Whigs. Swift branded them *the ruined party* and
resorted to ridicule. 'Some of these gentlemen', he wrote, referring
to the rumour-mongers, 'are employed to shake their heads in
proper companies; to doubt where all this will end; to be in
mighty pain for the nation; to shew how impossible it is, that the
public credit can be supported: to pray that all may do well in
whatever hands; but very much to doubt that the Pretender is at
the bottom. I know not anything so nearly resembling this behaviour, as what I have often seen among the friends of a sick man,
whose interest it is that he should die: The Physicians protest they
see no danger; the symptoms are good, the medicines answer ex-
pectation; yet still they are not to be comforted; they whisper, he
is a gone man; it is not possible he should hold out; he has perfect
death in his face; they never liked this doctor: At last the patient

recovers, and their joy is as false as their grief.' Swift in the *Examiner* derided the new hopes of the Whigs as readily as he answered their arguments. But his hints to Stella revealed how fitful was his own confidence.

What would he have written if he had known the truth! In the same week when he made sport with the charge that Harley and St. John were in league with the Pretender, the Abbé Gaultier arrived at Versailles and straightway had an interview with the Marquis of Torcy, King Louis's Secretary of State. During his long sojourn in England Gaultier had been instructed to conduct himself with the utmost discretion lest he might be considered a spy. He performed his religious duties in the household of the Austrian Ambassador with such impeccable piety that, when he arrived in Paris, Torcy was undecided how much faith could be reposed in his own agent. 'Do you chuse peace?' asked Gaultier. 'I am come to enable you to conclude it independently of the Dutch, a people unworthy of the King's favour, and of the honour he has so often done them, of applying to them, for the pacification of Europe.' Torcy already knew something of the mind of the new Ministry in London, but he was still staggered by the good fortune which had befallen his country. 'To ask his majesty's minister at that time whether he chused to have peace', he wrote, 'was the same thing as to ask a person lingering under a dangerous malady, whether he chused to recover. Yet as there are multitudes of quacks of all sorts, it was prudent not to be over-sanguine, but to know the purpose of the Abbé Gaultier's mission and by what means he intended to proceed.'

Gaultier was instructed to return with an encouraging reply, but not before he had been granted an interview with the Duke of Berwick, Marlborough's nephew who served at the Court of St. Germain's. Gaultier 'told me', wrote Berwick, 'that he had orders to speak to me about the Pretender's affairs, and to concert with me the means of restoring him'. An introduction to the Pretender himself was therefore arranged. 'These preliminaries being settled,' continues Berwick, 'we consulted upon the means of executing the business: but the Abbé could not, at this time, enter into any great detail, inasmuch as [Harley] had not yet fully explained his intentions to him; and it was necessary that the peace should previously be concluded, without which, the present ministry could not venture to open a matter which required so much nicety to manage. Though it appeared to me, that one of these points was no hindrance to the other, yet, in order to shew that we would omit nothing, and to give proofs of our sincerity, we wrote to all the Jacobites to join with the court. This contributed greatly to make the Queen's party so superior in the House of Commons, that everything was carried there according to their wishes.'

It is not recorded how speedily these curious instructions from England's enemies to English and Scottish Members of Parliament were dispatched or what precise results they achieved. Berwick was probably deceived about the Jacobite strength in the Commons just as Gaultier may have exaggerated the firmness of the offer he was entitled to make on behalf of Harley. Harley in turn may have argued to himself that a prospect conveyed to the Pretender through the media of Lord Jersey and the Abbé Gaultier could easily be repudiated once it had served its purpose of helping smooth the path towards peace. The web he was weaving had become splendidly intricate. In the very week when he received Gaultier's report he must have read and admired the scorn heaped by Swift on those who charged him with Jacobite sympathies. And Swift, the bosom companion of Harley, drunk and sober, night after night, went to his grave believing that Harley had never soiled his hands in an intrigue with the Pretender.

Even without Gaultier's assistance, the Marquis of Torcy was probably as well informed about the affairs of the English court as most people in London. Ever since the change of Ministry he, like so many others, had been fascinated by the position of the Duke of Marlborough. He understood Harley's dilemma better almost than Harley understood it himself. 'To continue that general in command of the army', he wrote, 'was a point of dangerous consequence; but it was difficult to dismiss him; his reputation was too well established, and he had not been charged as yet with any capital fault. No other general in England possessed the same abilities, nor would have been so much trusted by the allies. The new ministers limited his authority: this was an instance of their ill-will towards the general, which convinced him that he was feared, and at the same time that they could not do without him. He was provoked at the treatment shown to his wife, to his relations, and friends, and at seeing his enemies chosen to fill up their places. He was further provoked by their abridging him of part of that power which he had exercised the precedent years; *but he still had enough to be revenged.*' That last thought had occurred to many others, including Marlborough himself. Torcy added the further judgement: 'The only way to reduce him to the rank of a private subject, was to conclude a peace.' However harsh the judgement on Harley, it is hard to believe that the hope of removing Marlborough was his primary incentive for seeking peace. None the less Torcy had analysed correctly the new emphasis now given to the old, perpetual dilemma about the future of the Duke. Could all the complicated processes required to make a peace treaty be set in motion before Marlborough exerted his remaining powers to secure revenge? Harley had doubts, and one of his anxieties, expressed through Gaultier to Torcy, was that any peace parleys should not take place in England for fear of the patriotic opposition which Marlborough and the Whigs might still be able to excite.

The Duke himself continued to display an inhuman self-restraint. Within a few days of his return to London he had to face what was by inference and innuendo at least a challenge to his whole strategy and reputation. The place chosen for the attack was the House of Lords where previously—with the single exception of the slight inflicted upon him just after the election—his victories had been most fulsomely celebrated and where the Whig power had seemed most firmly established. Temporarily at least the knowledge of the way the wind was blowing at the court had given the Tories a majority. But there, if anywhere, the initial signs of Whig recovery must be looked for. Much might depend on the manner in which the Duke comported himself. He had to keep together his friends without provoking his enemies. Following a request from the Queen—doubtless inspired by Harley and St. John—the Lords had decided to stage a grand inquest into the defeat in Spain, news of which had reached London at Christmastime. Such an investigation suited the Tories perfectly. Not only was Stanhope—the General who had been defeated and captured —a prominent Whig. More important, it had always been part of the Tory case that the Spanish theatre had been starved of troops and supplies to feed the inordinate demands of Marlborough in Flanders. Moreover, two and three years before, victories had been gained in Spain under the dashing leadership of Lord Peterborough whom the Tories had long been cultivating as a rival to Marlborough for military honours. He had been abruptly called home on the instructions of Marlborough's son-in-law, Sunderland. His command was taken over by the Huguenot General, the Earl of Galway, a comrade-in-arms of King William, who could scarcely speak English and who, like Stanhope, had suffered misfortune or betrayed Whiggish incompetence in the field. No element was lacking for the import of prejudice, and the fact that the inquiry was directed to the details of the two-year-old campaign rather than the immediate military crisis was a proof that votes in the House of Lords were the real stake in the argument.

The Earl of Galway, with the evidence of his wounds still upon him, was brought to the bar of the Lords where he begged leave on account of his poor English to put his case in writing. One of his fellow-Generals, also arraigned by the Lords, made his point more impertinently. He complained that 'when he was in the Army, he kept no Register; and carry'd neither Pen nor Ink about him, but only a Sword, which he used the best he could upon Occasion'. Marlborough could not sit silent at such a scene. After some of the Whig Lords had come to the defence of Galway, he spoke 'with the utmost concern, and even tears in his eyes'. It was 'somewhat strange', he said, 'that Generals, who had acted to the best of their Understandings, and had lost their limbs in the Service, should be examined like Offenders, about insignificant Things: And he could not imagine the Meaning of such Proceedings, nor where they would stop'. Such pleas could not halt the Tory search for scapegoats. The Queen herself listened to the debates; no sign of displeasure was forthcoming when some of her most faithful soldiers were mercilessly pilloried. One observer marvelled at the change in the political complexion of the House of Lords. 'The Tories', he said, 'have such a majority (there) . . . that they carry what they please, much to the surprise of the late Ministers and their friends, who thought themselves sure of majority of 14 at least which was the number the Tories carried their first question.' The majority was sufficient to carry all the other questions. Marlborough made a clear-cut defence both of his own conduct and of those who had acted in Spain in conformity with his advice. 'My lords,' he said, 'my intentions were always honest and sincere, to contribute all that lay in my power, to bring this heavy and expensive war to an end. God Almighty has blessed my endeavours with success; but if men are to be censured when they give their opinions to the best of their understandings, I must expect to be found fault with as well as the rest.'

The Duke's readiness to throw his own reputation into the scales availed nothing. By a comfortable majority of ten or a dozen what amounted to a vote of censure on the previous administration was passed. Galway himself was censured with only thirty-six of the great Whig peers daring to enter a protest. Peterborough was acclaimed for his matchless services to the nation, and a touch of malice—aimed directly at Marlborough—was added when praise was given to the manner in which Peterborough accepted public thanks 'unalloyed by any other reward'. And yet something had been gained by Marlborough's demeanour. Compared with the triumphs of a year before, the scene for him must have been deeply humiliating. But, recalling the atmosphere just after the election or even when the Lords' debate opened, the Duke could fairly claim that he had achieved a worthwhile shift of the mood in his favour. As the debate proceeded the temperature cooled. Some of his suggestions on procedure were adopted, however ungraciously. At the conclusion of the whole affair the hopes or fears that Marlborough would resign had abated. 'I believe', wrote the same observer who had gloatingly described some of his most painful moments during the debate, 'the Ministry is willing to make the Duke easie as to his command in the Army, if he does not insist (!) to advise who shall be employed here at home.' It was not, however, the magnanimity of the Ministers which had decided the matter. Both the Ministers and Marlborough had a solid interest in ensuring that he stayed at his post. His difficulty was to retain the office without forfeiting his dignity, and in the Lords' debate he overcame it superbly.

A similar achievement was impossible in the other business he had to transact towards the end of January. The moment he had dreaded between Sarah and the Queen had come. Even before his return home he had been weighed down by forebodings, but the manner in which they were fulfilled made the ordeal all the worse. A rumour reached him that Anne was willing to relent. When Marlborough's concern about her attitude to the Duchess was represented to her she was said to have shown 'great tenderness'. He had at once sought an audience, taking with him a letter from Sarah. While he was abroad Sarah had been irked by his willingness to continue in the service of the Tory Ministry. But all her doubts had now been dissipated. Nothing must be allowed to stand in his way. His health was near breaking-point; his political schemes required that he should retain his command. Sarah's mind was at one with his. In such a mood and playing for such considerable stakes she could achieve the incredible feat of an act of humility. Her pride was sacrificed in the effort to make the letter to the Queen a successful gesture of reconciliation. 'Though I never thought of troubling your Majesty in this manner again,' she wrote, 'yet the circumstances I see my Lord Marlborough in, and the apprehension I have that he cannot live six months, if there is not some end put to his suffering on my account, makes it impossible for me to resist doing everything in my power to ease him . . .' Sarah apologized for her past misdemeanours; she made pledges for the future. Never again would she plague the Queen with her hectoring importunities. The Duke added his own entreaties. His sole request was that the Duchess should retain the gold key of her office as Groom of the Stole until the war was over and both he and the Duchess could retire together honourably from the Queen's service. But the Queen was adamant. A Stuart monarch could not conceive the idea of tolerance, much less forgiveness—no, not even towards one who had served her so brilliantly. Marlborough pleaded on his knees. But the royal demand became more peremptory than ever. The gold key must be restored to her within two days and until that was done she would discuss no other business with her Captain-General. A few hours later he was picking up the gold key from the floor where Sarah had flung it in disgust.

A reference to this pitiable scene appears in St. John's correspondence with John Drummond at The Hague. It reveals how bitter was the animosity felt by St. John towards the Duke and the Duchess and how formidable, by the same token, was Marlborough's authority. How gratifying it would have been to see the Queen treat Marlborough with the same contumely she showed towards Sarah and how readily she might have been brought to the deed since she risked so much with Marlborough to work her will on the Duchess! But neither St. John nor Harley dared to make the challenge to Marlborough decisive. 'As to the great man,' wrote St. John, 'he acts, in my opinion, a little and an ill-judged part: I should be tedious if I descended to particulars.' Then came the assurance that 'the Queen and those who are in her entire confidence, are desirous to please our friends in Holland'. So Marlborough would be continued at the head of the army and supplied with all his needs. But the tedious particulars could not be held back: 'He was told, that his true interest consisted in getting rid of his wife, who was grown to be irreconcilable with the Queen, as soon as he could, and with the best grace he could. Instead of this, he teazed the Queen, and made the utmost effort to keep this woman in her places ... however, he now pretends to make a merit of this resignation. He has been told that he must draw a line between all that is past, and all that is to come, and that he must begin entirely upon a new foot; that if he looked back to make complaints, he would have more retorted on him than it was possible to answer; that, if he would make his former conduct the rule of his future behaviour, he would render his interests incompatible with those of the Queen. What is the effect of all this plain dealing?—he submits, he yields, he promises to comply, but he struggles to alleviate Meredyth's disgrace and to make the Queen a less figure by going back, than she could have done by taking no notice at all of the insolence of him and his comrades.' St. John was not convinced that Marlborough's signs of complaisance marked a real conversion. 'The exterior is a little mended; but at heart the same sentiments remain, and these are heightened and enflamed by what he called provocations.' In other words, St. John, like Torcy, believed that Marlborough might be capable of revenge. 'We shall do what we can to support him in the command of the army, without betraying our mistress; and unless he is infatuated, he will help us in our design; for you must know, that the moment he leaves the service, and loses the protection of the court, such scenes will open as no victories can varnish over.' This last sentence was evidence that St. John, and perhaps Harley too, had contemplated what action would be necessary if the Duke did resign or was dismissed. An impeachment on the grandest scale would be needed to be set in train! St. John's political temperament, no less than his personal tastes, urged him towards an open collision with the Duke. But he was condemned to practise a disgruntled patience. It was impossible to live without Marlborough but how long would they be allowed to live with him? The task was made no easier by the armour-plated composure with which Marlborough brushed aside all insults and provocations, including even the debasement of his own wife, who a few years before had been the most powerful woman in Europe.

Swift must have been among those who were impressed by Marlborough's performance at this critical hour. No longer was knowledge of his chosen opponent confined to the second-hand reports he received from Harley and St. John. He had lived in the same London at the moment when Marlborough was reasserting his sway; he had heard the accounts of the Lords' debates; he was able to measure his man more accurately. His next attack was more skilfully delivered than the first shot he had fired in November. Even Marlborough's friends found it difficult to deny the charge of avarice so frequently made against him. The Whig journals treated the topic guardedly, while every Tory scribbler shrieked his denunciations of the miser. Swift saw how the exposure of this vice could be exploited to present the whole Ministerial case for curtailing Marlborough's power without stripping him of it completely. His *Examiner*, published on February 8th, kept the balance superbly:

'To MARCUS CRASSUS, Health:

' If you apply as you ought, what I now write, you will be more obliged to me than to all the World, hardly excepting your Parents, or your Country. I intend to tell you, without Disguise or Prejudice, the Opinions which the World hath entertained of you. And, to let you see I write this without any Sort of ill Will, you shall first hear the Sentiments they have to your Advantage. No Man disputes the Gracefulness of your Person; you are allowed to have a good and clear Understanding, cultivated by the Knowledge of Men and Manners, although not by *Literature*. You are no ill Orator in the Senate; you are said to excel in the Art of bridling and subduing your Anger, and stifling or concealing your Resentments. You have been a most successful General, of long Experience, great Conduct, and much Personal Courage; you have gained many important Victories for the Commonwealth, and forced the strongest Towns in *Mesopotamia* to surrender; for which, frequent *Supplications* have been decreed by the Senate. Yet with all these Qualities, and this Merit, give me Leave to say, you are neither beloved by the *Patricians* or *Plebeians* at home, nor by the Officers or private Soldiers of your own Army abroad. And, do you know, CRASSUS, that this is owing to a Fault, of which you may cure yourself by one Minute's Reflection? What shall I say? You are the richest Person in the Commonwealth; you have no Male Child, your Daughters are all married to wealthy *Patricians*; you are far in the Decline of Life; and yet you are deeply stained with that odious and ignoble Vice of *Covetousness*. 'Tis affirmed, that you descend even to the meanest and most scandalous Degrees of it; and while you possess so many Millions; while you are acquiring so many more, you are sollicitous how to save a single *Sesterce*, of which a hundred ignominious Instances are produced, and in all Mens Mouths. I will only mention that Passage of the *Buskins*, which after abundance of Persuasion, you would hardly suffer to be cut from your Legs, when they were so wet and cold, that to have kept them on, would have endangered your Life.

'Instead of using the common Arguments to dissuade you from this Weakness, I will endeavour to convince you, that you are really guilty of it; and leave the Cure to your own good Sense. For, perhaps, you are not yet persuaded that this is your Crime; you have probably never yet been reproached for it to your Face; and what you are now told, comes from one unknown, and it may be, from an Enemy. You will allow your self indeed to be prudent in the Management of your Fortune; you are not a Prodigal, like *Clodius* or *Catiline*, but surely that deserves not the Name of *Avarice*. I will inform you how to be convinced. Disguise your Person; go among the common People in *Rome*; introduce Discourses about your self; inquire your own Character; do the same in your Camp, walk about it in the Evening, hearken at every Tent; and, if you do not hear every Mouth Censuring, Lamenting, Cursing this Vice in you, and even you for this Vice, conclude your self innocent. If you be not yet persuaded, send for *Atticus, Servius Sulpicius, Cato,* or *Brutus*; they are all your Friends; conjure them to tell you ingenuously which is your great Fault, and which they would chiefly wish you to correct; if they do not all agree in their Verdict, *in the Name of all the Gods*, you are acquitted.

'When your Adversaries reflect how far you are gone in this Vice, they are tempted to talk as if we owed our Success, not to your Courage or Conduct, but to those *Veteran* Troops you command; who are able to conquer under any *General*, with so many brave and experienced Officers to lead them. Besides, we know the Consequences your Avarice hath often occasioned. The Soldier hath been starving for Bread, surrounded with Plenty, and in an Enemies Country, but all under *Safeguards* and *Contributions*; which, if you had sometimes pleased to exchange for *Provisions*, might at the Expence of a few *Talents* in a Campaign, have so endeared you to the Army, that they would have desired you to lead them to the utmost Limits of *Asia*. But you rather chose to confine your Conquests within the fruitful country of *Mesopotamia*, where Plenty of Money might be raised. How far that fatal Greediness of Gold may have influenced you, in breaking off the Treaty with the old *Parthian* King *Orodes*, you best can tell; your Enemies charge you with it; your Friends offer nothing material in your Defence; and all agree, there is nothing so pernicious, which the Extremes of Avarice may not be able to inspire.

'The Moment you quit this Vice, you will be a truly Great Man; and still there will Imperfections enough remain to convince us, you are not a *God.* Farewell.'

The alteration in the emphasis of the *Examiner's* campaign against the Duke did not pass unnoticed. A few days later Swift was talking to Lord Rivers. No one outside the innermost circle knew the real author; so Lord Rivers felt free to expatiate to Swift on the crime committed by the *Examiner* in 'speaking civilly of the Duke of Marlborough'. The tribute to his generalship, coupled no doubt with growing suspicion that the Ministry had resolved not to risk his dismissal, was too much for the Tories to swallow, and Lord Rivers was that most aggressive of Tories, a Whig convert. The Whig journal, the *Medley,* naturally made play with this change of tune. The *Examiner* 'appears, by his last Paper,' it wrote, 'to be in so desperate a Condition, that all his Friends should in good earnest look after him, lest, like the Weasel in the Fable, whilst he endeavours to bite the Tile, he should happen to cut his own Tongue. Such is the common Fate of all impudent Dealers in Calumny, who are justly exposed in that Emblem. But of all that ever made it their Business to defame, there never was such a Bungler sure as my Friend. He writes a letter now to Crassus, as a man mark'd out for Destruction, because that hint was given him six Months ago; and does not seem to know yet that he is still employ'd, and that in attacking him, he affronts the Q—n, and differs with his own Majority of Nine Parts in Ten of the Kingdom, who all desire the service of the General. Such an incorrigible person is this Examiner . . .'

Swift knew that the charge of inconsistency had some basis. Having launched their attack on the Duke, he and his friends had drawn back, partly perhaps on Swift's persuasion. When he reported Lord Rivers's conversation to St. John, the Minister cursed the hotheads for their recklessness. Swift himself replied to the *Medley*'s attack with unaccustomed mildness. 'Nobody that I know of', he wrote, 'did ever dispute the Duke of Marlborough's courage, conduct or success. They have always been unquestionable, and will continue to be so, in spite of the malice of his enemies or, which is yet more, the *weakness of his advocates.* The nation only wished to see him taken out of ill-hands, and put into better.' Thereupon the *Examiner* made a vow 'to banish controversy as much as possible . . . I am worried on one side by the

Whigs for being too severe and by the Tories on the other for being too gentle'.

Swift's independence was, of course, a reflection of the dilemmas facing the Ministers. But partly, too, it was assisted by a growing awareness of how much his services were valued. A bare three months had passed since his first meeting with Harley and St. John, but he left them in no doubt that he must be treated as an equal. Harley made the mistake of sending him a bank bill for £50 as an acknowledgement of the *Examiners*. Swift returned it with contempt and took the most elaborate steps to show how deep was his displeasure. 'If we let these great ministers pretend too much,' he told Stella, 'there will be no governing them.' The great ministers never had the nerve to make the same error again. Instead, having overflowed with their apologies, they called him Jonathan with an ever more caressing familiarity and invited him to their most intimate dinners every Saturday night. A few days later (or at least this was his boast to Stella) Swift sent Mr. Harley into the House of Commons to inform Mr. St. John that he would not be able to dine that night if St. John intended to dine too late. The Vicar of Laracor had certainly arrived! It is ironic to remember that Swift shared Marlborough's love of money. But how much stronger was his character in resisting its temptations! One motive, if not the major one, in determining Marlborough's attitude was his desire to keep his income of £60,000 a year and see Blenheim Palace finished at the expense of the State. One reason why the author of the *Letter to Crassus* was so formidable was that he sent back Harley's £50 and extorted in return a priceless addition of respect and influence.

The prophecy that February would prove a warm month showed every sign of being fulfilled. While the House of Lords was conducting its inquest into the Spanish campaign and while the Ministers reconciled themselves to the continuation of Marlborough's command, the Tory majority in the House of Commons forced through a whole series of measures either with or without the connivance of Harley and St. John. They repealed the Naturalization Act whereby the Whigs had agreed to permit thousands of Protestant refugees to enter the country. They passed a Bill to resume the royal grants bestowed by William III on friends of the Revolution. They instituted charges for peculation against the former Whig Minister, Robert Walpole. The Whig Bishop,

Burnet, bewailed the passage of another measure 'not much to the honour of those who promoted it for the importation of French wine'. His objection, needless to say, was based on grounds of patriotism rather than temperance. 'The interest of the nation lay against this so visibly, that nothing but the delicate palates of those who loved that liquor could have carried such a motion through the two houses.' More significant was the attempt to revive an old Tory favourite—the Place Bill—designed to limit the offices under the Crown which could be held by members of Parliament. Several of these measures were successfully opposed by the Whigs in the House of Lords; but the Tory members knew—as had been proved in the debates about Spain—that the court and the Ministers commanded a majority in the Lords if they chose to exert it. The suspicion grew that the Ministers were lukewarm in their Tory faith. St. John realized better than Harley the need to satisfy these clamours. He proposed, instead of the Place Bill, a Landed Property Qualification Bill which made the possession of specified acres of land a qualification for sitting in the Commons. His excuse was 'that we might see a time when the moneyed men might bid fair to keep out of that house all the landed men, and he had heard of Societies of them that jointed Stocks to bring in members'. But the Tories needed no excuse. The Bill was rushed through both houses, the Whigs fearing that it might cost them two hundred seats. In fact, the measure—not repealed until the reign of Queen Victoria—proved ineffective in practice. But the aim was clear; this was just one item in the Tory plan to smash the Whigs for ever. Its main immediate result was to improve the standing of St. John with the high-flying Tories and encourage him in the belief that he could 'set up to govern the House'. But even he was still frowned upon by many as a moderate.

'The party of the October Club is dominant in the Lower House.' That was Marlborough's view and, if it was correct, the most sinister implication followed. One observer dismissed members of the Club as 'self-contradictory, moonblind High-Flyers" comparing them with 'the tinker of Exeter who comforted himself on being hung in the reflection that he had made some noise in the world'. But Marlborough believed that most of the Octobrists were Jacobites. 'This party of the Prince of Wales is very strong. No one dares speak openly for him. That would be treason. But we who know the ground know also the intentions and motives which

Jonathan Swift:

'He was an *honest man* I'll swear –
Why Sir, I differ from you there,
For, I have heard another Story.
He was a most *confounded Tory*.'

The Duke of Marlborough:

'the greatest subject in Christendom'

The Duchess of Marlborough:

'three furies reigned within her breast'

Thomas,
Earl of Wharton:

'the most universal villain
I ever knew'

Stella,
Esther Johnson:

agreeable bitch'

Daniel Defoe:

'a stupid, illiterate scribbler'

Henry St John, Viscount Bolingbroke:

'you were my hero'

Robert Harley, Earl of Oxford:

'A person of as much virtue as can possibly consist with
the Love of Power.'

The Duke of Somerset:

'Not a grain (of Judgement); hardly commonsense.'

The Duchess of Somerset:

'rom her red Locks her
Mouth with Venom fills'

Queen Anne:

'a Royal Prude'

cause the different manœuvres we see now in England.' Such at least was the warning he gave to the envoy of the Elector of Hanover. Something may be allowed for his eagerness to win favour in that quarter. But many others concurred in his verdict. Every week in the new year the members of the October Club seemed to grow in numbers and ambition. Except for St. John, none of the Ministers showed the capacity to lead instead of being pushed. 'No one takes the direction and all drifts at hazard,' said Marlborough. And no one could foretell how daring the October Club might become and how far-reaching were its final aims.

Immediately, the issue of the Pretender was not the stake. First, the Whigs must be made impotent. It was this objective which gave the October Club its strength; for, in wishing to root out the remnants of Whig power, Jacobites and non-Jacobites in the Tory ranks could unite. 'In the House of Commons', wrote Bishop Burnet, 'there appeared a new combination of Tories of the highest form, who thought the court was yet in some management with the Whigs, and did not come up to their height, which they imputed to Mr. Harley; so they began to form themselves in opposition to him, and expressed their jealousy of him on several occasions, sometimes publicly.' Among the most notable of the Tories who wished to concentrate on this limited objective was the Earl of Nottingham. Ever since the Revolution he had regarded himself as the arch-champion of the Church, the keeper of the Tory conscience. No one could dismiss him as an over-enthusiastic upstart, with his head turned by October ale. He was diligent and determined. 'He hath also', admitted his enemies, 'the exterior Air of Business and Application enough to make him very capable. In his Habit and Manners very formal, a tall, thin, very black man, like a Spaniard or a Jew.' He was eloquent, learned, and richly respected for his integrity among the Tories. When such a leader delivered his grave judgements tremendous force was added to the slogans of the October Club. Harley had denied him the office to which he felt entitled. So, like Marlborough, if for very different reasons, Nottingham watched the drift of the new administration with lugubrious disdain. He agreed to meet five or six of the chief Ministers, Harley and St. John included, 'where he desired to know what we designed to do, for as yet, he said, we had done nothing'. Lord Dartmouth protested that 'the dissolving of the parliament and the turning out all the Whig Ministers' was surely 'something'. But Nottingham protested 'that was nothing, if we did not make it impracticable for them ever to rise again'. If the Whig Ministers were not prosecuted it would be assumed that the new Ministers were protecting them. The interview broke up with no rapprochement achieved. Harley's mildness had made another enemy.

Swift was now seriously alarmed. He could understand exactly the need for an accommodation with Marlborough. But could not the adoption of one policy so distasteful to the Tories be combined with an attempt to satisfy some other of their demands? Why were any Whigs at all retained in the Queen's service? For example, the Duke of Somerset kept his place at the court, despite the burst of ill-temper he had shown towards Harley at the time of the dissolution, and despite his ostentatious exertions on behalf of Whig candidates at the election. The Tories, said Swift, 'could not believe Mr. Harley was in earnest; but that he designed to constitute a motley comprehensive administration, which, they said, the Kingdom would never endure'. Several of the leading Tories approached Swift in the hope that he in turn could shake Harley from his sloth. Harley's explanations left Swift more mystified than ever. Instead of advancing powerful reasons of state for the risks he ran in defying so large a body of his followers, he took refuge in 'the general reasons of politicians'. He talked of 'the necessity of keeping men in hopes, the danger of disobliging those who must remain unprovided for, and the like usual topics among statesmen'. Swift was unconvinced. He did not then know that a stronger reason than anything attributable solely to Harley's natural disposition restrained him from acting too boldly. A subtle change had taken place in the attitude of the Queen. Her obstinacy had not been exhausted in her dealings with the Marlboroughs. Harley, too, was given a taste of her will-power and within the next week or two he began to discover the reason. Mrs. Masham's influence with the Queen was still strong; but it was weakening. The Duchess of Somerset had been appointed to succeed the Duchess of Marlborough as Groom of the Stole. 'She had more personal credit than all the Queen's servants put together. . . . As soon as she was fixed in her station, the Queen, following the course of her own nature, grew daily more difficult and uncomplying.'

As if Harley's embarrassments were not complicated enough already, a new one was gratuitously added. St. John was chafing under the restraint imposed by Harley's temperament and the tiresome claim that the opinions of men like the Duke of Somerset must still be respected. St. John sensed the spirit of the House of Commons. Harley, he feared, would let opportunity slip through his fingers. He himself, on the other hand, was bursting with energy. He longed to master events instead of waiting upon them. As yet he did not know of the approaches to the French court which Harley had initiated. He had been forced to acknowledge the wisdom of coming to terms with Marlborough. Therefore he looked for drama elsewhere. For some time he had played with the idea of an expedition to Quebec and an attack on French Canada. The Tories had always advocated a maritime war as a much less costly enterprise than the endless land fighting in Flanders. If the conquest could be achieved the glory would be St. John's or at least he might share it with Colonel Hill, the brother of Mrs. Masham, whom he proposed to place in charge of the troops. 'Honest Jack Hill' had no claims to military distinction, having owed his earlier promotion a few months before to Abigail's influence with the Queen and the fully justified belief of her Ministers that his advancement would enrage the Duke. But St. John saw his chance of increasing his favour with Abigail and, therefore, with the Queen. Early in the new year he started pressing for a decision about his Quebec scheme. Harley was deeply suspicious. He opposed the project on military grounds, wondered what intrigue was being conducted behind his back and had reason to suspect that part of St. John's motive was to recoup his own personal fortune from the pickings to be drawn from the management of the army contracts. The breach which had opened between them was still hidden from Swift. Indeed, the one thought which gave him comfort during those February days of mounting tension was that 'I see them (the Ministers) so perfectly easy and I believe they could not be so if they had any fear in their heart'. Obviously he was deceived. St. John's ardent nature was excited by the new horizons beckoning him forward. Harley carried the cares of state lightly and would never allow his load of intrigues to spoil his pleasures. The strange fact about this triumvirate which met every Saturday night to discuss the nation's policy was that the Vicar of Laracor had a real claim to be the most serious politician of the three.

The best service he could do was to soften or divert the rising anger of the October Club. Something could still be achieved by ridiculing the Whigs. He mocked the zeal of their journals in celebrating the accomplished administration and financial probity of the previous Ministry, taking leave to doubt whether the men concerned would really be grateful for the notice directed towards their least evident qualities. He recalled the story of 'a gentleman who fought another for calling him son of a whore; but the lady desired her son to make no more quarrels upon that subject *because it was true*'. Swift had much sympathy with the demand for a more aggressive attack on the Whigs, but in the *Examiner* during February he often turned aside from the congenial sport of Whig-baiting to tackle a much more difficult problem. 'I well know', he wrote, 'with how tender a hand this should be touched; yet at the same time I think it my duty to warn the friends as well as expose the enemies of the public weal.' Two months earlier to have written in such terms would have been unthinkable. But now the danger was that the great Tory majority might destroy itself if the October Club moved too fast or the Ministers too slowly. 'Those who wish well to the public', he wrote in the *Examiner* of February 22nd, 'and would gladly contribute to its service are apt to differ in their opinions about the methods of promoting it, and when their party flourishes, are sometimes envious at those in power, ready to overvalue their own merit and be impatient till it is rewarded by the measure they have prescribed for themselves. There is a further topic of contention, which a ruling power is apt to fall into, in relation to retrospections and enquiry into past miscarriages; wherein some are thought too warm and zealous; others too cool and remiss; while in the meantime these divisions are industriously fomented by the discarded faction.'

That such a warning should have been made in the *Examiner* was startling enough; for the *Examiner* was accepted as the voice of the Government. Every other witness testifies that Swift's fears were well founded. The October Club men did not hesitate to speak openly of their intentions. Come what may, they would execute a thorough purge of the Whigs. An attempt was made to curb their impetuosity by dispatching some of the older members of the Tory party to the Club meetings. They 'send the old Fellows among them, but damn they won't be bit so'. Neither 'weadles or threats' availed. The only conceivable threat, it seemed, was another dissolution. But the 'young men of estates' were sure it would never be executed. They believed they knew better than Harley the mood of their followers in the country; a new election would merely mean that they would all be re-elected. Marlborough was well aware how distasteful this extremism must be to Harley himself, but he had no confidence that he could withstand the pressure. 'The Tory Party (or rather the Octobrists) is so strong in the Lower House', said the Duke, 'that it is to be feared that Harley, who will always sacrifice everything to his ambition and private interests, will be obliged, if he is to keep his place, to devote himself to them, and to embrace all their schemes; and then the Prince of Wales business might move so quickly that there would no longer be any remedy.' It was a good guess; Marlborough, of course, knew nothing of the Abbé Gaultier's mission to Paris and his talks with the Pretender.

Yet, despite his serious estimate of the strength of the October Club and of Harley's weakness in the face of it, the Duke was not despondent. At the end of February he returned to Holland with a special message from the Queen commending him to the States-General and a firm guarantee that his troops would be supplied. Even St. John claimed in a letter to John Drummond: 'I flatter myself that his Grace will own that I have acted a fair and friendly part with respect to him.' In other words, Marlborough had every reason to expect that his authority was safe for another campaign. He talked freely to the envoy of the Elector of Hanover and vowed his loyalty in seeking to protect the succession. The hour for retaliation was not yet. He was opposed to 'miserable palliatives' for dealing with the situation. 'We must have a cure', he says, 'which goes to the source of the evil, and which must be applied when the real moment comes.' St. John was deluded if he imagined for a moment that Marlborough's meekness was a sign of surrender to the Tories; Torcy had interpreted the Captain-General's mind more discerningly. Meantime, the Whigs and the Whig journals in London were recovering from the collapse of their influence in the previous autumn. All was not lost. Their leader, Lord Somers, was known to have had some agreeable interviews with the Queen. Harley, for all his financial skill, was still in difficulties with the City. Even the *Examiner* was showing signs of nerves. And the improved spirits among the Whigs would have been still more lively if they had known that Harley and St. John were at loggerheads, that Nottingham had come near to despairing of both, and that the Duchess of Somerset was, from the Whig point of view, not the useless sycophant that Sarah in her pique tried to make her friends believe.

Harley was in real danger. The Queen, the Duke, the Earl of Nottingham, the Duchess of Somerset, St. John, the Whigs, the October Club—with all of these critical figures on the political stage the relations of the Queen's first Minister were strained or rapidly deteriorating. Two of his closest friends saw the situation in strikingly similar and darkening colours. John Drummond at The Hague wrote to him on February 28th: 'I have complaints of you from the Tory side, who I fear want to drive things too suddenly and to extremities. I hope you will agree amongst yourselves and then nothing can hurt you, if otherwise, everything will; and a watchful diligent enemy will make good use of your divisions for their advantage.' Swift wrote to Stella on the night of March 4th. His alarm was now unmistakable and unqualified. 'This Kingdom', he said, 'is certainly ruined as much as was ever any bankrupt merchant. We must have *Peace*, let it be a bad one or a good one, though nobody dares talk of it. The nearer I look upon things, the worse I like them. I believe the confederacy will soon break to pieces; and our factions at home increase. The ministry is upon a very narrow bottom, and stands like an Isthmus between the Whigs on the one side, and violent Tories on the other. They are able seamen, but the tempest is too great, the ship too rotten, and the crew all against them. Lord Somers has been twice in the queen's closet, once very lately; and your duchess of Somerset, who now has the key, is a most insinuating woman, and I believe they will endeavour to play the same game that has been played against them.—I have told them of all this, which they know already, but they cannot help it. They have cautioned the queen so much against being governed, that she observes it too much. I could talk till tomorrow upon these things, but they make me melancholy. I could not but observe that lately, after much conversation with Mr. Harley, though he is the most fearless man alive, and the least apt to despond, he confessed to me, that uttering his mind to me gave him ease.'

Matters had indeed reached a serious pass when the secretive, equable Harley needed a confessor for his fears.

CHAPTER NINE

The Rivals

(March 8th—June 12th, 1711)

'The Emperor had a mind one day to entertain me with several of the country shows, wherein they exceed all nations I have known, both for dexterity and magnificence. I was diverted with none so much as that of the rope dancers, performed upon a slender white thread, extended about two foot, and twelve inches from the ground . . . This diversion is only practised by those persons who are candidates for great employments, and high favour, at court. They are trained in this art from their youth, and are not always of noble birth, or liberal education. When a great office is vacant either by death or disgrace (which often happens), five or six of those candidates petition the Emperor to entertain his Majesty and the court with a dance on the rope, and whoever jumps the highest without falling succeeds in the office. Very often the chief ministers themselves are commanded to show their skill, and to convince the Emperor that they have not lost their faculty. Flimnap, the Treasurer, is allowed to cut a caper on the straight rope, at least an inch higher than any other lord in the whole empire.'—*Gulliver's Travels, A Voyage to Lilliput.*

ANTOINE DE GUISCARD, or as he affected to call himself the Marquis de Guiscard (his real name was the Abbé de la Bourlie), was a French adventurer who ended a career of romance and treason by changing the face of English politics in a single afternoon.

As the younger son in a distinguished French family Guiscard was destined for the Church. 'But when he enter'd the world, he soon discover'd a bold, daring, free spirit, and violent Propensity to Voluptuousness; particularly an Unruly Passion for the Fair Sex, which, together with the Advantages of his Noble Birth, the Countenance of the Court, and a Plentiful Income (being Possess'd of Church Preferments to the Value of above 2000 *l.* Sterling, a Year) let him into all the Extravagancies of Youth; so that he was Listed among the *French Petits Maîtres*, or Rakes of Quality. In a short time he became one of the Chief of those illustrious Debauchees; and that he might have more Opportunities to gratify his Vicious Inclinations, he follow'd his brothers in the Field, and made two or three Campaigns in Flanders.'

For some offence too shocking to be revealed even in his own garrulous tributes to his own prowess, he was denounced by the French court and driven from the country. His first idea for revenge was to espouse the cause of the Protestant rebels against King Louis in the Cevennes. When this failed, he set out on an extraordinary tour of the allied courts in which he upheld with unfailing devotion the interests of Antoine de Guiscard. He turned up at Turin, Vienna and The Hague, undertook diplomatic missions on behalf of the allies, and at the battle of Almanza in Spain acquitted himself as a Lieutenant-General in the Austrian army. Somehow he wheedled a pension out of the Dutch as a reward for his military exploits. Eventually he settled in London where he flaunted his imposing introductions from famous men in other capitals to gain the command of an English regiment of refugees recruited for the purpose of unleashing a diversionary attack on the French coast. Since the appointment was made by the hard-headed Godolphin, Guiscard's powers of persuasion must have been considerable. But the project languished. Occasionally he journeyed to Holland to press his schemes on Marlborough and the Dutch Government. At last everyone grew weary of his grandiose talk. Even with Henry St. John, who felt a temperamental kinship with him and readily joined his carousals, a quarrel could not be averted; the story was that they had shared the same mistress and disputed the paternity of her bastard child. For a little while longer the wonderful confidence trick worked. Guiscard 'took and furnished a House; set up an Equipage; stored his Cellar with the best Wines; and kept a good Table: Fondly hoping, I suppose, by this splendid Way of Living, to buoy up his sinking credit and screen himself from Contempt'. But the Dutch cancelled his pension; his chief patron in London, the Ambassador from Savoy, died; and finally his regiment, which had never fought a battle, was disbanded. St. John suggested he should be given an annuity of £500 a year as compensation. Harley, who strongly disapproved of St. John's companion, reduced the figure to £400.

Guiscard saw that the game was nearly up. The horrors of

sobriety and chastity, if not actual poverty, stared him in the face. In desperation he resolved to betray the English as he had once betrayed the French. He opened a correspondence with a banker in Paris. The incriminating letters fell into the hands of Harley, who promptly wrote to Marlborough but refrained from taking immediate action against Guiscard in the hope of being able to unmask any other parties to his treason. Swift knew Guiscard well; probably they had met in the company of St. John. On March 8th —the anniversary of Queen Anne's Accession Day—the broad-minded Vicar of Laracor was walking with the holiday crowds down the Mall where he noticed Guiscard among the others enjoying the parade.

That same afternoon Harley was crossing the park to visit the Queen at St. James's Palace. He too saw Guiscard and decided to hold his hand no longer. A warrant for his arrest, signed among others by St. John, was issued, and the Lords of the Cabinet Council were urgently summoned to St. John's office at the Cockpit to conduct the investigation. At first Guiscard denied every charge that he had been in secret communication with France. Confronted with his own letters, he asked to speak with St. John alone. Perhaps he believed that his insinuating tongue— assisted by a mild threat of blackmail—could still save him. When the request was refused he showed signs of rage and despair. The messengers were told to take him away. 'This is harsh usage,' he cried; 'am I not to be allowed a word?' Before an answer could be given, he found an opportunity to move closer to Harley and to stoop down towards him as if to whisper in his ear. Suddenly he whipped out a penknife and plunged it into the Minister's breast. The blow was parried by the heavy coat embroidered with silver and gold which Harley had put on only an hour or two before when he visited the Queen. Without that lucky armour, the stroke might have been mortal. As it was, the penknife broke on a bone, and after a second blow Harley sank to the ground. For one moment of indescribable confusion it appeared that the Queen's first Minister had been murdered in the presence of all his Cabinet colleagues. During the next few seconds swords were drawn, chairs were hurled across the room and a multitude of wounds and bruises were inflicted on the wretched Guiscard. He himself rushed on St. John, overturned a table and broke the sword which might have ended his life on the spot. At last with the help of some strong-armed servants he was subdued. Harley was the only man in the room who kept his calm. He picked himself up, plucked the blade from his breast and borrowed a handkerchief to stanch his wound. A doctor had been hastened to the scene. Once his own wounds were attended to, Harley had enough composure to invite him to dress those of his assailant. Guiscard vainly asked that he should be killed there and then by the sword of a gentleman. Instead he was hustled off to Newgate prison while the bleeding Harley was carried in a sedan to his home in the Strand—but not before he had coolly sent word to his sister to continue her dinner engagement without him.

That night something near panic swept across London. St. John raced like a man demented to the palace to inform Mrs. Masham and the Queen; until reassured by the doctor, Anne refused to believe that her Minister was not dead. The Duke of Argyll, who had rushed from a dinner-party to the Cockpit once the news was known, turned up later at Will's coffee-house to feed the appetite for rumour. He had reached the scene of the crime in time to hear the screams of protest from Guiscard. Guiscard had said—so Argyll reported—that St. John, not Harley, was the man he really wished to stab; for St. John, like the Duke of Marlborough who was also named, had treated him shamefully and if he had had his choice he would have stabbed them both. Much wilder tales were now spreading throughout the town. A French spy had killed Harley. A tremendous plot had been unearthed. The Queen had been attacked. The Pretender had sailed from Brest. An invading army had landed on the English coast. If proof were needed, was it not undeniable that the guards round St. James's Palace had been doubled?

For Jonathan Swift the truth was horrifying enough. He too had had his dinner-party interrupted. First he had called at St. John's house where Mrs. St. John had told him half the story. Then he had gone to Harley's where he had learnt that his friend was still alive. That night he wrote to Archbishop King despite 'the violent pain I am in, greater than ever I felt in my life'. Swift knew that Harley had been ill even before the assault. Certainly he could not be out of danger and if he died the consequences might be catastrophic. 'Time will show', he wrote, 'who is at the bottom of all this; but nothing could happen so unluckily to England, at this juncture, as Mr. Harley's death; when he has all the schemes for the greatest part of the supplies in her head, and the Parliament cannot stir a step without him.' Yet political perils were not uppermost in his mind at that hour. Swift truly loved the man. 'My heart is almost broken,' he wrote to Stella, '. . . I am in mortal pain for him . . . Pray pardon my distraction; I now think of all his kindness to me—The poor creature now lies stabbed in his bed by a desperate French popish villain . . . Pity me; I want it.'

Swift's distress was genuine, but his eagerness for news from the bedside could not blunt his appreciation of the political deliverance which providence had offered. Next day both Houses of Parliament agreed upon an Address to the Queen 'wherein they expressed their great Concern for the most barbarous and villainous Attempt, made upon the person of Robert Harley Esq., adding, That they had Reason to believe, that his Fidelity to Her Majesty, and Zeal for her Service, had drawn upon him the Hatred of all the Abbettors of Popery and Faction: And besought Her Majesty, to take all possible Care of her Sacred Person; and for that Purpose, to give Directions for causing Papists to be remov'd from the Cities of London and Westminster'. A few days later the *Examiner* was on the warpath. No subtlety was needed to underline the moral of the incredible scene at the Cockpit. A French papist, a Popish spy, had destroyed at one stroke the old Whig charge that Harley and the new Ministers were the friends of France, or at least that their policies served the interests of King Louis and the machinations of the Pope. This was not the first time that Harley had unmasked a traitor. Once before—in the Greg case in 1708— he had discovered an underling in his office engaged in secret correspondence with Paris. On that occasion the Whigs had done their worst to turn the revelation against Harley himself and had indeed succeeded in driving him from office. They—like Guiscard —would have killed him if they could! 'If there be really so great a difference in principle between the high-flying Whigs and the friends of France,' said the *Examiner*, 'I cannot but repeat the question, how come they to join in the destruction of the same man? Can his death be possibly for the interest of both? or have they both the same quarrel against him, that he is perpetually discovering and preventing the treacherous designs of our enemies? However it be, this great minister may now say with St. Paul, that he hath been "in perils by his own countrymen, and in perils by strangers".' Such was the ferocity with which the *Examiner*

turned the assault on Harley against the Whigs. And how intrepid
had been Harley's demeanour in face of the attack! But more
significant in this particular issue of the paper than any argument
was the news divulged by the writer or the rumours he appeared to
confirm. The charge was directly made that Guiscard had been
invited over to England and given his military command by 'a
great man of the late ministry'. It was further charged that he had
attempted to murder St. John as well as Harley: indeed those who
'could not be thoroughly informed' were now enlightened by a
few words from Guiscard's own mouth. 'The murderer confessed in
Newgate, that his chief design was against Mr. Secretary St. John
who happened to change seats with Mr. Harley for more convenience
of examining the criminal: and being asked what provoked him to
stab the Chancellor, he said, that not being able to come at the
Secretary, as he intended, it was some satisfaction to murder the
person whom he thought Mr. St. John loved best.' Finally 'he had
intentions of a deeper dye than those he happened to execute'. For
days previously he had been a visitor at the backstairs of the palace.
Was it not obvious that his real quarry had been the Queen? How
much the country owed to the men who had thwarted so devilish
a design! And how flattering was the tribute to the patriotism of
Harley or St. John that they, second only to the beloved monarch
herself, should be selected targets for a French papist's dagger!

Almost every *Examiner* Swift wrote drew a furious response
from the Whig journals, but none aroused quite the same intense
anger as his exploitation of the stabbing. His old antagonist on the
Medley replied with some effect to 'this incorrigible Blunderer and
most abandoned Scribbler' who dared brand the Whig leaders as
would-be murderers. Brushing aside the attempt to confuse the
issue by raising the case of Greg, the *Medley* issued a direct
challenge. Let him substantiate his claim that Guiscard had been
invited over by the Whigs; 'if he wou'd but prove that one
Particular, I wou'd forgive him all the Lyes past, and yet to come.'
If past association with Guiscard was to be made the ground of the
smear, did not everyone know that St. John was 'his most zealous
friend'? And was there not an obvious logical absurdity in the
Examiner's case? The Whigs and a French papist concurred—so
the *Examiner* had argued—'both agreeing in the great end of taking
away Mr. Harley's life'. Yet a sentence or two later the claim had
been made that St. John, not Harley, was the intended victim. It

was a damaging hit and in his next *Examiner* Swift did his best to blur the dilemma. Conveniently forgetting the actual words used, he claimed to have done no more than report without confirmation or denial what Guiscard had confessed. How like the Whigs to shirk the real charge! 'They take abundance of pains to clear Guiscard from a design against Mr. Harley's life, but offer not one argument to clear their other friends, who in the business of Greg were equally guilty of the same design against the same person; whose tongues were very swords and whose pen-knives were axes.'

Swift had stumbled on a piece of political dynamite; that was the real cause for his confusion. St. John had approved his original account of the Guiscard attack; probably he supplied the information—which may well have been true—that he (St. John) was the Minister Guiscard really wanted to kill. The implication was clear. St. John deserved at least to share the martyr's crown. Harley's friends and probably Harley himself were not so ready to forgo any part of the glory. Swift may have learnt something of their displeasure when he dined with Erasmus Lewis two days after the *Examiner* was published. The conflicting testimony about Guiscard's intentions seems trivial enough, but years later Swift was emphatic in tracing the feud between Harley and St. John back to this event. At the time, the animosity provoked by it was hot enough to make him abandon the idea of writing a special pamphlet on the Guiscard story. Swift could not please both his masters at the same time; so the task was given to another hand. And suddenly a veil had fallen from his eyes. He loved Harley and admired St. John. The whole tremendous enterprise on which the three were engaged depended on their staying together. But now for the first time he saw his two friends as rivals. Beneath the carefree intimacy which had given him his hours of greatest delight, he detected a germ of bitterness. The agonizing discovery was made all the worse because Swift saw the vices of each as clearly as their virtues. For him this cloud no bigger than a man's hand darkened the whole brilliant landscape of Tory triumph opened up by the Guiscard affair.

During the weeks of Harley's illness, Swift saw more of St. John than ever before. They met several times a week and a special arrangement was made that they should dine together every Sunday. The beginnings of their friendship had been founded on St. John's charm and flattery. 'We were determined to get you; you were the only one we were afraid of,' he told Swift. No compliment could have been more skilfully designed. In the days after the Guiscard excitement the relationship grew much closer. Swift felt able to chide Mr. Secretary for his excessive addiction to champagne and burgundy, and for a while it seems the reproof had some effect; he was less successful, however, in restraining the 'other liberties', not to 'be reconciled to religion and morals', which St. John was said 'to allow himself'. On one occasion, obsessed perhaps by the affairs of state or the growing envy of Harley, St. John lapsed from the normal candour and ceremony with which he treated the author of the *Examiner*. Swift was quick to insist upon his own terms of companionship. 'One thing I warned him of,' he boasted to Stella. 'Never to appear cold to me, for I would not be treated like a schoolboy . . . that I expected every great minister, who honoured me with his acquaintance, if he heard or saw anything to my disadvantage, would let me know it in plain words, and not put me in pain to guess by the change and coldness in his countenance or behaviour; for it was what I would hardly bear from a crowned head, and I thought no subject's favour was worth it.' Even if the rebuke was not in fact so sternly delivered, St. John never made the same mistake again. Those engaging talents which he had once used to win the affection of the Duke of Marlborough were lavished ever more profusely on the Vicar of Laracor.

St. John, in Swift's eyes, had 'the choicest gifts that God hath yet thought fit to bestow upon the children of men; a strong memory, a clear judgement, a vast range of wit and fancy, a thorough comprehension, an invincible eloquence, with a most agreeable elocution'. His faults were a tincture of affectation and an aggressive ambition. Above all—and for this Swift would absolve all his sins—he had the bearing of one determined to master events and this resolute spirit was supported by a prodigious industry. St. John could rouse the Commons with his fire and his rhetoric; yet at the same time 'he would plod whole days and nights, like the lowest clerk in an office'. The combination of all these qualities amounted to genius. Others well accustomed to political life were dazzled by the shafts from this blazing sun; it is not surprising that Swift was alarmed at the idea of seeing the Government deprived of St. John's energy or lashed by his tongue in opposition. If he was now estranged, might not the breach be due to the incorrigible refusal of Robert Harley to open his heart to all but a few; perhaps to all but Swift?

That was Harley's great fault—'the air of secrecy in his manner and countenance, by no means proper for a great minister, because it warns all men to prepare against it.' And yet when the outward mask was pierced, how rare among all the great men whose company Swift had enjoyed were the qualities which Harley revealed. The love of power was the disease of politicians; Swift himself was infected by it. Harley alone seemed immune from its temptations. 'He is the only instance that ever fell within my memory, or observation, of a person passing from private life, through the several stages of greatness, without any perceivable impression upon his temper or behaviour.' He seemed above fear, careless of fame, contemptuous of all the attacks upon him. Swift admired such equanimity all the more since he himself could never attain it. Others were enraged by the libels which Grub Street unloosed upon them; Swift knew how they could sting. But Harley enjoyed reading the scurrilities of his assailants, scrutinizing them all with the professional eye of a man who could enlist more successful exponents of the art. No doubt it was this display of bland indifference to his enemies and even some of his friends which encouraged the most familiar charge against him—that he was lazy, procrastinating, incapable of decision. Years later St. John still poured out his scorn against Harley when the anger he felt against most others had mellowed. The seed of that hatred was planted in those weeks when Harley lay on his sick-bed and St. John's jealousy was fed by the knowledge of how near supreme power had come within the grasp of hands so much more capable of exercising it. 'A man', he wrote, 'who substitutes artifice in the place of ability, who instead of leading parties and governing accidents is eternally agitated backwards and forwards by both, who begins every day something new, and carries nothing to perfection, may impose a while on the world; but a little sooner or a little later the mystery will be revealed, and nothing will be found to be couched under it but a thread of pitiful expedients, the ultimate end of which never extended farther than living from day to day.'

Was this the true portrait? Such must often have been the appearance. But against the Harley of March 1711, the indictment was false. He more than any other man had carried through the revolution in the Queen's affairs. He had come near to success in restoring the public credit. He had set in motion the negotiations for a Peace. He had resisted the clamours of the October Club which might so easily have spoilt the whole design. He had applied his mind with the most tortuous diligence to shape public opinion; when Jonathan Swift left at one door, Daniel Defoe entered at the other, and neither ever knew for sure they had been employed by the same master. Before Guiscard's attack a mountain of troubles were weighing heavily upon him; but even without that stroke of good fortune, so skilfully exploited, who can tell that his ingenuity would not have been able to contrive a release?

As he lay sick Harley must have relished anew the victories to be garnered by a well-timed inertia. In the first hour after the attack even St. John admitted that his life was 'absolutely necessary'. Day by day, without lifting a finger, he saw his prestige recover. Guiscard died of his wounds at Newgate, and the body was pickled in a trough for a fortnight to delight the spectators at twopence a time, until on the Queen's order the disgusting exhibition was stopped. Every macabre incident reported from the prison added to the sympathy for the stricken statesman. On the day after the burial Swift declared: 'All things are at a stop in parliament for want of Mr. Harley; they cannot stir an inch without him in their most material affairs.' And Mr. Harley showed no impatience to return to the scene where for a while his silence made conquests denied to the greatest orator of the century.

*   *   *

It is wellnigh impossible to disentangle all the tortuous parliamentary and personal manœuvres conducted during the two or three months after the stabbing of Harley. St. John's intuition urged him to act on the belief that his hour had come. He was tantalized by the opportunities suddenly presented to him for exercising complete mastery over the affairs of the Government. But often when he stepped forward to seize them the re-emerging authority of Harley stood across his path. The clash of temperament between the two men developed within a matter of weeks into a rasping antagonism. St. John had every reason to believe that he understood better than Harley the prevailing mood among the Tories in the House of Commons. He shared their ambitions more whole-heartedly and realized that these could only be fulfilled by the boldest strokes of policy. But he could not compete with his rival in the committee-room and the ante-chamber, and only learnt by hard rebuffs which came near to toppling him from his place altogether what care was needed to keep together the heterogeneous elements Harley had assembled. All the outward signs suggested that the improving nerve and cohesion of the Whigs had been broken. The administration should have gained a corresponding acquisition of strength. But the stresses between the chief Ministers stopped them from reaping the full harvest of advantage.

Swift did his best in the *Examiner* to foster the notion that the ferocious party animosities of previous months were fading. He was fulsome in his tributes to the new Parliament. 'It is acknowledged', he wrote in the *Examiner* at the end of March, 'that this excellent assembly hath entirely recovered the honour of Parliaments, which had been unhappily prostituted for some years past by the factious proceedings of an unnatural majority, in concert with a most corrupt administration.' Even the moderate Whigs were learning to appreciate what had been done. Swift cited as sure evidence of the new temper the readiness of the Commons to comfort one of the leading Tories, 'their most worthy Speaker who having unfortunately lost his eldest son, the assembly, moved with a generous pity for so sensible an affliction, adjourned themselves for a week, that so good a servant of the public might have some interval to wipe away a father's tears'. It was 'very handsomely done' and certainly if Junto Whigs and rampant Octobrists had truly been willing to forget their quarrels in the presence of an old man's grief the display would have been impressive indeed. But Swift confessed to Stella that there was possibly another reason. Without Harley the business of the Commons became hopelessly muddled; an adjournment would bring nearer the moment of his return. Altogether, for a few weeks even the *Examiner* seemed to lose something of its spirit and sense of direction. Doubtless Swift was distracted by the cleavage between St. John and Harley. And in the House of Commons itself the rumblings of discontent among the Tories had been muted but not killed by the blow from Guiscard.

Of all the forces which had threatened the destruction of Harley at the beginning of March the most serious came from the October Club. If this well-knit body of intransigents imposed its will both moderate Tories and moderate Whigs would be alienated. The Queen, too—now increasingly under the influence of the

Duchess of Somerset—might be persuaded to withhold her sympathy from the administration. The attack on Harley naturally softened the opposition of the October Men towards him. But in his *Review*, which appeared a week after the stabbing, Daniel Defoe testified that their raging temper was still unappeased. No doubt to avoid the risk of a second pillory Defoe pretended that these 'October Men' whose ambitions he sought to expose were not Members of Parliament themselves. He satirized the raucous group inside the Commons by describing the 'drunkenness and tumult' practised by the mob outside. 'These,' he wrote, 'are mighty busie now, Railing at the Proceedings of the *Parliament*, and tell us, that if they were Members, they would do something else, before they gave Supplies; they would Enquire how the Money was spent before they gave more—If there be any Cheats and Frauds, they care not to be put off with detecting a few small beer Brewers but they would push at Impeachments of all the Old Ministry, and calling to Account, *even right or wrong*, everyone they dislike: They say the Old Ministry either deserve to be Hang'd, or else did not deserve to be turned out; they damn the *Examiner* for a Coxcomb, who heaps Crimes upon their Heads, and says nothing of Punishment; they are horridly provok'd at the Duke of M————h for not Resigning his Posts, and say he has a mean Soul; they Affront the Queen for stooping to Employ him again, and they could Assassinate Mr. *Harley* a second time as Minister of State, for Advising to put the Army into the same Hands. Tis our infinite Happiness, that none of these are Parliament Men; for no doubt had they been in the House, they would have run Things up to a desperate height.'

The worst perils of that 'desperate height' had been avoided—thanks partly to Guiscard. But the October Men looked always for fresh means of satisfying their passions. One of their chief grievances concerned the weight of taxation and when, in the absence of Harley, the Government proposed a new tax on leather, they staged a revolt. The Ministers were 'thunderstruck' to see themselves defeated in the lobbies by no less than forty votes. St. John was forced to lecture the men he sought to lead on the dangers of jeopardizing the supplies and undoing all the work so painfully accomplished in building up the public credit. It was necessary to reverse the decision. 'Someone did bestir themselves, the business was brought in by another title, a duty upon raw hides instead of leather. For the passing of it there was 170 odd against 80 odd, wch accations much speculation how so many men in one night shou'd be brought over.' And this was not the only speculation which buzzed in the corridors of the Commons that night. The absent leader, it was said, would never have courted such an indignity for himself or his followers. He would have guessed what was happening and postponed the introduction of the measure until the machine had been properly oiled. 'Several Politicians that cou'd not endure Mr. Harley say they see now there's no man the Court imploys has address enough to manage the House of Commons but him.' How the report of that general verdict, if it ever reached him, must have infuriated St. John! He had been forced to squander a little of his own precious popularity in order to restore discipline. Harley derived all the benefit, and yet it was Harley's obstruction of the October Club's plan, backed by St. John, for a more thoroughgoing removal of the Whigs which was the real source of their rampaging tactics. Swift, like St. John, had some sympathy with their complaints. But now all must wait on Harley's return. One night the October Club leaders invited Swift to dine with them. He made his excuses 'adorned with about thirty compliments, and got off as fast as I could. It would have been a most improper thing for me to dine there, considering my friendship with the ministry'. Such were the strained relations between the Ministers and the men in the Commons on whom they must rely for their majority. It was surely frustrating for St. John to know the lead they wanted and to be unable to give it, to suffer reproaches for his share of responsibility while he was still denied the final power to govern.

He turned more hopefully from parliamentary setbacks to his scheme for the expedition to Quebec. With Harley ill, the project could be pressed forward so far that any opposition from his colleagues could be overborne. A considerable armada, comprising ten ships of the line, thirty-one transports and five thousand troops, was assembled in the English Channel. This was to be the strongest military force which had ever crossed the Atlantic. St. John boasted with full justice 'a sort of paternal concern for the success of it'; every detail had gone through his hands. Harley remained rootedly opposed to the whole idea. He roused himself sufficiently to send Lord Rochester to the Queen with a 'dying request' that she should forbid it. But the plea came too late. Mrs. Masham's brother, Brigadier John Hill, had already been appointed to the command of the troops. Another favourite of the Tories, Rear-Admiral Walker, was to be in charge of the ships. Anne rejected the entreaties of Harley and Rochester, and possibly their apparent eagerness to rob Brigadier Hill of his first meed of military glory raised St. John in her estimation as it certainly did in Mrs. Masham's. When the news of Harley's intervention reached St. John he professed his surprise and discovered a creditable reason for backing the enterprise. 'The worse condition we are in,' he wrote to Harley, 'the worse peace we are likely to obtain; the more reason there is in my humble opinion that the intended expedition should be pushed.' Harley from his sick-bed could not withstand the masterful enthusiasm of St. John who designed to win Canada and Abigail by the same stroke. And St. John had stored up for himself—if the plan proved successful—a triumph which would more than compensate for all the irritations he had suffered since the wounding of Harley. At the end of April the fleet sailed. Despite the elaborate plans for secrecy, Swift knew a great deal about it. Every week he was gaining more of St. John's confidence. He could not fail to be impressed by such proofs of determination and daring. Yet he could not shake off the suspicion that a superior wisdom or at least a more winning temper was possessed by Harley. He could not stifle the foreboding that the old comradeship between his two friends might never be repaired.

If Swift had known something of the other great issue which arose at the time when the argument over Quebec was reaching its climax, his trust in Harley might have been considerably diminished. Ever since the election one chief aspiration had governed his thoughts and much of his writings: the supreme need for peace. That was the prize which could banish the dilemmas of Ministers and entrench them in power for a generation. It was, moreover, hatred of war which supplied the fierce edge to the *Examiner*'s invective against Marlborough and the moneyed men. In the middle of April an event occurred which made many observers consider afresh how peace could be secured. The young Austrian Emperor Joseph I died. His brother and likely heir was the Austrian Archduke Charles III whom the allies had vainly striven for so long to establish as the King of Spain. Was it really in the interests of England that the war should be endlessly prolonged to impose on the Spaniards a monarch they so heartily detested? The military set-backs of the previous year had shown how arduous the enterprise was certain to be. And now, with the Emperor's death, the fact was reinforced that even if the campaign proved successful the result could only be a vast extension of the Austrian Empire. The House of Austria was not loved in England. Plentiful illustrations could be produced to prove how fickle had been the assistance of the Austrians as allies, and among the English Ministers St. John in particular revealed a streak of fury in his contempt for them. The Queen's message to Parliament on the Emperor's death observed all the proper etiquette. England's support for the Archduke in his claim to the imperial crown was suitably declared. But the message also 'gave the Discerning a Glimpse of the Project of the New Ministry . . . to make a Peace by yielding Spain'. Swift could count himself among the discerning. He at once concluded that the Emperor's death would 'cause great alterations in Europe, and, I believe, will hasten a Peace'.

What Swift did not know—what indeed even St. John did not know—was that in the middle of April a sensational advance had been made in the actual overtures for a peace. The journeyings of the Abbé Gaultier between London and Versailles were at last promising results. The Abbé himself had been surprised at the failure of the French King to seize more eagerly the tentative offers conveyed from Harley to the French court. Did they not realize the risks of letting the chance slip? Did they not appreciate that a fresh victory for the Duke of Marlborough might rob them of the terms now available and that a change in fortune could easily bring a reassertion of the Whig power in Whitehall? Clearly the Abbé underrated the French nerve. The Marquis of Torcy knew well enough how immensely advantageous for France had been the change of government in England; he knew that Marlborough might still be reckoning on a full recovery of his power. But he also knew that any sign of weakness would injure the terms he could secure. He was not prepared to become an abject suitor for peace. Instead, he sent Gaultier back with an offer of terms sufficiently enticing to keep the discussion open yet sufficiently stiff to indicate that the French King was not contemplating unconditional surrender. Gaultier reported in London on April 21st. Hitherto only two among the English Ministers—the Duke of Shrewsbury and Harley—had known about his mission. Harley was in favour of keeping the secret still. He wanted to send another secret emissary to Holland to test the reaction of the Dutch. Perhaps he hated the idea of allowing St. John a finger in the great matter which would shape foreign policy and the whole future of the administration; perhaps he could not escape from his inveterate habit of intrigue. But Shrewsbury stressed the dangers of such a course. The news was bound to leak out at The Hague or in Paris and the anger among other members of the Cabinet could easily be foreseen. For a few days the argument continued. Then at last it was agreed that the Queen should reveal the document brought by Gaultier to the members of her Council 'as a paper coming to her hands without saying how'. Harley had been forced to relinquish his hold on this essential lever, although he still tried to insist that an agent answerable alone to the Queen, to Shrewsbury and himself should conduct the business in Holland.

St. John had every right to feel aggrieved at the work done behind his back by his most intimate colleagues at the very period when he was bearing on his shoulders the brunt of the administration's burdens. But he wasted no time in recrimination. At moments of crisis he showed the stature of a statesman, recognizing at once the critical nature of the opportunity. He could not claim any special title to undertake the business of peacemaking; by custom at least the task could more properly be assumed by his fellow Secretary of State, Lord Dartmouth. The demarcation line between the duties of the two Secretaries was most clumsily drawn, but as Secretary for the Southern Department, as it was called, Lord Dartmouth had the better right to take control over correspondence with The Hague. With one sweep of his hand St. John brushed aside these procedural cobwebs. On the very next day after he had heard the news he dispatched three important letters.

One went to Lord Raby, the newly appointed ambassador in Holland, appraising him of the approach from France, instructing him to reveal the matter to the Dutch, but urging—on the Queen's authority—that the strictest secrecy must still be maintained. 'The Duke of Marlborough', he said, 'has no communication from hence of this affair; I suppose he will have none from The Hague.' Raby was also ordered to watch carefully for any underhand moves by the Dutch to seek separate advantages for themselves from the French; St. John knew his own game and was all the more suspicious that others might try to play it as well. A sharp reminder followed that this new business superseded in importance anything that had gone before. In some earlier epistle Raby had bored the busy St. John with a recital of the indignities he had suffered at the hands of the Duke of Marlborough and other friends of the Whigs in Holland. This was no time to worry about Whig manners and diplomatic etiquette. Nothing counted beside the prospect of peace. St. John's second letter—to his old agent, John Drummond—was designed to assist the same purpose. A veto from Shrewsbury and the Queen prevented him from divulging the news about Gaultier's mission to Drummond, but there was other good work he could do. Some of the Tory officers—notably Lord Orrery—were still pursuing their old vendetta against the Duke of Marlborough. But, again, this was no time for personal feuds. The Duke's services in sustaining the battle-front while negotiations proceeded were now more vital than ever. If the Ministers at home could swallow their pride to win the point of substance, the underlings with their petty animosities must not be allowed to interfere. Everything must be done to retain Marlborough's good-will; Drummond should see to it. Finally, the third letter was addressed to the Duke himself. No hint was given of the peace initiative. But, for the rest, St. John was resolved to make relations with him as smooth as possible. Ever since Marlborough had returned to the head of the army, St. John had done his best to restore confidence between him and the new Ministry. Now he added flattery to the promises of good faith. 'My care', he wrote 'can be of no great service to your Grace, though you are pleased to ask it; but the best offices in my power you shall at all times be sure of. With respect to the common cause, you have, my Lord, a hard game to play; but with respect to yourself, and your own reputation, I think you have not. Every man is so apprized that the whole strength of France is now opposed to you, that if you should be able to do anything, you would outgo almost our hopes; and if you are able to do nothing (which God forbid) I dare say no blame will be ascribed to you.'

Thus, from the first hour when he heard the exciting news from France, St. John applied his mind to the double objective of enabling the peace discussions to fructify and of sustaining the armed power without which they might so easily prove abortive. The haphazard, slipshod discussions conducted by Gaultier on Harley's directions were taken over by a man who preferred action to talk. Torcy was confronted by a mettle as tough as his own. If Swift had known, how could he have withheld from St. John the devotion which he still accorded more lavishly to Harley?

The superabundant energy with which St. John drove forward his expedition to Quebec, the campaign in Flanders and the negotiations for peace appears all the more remarkable in view of the parliamentary crisis which broke over his head during these same weeks. The incident is the most curious and inexplicable in the whole of St. John's career. But, whatever the explanation, it is impossible not to admire the audacity with which he surmounted it.

Ever since Harley and his associates had assumed office no topic had aroused more interest among the Tories than the financial operations of the previous administration. The charge of corruption on a monumental scale had been freely bandied about by the Tory leaders, but once they were in office no sign appeared that action was intended. Nothing angered the October Club more than this insufferable reticence. All their hatred of the moneyed men and the merchants was bound up with their belief that the whole Whig tribe, headed by Marlborough and his Duchess, had dipped their hands deep into the public coffers. But now their own leaders foiled every attempt to unmask the profiteers who had grown fat on the land taxes stolen from the Tory squires. Week by week passed and nothing happened. Then at last, despite a rumour of opposition from Harley, a Commission was proposed to examine the public accounts. St. John won favour by backing the October Club demand. 'None', he said, 'but those who were the enemies to their country, or who would themselves plunder the Treasury, would be so bold as to oppose it.' When Sir Robert Walpole spoke on behalf of the Whigs against the Commission, suspicions were increased. Harley's supposed doubts were swept aside and a Commission stuffed with Tories and with Harley's own brother as auditor was appointed. Their report to the House of Commons exceeded the wildest dreams of the most determined muckrakers. For the report stated that up till Christmas 1710 the enormous and particular sum of £35,302,107. 18s. 9d. was unaccounted for.

Naturally enough, a tremendous outcry was let loose by this revelation. The impression at first created and sedulously spread by the Tory journals was that the whole of this vast sum—equal to the total revenue of the country for several years on end—had gone direct into the pockets of Lord Godolphin and his friends.

If the report were true, impeachments must soon follow and the great Whig financiers could be indicted amid nation-wide derision. The excitement in the October Club can be imagined. Nothing half so good had happened since the election; for a week or two all else on the political scene was lost in the shadow of the case of the £35 millions. But the report was *not* true. Most of the missing millions could be accounted for by delays in book-keeping. The Commission had uncovered a gigantic mare's nest. And yet even when the technical facts which exposed the main scare for what it was had been comprehended, a big enough stench remained. Every penny of the £35 millions could not be explained away so simply. Here surely was an issue on which St. John could exert his demagogic powers to the limit. He had courted the October Club before; now he could stand forth as their unquestioned champion.

To the amazement of every observer, he did the exact opposite. If the examination was to be pressed one of the chief victims would be James Brydges, who had served St. John as Paymaster-General of the forces when he was at the War Office. St. John resolved to stand by Brydges and attack as trumpery nonsense the whole proposal for further detailed investigation. It is hard to believe that a quixotic care for the interests of his friend was his paramount motive in casting aside so rich a parliamentary opportunity and risking so much on the outcome. Perhaps he had some excellent reason for fearing an inquiry into his own past financial dealings; perhaps he had shared the considerable loot which Brydges managed to acquire as Paymaster. Not a scrap of evidence exists to explain the mystery. What is known is that, once he had set his face against the clamours of the October Club, St. John hurled himself into the debates with all his customary ardour. Just at the moment when he needed parliamentary backing in his tussle with Harley he had the mortification of seeing the Commons reject his advice and declare that 'the not compelling the several Accountants truly to pass their respective accounts, had been a notorious breach of trust in those that of late years had had the management of the treasury, and an high injustice to the nation'.

St. John's stock slumped. Swift feared that any moment he would be forced out of office. In the very week when he gathered into his hands the reins of European diplomacy he was nearly unhorsed in the Parliament where his reputation had been founded. Swift must have felt the poignancy of the scene. How savagely could he himself have exploited the scandal of the £35 millions in the columns of the *Examiner*! In fact his few references to the subject were casual and reserved. A lashing of the Whigs would be too expensively paid for if it sundered his own friendship with St. John and St. John's links with the Ministry. Swift, the journalist, gave way to Swift, the politician. Everything hinged on keeping Harley and St. John together in the same team. And if anyone could heal the breach Swift was the person to do it.

*   *   *

St. John's crisis coincided with the return of Harley after his illness. He came back like a conqueror. During the two months of his absence, the House of Commons—even his enemies in the October Club—had learnt how much they owed to his skilful management. Daniel Defoe hailed him as an agent of providence. 'Why', he wrote, 'was he (Guiscard) Permitted to Assault, and not Permitted to Effect his Design; what Armour Guarded the Precious Part; what Restrain'd the Point; why Directed just to the Onely Little Solid part That was in The wounded place, But to bear Witness to this Glorious Truth, That Verily There is a God That Governs The Earth, That The Hairs of Our head are Numbred, and Not a Sparrow falls to the Ground etc.?' A flood of poems and pamphlets had given thanks for Harley's deliverance in language no less sanctimonious.

One pamphlet came from the pen of Mrs. Manley, the notorious author of the *New Atlantis*. She was now the mistress of Swift's printer, John Barber, and to her Swift had given the facts about the case which he refrained from writing himself for fear of offending either St. John or Harley in the apportionment of the glory. Mrs. Manley, no doubt on Swift's instruction, held the balance as carefully as possible. Guiscard, she said, had sought 'the destruction of those two dreadful enemies of France, Mr. Harley and Mr. St. John'. They were 'the two important lives that gave dread and anguish' to King Louis XIV. But after all it was Harley who had actually been stabbed. 'Is it not obvious to all England, what had been our distress in the confusion wherein so long a run of mismanagement has plunged us, if Heaven had permitted the knife of a barbarous foreigner to have robbed us of a minister, whose conduct, wise, stedfast, vigorous, extricates our affairs, and embroils the enemies! Does not the flourishing church of England owe him all things for her deliverance from presbytery and atheism . . . Is not even our gracious sovereign indebted to him for scattering those persons from about her, whose excessive tyranny strove to ruin all those who aimed to come at the Queen but by them? Does he not sacrifice his quiet to the good of his country, without enriching his own family with her treasures, or decking himself with her honours, though she has none but what, with pride and joy, she is ready to bestow upon him? Was not his blood (even now devoted to the restless genius of France) spilt in dread of his pursuits and endeavours to reduce that monarch to humanity and reason . . . His actions have had their foundation in solid judgement, propped by a most extensive genius, unlimited foresight and immovable prudence. France records her Richlieu, Mazarine and Louroy; we talk with veneration of the Cecils; but posterity shall boast of Harley as a prodigy, in whome the spring is as pure as the stream. . . .'

Thus Mrs. Manley acclaimed the national hero who only seven weeks before had felt himself encompassed by so many enemies that he feared for his survival. Her rhetoric may sound absurd, but indeed Harley's sudden popularity knew no limits. When he returned to the House of Commons on April 26th, members crowded round him with their congratulations; and the Speaker groped for words of ecstasy to match Mrs. Manley's. And, as the next few weeks proved, the ovation was no more than the outward sign of a political strength solidly rooted in the sentiments of a vast number of Harley's fellow-countrymen. It was barely a year since he had started, on the Queen's prompting, to challenge the tyranny of the Whig Lords, sustained by the prestige of Marlborough. He was then a man out of office, hated by the Whigs, branded by them as a near-traitor, suspected by the Tories and distrusted on every side. Now he wielded power such as no previous Minister had acquired throughout the whole of Queen Anne's reign. In all the devious courses he had been compelled to pursue he had never put a foot wrong. Certainly Guiscard had come to his aid when for a moment all his schemes were threatened with ruin. But none could attribute so immense a success solely to luck. Keeping his own counsel at every stage, and risking his hardly-gained measure of popular approval rather than drive issues to extremes, he had held together the strange assortment of political forces and made possible the exploitation of the gift which Guiscard had bestowed. To be hailed as the patriotic champion of his country against France at the very moment when Gaultier on his behalf was speaking words of encouragement into the ears of the Pretender; to have extorted in unison the assurance from Whig moderates and October men that he was the indispensable leader; to hear from the Duke of Marlborough who had once vowed eternal detestation of Mr. Harley that 'I will be uneasy until you are recovered'—this was no mere accidental achievement. Only St. John dared to scowl. But perhaps he knew his 'dear Master' better than all the others. Perhaps, along with his personal feud, he also began to understand that the qualities required to rule the Commons and the court would not suffice to reshape the affairs of Europe.

No doubt was possible about one of the miracles which Harley had worked. When he assumed office a first-class financial crisis was in the making. Every tremor in the political scene jolted the public credit, and the Whigs were never slow in offering their prophecies of doom. 'To hear some of those worthy reasoners talking of credit,' wrote Swift, in the *Examiner* during April, 'that she is so nice, so squeamish, so capricious; you would think they were describing a lady troubled with vapours or the colick, to be only removed by a course of steel, and swallowing a bullet. By the narrowness of their thoughts, one would imagine they conceived the world to be no wider than Exchange Alley. It is probable they may have such a sickly dame among them, and it is well if she has no worse diseases, considering what hands she passes through. But the national credit is of another complexion; of sound health, and an even temper, her life and existence being a quintessence drawn from the vitals of the whole kingdom. And we find these money politicians, after all their noise, to be of the same opinion, by the court they pay her, when she lately appeared to them in the form of a *lottery*'. This line of argument no doubt served well enough for propaganda; it contained its grain of truth. Two lotteries, one raising £1,500,000 and another £2,000,000, had provided one of the means by which Harley had bolstered the nation's finances. But the Government's credit was still shaky. On the day before Guiscard's attack Harley had to warn the Commons of a new crisis. 'It was absolutely necessary', he reported, 'that the House should fall into some method for finding a fund for this great debt, which amounted to above £9,000,000, and concluded with a motion that the House should grant a supply for this purpose'. The Whigs ridiculed the proposition. The Chancellor, said Godolphin, had hung a millstone about his neck. During his absence the situation got worse. The October Club, as we have seen, thought they could impose their own will about the new taxes desired by the Government, and, while they were recklessly upsetting the Budget, fresh confirmation was offered of the hold which the Whigs still retained in the City of London. Elections for the directors of the Bank of England had been conducted like a modern by-election campaign. Every attempt was made—with the assistance of Dr. Sacheverell in person—to wrest some control over that governing institution for the Tories. But the machinations failed. Here at least the Whig ascendancy was unchallengeable. Well might Swift ask: 'What people, then, are these in a corner, to whom the constitution must truckle? If the whole nation's credit cannot supply funds for the war, without humble application from the entire legislature to a few retailers of money, it is high time we should sue for peace. . . . Must our laws from henceforward pass the Bank and East India Company, or have their royal assent before they are in force?' The question was mocking but also plaintive.

Finance was, in truth, the fatal weakness of the Tory administration which in most other respects had proved itself impregnable. Some bold plan of escape from this ever-present anxiety was required and on his return to official duties Harley produced it. He brought forward a scheme to consolidate the floating debt and combine it with the formation of a South Sea Company. The state's creditors would become the first shareholders in the new enterprise. Guaranteed interest at 6 per cent would be paid and the duties on certain commodities would be allotted to the new company in perpetuity. If, as was hinted, the profitable slave trade would soon be wrested from France, vast fortunes could be garnered in the South Seas. No doubt there was also the thought at the back of Harley's mind that a financial rival to the Bank of England and the East India Company, dominated by the Whigs, could thus be established. Altogether, the project had been most skilfully devised to satisfy a number of political and financial necessities. 'The Project of satisfying all publick Debts, which many thought would be attended with insuperable Difficulties, did wonderfully advance the Reputation of Mr. Harley, secured him in the favour of his Royal Mistress; and endeared him to the Whole Nation; Every Body being more or less concern'd in the

Payment of those Debts.' This was the verdict of an observer by
no means Tory in sympathy. True, it was an exaggeration; most
of the Whigs and many investors were on reflection not so enthusi-
astic. But the immediate effect was electric. Harley's real achievement was that he had enticed a sufficient number of City men away
from the rigid belief that only by a Whig restoration could their
money be secured. The Duchess of Marlborough paid her unwilling tribute to 'the Sorcerer'. Even St. John was impressed. On
the night when the plan was divulged the bells rang and bonfires
were lit in the City of London. No such music from that quarter
had greeted a Tory statesman for a generation or more.

Fortune favoured the cunning. Within a few days of Harley's
recovery, the Earl of Rochester, President of the Council, uncle
of the Queen and a most powerful figure among the Tories,
suddenly died. For several months past he had worked closely
with Harley, exerting his influence to withstand the pressures of
the October Club. But Rochester remained a high Tory. Never
could the political menace from this group among the Tories be
disregarded. If at any moment Rochester had chosen to put
himself at the head of an October Club agitation the threat would
have been formidable. This was well understood by George
Lockhart, one of the most aggressive of the Scottish Tories.
Rochester's death, he said, was 'an unspeakable loss'. He was 'a
great check upon Mr. Harley, as he had the greatest interest with
the Tories, was most confided in by them and properly the head
of the party. After his death Mr. Harley . . . being free from this
rival, stood in awe of none, and being the first Minister and chief
favourite, acted without controul whilst the Tories, like a parcel of
sheep without a shepherd or a ship without a ruther, spent their
fire in random shots, and presented no certain measure'.

Rochester's death had in fact opened the way for a general
reconstruction of the Ministry. Harley's friends and Harley himself lost no time in useless mourning. Before Rochester was in his
grave one of Harley's closest associates sent him an elaborate document dissecting the anatomy of Harley's forces and stressing the
point that he had already achieved one of his most persistent
objectives—liberation from any dependence on the high-flying
Tories. After the Earl of Rochester, the biggest name among the
Tories was the Earl of Nottingham. Nottingham had hitherto been
excluded from the administration; the recruitment of his backing

might appear an obvious resort for making good the loss of Rochester's influence. But why—so Harley's adviser insisted—should Harley stoop to such devices? Why should he not hold the scales in his own hand? If a Tory name was needed why not consider a man much more amenable and moderate such as the Duke of Buckingham? 'John of Bucks' was commended as a candidate for the Ministry on the most novel grounds; he could always be turned out again without giving offence to anybody and even amid general applause. In other words, the indispensable leader was encouraged not to share his victory with any but those who would prove his obedient servants.

'A prudent letter' was Harley's comment on this flattering advice, and in the weeks that followed the rush to support him bore the marks of something near hysteria. Some did not hesitate to portray him as a national saviour who might banish to oblivion those fierce party quarrels which had come so near to ruining the nation. Prominent men among the moderate Whigs no less than among the Tories urged the Queen to thrust fresh honours upon him. Hitherto he had exercised his power as Chancellor of the Exchequer; since the dismissal of Godolphin the Treasury had been in commission. At the end of May, Harley was appointed Lord Treasurer and raised to the peerage as the Earl of Oxford.[1] He was now indisputably the Prime Minister, the first statesman in English history to establish the title in general parlance. Swift was overjoyed at his friend's advancement. 'This man has grown by persecutions, turnings out and stabbing. What waiting, and crowding, and bowing, will be at his levee? Yet if human nature can be capable of so much constancy, I should believe he will be the same man still, bating the necessary forms of grandeur he must keep in.'

St. John was one of the few who refused to bow the knee before the new god. He was scornful of the pompous preamble to the patent creating him a peer which Harley allowed to be circulated. For weeks after his recovery Harley rarely appeared at the Council or the Treasury or the House of Commons. 'A perfect stagnation,' according to St. John, settled on the nation's business. Yet he was far from despairing; that mood was never part of his nature. Despite all the desperate risks he had run during the past

[1] Henceforward Harley should be referred to as Oxford, but I have continued to use the name with which readers of this book have been familiar.

two months he had his compensation. For the first time he had tasted real power and he had, too, the evidence from Harley's swift move from the depths to the heights that dazzling new horizons might suddenly open for himself if only he showed the necessary patience and courage. 'Our friend, Mr. Harley,' he wrote on June 12th, the day of the prorogation of Parliament, 'is now Earl of Oxford and High Treasurer. This great advancement is, what the labour he has gone through, the danger he has run, and the services he has performed seems to deserve. But he stands on slippery ground, and envy is always near the great to fling up their heels on the least trip which they make.'

The slippery ground was not noticeable to any other eye. As the gruelling session ended (St. John confessed himself 'half murdered' by it), nothing seemed to mar the glow of Harley's success. In particular he seemed to have destroyed the base on which any Tory rival might take his stand. For all the occasional forays of the Whigs in the Lords or the Commons, it was the veiled struggle with the October Club which had dominated the parliamentary scene. They alone had the power, as many had the wish, to break Harley and substitute a leader with a spirit better attuned to the Tory temper in the country. At the end of February they had nearly done it. Thenceforward they achieved nothing but the 'random shots' so pathetically described by George Lockhart. When the great moment came for which they had impatiently waited—the moment of government reconstruction when the last Whig could be expelled from any post of influence—their impetus had gone. St. John did his best to press the demand. But he was isolated, injured by his aberration over the Brydges affair, condemned to work for his own survival instead of mustering his resources to gain fresh allies in the councils of the government. A few minor posts for Tory high-flyers were the only sops thrown to the October Club. In general they had suffered crushing defeat. 'By silent quiet steps, in a little time,' wrote Daniel Defoe, 'he [Harley] so effectually separated these Gentlemen, that in less than Six months, the Name of the October Club was forgotten in the World, as if such a thing had never been heard of.'

Defoe exaggerated, but the truth was that the young men from the country estates who had flocked to Westminster with such enthusiasm seven months before had been no match for the old parliamentary hands who knew so well how to guide these torrents into the sand. The October Club zealots thought they could change the world, but they soon found themselves lost in the maze of precedent and procedure. Among their number, George Lockhart, who had come from Scotland on a crusade to destroy Whigs, make a peace and pave the way for a Jacobite restoration, saw the session end in complete disillusion. He was not impressed by the much-vaunted liberties of Englishmen in their famous House of Commons. 'For tho' all of them are vested with equal powers,' he lamented, 'a very few of the most active and pragmatical, by persuading the rest that nothing is done without them, do lead them by the nose and make meer tools of them to serve their own ends.' When the October Men had met at their long tables in the Bell Tavern in the previous November, swearing eternal loyalty to one another and vowing to consign the upstart Whigs to perdition, no one could have guessed that their will would have broken by the following June. This was a principal feature of Harley's success and most observers were content to marvel at the spectacle.

St. John was *not* content. He had always sympathized with the aims of the October Club and the instinct cannot be attributed solely to the demagogue's desire to please. Was it really wise to treat the Whigs with such leniency? Great obstacles had still to be overcome and perhaps the vigour of the October Club would be worth more than all the wavering allies whom Harley had been able to weld together. 'Those Junto pigmies, if not destroyed, will grow up to giants,' Lord Peterborough had warned Swift not so long before. Lord Wharton and his friends would have been pleased to back the prophecy with a considerable wager. They were down but not out. As the October Men rightly guessed, nothing but death itself could destroy pride and ambition on so inordinate a scale.

Swift, as we have seen, could never suppress his sympathy with the October Club's aims; he too itched to see all the Whigs robbed of their fleshpots and condemned to the wilderness. On almost every political issue he sided with St. John; Harley's arguments for restraint he had usually found unconvincing. But the man's charm was irresistible. After a few hours with Harley his doubts were composed once more; plausible excuses for complacency were always available. 'When the sons of Aeolus had almost sunk the ship with the tempests they raised, it was necessary to smooth the ocean, and secure the vessel, instead of pursuing the offenders,' said the *Examiner*. That the ocean had been smoothed and the vessel secured with Harley at the helm in a manner exceeding anything the most optimistic could have expected, none could deny. So, when the Parliament ended its labours for the session, Swift concluded that he could safely relinquish his work for the *Examiner*. 'And now I conceive the main design I had in writing these papers is fully executed. A great majority of the nation is at length thoroughly convinced, that the Queen proceeded with the highest wisdom, in changing her ministry and Parliament.' Stella was warned that she would hardly find the *Examiners* so good—'I prophesy they will be trash for the future'—and one night in the middle of June Swift had a special celebration with Harley who had excellent reasons for showing the best of humours. But no word was breathed of a return to Laracor, and day by day Swift found himself more deeply engaged with St. John. Among the stakes in the contest between Harley and St. John few were more considerable than the heart and mind of Jonathan Swift. Harley had captured his heart but his mind was more and more attracted by the intoxicating visions of St. John.

The last issues of the *Examiner* from Swift's pen, before he handed over the task to Mrs. Manley, were not marked by quite the same sharpness which had made the paper so powerful a weapon in the hands of the Government. More and more, and in defiance of his own haughty resolution, Swift found himself engaged in controversy with the inhabitants of Grub Street. Many of them he disregarded altogether, notably Daniel Defoe and his *Review* which was always ready to pick a quarrel with the *Examiner* even when both authors were employed by Harley. But the *Medley*, the *Observator* and that 'little whiffling Frenchman', Abel Boyer, were assailed with a searing contempt. Swift professed himself amazed at 'the flaming licentiousness of several weekly papers'. Such scurrility against the men in power 'would not be suffered in any other country in Christendom'. On one occasion he congratulated himself that never once had he 'invoked the assistance of the gaol or the pillory, which upon the least provocation, was the usual style' during the days of the Whig tyranny. A few weeks later he 'could not forbear asserting, as my opinion, for a ministry to endure such open calumny, without calling the author to account, is next to deserving it'. There was, it seems, a line to be drawn between liberty and licence, but fortunately Swift never used his matchless powers of verbal precision to define this mystical distinction which has baffled the lovers of censorship throughout the subsequent centuries.

The Duke of Marlborough had the most positive ideas on this same subject. Early in March he must have seen the *Examiner* No. 26, containing the famous *Letter to Crassus*. He voiced his complaints to St. John who, as he believed, 'governed the prints'. 'I had not in truth read the *Examiner* which your Grace mentions,' replied the busy Secretary of State, who had probably relished every paragraph of the offending article in Swift's company a few nights before, 'but I will take the best care I can to have honour done you, and no reflection upon you. It is a hard matter to keep the minds of men, when they are thoroughly heated, from pushing every subject too far; and no man is more heartily sorry than I am for those occasions which have been given of raising the ferment. Your Grace may be assured of my services in every instance; and I shall be glad to see you (which it is in your power to be) the subject of universal panegyric.' A week later Marlborough was assured that 'the proper hint' had been given to the *Examiner* and, indeed, thereafter, apart from an occasional stab at the Duchess, the paper had refrained from any provocation directed clearly at the Duke. Whether St. John's representations were responsible for the change is more doubtful. Swift himself understood that a new epoch in the Ministers' relations with Marlborough had been opened when they sent him back with their blessing to the battle-field. Perhaps it was this withdrawal of his chief enemy from the arena which helped to diminish the attraction of his work for the *Examiner*. In any case his discussions with St. John had convinced him he was required for a more important duty.

At the beginning of June he bade farewell to Grub Street. 'Those little barking pens', he wrote, 'which have so constantly pursued me I take to be of no further consequence to what I have writ, than the scoffing slaves of old, placed behind the chariot, to put the general in mind of his mortality; which was but a thing of form, and made no stop or disturbance in the shew. However, if those perpetual snarlers against me, had the same design I must own they have effectually compassed it; since nothing can well be more mortifying than to reflect that I am of the same species with creatures capable of uttering so much scurrility, dullness, falsehood, and impertinence, to the scandal and disgrace of human nature.'

* * *

While the intricate political drama was enacted in London, the Duke of Marlborough was preparing for another military campaign. He figured, too, in the strangest of all the rivalries between Harley and St. John. A few months before, each had sought to outdo the other in expressing their venom against the man they feared to overthrow. But now all was changed. From the day Marlborough left the shores of England to resume his command, St. John was profuse in his offers of friendship. His promise to warn the *Examiner* was but one small sign. Week by week he wrote to the Duke inviting him not to hesitate in asking for assistance and overflowing in his pledges of respect and affection. 'I hope never to see again', he said, 'the time when I shall be obliged to embark in a separate interest.' By every immediate test the professions seemed genuine. St. John sought out Marlborough's aides, Colonel Cadogan and John Craggs, and gave the same assurances to them. And to all his other correspondents in Holland—Drummond, Raby and Orrery—he displayed the same attitude. All of them were urged, indeed instructed, to forget their past antagonisms towards the Duke, to 'live easily with him', and to offer every proof that the old rancour was dead. Harley was no less assiduous. Steps were taken by him to end the old grievance about the incitement of officers against their Commander-in-Chief and, with a sure instinct, the Duke was wooed with the assurance that orders would quickly be given for the completion of Blenheim Palace in Woodstock Park. Some historians have suggested that this most curious competition was due to a desire on the part of both St. John and Harley to win Marlborough as a personal ally in whatever political combinations might later develop. Both knew how the Duke detested party strife. As a champion of moderation, he might prove a natural associate for Harley. St. John, on the other hand, may have thought it wise to counter any such manœuvre in good time. He had once been the intimate companion of Marlborough; flattery and fair dealing might restore the old friendship. But, in truth, there were other obvious reasons for seeking good relations. All the signs suggested that the peace could not be won without another year of war.

Marlborough in turn seemed ready to forget the old sores. To St. John he wrote every few days in the most amiable terms and with the utmost detail. To Harley special thanks was due for the news about Blenheim. Never would he forget such kindness. I 'pray you will believe it shall always be my endeavour to make all possible return for your friendship and good offices, of which you continue to give me such convincing proofs, as well by the provision you make for the public service, in which I have my lot, as for that part of my private concerns'. Never in particular would he forget Harley's display of 'sincerity'.

To sustain the tone of this touching correspondence it was necessary to impart some cautionary words to Sarah. She insisted, despite all warnings, in spattering her letters to the Duke with the names of all the Ministers, in particular the unspeakable Mr. Harley. Unfortunately for the literature of invective, these letters have been destroyed. Marlborough was taking no chances. His fear was that they were opened in transit by the Ministers' agents and to this he partly attributed the constant attacks in the *Examiner* and other journals, 'the villainous way of printing that stabs me to the heart'. So he pleaded with Sarah to be more careful. As for his true thoughts about the Ministers, she could 'be assured that I know them so perfectly well that I shall always be upon my guard. But whilst I serve I must endeavour not to displease; for they have it so much in their power to vex me that I must beg you will, for my sake, be careful in your discourse, as well as in your letters. . . . My thoughts are that you and I should endeavour all we can not to have enemies; for if we flatter ourselves with the having many friends, it is not to be expected when favour is lost, as ours is entirely'. Marlborough, it appears, had not altogether forgotten the past. But the campaign on which he was soon to embark promised to be the most frustrating of his career. He wanted political peace at home and was quite ready to pay for it by abandoning his ancient grudges against Harley and St. John. Sarah's doings did not add to his equanimity. On her dismissal from office she had been compelled to leave her lodgings in St. James's Palace which were soon to be taken over by the Queen. Sarah had given orders for the removal of the brass locks from the doors, the mirrors and the marble chimney-pieces which she had paid for herself. The news of these instructions had outraged the Queen and some hint of her anger had reached Marlborough. 'I beg', he wrote to Sarah in a mood of daring compromise, 'you will not remove any of the marble chimney-pieces'. Obviously Sarah did not delude herself that the old wounds were healed. Obviously she persisted in warning her husband against the perils of self-deception. Either to mollify her or because he was genuinely on his guard, Marlborough implied that the warnings were superfluous. But the weight of his correspondence with Harley and St. John suggests that their wooing was successful. At least Marlborough had grounds for believing that a fresh and stable association had been established between the three men upon whom the fate of England depended. The warrant for the building of Blenheim had been signed and the work on that 'monument of Her Majesty's goodness' was going forward at last. That was surely an agreeable sign to set against the broken locks on St. James's Palace.

But if, apart from Sarah, all the news from London was favourable, the same could not be said about the prospects for the war. The French armies looked stronger than anything Marlborough could muster. Gone, or nearly gone, was the chance that in another single campaign the French resistance could be pulverized. And if he failed or appeared to fail, how firmly could he rely on the loyalty of his new friends who had once raised such a clamour against the 'butcher's bill' of Malplaquet? The French troops had shown a wonderful resilience and, thanks no doubt chiefly to the political changes in London, that same spirit seemed to emanate from Louis's court at Versailles. For a while the Duke was comforted by the arrival of his trusted comrade-in-arms, Prince Eugene. Then came an unforeseen and terrible blow. So far from hastening a settlement the death of the Emperor had the opposite result. King Louis was encouraged to stage a diversionary attack across the Rhine towards Vienna and in the early weeks of June Eugene and his army were recalled to parry the attack. In the Duke's camp, a good peace—any peace—seemed further off than ever.

Marlborough, it seems—strangely, in view of his normally expert sources of intelligence—had still no inkling of the reports which Gaultier had brought back to London. Jonathan Swift was soon to be better informed. For a week or two he enjoyed a holiday at Wicomb 'wholly disengaged . . . from all public thoughts'. Then he returned to hear from St. John the first hint of the great developments which had not been divulged to the Captain-General. And while Marlborough went to war, Swift started sharpening his weapons for a more serious combat than he had ever contemplated before.

CHAPTER TEN

The Secret Peace

(June 12th—November 26th, 1711)

> 'He wondered to hear me talk of such chargeable and
> expensive wars; that certainly we must be a quarrel-
> some people, or live with very bad neighbours, and that
> our generals must needs be richer than our kings. He
> asked what business we had out of our own islands,
> unless upon the score of trade or treaty, or to defend
> the coasts with our fleet.—*Gulliver's Travels, A Voyage
> to Brobdingnag.*

PEACE WAS THE WORD on everyone's lips in the London
coffee-houses during that June of 1711 when the Duke of
Marlborough was marshalling his armies for the tenth campaign. But no one outside the tiny handful of Ministers admitted
to the secret could even begin to guess how the word might be
translated to the deed. A few days after the Queen had prorogued
Parliament—having expressed her special thanks for the sustenance provided to make possible the persecution of the war—Daniel
Defoe reported that the prospect of peace was 'all the discourse'
among the 'Stock-Jobbers, State-Jobbers and meer Street Politicians'. But he could find no foundation for their chatter. Apart
from the fact that the armies were not yet directly engaged in
battle, the only authority for the rumour was that '*they talk of it*'.
Defoe was unimpressed; he eagerly flaunted his superior knowledge to expose 'the chimera'.

More remarkable than his caution was the mood of scepticism
displayed towards these same rumours by the Duke of Marlborough. Early in June James Brydges, from his office in Whitehall, sent the Duke a secret message. 'It is looked upon here as
certain,' he said, 'that there are Propositions in agitation for a
General Peace. Your Grace must undoubtedly be apprised of them
if there are, tho ye treaty is carried on with ye utmost secrecy, if
there is one, I am inclined to believe, that ye Message which was
sent with so much privacy about three weeks ago to Holland was

upon that account.' Brydges's information happened to be correct. But, as far as we know, Marlborough took no steps to warn or consult with his friends at Hanover or The Hague, in Vienna or in London. Instead, he appeared to accept at their face value the assurances of good faith which St. John and Harley continued to shower upon him. He was obsessed by the military difficulties of the immediate campaign ahead and was already resigning himself to the view that yet another campaign might be required if the full harvest of military victory was to be garnered. The French General, Villars, had spent the winter and the spring perfecting his defensive system. The story ran that Marlborough had purchased a new scarlet coat of a cut which the tailor had described as *ne plus ultra*. Villars appropriated the phrase and boastfully applied it to his own defensive lines. Not for many months had the French shown such arrogance. A few more weeks passed and still no sign appeared that the posture of affairs was likely to be altered by military action. By the beginning of July Marlborough had devised a more ambitious plan to counter the French strategy. If little spectacular could be accomplished that summer and autumn, more might be achieved—possibly forcing the French to accept a peace that winter—by a project for keeping the allied armies ready in the field throughout the winter months with a threat of delivering a real offensive early in the following year. Since the expense would be considerable, the scheme called for detailed examination. Marlborough proposed to Harley that he should send his friend Lord Stair to London to discuss it. His idea was not limited to the military plane; probably he hoped that the better relations between himself and the Ministers at home might now be consolidated into a more settled and comprehensive understanding. Together, if the necessary fortitude and patience were forthcoming, they could contrive a situation where terms could be dictated to the French. Harley's reply was encouraging: 'I will not omit anything in my power, which may testify my zeal for the public, and my particular honour and esteem for your grace, and I doubt not, but when the lord you mention comes, I shall satisfy him of the sincerity of my intentions towards your grace.' When his old enemies spoke in so courteous a tone, the Duke might be pardoned for discounting the rumours of a 'peace' plot to which he was not a party.

Defoe also liked to believe that he was in Harley's confidence;

he became more aggressive in his attack on the rumour-mongers. In the first week of July he denounced as 'a Malicious Invective upon the Queen and the present Administration' any suggestion that Peace was to be made upon 'mean, precarious and dishonourable Terms'. Parliament had once advised the Queen not to sheathe the sword until the Spanish monarchy was restored to the House of Austria, and the Queen in reply had insisted that no peace would be safe without it. How insolent it was to suggest that a settlement which failed to secure these conditions was being contemplated now that Parliament had been shuffled out of the way!

No doubt Harley was happy to see his honour so readily defended; some of the opponents of the peace might be put off their guard. Possibly his assurances to Marlborough were sincere; who could tell whether a still closer accommodation with the Duke might not yet be most desirable or even necessary? It was St. John who resolved to press matters more vigorously, and he did so with a marvellous dexterity. To the Duke he expressed his confidence in the success of the military campaign. To the Dutch he sent repeated appeals that they should repose the utmost confidence in the Queen's Ministers. To his most intimate friends he revealed his soaring hopes that news of a splendid victory would soon come from Canada; the expedition to Quebec could bring fresh credit to the administration and assist in enforcing the peace on good terms. Of course, the peace *was* the supreme objective; St. John searched persistently for means of bringing it to reality. He did not hide his scorn for those with weaker nerves than his own. At one moment the rumours of peace caused alarm among the City men; at another the public credit was shaken by one of the periodic reports that the Pretender had embarked on an expedition from Brest. St. John was contemptuous of 'those of little genius and narrow soul, apt to take umbrage and to be startled at every trifle'.

He was not satisfied, like Harley, to play tricks with the public opinion of the coffee-houses which might blow one way or the other and bedevil their plans. He wanted to mould that opinion to his will. At the end of June and the beginning of July he was more than ever deeply engaged in consultation with Swift. One sign of their growing intimacy was the formation of the Brothers Club at which a dozen of St. John's closest friends—significantly Harley was excluded—agreed to meet and dine together every Thursday.

The idea was St. John's; Swift was left to frame the rules and make the arrangements. Yet Swift and St. John soon had business together which could not best be transacted even in this most private circle. The idea was mooted that when St. John moved with the court to Windsor, Swift should come with him to St. John's house where there was 'just room enough for him and me'. Swift himself was still on excellent terms with Harley and never failed to admire his unruffled demeanour in the face of all irritations. 'It seems to me', he wrote on July 12th, 'that the Ministry lie under a grievous dilemma, from the difficulty of continuing the war, and the danger of an ill peace; which I doubt whether all their credit with the Queen and country would support them under.' When so passionate a supporter of peace as Swift was dubious about the means of achieving it, the hazards may be measured. Harley's way was to wait on events with slothful smugness. 'He was saying a thing to me some days ago which I believe is the great maxim he proceeds by,' wrote Swift, 'that wisdom in public affairs was not, what is commonly believed, the forming of schemes with remote views; but the making use of such incidents as happen.' Through the hours of a drowsy evening, Swift could be beguiled by such a doctrine, especially when it came from the man who had so often exploited a sudden turn in events to suit his purpose. But a night or two later, when he was writing to Stella, or after a few hours in the company of St. John, the enchantment faded. The rough obstacles ahead were starkly clarified once more. Great issues of war and peace re-emerged in their grand perspective, and St. John's attraction was that he relished the coming struggle which Harley appeared all too ready to dismiss from his reckoning. In the middle of July Swift went to Windsor. There he played his part at the court, talked on equal terms with duchesses, even hunted in Windsor Park, with 'the Queen following in a chaise with one horse, which she drives herself, and drives furiously, like Jehu, and is a mighty hunter, like Nimrod'. But his most precious time was spent closeted with Mr. Secretary. More and more St. John was absorbed in directing the affairs of the nation and of Europe. But he always had time for Swift.

It is not hard to imagine the theme of those discussions which Swift found more engrossing than all the splendours of the court. Everything, indeed, depended on the peace. Once it was achieved no limit need be set to the ambitions of the Ministers. They would

be the masters of the scene at home and abroad and would possess
the necessary prestige to execute the full counter-revolution which
the Tory majority in the Commons demanded. And even if these
grandiose prospects had not beckoned so enticingly, immediate
necessity enforced the same logic. Marlborough's hint that no
dramatic victory in Flanders could be expected that year encouraged the natural Tory thrust to end the fighting. Even if he was
proved to be unduly pessimistic, how could the capture of a few
fortresses or even a major battle in Flanders change the aspect of
affairs in Spain where, after all, the fatal stumbling-block had
appeared on which previous peace negotiations had foundered?
Three years before, St. John had despaired of ever winning decisive
victory in Spain; all the intervening developments in that theatre
had confirmed his foresight. General Stanhope himself did not
share the blind optimism or complacency of his Whig friends at
home. He had indeed (so St. John recalled years later) sent back
reports that 'nothing could be done more in Spain, the general
attachment of the people to Philip, and their aversion to Charles
considered; that armies of twenty or thirty thousand men might
walk about that country till doomsday, so he expressed himself,
without effect: that wherever they came, the people would submit
to Charles the third out of terror, and as soon as they were gone,
proclaim Philip the fifth again out of affection: that to conquer
Spain required a great army: and to keep it, a greater'. Those were
the gloomy prognostications of a General wedded to the strategy
and fortunes of the Whigs, and now this same General was a
captive in the hands of the Spaniards. 'Was it possible, after this,'
asked St. John, 'to think in good earnest of conquering Spain?'
Surely only one answer was conceivable. And yet in the midsummer of 1711 this was by no means the common assumption.
Defoe, as we have seen, considered that he was exposing a slander
against the Ministers when he rebutted the charge that a peace
without victory in Spain might be tolerated. 'He who had judged
by appearances of things on one side at that time', wrote St.
John, 'would have been apt to think, that putting an end to the
war or to Magna Charta, was the same thing'. Many refused to
face the stubborn facts about the dismal outlook in Spain. Lord
Peterborough, for example—the friend of the Tories who had been
acclaimed by them as the infallible expert on Spanish affairs—
was still convinced that the situation there could be transformed by

a touch of his own magical genius. In short, the war party was still immensely strong. A general case for peace had been presented; no one engaged in the public debate had yet come down to particulars. Neither in the election campaign nor in the official utterances of the Queen or her Ministers nor even in the pages of the *Examiner* had anyone dared to analyse the terms on which peace could be secured and the risks which must be courted to gain it.

These were the obvious topics of discussion between St. John and Swift. Between desultory, endless war and the glittering prospects of peace there lay a fearful chasm. Public opinion must be rallied to make feasible the passage across it. St. John began to feel that the whole burden rested on himself. Swift more than anyone else he must have valued as a kindred spirit in the enterprise, the more so since Harley seemed content to bask in his newly-recovered popularity without caring how precarious it might be. And yet—so great were the risks—when the next positive step was taken, not even Swift was allowed to know. St. John was resolved to make a peace. He tackled the job with buoyant enthusiasm. Yet he did not forget that if the plan misfired his own head might not be safe.

When at the end of April St. John had communicated to the Dutch the proposals from King Louis brought over by the Abbé Gaultier the reaction among the great officials who served the States-General and largely governed the policies of the Republic was less violent or suspicious than might have been expected. The two most prominent among them were the Grand Pensionary, Anthony Heinsius, and the Pensionary of Amsterdam, Willem Buys. A rivalry between them complicated the task of devising a consistent Dutch policy to meet the new situation. Heinsius, an old man of seventy who had given a lifetime of loyal support to the dual task of building a Dutch barrier against France and sustaining the English alliance, had naturally found the change of government in London highly distasteful; hatred of the Dutch was an old Tory sentiment and the humiliations heaped on Marlborough had threatened to put in jeopardy the English support for the war in Flanders. It was the Whigs who had signed the Barrier Treaty assuring the Dutch that no peace would be accepted unless their war aims were secured; naturally their overthrow had bred suspicions at The Hague, and Heinsius soon learnt that St. John professed no rigid allegiance to the terms of the Barrier Treaty. Willem Buys, garrulous and secretive by turns, was the spokesman of a more pacific party. He took some pains to ingratiate himself with the representatives of the new English Ministry at The Hague as a more accommodating colleague than Heinsius; he was even dubbed by the Whigs 'a Tory Dutchman'. In fact, Heinsius wanted peace no less than Buys if he could get it on satisfactory terms, and Buys could not safely manœuvre so far that he put Dutch interests in danger. Despite their natural fears about English policy, it was still true that Marlborough had been sent back to command the armies. The Dutch leaders were unaware that the peace proposals had originated, not in Versailles, but in Whitehall. They knew nothing of Gaultier's comings and goings. So, in response to St. John's communication, they undertook no diplomatic *démarche* to insist on their rights. Instead, Heinsius was content to reply that the States-General was ready to negotiate, wishing only that the preliminary propositions should be more clearly defined than those which had come supposedly from King Louis: why not, he asked, revive the original terms which had proved abortive at the Gertruydenberg negotiations in 1709?

For St. John this response was most gratifying. A head-on clash with the Dutch had been avoided at a moment when it could have brought disaster; yet sufficient evidence of Dutch obstinacy had been elicited to assist him in convincing his colleagues that England must act alone. It was not his idea that the next step should be to recall a large-scale conference where the Dutch would retain the power of veto; that procedure might cast away all the advantages already secured by the Gaultier mission. Nor was he content that the critical negotiations should be left in the hands of Gaultier, receiving his instructions from the Ministers at second-hand through such a dubious go-between as Lord Jersey. The time had come for more resourceful action. It was therefore decided to send to France a more reliable emissary, an intimate member of the innermost Tory clique. Matthew Prior was the man chosen. Queen Anne thought it wrong 'to send people abroad of meane extraction', but she complied with the pleadings of her Ministers. That compliance was essential, for it was part of the Ministers' plan to dispatch their obedient servant on the authority of the Queen alone. If the Prior mission miscarried, if by any misfortune the secret got out, no single Minister could be held responsible.

'Mr. Prior', said the document written in St. John's hand-writing but signed by the Queen, 'is fully instructed and authorised to communicate to France our preliminary demands, and to bring back the answer.' Thus the Ministers embarked on their peace-making adventure behind the shield of the Queen.

All the circumstances surrounding the Prior mission illustrate how hazardous was the task of translating a vague sentiment for peace into practical measures. Prior and Gaultier were taken to Dover. They crossed to Calais in a hired fishing-boat. Protected by fictitious names—in his instructions Prior was described simply as 'the man', on his passport he was described as 'Jeremy Mathews' —they journeyed to Fontainebleau, there to parley with the Marquis of Torcy and later to be granted an audience with the Grand Monarch himself. Swift during those last weeks of July was the daily companion of St. John. They lived together at Windsor, walked together in the park for three or four hours at a time, or travelled across country to visit St. John's estate at Buckleberry. 'We were engaging in deep discourse', Swift wrote, 'and I was endeavouring to settle some points of the greatest consequence; and had wormed myself pretty well into him, when his under-secretary came in (who lodges in the same house with us) and interrupted all my schemes.' The two men had secrets to discuss which could not proceed in the presence of St. John's own Under-Secretary; yet the great secret of Prior's mission was withheld even from Swift.

One purpose of all these elaborate precautions was to ensure that no hint of the plan should reach the ears of the Duke of Marl-borough. If the forces opposed to peace at home and abroad were to be rallied in time, he was the man to do it. For weeks past Harley and St. John had competed with one another in disarming his suspicions. Now that fresh dangers were being courted with the Prior mission the deception was practised with an ever more delicate artistry. No open complaint on the part of the Duke was possible; the pledges of support from the two Ministers were too pressing and frequent. He was half or more than half convinced. But one lingering source of doubt remained—the stream of Grub Street libels which still percolated across to Holland. Marlborough could not finally suppress the thought that these attacks were engineered by the same St. John who attended to his military requirements with such exemplary promptitude. A close friend of the Duke at The Hague called Harry Watkins pleaded to John Drummond that action was needed 'to take off the *Examiner*, for he is grown our greatest grievance, and sours all other enjoyments'. In fact, the *Examiner* had refrained for several weeks from any renewed baiting of the Duke or the Duchess. But wounds inflicted by Swift did not heal quickly and doubtless it was the memory of these which kept alive the Duke's resentment. 'I tell my great man', said Watkins, 'he carries his point too far in suspecting those arrows come from the same quiver that has for some time past furnished very obliging pens.' Marlborough was conscious of the counter-charge that he was responsible for encouraging the *Medley* to harry the Tory Ministers. The mention of it destroyed his normal composure and in a flaming passion he replied: 'I wish the devil had the *Medley* and the *Examiner* together.'

A week or two later the *Examiner* did in fact lapse from the painful discretion sustained for some months previously. A blow was struck at the sorest point. Mrs. Manley took her readers on a tour of 'the House of Pride'; in other words the half-completed Blenheim Palace in Woodstock Park. 'This dazzling, unwieldly structure', she wrote, 'was built amidst the Tears and Groans of a People Harass'd with a lingring war, to gratifie the Ambition of a Subject, whilst the *Sovereign's Palace* lay in *Ashes*. It was dedicated, from the first Foundation, to the Goddess of Pride; the Building excessive *costly*, but not *artful*; the *Architect* seem'd to consider how to be most profuse and therefore neglected an advantageous Eminence (made proper by Nature) to build one a quarter of a Mile short of it, at the vain expense of Fifty Millions of Sesterces. There were to be seen stately *Towers*, noble *Porticos*, ample *Piazzas*, and well-turned Pillars, without one handsome Room, unless you will call the kitchens and cellars such, which part of the House happens to be of very little or no use to the *Parsimonious* Founder.' This effusion was a prelude to an equally offensive assault on the Duchess. It was written in the same month when the Duke received the news that further orders had been given by Harley for the completion of Blenheim. And on the very day it appeared Mrs. Manley applied to Harley for a pension as a recognition of her past services. Someone—and the suspicion points directly at Swift—must have told her those barbed details about Blenheim. Harley or St. John in turn must have told him how absurdly sensitive was the Duke on every matter affecting his great obsession. Perhaps also Drummond reported to his superiors in London the conversation he had had with Marlborough's outraged friend, Harry Watkins. For a week later (at the end of July) the *Examiner* was closed down and Mrs. Manley was driven by her 'infirmities and misfortunes' to seek refuge in 'a cheaper part of the Kingdom'. But she did eventually get her pension from the man who had solemnly pledged to serve the Duke with unfailing, almost sycophantic devotion. If Marlborough had known how much energy the Ministers spent in these secretive occupations, he would surely have been roused to protect himself. But, for all his doubts, the men who directed the *Examiner* were never unmasked by their victims. Only when all the actors in the drama were dead was it possible to appreciate fully how pervasive was the influence which the London press exerted; how unerringly the arrows shot from Grub Street found their target in the breast of the Captain-General.

If the closing down of the *Examiner* was one evidence of the sacrifice which the Ministers were prepared to make in the attempt to appease the Duke, there were plenty of others. While Matthew Prior was on the way to Paris, Lord Stair arrived in London. He was at once presented to the Queen who was 'very inquisitive as to your Grace's health'. Harley and St. John were equally gracious. A few days later St. John reported to the Duke that his detailed plans had been received most favourably; little remained, it seemed, except for the Queen to give her final blessing. 'I have since waited on my Lord Stair in town, and have spoke with all the openness and sincerity imaginable to him, as I make no doubt but he does me the justice to inform your Grace.' A few days later again the news arrived in London that the military front had suddenly become alive and that Marlborough had executed one of the most skilful manœuvres of his career. He had passed the lines of *ne plus ultra* without losing the life of a single soldier, achieving a position from which fresh military advantages might be extorted. St. John hastened to offer his congratulations. 'The hardest battles you have fought', he wrote on July 31st, 'and the greatest victories you have won cannot afford more honourable testimonies of your Grace's superior capacity, and of your indefatigable zeal for the public service, than your late success. For my own share, I have the joy which every honest man must feel when the common enemy receives a blow; and I have the additional satisfaction of a faithful friend in thinking that it was your Grace who gave it.' Fresh assurances followed that the project unfolded by Lord Stair was receiving detailed attention. 'And give me leave to add', said St. John, 'that for many reasons, your actions will have, at this point of time, a very uncommon lustre. I most ardently desire that uninterrupted prosperity may attend you, and that you may conclude this campaign to your entire satisfaction, in every respect, abroad and at home.' During the days that followed, as the news of military success was confirmed, St. John's praise for Marlborough's accomplishments knew no bounds. Not only to the Duke's friends was he most ready with his compliments; to his confidant, Drummond, he was hardly less ecstatic. 'I look on the progress which the Duke of Marlborough has lately made to be really honourable to him and mortifying to the enemy. The event cannot be ascribed to superior numbers, or to any accident. It is owing to genius and to conduct.' And when the critics raised their voices and Marlborough himself was aggrieved at the gibe that he had failed through negligence or incapacity to fight a more significant battle, St. John was among the first to repudiate the calumny.

It is not surprising that St. John's show of friendship appeared convincing to Marlborough; even today his words persuade. The inspired touches of flattery, the elaborate round-about compliments which could only reach the Duke's ear at second- or third-hand—as surely they were designed to do—almost convince us that St. John truly contemplated a solid alliance with the Duke. Was it all deception? Of course he had good reason for rejoicing that military pressure was being exerted on the French. He had always known that for a period at least the military campaign and the peace negotiations must be driven forward in double harness. But the special flavour of personal devotion to the Duke combined with the pledges to Lord Stair—were these not signs that St. John genuinely thought in terms of fulfilling his whole scheme in loyal association with the Duke?

It is a conceivable theory; but the objections are wellnigh overwhelming. St. John's apologia, written years later, tells against it. He was talking during the same weeks a very different language to Jonathan Swift. He was waiting anxiously for the report from Prior. And on that last day of July, when he expressed his undying allegiance to the Duke, another letter was written which soon revived in St. John's mind the fear that Marlborough was still potentially the most dangerous of his enemies. Count Gallas, the Austrian Ambassador in London, was the author of this decisive document. For months he had been alarmed by developments at the English court. His friends were among the Whigs and he deeply distrusted the loyalty of the new Ministers to the causes for which the war had been fought. Gallas smelt treachery, and the arch-traitor, in his estimate, was St. John. He admired St. John for his insight and diligence—'he investigates everything, takes everything in'—despised him for his debauchery, marvelled at his capacity to pursue his tastes without weakening his talents, and wondered where his 'arrogant and excessive fiery temper' would lead him and his country and the Grand Alliance whose fortunes he now so largely governed. All this he revealed to his masters in Vienna—*and to St. John*! For in the summer of 1711, St. John bribed the first secretary at the Austrian embassy to betray his ambassador and thereby laid his hands on the code which could unravel the most secret and perspicacious assessments of the situation at the English court made by the Austrian envoy. Gallas had pleaded with the Emperor to send to London an emissary with sufficient prestige to frustrate the policies on which the Queen had been persuaded to embark. The likely choice for the mission was Prince Eugene, Marlborough's comrade-in-arms. If Eugene set foot in Whitehall the Whigs and every other enemy of the peace would have a champion second only to Marlborough himself. The secret negotiations would be transformed overnight into a public debate capable of shaking the whole Kingdom and wrecking the peace. As the Gallas reports to Vienna arrived punctually on his desk, St. John must have known that time was not on his side. His enemies would soon be sounding the alarm. If he had forgotten how bitterly he was hated, here was the clinching proof. It is not surprising that he was goaded to frenzy by the phlegmatic Harley who spent his time calculating so nicely the most astute means of filling the latest vacancy in his administration, but who—as Gallas reported—would rarely apply his mind to the surging crisis of Europe. It would be pleasant to make a good peace in friendly collaboration with the Duke of Marlborough. Count Gallas's report gave warning to St. John how idle or deceptive that dream might be. At the greatest moments in history, statesmen must cease to compromise and calculate. They must choose, and risk fierce and deep-seated divisions in the state. St. John had the nerve to face the challenge even while he continued to practise a little longer the expert chicanery which concealed his choice.

*   *   *

By the first days of August Matthew Prior had completed his task in Paris. He had done his work well. Acting on St. John's instructions, he brought the prospect of peace within the arena of practical politics.

Before Prior's mission the negotiations conducted earlier by the Abbé Gaultier had produced the general framework for a peace. Gaultier had received his orders from Lord Jersey who in turn had acted for Harley. Jersey was a near Jacobite, his wife was a Roman Catholic, and in January—on Gaultier's advice—the Marquis of Torcy was persuaded to pay him £3,000 a year for his services. He was not even a member of the English Ministry for which he acted, although the rumour ran that he would soon be given an official post. The miracle was that discussions conducted in such a fashion had achieved so much. Three general propositions had been established. A barrier was to be erected in the Netherlands sufficient to guarantee the Dutch their security, although the inference was that the terms of the Barrier Treaty of 1709 were not necessarily to be fulfilled either in the letter or the spirit; England was to agree that King Philip V would be recognized as King of Spain and the Indies; and in reward for this concession England was to secure immense commercial advantages in Europe and America. During the exchanges from which these general ideas had emerged, other inferences had become apparent. The transaction was to be conducted secretly between France and Britain; Holland would be compelled to accept the agreed decision. England's other chief ally, Austria, was to be treated with a similar lack of consideration. Finally—although none knew how deeply, if at all, Harley was committed to this longer-term objective—Jersey, Gaultier and Torcy acted on the assumption that the peace might lead to a Jacobite restoration on the death of Queen Anne.

Such was the state of the negotiations when St. John was admitted to the secret in April. By the time he and Harley had dispatched Prior to Paris in July many of the propositions had been formulated with much greater precision. Lip-service was still paid to the ideal that 'we would make no peace but what should be to the satisfaction of our allies'. But the secret negotiation was itself a breach of that obligation, and the demands made on behalf of England, listed in much more detail than any of the other proposed items, underlined the duplicity of the whole proceeding. A long series of commercial advantages were demanded; for example, Gibralter and Port Mahon were to be conceded as a permanent security for England's Mediterranean trade; the fortifications of Dunkirk, long a threat to English merchants owing to the protection they gave to French privateers, were to be dismantled; the *Assiento* or monopoly of the Spanish-American slave trade was to be taken from the French and granted to the South Sea Company which Harley had founded with such a blare of trumpets a few months before. It was also insisted 'that all things in America should continue in the possession of those they should be found to be in at the conclusion of the peace.' How overflowing would be the acclaim for this particular clause when—as St. John confidently expected—the nation would awake one morning to learn that all Canada lay at the feet of Admiral Walker and Brigadier Hill! Altogether, St. John's terms for peace could open up a new world of riches for the merchants of England. If these terms could be secured even the City of London might be weaned from its Whig allegiance.

This, then, was the scheme presented with firm and accomplished politeness by Matthew Prior to Torcy and the French court. At first Torcy was horrified. No longer was he dealing with the Jersey he had bribed and the amenable Gaultier. Instead, England was demanding 'such considerable advantages as must absolutely ruin all commerce but her own'. The argument continued for several days. Prior was not to be frightened by hints that the Dutch also had been seeking a separate peace on their own account. He would not alter or abate his demands by one jot. Always he took refuge in the letter of his instructions that he was not empowered to negotiate. The consolation for the French was that he also made clear how eager were the English Ministers to make a peace and how readily they would betray their Dutch and Austrian allies to secure it—always provided that 'the secret shall be inviolably kept, till allowed to be divulged by the mutual consent of both parties concerned'. The bait was too tempting, even when it was obvious that the men who dangled it had strong nerves and stubborn aims. Matthew Prior combined obstinacy and friendship with a skill which St. John himself could not have excelled. Only one course seemed possible. Despite all the dangers, the talks must be transferred to England where the French might hope to negotiate instead of accepting what had begun to look more like a dictate. King Louis was not able to approve some of the 'terrible articles' which Prior had brought over, but he was willing to send his own emissary, M. Mesnager, to London to seek a reasonable accommodation.

So, at the beginning of August, Prior left Paris as secretly as he had come, accompanied by Gaultier and Mesnager. They crossed safely from Calais to Deal and had started out on the road to London. But their precautions were too clever; they had aroused the suspicions of an officious customs officer called John Macky who had often been employed in secret service jobs for the Government. He recognized Prior as an old acquaintance and wondered why this travelling companion of two Frenchmen had tried to pass himself off as an unknown Jeremy Mathews. At Canterbury all three were arrested and detained. The news of Macky's efficiency was reported to St. John and a hectic message from him was necessary to secure Prior's release. Thereupon also (according to his own account) Macky set out on a desperate ride to Tonbridge where he had friends who could pass on the information to Lord Sunderland and Count Gallas. Before leaving, however, he dispatched an express message to the Duke of Marlborough, acquainting him with his strange discovery. How true in every particular is Macky's report of the incident it is hard to tell; it may have been coloured by the fact that soon afterwards he was thrown in gaol and kept there during Her Majesty's pleasure. One fact is certain. St. John knew now that his secret might stay a secret only for a matter of days.

Only after this nerve-racking interruption was Prior able to complete his journey and help conduct his French friends to their destination at Windsor. On the night of August 12th he had supper at the house of Mr. Masham with Harley, St. John and Jonathan Swift. The news of his misadventure at Canterbury had not leaked out yet and by an incredible feat of reticence the Ministers succeeded in outlawing from the conversation in the presence of Swift any reference to Prior's activities in the previous weeks. St. John was on tenterhooks; how long could the story be concealed?

As it happened, for the moment he was lucky. For that night the four men had another topic, hardly less enthralling, to discuss which kept them awake and excited until well past two in the morning.

*　　*　　*

Once more St. John had shown his boldness. His sense of urgency was not limited to the diplomatic task. He, like many others, had long wished to see the Ministry reconstructed on a more solidly Tory footing. But Harley still preferred half-measures and postponement. After his own elevation to the peerage and the Lord Treasurership, he revealed little awareness of the perils which might be ahead if some of his Ministerial colleagues showed themselves tepid in the cause of peacemaking or if the Whigs mustered enough nerve to exploit their timidity. Even Swift's patience with his hero was sorely tested.

After the death of Lord Rochester in May, an obvious opportunity presented itself. Harley's closest associates were ready with advice, but nothing was done. A further opportunity occurred when in the middle of July Harley's chief confederate among the Whig Lords, the Duke of Newcastle, was killed after a fall from his horse. Who would succeed him as Lord Privy Seal? London buzzed with rumours. The Dukes of Buckingham, Shrewsbury, and Leeds, the Earl of Nottingham, the Lord Guernsey, (Nottingham's brother), the Earls of Clarendon and Jersey, were all mentioned as possible Tory candidates for the vacant offices. On the other hand—so the rumour ran—the Duke and Duchess of Somerset 'made great interest for the Lord Somers' and had even come near to persuading the Queen and Harley that this idea, which entailed a reconciliation with the most eminent (and the most bribable) of the Junto Whigs, was both feasible and desirable. The Duke of Shrewsbury, who had forfeited so much of his credit with his old Whig friends to work with Harley, made no effort to hide his disgust. St. John was outraged; these manœuvres might destroy any chance of making the peace talks succeed. Why must Harley attempt these tight-rope acrobatics when a single slip could bring catastrophe? Was it merely due to his 'trimming disposition'? Could the Tories be expected to sit quiet under the offensive hint dropped so tactlessly by Harley—after the manner in which Prime Ministers are often inclined to try the patience of their most devoted and aspiring followers—that he was 'at a loss to find persons qualified for several places'? Or was there real truth in the suggestion that 'the Queen interposes'?

If this last thought ever reached St. John's ears, it must have given a fresh spur to action. He had long suspected the Duke of Somerset. Ever since that great nobleman had flounced out of London in protest at the news of the dissolution of the Parliament in the previous year he had been an uneasy and unwelcome associate of the new Ministers. Now the story was that he was busy working against them. Stupid and insanely proud though he might be, his influence could not be despised. No one was closer to the Queen than the Duchess of Somerset; she shared none of her husband's failings; friend and foe alike paid tribute to her cunning and graceful temper. Since the Tories owed their rise to power partly to Mrs. Masham's friendship with the Queen, they were naturally sensitive and jealous at the thought that their own favourite might be ousted by another. Swift was hugely impressed by these signs of successful Whig infiltration; 'to make a stratagem succeed a second time, and this even against those who first tried it upon them'—this surely was 'a plain demonstration of their superior skill at intrigue'. Whatever the truth about these machinations or the Duchess of Somerset's part in them, St. John felt himself the victim of a persistent hostility emanating from the court. In the Tory imagination, the vision of the sinister, captivating, ever-vigilant Duchess of Somerset swelled to monstrous proportions. All but Harley were alarmed by the apparition. No doubt he comforted himself with the thought that if a crisis came he could manipulate the Duke and even the Duchess as he had so many others before them and, in any case, the counterweight of some Whiggish influence at the court was needed if his balancing trick was still to be sustained. But St. John scorned or feared these nice calculations. The occasion arose when he could sweep them aside; either from growing fury with Harley's delays or from sudden hot temper, he seized it with both hands. While the Queen was at Windsor it was the custom of the Duke of Somerset to stay at the court during the week and depart when the other Ministers arrived at the week-end. On Saturday, August 12th, he changed his routine and turned up that night at the Cabinet council— the very council, perhaps, when St. John intended to report on Prior's mission and devise the next instructions for the peace talks with Mesnager. St. John refused to join the council in the presence

of the Duke, and as a result of his protest the meeting was abandoned. He told a friend that he would not sit with a man who had
so often betrayed them.

This was the sensational item of news which kept Harley, St.
John, Prior and Swift talking so late around Mr. Masham's table
on the night of August 12th. Next day the council was held without
the assistance of the Duke of Somerset; he spent the day at Ascot
where two days before a new race-course had been opened under
royal patronage. St. John, in Swift's words, had 'declared open
war'. To secure the peace and win untrammelled power for the
Tories and himself he would risk making immortal enemies—even
if the mighty Duchess of Somerset must be counted among them.
The risk was the greater since just at this moment another hazard
was added to the course which the men who wished to change the
face of Europe must run in the critical weeks ahead. Mrs. Masham
was about to have a baby. For a while her watchful eye would be
removed from the Queen's bedchamber and the sway of the Duchess would be left undisputed. But the great world could not wait
even for such momentous interruptions as Mrs. Masham's confinement ('God send her a good time; her death would be a
terrible thing,' wrote Swift). For Somerset had been changed from
a testy neutral into a bitter enemy; very soon, within a matter of
days or even hours, he would be seeking allies among the Whigs.
The perils which already lurked in the disclosure of Prior's mission
were multiplied. Once more for St. John the stakes were mounting.
Victory, if attainable at all, must be speedy and complete.

Had St. John over-reached himself? For a week or two after his
challenge to the Duke of Somerset some signs suggested that he
had. Harley disapproved of these brusque tactics. One indication
of his displeasure was the effort he made to win Swift away from
his ever-growing intimacy with St. John. Swift still regarded the
Lord Treasurer as 'much the greatest Minister I ever knew';
whenever Harley exerted himself, the Vicar of Laracor's strongest
tie of affection was quickly revived. But Swift was also convinced
that St. John was indispensable: 'I do not see well how they can
be without the Secretary who has very great abilities both for the
cabinet and Parliament.' He worked ceaselessly for a reconciliation. 'Do you know', he wrote to Stella, 'that I have ventured all
my credit with these great ministers to clear some misunderstand-
ings betwixt them: and if there be no breach, I ought to have the

merit of it? Tis a plaguy ticklish piece of work, and a man hazards losing to both sides.'

The ancient dispute about the proper composition of the Ministry, now sharply exacerbated by the exclusion of Somerset from the Cabinet council, was not the only one between the two men. 'They vary a little about their notions of a certain General. I will say no more at this distance,' reported Swift cautiously to Archbishop King. How precisely their notions diverged on that perennial and all-important theme it is possible only to guess. Outwardly both strove to improve still further the good relations now restored with the Duke. On August 17th St. John acknowledged 'with abundance of thanks, the favour of your Grace's private letters; and I hear with great pleasure how successfully you proceed in the difficult task which you have undertaken'. Renewed promises were given that Marlborough's project for the coming winter would soon be confirmed by the payment of the necessary money. 'I am truly concerned for your Grace's health which I heartily wish may be restored, and that you may long live to enjoy the blessings of an honourable peace, which will, whenever it is made, be due to the fatigues and dangers of the war which you have sustained.' But St. John's protestations of friendship for the Duke were combined with continued efforts to keep him in ignorance of the true nature of the peace talks. Perhaps this was the more fundamental cause of the quarrel. Harley may still have hoped that an accommodation with the Duke was possible; if so, an attempt should be made to enlist his sympathy by a carefully contrived release of the secret. Moreover, Marlborough's support might have its value for him to counteract the overbearing influence of St. John. St. John preferred shock tactics; let the business with King Louis's representative be concluded first; then the Duke and all other such potential allies of the Whigs as Count Gallas would be confronted with a *fait accompli*. St. John's idea was to mobilize his strength for a struggle; Harley still pinned his faith to the arts of persuasion. St. John was loath to admit more participants than were absolutely necessary to a knowledge of the French negotiations. Harley looked on with some jealousy as the assiduous Secretary of State, speaking perfect French and in daily contact with Prior and Mesnager, firmly grasped the key to events in his hands. Swift's task in smoothing the animosities between them was made all the more 'ticklish' since as yet he, like Marlborough, had to be content with second-hand reports of the greatest developments behind the scenes.

But, thanks to Prior's misadventure at Deal, neither St. John nor Harley were able to keep their manœuvres strictly private. While the coffee-house politicians were still speculating about St. John's clash with Somerset, news of Prior's mission to Paris began to filter through. The ever-watchful Count Gallas was one of the first to get wind of it; he at once demanded an explanation from Harley. 'There was no reason for alarm (so Harley was reported to have answered). For the Queen would never make a Peace, derogatory to any Engagements She had with Her Allies.' But the time was past when these soporifics could suffice. A report of Prior's arrest had leaked to Holland (perhaps John Macky's message had reached its destination) and John Drummond wrote urgently to his masters to ask how he should pacify the suspicions of the Dutch.

Total concealment was no longer feasible; something must be done to still the alarm while the discussions with Mesnager continued. On August 23rd a remarkable article appeared in the *Postboy*, another of the journals suspected of taking its directions from St. John. The article amounted to an admission that some 'clandestine negotiations' had in fact been taking place. But the excuse was offered that the Dutch themselves had been seeking separate negotiations with the French, and the impression was conveyed that the English Ministers were unshakably determined to protect English interests. Never would they be outwitted by the tricksters of Versailles—'The Britains still turned a deaf Ear to the melodious Accents of that deluding Syren.' Not all, however, were deceived by this daring prevarication. The *Postboy*, said Abel Boyer, the rival Whig journalist, was such a scandalous sheet that normally few people took much notice of it. But this particular article was written with 'a better Stile, a cleaner Turn, and more Art'. The idea obviously was to put a more favourable construction on the clandestine negotiations, to fly a kite for the Ministers, 'to feel the Pulse of the Nation'. James Brydges had no difficulty in reading between the lines. On the night the *Postboy* article appeared, he wrote to the Duke of Marlborough: 'We have a strong report in town of a secret negotiation of peace being carried on, and that which confirms people in this opinion is the search that was lately made of some persons as they landed upon coming over from France, but were released again upon their producing passes from the Secretary of State and all their papers delivered to them . . . Mr. Prior was declared to be one of their number. I would not trouble your Grace with a matter of town talk if I had not a reason to look upon it as being true and that he went over almost three weeks ago with Monsieur de Torcy's secretary, and whether the treaty has been desired by the French and what promises have been offered or asked I am wholly a stranger to.' Next day, in his letter to Stella, Swift made the first mention of the matter which so strangely had not been divulged even to him: 'Prior has been out of town these two months, nobody knows where, and is lately returned. People confidently affirm he has been in France, and I half believe it. It is said, he was sent by the ministry, and for some overtures towards Peace. The secretary pretends he knows nothing of it.'

The Secretary had every reason for anxiety. All his elaborate efforts to prevent a premature disclosure of the peace talks were breaking down. Harley was muttering discontentedly, and perhaps contemplating a bolder stroke against him. The Duke of Shrewsbury was losing his nerve and complaining that the Allies would soon be raising a clamour against these backstairs methods. Yet St. John was not easily rattled. The taste of victory, the game itself, was too exhilarating. And on August 24th he had encouraging news from the other side of the Atlantic. Reports had been received at St. John's, Newfoundland, 'of the fleet under Mr. Hill, having sailed up the river of Canada to Quebec, whilst Colonel Nicholson was marched overland with the militia of the Queen's colonies, and the Indians, into New France. This disposition being exactly agreeable to their private instructions the news is, without dispute, authentic, and I believe you may depend on our being masters, at this time, of all North America'. St. John imagined he had won a second Blenheim in the New World. Such tidings called for a special celebration. That night Swift was walking in the Mall with a friend: 'and Mr. Secretary met us and took a turn or two, and then stole away, and we both believed it was to pick up some wench; and tomorrow he will be at the cabinet with the queen: so goes the world.'

Next morning St. John was in 'a mighty hurry'; he was off to Windsor. Swift saw him for a moment, but had no time to check the now well-established rumour about Prior. At the Cabinet council six men—Harley, St. John, Prior, Lord Jersey, the Duke of Shrewsbury and St. John's fellow-Secretary of State, Lord

Dartmouth—were appointed plentipotentiaries to conduct and sign the preliminaries of peace with Mesnager. These six, along with the Queen, alone knew how near the business had been brought to a consummation. They still enjoined the utmost secrecy on one another even though the speculation about Prior's journey could not be stifled altogether. Harley, however, felt it no longer possible to keep the Duke of Marlborough completely in the dark—he would hear the rumours from London; possibly he was already making inquiries on the basis of Macky's report: some explanation must be offered. 'I have delayed mentioning a particular of great moment,' wrote Harley on August 26th, 'because I have no cipher to write to your Grace, but I shall reserve the whole to send by Lord Stair. In general it is this: the French made an offer to the Queen of a general peace, and to do it by the canal of England. The Queen's answer was she would enter into no separate treaty, neither should it be transacted here; she had several things to demand for the good and quiet of her dominions, but she was resolved not to act without her allies, and particularly the States. They (the French) sent a paper in general promising satisfaction to all the allies, in barriers, in trade, and all other articles: this being thought too general, they have sent a man over to explain it: what he says will all be transmitted over by Lord Raby.' Considering the decision reached at the Cabinet council only the day before, Harley's first intimation to the Duke of the peace negotiations in which he had been engaged over a period of some eight months could hardly have been more disingenuous. Even so he went further in revealing the truth than St. John would have advised. 'I can say no more than this,' added Harley with a characteristic smirk of combined humility and deceit, 'that I shall leave it to my actions to speak for me, and so give your Grace demonstration that I am the same man towards you as I was the first day I had the honour of your acquaintance.'

Both Harley and St. John must have known that a common policy for dealing with the Duke had become imperative; yet more and more their temperaments and ambitions jarred, and they sought their separate ways. Swift was unusually dispirited as well as anxious. 'Burn all politicks!' was his verdict to Stella. (Doubtless she agreed with him.) 'The Whigs whisper', he wrote on August 27th, 'that our new ministry differ among themselves, and they begin to talk out Mr. Secretary: they have some reasons for their whispers, although I thought it was a greater secret. I do not much like the posture of things; I always apprehended, that any falling out would ruin them, and so I have told them several times. The Whigs are mighty full of hopes at present; and whatever is the matter all kinds of stocks fall. I have not yet talked with the secretary about Prior's journey. I should be apt to think it may foretell peace; and that is all we have to preserve us.'

Some easement for his fears was offered by the move at last made by Harley to carry through the long-awaited reconstruction of the Ministry. He had made up his mind, it was said, to secure the appointment of Lord Jersey to the office of Lord Privy Seal left vacant by the Duke of Newcastle's death. Then, on the day after his appointment to the committee of six, Lord Jersey himself died. Two days later Harley made it known that a successor had been chosen. John Robinson, Bishop of Bristol, had never been mentioned among the long list of eligible candidates so eagerly canvassed by their friends. But he was a perfect choice for Harley. He had a reputation as a moderate and, unlike Lord Jersey, had none of the Jacobite taint about him; on the other hand the elevation of a churchman to so important a secular post was bound to be most acceptable to the Tories. Harley had managed to extract some gain for himself from a duty which might so easily have embroiled him in fresh difficulties either with the high-flying Tories or the moderate Whigs whom he still sought to cultivate. He considered the situation still well within his control, despite the obstreperous ambition of St. John, the renewed vigour of the Junto Whigs, the pressure of the Octobrists and the unavoidable risks involved in the peacemaking.

Neither St. John nor Swift could share his contentment. One sign that something more than Harley's artifice might be needed to meet the new situation was the growing impudence of the coffee-house wits. That Matthew Prior, one of their own number, had been unmasked as the hero or the villain of some unfinished drama offered an opportunity too good to be missed. 'Matt's peace' became a favourite topic for ballads and poems.

> '*The news from abroad does a secret reveal*
> *Which has been confirmed both at Dover and Deal*
> *That our Master Mathews, once called Plain Matt,*
> *Has been doing in Paris the Lord knoweth what.*'

The same ballad-singer prophesied: 'Poor Matt in the pillory soon will be seen.' As yet the Whig journalists did not take the tale of his mission too seriously. But at that moment, while they scoffed and rhymed, Poor Matt was one of the plenipotentiaries acting directly on the authority of the Queen; Mesnager, the emissary of King Louis, was secreted in his house in Duke Street, Westminster, where the back door was left open at night so that Harley and St. John could arrive to continue the negotiations, safe from the prying eyes which had come so near to piercing the last flimsy veil of secrecy.

*　　*　　*

The miracle was that the great deception was still succeeding. Daniel Defoe, for example, like many others, was not much impressed by the rumours about Prior which reached his ears. He still poured scorn on the idea either that peace was imminent or that anyone would seek it on terms less advantageous than the French had offered a year before. 'That Spain', he wrote in his *Weekly Review* of September 1st, 'should be abandon'd, it certainly never enter'd any Men's Heads, that were not Mad; no Minister the King of France has, expects it; no Minister England ever had, could, without Distraction, think of venturing, and the suggesting it at this Time, I must acknowledge, I look upon as a Plot against the Allies, to render them Jealous of one another.' Harley and St. John knew so much better than their naïvely trusting servant. St. John probably did not know that Harley had broached the general topic to Marlborough, albeit in terms calculated to mollify his fears. At the beginning of September St. John was still insisting to Harley how vital it was that the Duke should 'not be in the secret of the peace'. Justifiably or unjustifiably, he even cited messages from Amsterdam suggesting that both Heinsius and Buys were also eager not to arouse Marlborough's slumbering suspicions. But to parry the dangers which must arise if the truth about the peace negotiations should get out too soon it was not enough to rely on luck. Fresh resort was made to the second line of defence already employed in the *Postboy*. Yes, peace negotiations were afoot, but no one need be alarmed. 'A General Peace', said the *Postboy* at the beginning of September, 'was upon the Anvil, which France proposes in Terms so very Advantageous, that 'tis probable it may take.'

At this point, Swift took a hand, possibly acting alone, probably with the connivance of St. John. He was hard at work on other business for St. John, but for a few days he put it aside to produce what he gleefully described to Stella as 'a project to bite the town'. On September 11th appeared a pamphlet with the elaborate title: *'A New Journey to Paris: Together with some Secret Transactions Between the Fr—h K—g, And an Eng— Gentleman. By the Sieur du Baudrier. Translated from the French. London. Printed for John Morphew, near Stationers Hall*, 1711.' 'This morning', Swift wrote to Stella, 'the printer sent me an account of Prior's journey; it makes a two-penny pamphlet; I suppose you will see it, for I dare engage it will run; tis a formal grave lie, from beginning to end.'

Lie or no lie, the *New Journey* left the Whig journalists puzzled how to retaliate. 'The generallity', wrote Abel Boyer with grudging admiration, 'expressing their Readiness, rather to bear the Burthen of Taxes sometime longer, than lose, by a precarious Peace, the Fruits of so many Victories and Conquests, gain'd in the Course of this Expensive, but Necessary War, it was thought fit to seem to strike in with the Humour of the People.' How could a Whig lay hold of this eel-like enemy? Here Prior was portrayed as the highly skilful and robust agent of a masterful government reducing the French to an abject state of pleading. The story was told with such a plethora of intimate detail that even today it is hard to believe the incidents so gravely described never actually occurred. The alleged author of the piece was a French valet berated in the introduction for giving himself airs above his station. Yet into his mouth were put some of the favourite Tory gibes against the Duke and Duchess of Marlborough ('In England, as I was informed, the wealth of the Kingdom was so divided among the people, that little or nothing was left to their sovereign; and that it was confidently told—though hardly believed in France—that some subjects had palaces more magnificent than Queen Anne herself.') How impudent to let an eavesdropping French rascal repeat the gossip from the London coffee-houses; somehow these jeers so casually interpolated acquired a new authenticity. Yet how difficult to come to grips with the argument, and how hopelessly ineffective to answer a joke with some ponderous contention!

These, however, were only the side glances. The main tale which Sieur du Baudrier had to tell was highly flattering to English pride. From behind the wainscot he overheard the furious controversy between Monsieur Prior and the representative of King Louis. 'Good God!' cried King Louis's spokesman. 'Were ever such demands made to a great monarch, unless you were at the gates of his Metropolis? For the love of God, Monsieur Prior, relax something, if your instructions permit you, else I shall despair of any good success in our negotiation? It is not enough that our King will abandon his grandson, but he must lend his own arms to pull him out of the throne? Why did you not open yourself to me at Boulogne? Why are you more inexorable here at Versailles? You have risen in your demands, by seeing Madame Maintenon's desire for a peace? As able as you are to continue the war, consider which is to be most preferred, the good of your country, or the particular advantage of your general; for he will be the only gainer among your subjects.' How often had Monsieur Prior heard that same sneer from the lips of St. John or Swift! But in the vineyard of Versailles where he later met the Grand Monarch himself, accompanied by Madame Maintenon, nothing could mitigate the superb effrontery with which he presented the ultimatum of Her Majesty's most patriotic Ministers. The terms (whatever they might be) must be accepted, all or none. Whether in fact they were accepted was left a mystery. For, on this resounding note, Monsieur Prior took his leave. 'I will make no reflections on this important affair,' wrote the anonymous translator who purported to introduce this French tract to the English public, 'nor upon the consequences we may expect from it: To reason upon secrets of State, without knowing all the springs and motions of them is too common a talent among us, and the foundation of a thousand errors.'

In this manner the Whig journalists who dared voice their suspicions about the peace were rebuked for their curiosity and ignorance. Even weeks later those who guessed the author—as the well-informed Abel Boyer did—were still scratching their heads. Was the story fictitious or genuine? Fictitious, thought Boyer; but how infuriating not to know for certain! Boyer detested Swift, denounced him as 'a Tantivy' who had changed parties for gain; '*Haughty* and *Stiff* with most Men, *Cringing* and *Obsequious* with those in Power'; successful in his cringing, too, except perhaps with Harley who (as Boyer comforted himself) was not so ready to play the high Tory game. If this wretch Swift was truly the author, what could be the meaning of it? No Whig had mocked the French

—including even the Grand Monarch himself—with a raillery so outrageous. And whether the pamphlet was true or false, the gnawing doubt remained; could it really be true that the Tories were negotiating a peace so glorious and honourable that no Whig would be left with grounds for complaint?

That was the inference presented to the public in this pamphlet with sensational impact. It 'furnished fools with something to talk of', said Swift; even the wisest would have difficulty in devising a retort. Swift had the satisfaction of knowing that the whole town was talking about it; a thousand copies were sold within twenty-four hours. On the day of publication St. John sent him an urgent message to come and dine at Prior's. Prior was angry, or at least affected to be so. 'Here is our English liberty!' he said as he showed the offending pamphlet to Swift. Swift read some of it, said he 'liked it mightily, and envied the rogue the thought; for had it come into my head, I would have certainly done it myself'. Many of the details divulged so brazenly were accurate—sufficiently so for Mesnager to tell Torcy that the truth of Prior's voyage had been revealed along with some falsehoods. Where had Swift got them? The obvious likelihood was that St. John had told him. To have been the agent who revealed at least part of the truth which all London hankered to know must have been for Swift a pleasant revenge for the caution of his friends in hiding it from him so long. 'I believe we shall have a peace,' he wrote that night; at last he could see a break in the clouds. But if others with very different ideas of England's honour and interest were still not too much alarmed, much of the credit was due to the camouflage which Swift supplied for the vital discussions now proceeding at Prior's house.

That night at Prior's (September 11th) St. John received a packet containing the latest news from the battlefield. The fortress of Bouchain had fallen to Marlborough's siege. Risking his own life to make the necessary reconnaissances and conducting the whole operation in the presence of a stronger French army commanded by the greatest of French generals, the Duke had achieved one of his most brilliant triumphs. Marlborough was prouder of this victory than of almost any other. St. John at once expressed his enthusiasm. The 'peace' party at Prior's broke up at ten o'clock. An hour later St. John sent to the Duke his thanks for 'the news which adds to your glory and our happiness: I have sent an express to Windsor with your Grace's letter to the Queen, the tower guns

I have ordered to fire, and I beg you to believe that I take such part in this success as becomes an honest man, and, my Lord, Your Grace's faithful Henry St. John'. Two days later something like a pledge was allied to the words of praise. 'There is nothing wanting to complete your glory, or the dishonour of the enemy,' he wrote, adding as proof that everything would be done to support the Duke's project for the ensuing winter even though the Dutch were showing hesitations. 'On the Queen's part,' insisted St. John, 'nothing will be neglected, as I hope my Lord Stair has satisfied you before this letter can come to your hands.'

As it happened, Lord Stair had not been completely deceived during his visit to London; for all the excessive courtesy shown towards him, he sensed a coldness in the atmosphere. Plans for Marlborough's project hung fire; promises were made, but the business was never concluded. In the end he returned to Marlborough's camp at Bouchain with what he described (years later) as 'a bamboozling letter' from Harley. If Marlborough was not bamboozled, at least he was kept quiescent. Considering the profound insight he had shown in analysing the English political scene to the Hanoverian envoy only a few months before, nothing is stranger than the lethargy which now settled upon him. Seemingly, Harley's earlier letter describing the overtures for peace had prompted no violent response. 'Nothing in the world', wrote Marlborough soon after the fall of Bouchain, 'can be more agreeable to my inclinations than to be in any way instrumental in the concluding, as soon as possible, such a peace as may be to the satisfaction of her majesty, and the good of my country.' Lord Stair's arrival did not rouse him from his mood of tolerance. Harley's deceit and St. John's flattery were too persuasive. Hard on the news that the tower guns were firing to celebrate a Marlborough victory as in the old days of Blenheim and Ramillies came further advice from Harley on 'the affair of the peace'. 'The sum of what is hitherto done is this,' Marlborough was told by Harley. 'Some in Holland having this summer, by divers ways, endeavoured to set on foot a negotiation for peace, and France not being prevailed with to begin with them sent a proposition directly to England. The Queen declared she would enter into no separate treaty, nor would receive anything she would not transmit to the States. Upon this, they sent a general offer of giving satisfaction to England, to Holland, to the emperor and all the allies, and to give a real surety for our commerce; but this being only in general, it was insisted upon that it should be explained, which they sent one to do, and he is ordered to prepare such a proposition, as may be fit to be transmitted to Holland, which is not yet done. This is the sub-stance of everything which hath passed. I suppose in very few days we shall show whether they are in earnest. This is kept as secret as it can be, though there is not one step taken which will not speedily be laid open in Holland. . . .' This cool, uncandid account of the affair was accompanied by the firmest promise yet that the winter project would be backed to the hilt: 'I will immediately issue such sums of money as you shall judge necessary, for making the re-quisite magazines.'

Harley's bamboozling letter achieved its intended effect with the Duke; Swift had put many inquisitive noses off the scent with his *New Journey*; when the tower guns fired, on St. John's orders, to celebrate Bouchain even the staunchest Whig might be pardoned for abating his suspicions. Yet all these devices, successful as they were in protecting the Ministers' secret a while longer, could not keep Grub Street in order. Throughout the weeks of September a trickle of political personages started back to London after the summer exodus; the coffee-houses became busier; speculation naturally centred on the talk about the peace. In particular the nerve of the Whig writers was stronger than that of their leaders, their suspicions less easily tamed. Swift had noted the recovery of their spirit at the end of August; during the weeks of September they grew more audacious. A friend of Harley's expressed his dis-gust: 'At the same time that the outed family (the Marlboroughs) are applauded above measure, and bloated on the success at Bou-chain, I find they double their malice against your Lordship, and spare no cost to encourage pamphlets against the Ministry. Tis a notion in the pamphlet shops that Whiggish libels sell best, so industrious are they to propagate scandal and falsehood. The tak-ing of Bouchain now animates them afresh, 'tis a mighty glorious thing for them to be as long taking a little town as our ancestors have been in reducing all France. . . .' Swift was naturally con-cerned. 'The pamphleteers begin to be very busy against the ministry,' he wrote on September 21st; 'I have begged Mr. Secre-tary to make examples of one or two of them; and he assures me he will. They are very bold and abusive.' Ironically, one of the first of whom St. John had to make an example was his own hireling, Abel

Roper, who ran the *Postboy*. Count Gallas complained directly to St. John of aspersions on the Emperor in the columns of the *Postboy*. Roper was summoned before the Under-Secretary and required to reveal the sources of his intelligence. He escaped with a caution, but continued—according to his rival Boyer—'his licentious and bold way of writing'.

Even more licentious and bold and—what was much worse in St. John's eyes—strongly Whiggish in sympathy was the sermon preached on September 11th at a Thanksgiving Service for Bouchain by Marlborough's chaplain, Dr. Francis Hare. Writing to a friend in Holland who had means of passing on information to the Duke, St. John for the first time in months gruffly replaced compliments with a threat. The intermediary between St. John's friend and the Duke was the same Harry Watkins who two months before had dared to raise complaints about the *Examiner*. 'You will do well to observe from what I write to you,' wrote St. John now as a final comment on the licence of the press in Britain, 'that the *Examiner* is silent, but that my Lord Marlborough's stupid Chaplain continues to spoil paper. They had best for their patron's sake, as well as their own, be quiet. I know how to set them in the pillory, and how to revive fellows that will write them to death.' He was better than his word. That same day Swift was complaining that he had 'a plaguy deal of business on my hands, and very little time to do it'.

Dr. Francis Hare was not quite so stupid as St. John claimed. Nor was his sermon confined solely, as St. John alleged, to 'one entire panegyric upon his Grace, and an invective, I think, against the Queen, and all who serve her'. Rather was it a sustained plea that the fruits of victory should not be thrown away by premature peacemaking. It came very near the bone. So St. John was gratified to be able to inform one of his correspondents that 'somebody or other has been provoked by it; an answer full of spirit has come out'; and 'the Duke of Marlborough had been used worse than ever he was'. His gratification was not so surprising since the somebody or other was Mrs. Manley who had been well briefed by Swift and probably by St. John himself. Together they made mincemeat of 'the Chaplain-General'.

Together they had revived the old vendetta against the Duke in language unheard since the *Examiner* went out of business. If Marlborough had had spies in Grub Street one small degree as efficient as those he employed across the battle lines, this warning should have been sufficient. Once more St. John had declared open war. Either the Duke of Marlborough must be cowed or he would be fought. Six weeks before, St. John had challenged the Duke of Somerset. No fatal consequences had followed, although many believed the Duchess continued to increase her influence at court. But to challenge the Duke of Marlborough was a more formidable enterprise. St. John believed that he was now in a better position to deliver it. His terrific labours of the previous two months were bearing fruit. 'I verily believe they are contriving a Peace as fast as they can, without which it will be impossible to subsist,' wrote Swift on September 23rd.

*　　*　　*

On Wednesday, the 26th of September (according to the report by Abel Boyer), 'some Mobb gathered about a House in the Street Call'd Pell-Mell, upon a Report, that two Ministers, lately arrived from France, were lodg'd there, whom they were curious to see'. If that mob wished to demonstrate against Popish spies or agents of King Louis, they or the Whig journalists who incited them were too late. Everything had now been agreed between the English Ministers and the French emissaries.

For nearly six weeks St. John had wrestled with Mesnager and several of his own colleagues to drive through the bargain. Considering how crowded were all his other occupations and dissipations the feat was prodigious. Week by week, his energies were distracted by the activities of the Duke and Duchess of Somerset, by the need to appease the Duke of Marlborough, by the clamour of the newspapers. Hardly a day passed without a long confabulation with Swift. Yet how precious was the secrecy he had managed to preserve by so much diligence; without it the discussions with Mesnager, intricate and awkward enough in themselves, would almost certainly have come to naught. When he first arrived, Mesnager still had some lingering doubts, despite Prior's mission, whether the English Ministers were really determined to make a peace. Once he met them face to face, the fear on their countenances, the quarrels between them, their exorbitant demands brought him near to the point when he considered returning home. But gradually the truth emerged in a clearer light. Perhaps the very lives of the men who treated with him more in the fashion of conspirators than statesmen were at stake. They must have a peace,

261

yes; but it must be one they could present to their countrymen as a triumph. Hence the rigid, sometimes extortionate, demands they made for the benefit of English commerce. Yet when Mesnager was on the point of yielding, some among their number, notably Shrewsbury, lost their will. How would the allies receive the news that England had grabbed such loot for herself behind their backs? Mesnager had no authority to make the concessions required; Gaultier had to be sent back to Versailles to get fresh instructions. On his return all seemed settled. Harley, with the aid of several glasses of claret, treated Mesnager as a friend and toasted the King of France as his good ally. But still there were further crises to be surmounted. At the eleventh hour other English Ministers—the Duke of Buckingham, Lord Poulett and the Bishop of Bristol—were brought into the talks and each 'to show his penetration' proposed new alterations in the terms already approved. Violent disputes arose over such various issues as the future of the Pretender and fishing rights in Newfoundland. Mesnager was pressed hard to exceed his authorized powers. In the end he was confronted with a threat—Pensionary Buys had been appointed to come to England; if the wrangling continued, a new and perhaps intransigent party would arrive at the bargaining table. Mesnager could threaten too; if he was forced to return to Paris for fresh instructions, how easily could 'some unlucky miscarriage' ruin the whole prospect. Throughout the whole proceedings—so Mesnager thought—only one English Minister held unshakably to his purpose. Nothing could disturb the resolution of St. John. He was bold in his demands; but his was the driving force which swept away one obstacle after another.

At last, on September 27th, the preliminaries were agreed. They took the form of three instruments. One signed by Mesnager, St. John and Dartmouth (with both the English Ministers expressly and guardedly insisting that they signed only on the specific instructions of the Queen) set out in the most elaborate detail in a secret document the concessions which France was prepared to make to England. 'This agreement', said St. John to the Queen with some truth, 'contains more advantages for your Majesty's Kingdom than were ever, perhaps, stipulated for any nation at any time.' A second document—for public consumption and signed by Mesnager alone—included an acknowledgement of Queen Anne's title and a guarantee of the Protestant succession; a vague promise of a Barrier for Holland; and similar stipulations favouring the House of Austria. A third paper dealt with the concessions to be granted to the Duke of Savoy, the Tory favourite among England's great allies in the Grand Alliance. These last two documents might not read too grimly at The Hague, in Vienna, in Hanover or Turin. Apart from securing the unconditional victory for Austria in Spain, which many now knew to be a vain endeavour, most of the war aims of the Alliance had been adumbrated in general terms. But the secret preliminaries insisted that England would enter the projected peace conference with all her vast commercial and strategic gains settled in advance. The Barrier Treaty of 1709 had guaranteed equal trading rights for the Dutch and a barrier of towns specified by name to guard their frontier; it contained a clause forbidding separate negotiations. In six weeks' work the Barrier Treaty had been torn to tatters. The whole accomplishment bore the stamp of St. John; energy, audacity, duplicity. Thanks to the exercise of those attributes, the prize of peace—and all that it could mean for his own power and ambition—was now within his grip.

Soon the story—or part of it—would get out. The allies must soon be told; every coffee-house was agog with rumours. But the cover of secrecy still had its advantages; time was needed to mobilize support for the deed that had been done; and, more immediately, who could tell what a Whig mob might not do if they unmasked Mesnager? On the day after the preliminaries were signed he was taken to Windsor where he supped with St. John, Prior and Swift. 'We have already settled all things with France,' wrote Swift, 'and very much to the honour and advantage of England; and the Queen is in mighty good humour. All this is a mighty secret; the people in general know that a Peace is forwarding.' Next day Mesnager was led up the backstairs of the castle to see the Queen; only a couple of sentinels and one of the Queen's attendants saw him come and go. A day later he was shepherded back to London by Prior, successfully shielded from 'the great number of spies, whom the Whigs had about the Queen'; fortunately the Duke of Somerset was still engaged at Ascot and Mrs. Masham had returned from her confinement to mount guard on the Duchess. Soon Mesnager was on his way back to Paris. Swift's 'mighty secret' was not kept long; 'Prior went away yesterday with his Frenchman,' he reported on September 28th, and 'a thousand reports are raised in this town'.

St. John and his colleagues could turn to face the storm. One of his first acts was to dispatch a letter, written before Mesnager was out of the country, to the Duke of Marlborough. Everything was now conclusively arranged for his winter project: 'The Queen will not only bear the proportion of the extraordinary expense of forage; but likewise contribute to the charge of stables, barracks and those other incidents, which naturally ought to be placed to her account.' Her Majesty was in a generous mood. Everything would be agreed according to Marlborough's wishes provided the Dutch could be persuaded to play their part. Not a word, however, was said about the peace. That was for other ears, and for them, too, St. John was overflowing with promises and pledges that England would serve her allies so much more faithfully than any of them deserved. This was his pose to all who must share at least a part of the secret—to all perhaps except Swift. He knew better. 'The Earl of Stafford', he wrote in September, 'is to go soon to Holland and let them know what we have been doing: and then there will be the devil and all to pay; but we'll make them swallow it with a pox.'

That night Swift sat up late with St. John on one of their ever more frequent 'nightly debauches'. By day he was furiously at work 'to finish something of weight I have upon my hands, and which must be done soon'. All his doubts had vanished; St. John's zest had captured him completely. On the last day of September he wrote excitedly to Stella: 'The Whigs are in a rage about the Peace; but we'll wherret them, I warrant, boys. Go, go, go to the dean's, and don't mind politics, young women, they are not good after the waters; they are stark naught; they strike up into the head. Go, get two black aces and fish for a manilo.' Five months after he had first set eyes on the peace transactions St. John had brought them to fruition, making himself in the process the most dynamic figure in the European drama. And Swift was at his side, more lovingly caressed than ever and charged with a task which St. John reckoned crucial to the whole of his scheme.

A sudden blow marred the moment of exhilaration. Every day St. John had been expecting news of the expedition to Quebec; it was partly his confidence that Canada would soon be an English colony which made him so insistent on the clauses affecting North America in his negotiations with Mesnager. He also knew the dangers of failure. He had been responsible for forcing through the plan in defiance of Harley and even to the point of depriving Marlborough of some of his troops in Flanders. Moreover, the whole project had never been sanctioned by Parliament. In writing to one of the Governors of the New England colonies which were required to assist the naval attack with a land expedition, St. John had emphasized how vulnerable he himself would be if the project failed, since he had not been 'back'd by those forms and orders, which are necessary as safeguards in a government, where the best designs are converted into crimes, if they want success'. But the thought of failure had never really entered St. John's head; it played no part in his gay temper. And indeed, despite the doubts felt by so many in England, there were good reasons for expecting success. The naval force commanded by Admiral Sir Hovenden Walker, hastily assembled though it had been, was formidable. The New England colonists were eager to assist the attack on French power in North America. St. John's idea was certainly not derisory, and the scraps of news which crossed the Atlantic during September gave no hint that all was not well. But on October 6th a ship detached from Admiral Walker's fleet brought the first news of disaster, and a few days later the remnants straggled back into Portsmouth harbour.

The combined naval genius and military courage of Admiral Walker and Brigadier Hill had achieved a total fiasco. First they had quarrelled with the New England colonists; then they had failed to secure the best pilots to navigate the St. Lawrence and neglected the advice of those they had; when the storms came, seven or eight transports had been wrecked and nearly a thousand men had lost their lives. Brigadier Hill had had no chance to reveal his military talents, for neither he nor his troops got within miles of the enemy; but when the choice had come between the attempt at recovery or retreat, the Brigadier quickly cast his vote in favour of abandoning the whole enterprise. 'Was it expected', asked Walker, 'that I should have commanded Wind and Weather? Or is it imaginable, that by Art Magick, I raised storms and form'd Foggs to drown so many Men . . .?' In fact, the folk-lore of the Quebec fishermen did preserve the story that the ships had been beckoned to their destruction by the incantations of a sorcerer and for generations the ghostly tale was told of how more of Marlborough's soldiers were lost on the rocks of the St. Lawrence than at the siege of Bouchain. The citizens of Quebec, more mundanely, attributed their deliverance to the intervention of the Mother of God. But, in truth, storms and fogs had not been unknown in those waters before and if a little more care had been taken with the pilots and the provisions, St. John might have won a victory to make him the hero of the nation. As it was, he was naturally 'mortified'. Mrs. Masham and Mrs. Hill were in tears. Swift had to persuade them to go to 'the musick-meeting' on the night the news arrived to shew the court that 'they were not cast down'. Harley bore the disaster with indecent fortitude; he was 'just as merry as usual'. The amazing achievement of the Tories was how quickly they managed to smother any fierce public protest; if Marlborough had organized such an unmitigated calamity the event would have been immortalized by Swift or at least by Mrs. Manley.

*   *   *

In the rush of the peacemaking, even the Quebec disaster lost its significance. St. John's boldest dream had been dissipated, but he had no time to spare for regrets or even to congratulate himself on his newly-reinforced bond of friendship with Mrs. Masham which was all that could be saved from the wreckage. He was deeply immersed in the next diplomatic task of organizing the peace conference.

Somehow, if possible, the allies whom he had treated so scurvily must be assembled around the same table with the plenipotentiaries of King Louis. Of course, they would be aggrieved, even outraged; St. John's confessions to Swift revealed his awareness that what had been agreed might prove extremely unpalatable to the Dutch, the Austrians and the others. But he was not to be deflected from his purpose; after the first shock they could be brought to see reason. For the Austrians, St. John cared little enough; time and again they had failed to supply the military forces promised for the common cause. Obviously they would object with the utmost violence to the abandonment of Charles III and his Spanish ambitions. Those objections could be borne; the main consideration here was to prevent the Emperor from playing the one effective card in his hand—a visit by Prince Eugene to London. Much more serious and intricate would be the handling of the Dutch. Harley and St. John had always believed that a conference on English soil would be too risky. It would give the Whigs so many openings for protest and sabotage. Holland would be a safer venue; but would the Dutch agree? They had been deeply engaged in the war; their very life as a nation might be involved in the terms of the peace. Obviously their anxieties would be profound; but a suitable combination of soft words and hard bargaining might enforce their collaboration. Such were the instructions imparted to the English Ambassador-extraordinary, Lord Strafford, as he left for The Hague. He carried with him the general preliminaries (but not the secret agreement) signed by Mesnager. These were certainly vague and St. John knew they would not be well received. Lord Strafford was therefore instructed to insist that 'no concessions whatsoever can tempt us to embrace the blessings of peace, unless our good friends and allies, the States-General, have all reasonable satisfaction as to their barrier, as to their trade, and in all other respects'. True, these preliminaries did not include the precise terms of the Barrier Treaty signed by the Whig Ministers only two years before. But the Dutch were invited not to risk the substance for the shadow. The Barrier Treaty was detested by others among England's allies no less than by the English Tories; only the care of the Ministers in keeping it as secret as possible had prevented an outburst of anti-Dutch sentiment. Possibly the Dutch might ask what private stipulations and agreements Britian had sought for herself; a likely question indeed! Lord Strafford was delicately briefed to side-step the accusation. Nothing had been agreed which could possibly clash with the interests of Holland and, moreover, everything had still to be confirmed around the conference table. If finally the Dutch were still determined to continue the war, England would concur, demanding only that she could no longer bear the disproportionate share of the burden which she had carried in recent years.

Thus, St. John planned—in the less diplomatic language of Swift—to 'make them swallow it with a pox'. Meantime Willem Buys set sail for England as the emissary of the Dutch Government. Even his pacific temper was ruffled by the rumours of the English intrigue reaching The Hague. His vanity matched his patriotism. No public outcry had as yet been made by the Dutch, but Buys confided his private hopes: Let him but have one audience with the Queen and a good settlement could soon be arranged; if not, so much the worse for the Queen's Ministers.

For all Buys' boasting, this was in fact the crux of the situation

which faced Harley and St. John in the month of October; could
the allies—the Austrians and the Dutch assisted by the Elector of
Hanover with all the leverage he exercised as the potential future
King of England—join forces with Marlborough and the Whigs to
overturn the Queen's Ministers? Harley had fallen ill again; his
chief activities were confined to a few approaches to the most prominent Whig and Tory leaders outside the administration, to those
whom he feared as possible enemies of the peace. Cautiously he
sought to enlist their support or ward off their hostility. Most of
them replied with equal caution. Once more the main brunt fell on
St. John; once more he discovered that his chief battles must be
fought in Grub Street. If the great Whig Lords in their country
houses still hesitated to sound the rallying-cry, if the Duke of
Marlborough was still gulled by the sweet words of the Tory
Ministers, no such reticence or delusion afflicted the Whig journalists. Swift and his companions on the Tory side were no less
active. 'I will ply the rogues warm,' he vowed, 'and whenever anything of theirs makes a noise, it shall have an answer.' Never before
in English history had the press played so notable a role as it did
in the month of October, 1711. Tory and Whig writers hurled
themselves at one another's throats until both St. John in Whitehall
and the Duke in Flanders found themselves embroiled in the Grub
Street war. The outcome would settle more than the expedition to
Quebec or the capture of Bouchain.

Once Lord Strafford was safely dispatched to Holland, St. John
revealed the terms of the preliminaries signed by Mesnager (excluding, of course, the secret agreement) to the representatives
of the allies in London. The response removed any doubts about
the hazards ahead. Count Gallas, in particular, was quick to show
his scorn. He 'treats the propositions very slightly, and only
condescends to take notice of them because they were sent by her
Majesty's order', wrote St. John. 'He calls the whole proceeding an
enigma, and, in short, speaks the language, which the impertinence
of an Austrian minister, improved by the encouragement and conversation of a saucy faction, might make one expect.' Even Count
Maffei, Ambassador of the Duke of Savoy, was discontented.
Having achieved so much, St. John was naturally aggrieved; signs
reappeared of the old fury against the prosecutors of the war which
had animated him at the time of the election campaign. 'Your
Excellency sees, by this time,' he wrote to Strafford, 'what the

artifices are, which will be employed to hinder this negotiation from succeeding, and our nation from rising above the character of a province to the alliance, which character ambition and avarice brought upon us, and presumptuous folly has made us pride ourselves in.'

One particular dilemma riled him with irritating persistence; with Swift's help he puzzled to find a solution. The general terms signed by Mesnager were carefully designed to commit the French to further negotiation without imposing a fatal bar to Dutch cooperation. Even so 'the enigma' stuck in Count Gallas's throat and the same reaction might be expected from the English Whigs. The sugar for the pill was the immense commercial advantage secured to England in the secret agreement. But necessarily, if the suspicion of the allies was not to be turned to rage, these clauses could not yet be made public. How was St. John to rally the Tories in England without inviting the wrath of the allies? Once more he resorted to the inspired leakage. On Thursay, October 11th, the *Postboy* carried a remarkable paragraph. 'We are inform'd', it said, 'from *undoubted Hands*, that the Treaty of Peace is so far advanc'd, that we have Hopes, *in a few Days Time*, We shall be able to inform the Publick of the Particulars; which are so GLORIOUS and ADVANTAGEOUS to the Nation and ALL the ALLIES, that it will be LASTING, SAFE, and HONOURABLE.' Two days later the *Postboy* published—again on the authority of the same well-informed sources or 'undoubted Hands'—an even more specific reference to the gains which England might expect. Abel Boyer was shrewd enough to guess that 'the Writers of the *Postboy*, or rather their Prompters behind the Curtain' intended to leak week by week news of the succulent morsels being garnished for the English merchants.

But two could play this game. On Saturday morning, October 13th, the *Daily Courant* published in full the Mesnager preliminaries, that is, all the preliminaries except those promising the commercial advantages to England. The news came from Count Gallas (or so the Ministers suspected—on the basis perhaps of proof supplied by their spies which they could not disclose); he had contrived a leakage more sensational than anything perpetrated by the *Postboy*. That night the *Postboy* attempted a reply; they rushed out 'a Postscript', revealing more titbits about England's gains and promising that 'the satisfaction and security' of all the rest of the allies was 'to be guaranteed at the General Congress'. But nothing for the moment could counter the effect of the *Daily Courant* revelations. Instead of the glorious victory forecast by the *Postboy*, the terms sounded flat and unprofitable and were indeed far less favourable to the allies than those which the French had so nearly accepted a year before. The shock was tremendous. Stocks on the exchange fell by several points. Even the friends of the Ministry were aghast. Count Gallas was able to report that 'the publication of the new scandalous preliminaries' has 'made the Tories and Whigs terrified and dumb'. Exaggeration was pardonable; for if the *Daily Courant* was believed and if these were in truth the terms which the English Ministers had approved, incalculable damage could be done to their prestige. Harley's anxiety was betrayed by a letter he wrote post-haste from his sick-bed to the Earl of Nottingham, the respected Tory leader who stood outside the administration and whose voice and vote might settle the fate of the Ministry in the House of Lords. The icy reply gave warning that Count Gallas and the Whigs might soon be gaining some strange allies to their 'saucy faction'. Nottingham was surprised by the honour of a letter, 'for I did not expect that your Lordship should have taken the trouble of communicating to me an affair of so vast importance as the settling the preliminaries of a Peace, of which I am not a competent judge, not having for some time been acquainted with any matter relating to the public administration. But as no man can wish better to his country than I do, so I am very glad to hear from your Lordship so good a character of this treaty as your Lordship gives it, for I may conclude that the accounts of it in the prints must be very imperfect, and your Lordship's favour therefore was much the greater because it gives me hopes of better things'.

St. John as usual believed in direct action. Nothing much could be done about the *Courant*; their only crime was to have printed the bare truth. But the time had surely come to curb the Whig journalists. Already a move had been made against one of them who had achieved the feat of libelling Jonathan Swift. 'A rogue that writes a newspaper called *The Protestant Postboy*', wrote Swift, 'has reflected on me in one of his papers. But the Secretary has taken him up, and he shall have a squeeze extraordinary. He says that an ambitious Tantivy, missing of his towering hopes of preferment in Ireland, is come over to vent his spleen on the late

Ministry etc. I'll *Tantivy* him with a vengeance.' In the middle of
October the campaign of proscription was intensified. 'I have discovered the author of another scandalous libel, who will be in
custody this afternoon; he will make the 13th I have seized and the
15th I have found out,' reported St. John to the Queen. Abel Boyer
was among those caught in the net. He was Whiggish in sympathy
but his writings were usually most circumspect and interlarded
with skilful tributes to the moderation and patriotism of the Prime
Minister. His lapse on this occasion was that (in his own words)
he took 'the opportunity to vindicate himself of the Reflection of
a *shameless* and most *contemptible* Ecclesiastical *Turn-Coat*, whose
tongue is as SWIFT to revile, as his Mind is SWIFT to change;
And yet who, by what strange strain of Politicks I know not,
happened at this time to be clandestinely countenanc'd'. Swift's
account of the same incident showed how little he cared that the
licence he practised himself should be preserved for others. 'One
Boyer, a French dog,' he wrote, 'has abused me in a pamphlet, and
I have got him up in a messenger's hands: the secretary promises
me to swinge him. . . . I must make that rogue an example for
warning to others.' But the warning, it seems, was of little avail.
Thanks to Harley's intervention, Boyer was not 'swinged'. And
even when the fourteen booksellers were brought before the bar of
the Queen's Bench Court to answer for their misdeeds—some of
which were indeed, on Boyer's admission, 'Scandalous Invectives
against the Ministry'—the Whigs were not cowed. They defended
themselves stoutly 'pleading with notable Vehemence against the
Severity of *Committing People without telling them their Crimes:
Urging that at this rate the Office of the Secretary of State would
become a* Spanish *Inquisition*'. Considering the fate which Defoe
had suffered in the pillory and in Newgate only half a dozen years
before, the Inquisition was comparatively mild. On the request of
the Attorney-General all the accused were bound over to behave
themselves. Yet how infuriating such harassment must have been
at so critical a moment when all the Tory libellers were left free to
pursue their filthy trade!

It was necessary to use other protections more reliable than
the laws of England, and the favourite among them was the shield
of irony. A few days after the *Daily Courant* disclosures a splendid
essay in this art appeared entitled *A Vindication of the present M—y
from the Clamours rais'd against them, upon Occasion of the NEW*

PRELIMINARIES. Only one explanation was possible of the Articles of Peace published with such a fanfare; they were spurious, the whole publication 'a Banter'. Only the most bitter enemy of the Ministry could suppose that such trifling terms would be acceptable. 'True tis no strange thing in a *French* Minister to shuffle, and prevaricate—a *Frenchman* is capable of offering such Articles but it would be strange, very strange in any English Minister to accept them; which 'tis pretended they have done: And 'Tis this Reason I make the Looseness and Antiquity of these Articles an Argument of their being spurious. For Proposals that have a Sense so very indeterminate, are, in effect, no Proposals at all; therefore 'tis impossible, even the Old M—y could think such Articles fit to be the Foundation of a Treaty of so much importance, and we have a Ministry too well skilled in the Arts of Language and the Power of Words to be so shamefully impos'd on by a much abler Man, than I take the Manager of these Articles to be.'

The Ministers did not welcome this ally who took up the cudgels on their behalf with the *Daily Courant*. St. John's messengers worked hard to discover the culprit. 'This Pamphlet', wrote Abel Boyer in the objective Annals of his time whose authorship he was not afraid to own, 'being writ in a master Stile, and with a peculiarly happy Turn of Wit, and Strength of Argument, was received with general Approbation, and many Thousand Copies of it were, in a few Days, bought up with uncommon Greediness; which was not a little increased by the strict Enquiry that was made after the Author, Printer and Publishers; which amounted to a Prohibition.' Who the author was is not known to this day. Some suspicion points at that French dog, Abel Boyer, who was not accustomed to pay to his fellow-journalists such exuberant tributes. A Huguenot refugee must be polite to his hosts but under the cover of anonymity he could still strike powerful blows against the enemies of his great cause. In any case no amount of warnings and prosecutions could check the flood of English journalism now pouring forth in an avalanche more turbulent than ever before.

St. John's attack on the booksellers was probably not expected to achieve dramatic results; it was more a sign that even his nerve was strained. In his cooler moments he knew that the printed word could best be answered by the printed word itself; had he not promised to revive fellows who would write the Whigs to death? Among those who escaped the fires of his Inquisition during that

October was Mrs. Manley. Under Swift's tutelage she now excelled herself. Swift accorded her all the glory but it is impossible to believe that the force of the new pamphlet was not supplied by himself and St. John acting in concert. Whatever hesitations might still restrain Harley, St. John had decided that the fight with the Whigs must involve a final trial of strength with Marlborough. It was best to take the offensive. 'I have instructed an under-spur leather to write so, that it is taken for mine,' wrote Swift, and the pamphlet *A New Vindication of the Duke of Marlborough* was proof of how well the instructions had been heeded. Mrs. Manley dismissed Bouchain as a victory of no military significance. She wrote bitterly of the contrast between the wretchedness produced by the war and the luxurious appurtenances of Blenheim Palace. In particular, she offered an ironic tabulation of the mortifications which the Captain-General had *not* been called upon to endure. It was the first precise warning of St. John's intended programme of action.

Mrs. Manley's diatribe (it was, of course, anonymous) was read by the Duke of Marlborough in his camp at Bouchain just before he departed for The Hague *en route* for England. He was stirred to fury and to action, and yet the action was inapposite and even ridiculous. The Duke understood nothing of Grub Street; he despised the public opinion which the Grub Street writers so largely dictated. If he had his way all these obstreperous mountebanks would have been clapped into the pillory, or, better still, into irons. How little did he know of his native land where even St. John did not dare to resort to such extremities! Probably the Duke and Queen Anne herself were the only two eminent figures of the time who still regarded the printing press as an invention of the devil, a wretched encumbrance on the political scene, which could easily be smashed or deprived of its striking power if only the Queen's Ministers showed a little resolution. The rest—great Whig Lords like Wharton and Somers no less than ambitious adventurers like St. John and Harley—realized, half consciously perhaps, that the practitioners of the new craft must be bought, bribed, encouraged, seduced, harassed maybe, but, in the main, tolerated. Public opinion with the press as its main engine, in the country at large and particularly in the London coffee-houses, was now a considerable force. It could help sway votes in Parliament, settle elections, sink the public credit or raise a mob on the streets. It had wrested some part of the real power in the state from Kings and courtiers and Captain-Generals. But Marlborough stubbornly refused to understand. Public opinion was an impudent upstart and the Grub Street specimens no part of the same human species as himself. This foolish disdain much more than his avarice was his real Achilles heel; and yet so unconscious of it was he that he actually paraded his weakness.

When he read Mrs. Manley's pamphlet he exploded with anger. It was natural enough that he should be infuriated by the jeers about Bouchain (the *Postboy* improved on Mrs. Manley by asserting that the 'Taking of the Place and that of a Pigeon-house, was the same Thing'); but was it not curious that he made no effort to gauge the political significance of her attack? Was it really so impossible to trace these outbursts to their source? If he had taken that much trouble how much more incisive would have been his appreciation of the political crisis in London. And did he really imagine that, while the Tories poured out their venom, the case for the war, for a decent peace, for himself and the cause he espoused, could be left to go by default? So he implied in some strictures to Sarah. But was this really his idea of how to wage a power struggle on which the whole future of Europe might depend? How superior and how futile; as well charge the ramparts of Bouchain without muskets and cannon!

However, Sarah did not share his lordly distaste for the printed word. With the aid of Arthur Maynwaring and the *Medley* she had long done her best to ensure that the Tories were not left the sole masters of the Grub Street battlefield. So, when Marlborough exploded at Mrs. Manley's scurrilities, he was greeted with a laugh and a sneer. St. John and Harley were not likely to believe that the mighty Duke along with his Duchess were guiltless of the crimes which they themselves practised so assiduously. St. John brushed aside his renewed plea for action against the libellers with a remark to the Queen that the Duke's own chaplain was involved in the same trade. To Harley the Duke was even more pressing. He affected to object to the Whig pamphlet extolling Bouchain no less than to Mrs. Manley's reply. 'The authors of these papers, as well the one as the other, are not only my enemies, they are yours too, my lord; they are enemies to the Queen, and poison to her subjects; and it would be worth the while to make a strict search after them that the punishment they deserve may be inflicted upon them.'

Harley's reply was a mixture of blandness and contempt. He too deplored this 'villainous way of libelling'. As Secretary of State he had 'by an impartial prosecution' silenced most of them. Unfortunately the Whigs had rushed to their support. However, 'I do assure your Grace I abhor the practice as mean and disingenuous. I have made it so familiar to myself, by some years experience, that as I know I am every week, if not every day, in some libel or other, so I would willingly compound that all the ill-natured scribblers should have licence to write ten times more against me, upon condition they would write against nobody else. I do assure your Grace I neither know nor desire to know any of the authors; and as I heartily wish this barbarous war was at an end, I shall be very ready to take any part in suppressing them'. This from the Harley who had released Defoe from prison, cultivated Swift as his most treasured dining companion, and even rescued the Whig spokesman, Boyer, from the clutches of St. John! For a moment we catch a glimpse of the great Duke of Marlborough as a child-in-arms pitted against sophisticated politicians. Sarah, too, was told of Marlborough's frenzy at Mrs. Manley's 'barbarous libel'. On the Duke's instructions Arthur Maynwaring, of all people, was sent to remonstrate with Harley personally. 'The Duke', said Harley, 'must not mind them. I myself am called a rogue in print every day. What is more,' he added, looking straight at Maynwaring, 'I know the man who does it; but I intend to live fairly with him.' If St. John and Harley ever had doubts about the efficacy of the work which Swift and his under-spur-leathers were doing, Marlborough's explosion must have removed them. The colossus was human after all. If he could be so easily wounded, could he not also be destroyed, and by the same weapons aimed at the same Achilles heel?

These were comforting thoughts for the Ministers amid all their mounting anxieties. And yet neither Harley nor St. John would be such fools as to set too great store upon them. Both knew the Duke well as soldier, courtier, supreme diplomat and guiding genius of the Grand Alliance—a very different man from the one stabbed to impotent passion by the pen of Mrs. Manley. How would he exert his power now that their machinations threatened the very basis of that Alliance? If St. John was resolved to fight him, Harley was not, and he had reason for his reticence. All the smiles and courtesies and promises of good faith exchanged between the Ministers and the Captain-General since the beginning of the year seemed to have borne good fruit. If the Duke had wanted to pick a quarrel, there were plenty of grounds for it; the peace preliminaries, for example, published in the *Daily Courant*, had not yet been communicated officially to the commander of the Queen's forces. Yet, except on the subject of Grub Street, the Duke seemed composed, almost compliant. Just before leaving the camp at Bouchain at the end of October, thanks to Harley's 'encouragement to enter into the strictest friendship', he begged 'friendly advice in what manner I am to govern myself'. 'You cannot but imagine,' he wrote, ''twould be a terrible mortification to pass by The Hague, with our plenipotentiaries there; and myself a stranger to their transactions; and what hope can I have of any countenance at home, if I am not thought fit to be trusted abroad.' No milder words could have been employed if any reference at all was to be made to the peace negotiations. Marlborough was now convinced that a peace would be sought that winter and that he himself would be excluded from the negotiating table. Yet still he insisted to Harley: 'My lord, I have put myself wholly into your hands, and shall be entirely guided by your advice, if you will be so kind as to favour me with it.' Perhaps he was old and tired and unfit for a great new political combat. Perhaps Harley's arts of persuasion had secured a new victim. Perhaps Marlborough could be truly convinced that peace was inevitable and that the terms secured were the best available. At least he might be content to leave the political arena to others. Harley was not one to shatter such prospects by a premature challenge. Let St. John sharpen his daggers, if he must; no one could stop him. But, in the name of sanity, why waken the sleeping giant?

Such was Harley's policy towards the Duke and no one could deny its degree of success. Others noted with sadness mixed with surprise the lack of energy and insight which seemed to afflict the Duke at this moment of crisis. Ever since the *Daily Courant* disclosures the spirit of the Whigs had been given a new impetus. Not merely were their journalists growing bolder every day. The great Whig Lords were meeting in their country houses; more hopefully than at any time since their dismissal from office a year before, they saw their chance of recovery. 'We have no quiet with the Whigs, they are so violent against a Peace; but I'll cool them with a vengeance, very soon,' wrote Swift on October 26th.

Yet, if the Whigs were noisy, why was Marlborough still quiet? Could not the master tactician see that it was now or never? For all Harley's persistent politeness towards himself, could he not understand that the Ministers were deeply committed to a treacherous peace and that having set their course they must drive it through with ruthless energy?

To the Whig chieftains another sign was given at the end of October that the fight was on. For weeks and even months one of their favourite meeting-places had been Leicester House, the home of Count Gallas. There they had prepared some of the Austrian memorials to the Queen. There they had assisted in devising the envoy's reports to the Emperor, 'the whole drift' of which was, said St. John (and he had good reason to know), 'to represent the Queen's word as not to be relied upon, to represent her Ministers, in the gross, as fools, knaves, and, in express terms, as enemies to the common cause'. There, too, under the cover of diplomatic privilege, had been set up a printing press for the production of pamphlets too hot to be handled elsewhere. The *Daily Courant* disclosures provided the last straw. It was, however, not so easy for the Ministers to show their resentment. Count Gallas could not be dismissed for the simple reason that the Emperor had already summoned him back to Vienna. Nevertheless on October 26th the Master of Ceremonies presented himself to the ambassador and announced that 'owing to the displeasure his conduct had caused, the Queen had forbidden him the Court and would explain her reasons to the Emperor'.

Normally such an affront to an ally might have been expected to arouse a storm from the Whigs and the stir was indeed considerable. But some at least who had been frequent visitors to Leicester House were not too eager to see the matter probed. Who could tell how precise might be the Ministers' knowledge of the activities conducted there? The incident reveals much about the temper of the times. Gallas had his own spies reporting to him on political developments in London. For years the French agent Gaultier served as a priest under this same roof. When he departed on his mission to France he left behind another agent who could supply St. John with news of the latest twist in Austrian diplomacy. And inside these protected, eavesdropping walls Lord Wharton and his friends nursed their hopes of a Whig resurgence. They, no less than St. John and Harley, found it hard, or took little trouble, to draw the line between politics and treason. So merciless was the contest, so great the risks which men ran to capture power in the English state. When Harley and St. John struck at Gallas, the Whigs knew that it was war to the knife.

Yet if the Whigs had lost one friend, another was gained. Pensionary Buys arrived from Holland. For weeks the more embarrassed and moderate defenders of the Ministry—Daniel Defoe, for example—had kept up their courage with a favourite jeer at the Whigs: if the peace in preparation was so bad and such a betrayal of England's allies, why were the Dutch meekly silent? To suggest they might be backward in defending their own interests was a kind of satire against the Dutch nation. Were the Whigs better Dutchmen than the Dutch themselves? In fact, the explanation was simple. No one in Holland realized how far the negotiations had proceeded and how scantily Dutch interests had been protected. Of course, the whole tone and method of the Tory Ministers caused anxiety, particularly in the mind of Heinsius, but only when the *Daily Courant* disclosures and Lord Strafford arrived in Holland did anxiety change to shock. Moreover, the Dutch dearly wanted peace if it could be had on safe terms. Had they not agreed to continue the war in 1709 only in return for the guarantees of their defence and commerce provided by the Barrier Treaty, pressed upon them by the Whigs and ratified by the Queen herself? For the Dutch to jeopardize either their Alliance or the peace would be a most dangerous procedure. Hence their inclination to accept the dubious word of St. John at its face value. But when Strafford arrived with Mesnager's preliminaries (not, be it noted, with the much more sinister secret agreement), a darker colour was put on all the rumours of Anglo-French intrigue. Even 'the Tory Dutchman', Buys, was aghast and momentarily reduced to silence. At once the terms of his commission were changed. Instead of being sent to inquire politely how far 'the pourparlers' had proceeded and what terms would be satisfactory for the Queen for a peacetime alliance, he was charged to present the Dutch objections to the whole procedure.

Buys, as we have seen, felt himself equal to the task. He did not know that his casual remarks about the Queen's Ministers were overheard by some French spy and recapitulated to Torcy who quickly passed them on to London. St. John was forewarned, and in truth the Dutch position was not strong. Against the firm common interest now established between Whitehall and Versailles, Buys had only two cards to play. The English desired that the general conference should take place in Holland. For that purpose it was necessary that the Dutch should issue passports to the plenipotentiaries appointed by the French King. No passports should be forthcoming until the Dutch were guaranteed their Barrier. For the rest, the Dutch knew, or thought they knew, how precarious was the authority of the English Ministers. A waiting game was the one to play and the talkative Buys did not lack topics of conversation. Could Mr. St. John tell him the history of the negotiations? Why should not the two friendly maritime powers return to the principle of preliminary agreement between themselves before risking a rupture in the presence of the enemy? Had the English Ministers made any other agreements protecting their own interests? 'I took an air of frankness,' said St. John in describing one of his meetings with the prickly Pensionary, but 'he looked as if he believed me but by halves'. For such negotiation the Queen had a better technique, the old stubborn grain of a Stuart monarch who had made up her mind. Against this rock the eloquence of Buys beat in vain. And yet his own instructions and the necessities of his nation were hardly less adamant. There was one way out of the dilemma. If St. John had agreed to abide by the terms of the Barrier Treaty, Buys and the Dutch would have become overnight as strong peacemongers as himself. But that would have involved reopening the discussions with the French and a surrender of part of the English commercial gains, particularly the *Assiento*, secured in the secret agreement.

St. John would not yield. Even the faithful servant of the Tories, Lord Strafford, at that moment engaged in simultaneous discussions with Heinsius at The Hague, felt the Ministers were pressing the Dutch too hard. He was aggrieved, moreover, that nothing had been included in his own instructions about the secret clauses which made Heinsius so inquisitive. 'If the separate article was omitted to be given you, it was a pure mistake,' wrote St. John, adding with barefaced audacity: 'As to any separate treaty with France, there is no such thing; the Queen would never think of taking so dishonourable a course.' Strafford and everyone else should understand the main point. 'We want a peace, and the sense of the nation is for it, whatever noise may be made about London, by those who find their private account in the universal calamity.' The noise was certainly growing and the presence of Buys helped to make it still louder. Special precautions were taken by the Ministers to ensure that the Dutch negotiations were kept secret. But secret diplomacy did not suit the style and purpose of Willem Buys. According to the reports reaching Versailles, 'all malcontents, whether English, or foreigners, were welcome to his house, he took pains to invite them all, perfectly discharging his commission, that of blowing the coals, and using all his endeavours, either to ruin the new ministers, or to restore their rivals'. Much must be allowed for embroidery as the news crossed the Channel. But the truth remained; by the end of October Buys was still resisting all blandishments and threats. Perhaps the Tory Dutchman was a good Whig after all.

Good news for the Whigs came from one other quarter and that the most important of all. If the Austrians were up in arms and the Dutch had doubts, how much more could be expected from George Louis, Elector of Hanover and a man who might one day have the power to teach these Tory friends of France with their Jacobite sympathies a lesson they would never forget. He had been well tutored in anti-French, even Whiggish, sentiments by his mother, the Electress Sophia. Someone once taunted her with belonging to 'Marlborough's party'. Her answer showed plainly enough the principles or prejudices ruling at the Hanoverian court. 'If the Queen', she replied, 'had made an ape her general, and this ape had won so many victories, I should be on the side of the ape.' No detailed scrutiny was required to enable her to pass judgement on the peace preliminaries. If the Elector himself lacked resolution, she could supply the sinews for a struggle. As it happened, no such stiffening was required. Marlborough himself had completed the education which the Electress had begun; Grub Street might be neglected by the Duke but not a man with royal blood in his veins who might one day sit on the throne of England. Some day, he had always believed, the Elector might be able to tip the tender balance in English politics. Perhaps that moment had come. That was also the fear of the Tories who had painfully striven over months to counteract the persistent wooing of the Elector by the Duke. Once the preliminaries were signed with Mesnager, Lord Rivers was sent to Hanover to present the document in the most favourable light. His reception was frosty. The rumours seeped back via The Hague to London. The Elector was not yet King of England. He could not settle the issue of peace and war. But he did intend to send the formidable Baron von Bothmar as his envoy to London, and lest Harley should have doubts in the interval about the Elector's opinion a message was dispatched in terms much more peremptory than the Dutch dared employ. If after all the exertions of the war Spain was now to be surrendered to King Louis's grandson, France would once more be in a position 'to give the law to Europe'.

*   *   *

The stage was almost set. Sooner or later the great debate must be transferred from Grub Street and the chancelleries to the floor of the British Parliament. The date for the reassembly of Parliament had in fact been fixed for November 13th. St. John had always been the advocate of speed. Every week counted; every day gave the opportunity to the Whigs to mobilize their forces at home and abroad. By all the reckoning of the previous session, the Tories could count on majorities in both Houses. And yet this was not quite the scene he had hoped for. Buys was still haggling; and how could the grand announcement of a Peace Congress be made by the Queen while the Dutch still withheld the passports? Harley was ill, and, for all St. John's growing impatience with him, was it not too risky to allow the Parliament to meet without his expert management? St. John believed that the sentiment for peace in the country was still flowing as strongly as ever, but his confidence was not shared by all his colleagues. Shrewsbury was jittery; he plied the Queen, Harley and the others with his scruples about the methods of peacemaking. Ugly reports were circulating that the Earl of Nottingham's vote might not be relied upon. The Tory majority in the Lords—if it really existed—could at best be counted on the fingers of two hands; any wavering would be fatal. And no one could doubt that the Whigs were mustering their strength. They were indeed flocking back to London while the lazy Tory squires stayed at home, muttering oaths against the moderation of Harley which had cheated them of their Whig scalps in the previous session. Thanks no doubt partly to the virulence of the Whig pamphlet campaign and the signs of fierce remonstrance from the allies, a nightmare seized the Tory hangers-on, and they bombarded Harley with their fears. They saw the benches of the Commons— and more still the Lords—lined with jubilant Whigs, swearing, as a few of them did, that they 'would have Harley's head'. Neither Harley nor St. John gave way to the panic. But they saw the case for delay. Fortunately for them, the Queen was ill. She might not be able to open her Parliament on the allotted date. The excuse was there if they wanted it—and if they could take the alternative risk of allowing Marlborough, Baron von Bothmar, perhaps even Prince Eugene, to arrive in London and add their voices to those of Lord Wharton and his fellow-Whig conspirators.

The mood of alarm had even percolated from London to far-away Laracor. Stella was not convinced by the optimism which Swift had felt a few weeks before. 'I believe you begin to think there will be no Peace,' he wrote on October 29th; 'the Whigs here are sure it cannot be, and stocks are fallen again. But I am confident there will, unless France plays us tricks; and you may venture a wager with any of your Whig acquaintance that we shall not have another campaign. You will get more by it than by ombre, sirrah.' But Swift had had little time to keep up with the latest news, no time to accept the invitations of duchesses, 'no time to dine with great folks', no time even to read the newspapers. He was hard at work on a new pamphlet. 'I won't tell you now; but the ministers reckon it will do abundance of good, and open the eyes of the nation, who are half bewitched against a Peace. Few of this generation can remember anything but war and taxes, and they think it is as it should be: whereas 'tis certain we are the most undone people in Europe, as I am afraid I shall make appear beyond all contradiction.' All the proofs had to be read by St. John and it was tiresome trying to catch him amid so many other preoccupations. Yet Swift glowed in his companionship. The beloved Harley had become 'the greatest procrastinator in the world', but 'I think Mr. St. John the greatest young man I ever knew; wit, capacity, beauty, quickness of apprehension, good learning, and an excellent taste; the best orator in the house of commons, admirable conversation, good nature, and good manners; generous and a despiser of money. His only fault is talking to his friends in way of complaint of too great a load of business, which looks a little like affectation; and he endeavours too much to mix the fine gentleman, and man of pleasure, with the man of business. What truth and sincerity he may have I know not; he is now but thirty-two and has been secretary above a year'. This was St. John at the peak. He was in a mood to ride any storm. Certainly it was not from panic that he applauded the delay in the recall of Parliament. A few days later—on November 7th—on another journey to the printer Swift heard the news. Parliament had been prorogued until November 27th; 'I suppose, either because the Queen has the gout; or that the Lord treasurer is not well, or that they would do something more towards a Peace.' Swift himself was relieved. By the 27th his own masterpiece would be ready to shake the world.

But another three weeks; was it really wise? Perhaps St. John's first instinct in favour of speed was right after all. The Duke, the Dutch, the Elector, the Emperor, the great Whig Lords—and half Grub Street; how powerful this combination might be and how perilously the extra days might give the opportunity for its strength to be consolidated! So much depended on the energy with which the Tory forces might be mobilized for the struggle, and their leader was a sick man who often appeared to be distracted from the main objective by the most inscrutable diversions of his own. The paramount aim should be to rally the Tories, to show a fighting spirit, to ensure that they arrived for the Parliamentary session in time, to give them some pledge that the old hesitations which had caused so much trouble with the October Club were now to be finally abandoned. There was more talk of putting out a few Whigs from their offices and rewarding the truly loyal supporters of the peace; but still nothing was done. No doubt was possible about the urgency of the situation. 'You have no time to lose,' wrote the Duke of Hamilton to Harley on November 13th; he was busy attempting to organize the Government's forces in Scotland. If messages were not sent out at once insisting on the presence of the Government's supporters at Westminster they would not be there to meet the Whig assault even on the later date of November 27th fixed for the meeting of the Parliament.

But Harley had other cares. His love of intrigue made him hesitate even at this critical juncture to stake all on a contest in the open daylight. He still preferred the dark alleys of politics. No one can determine for certain what was his purpose: as usual, he did not divulge it to anyone. He breathed no word to Swift despite their continued meetings on the friendliest terms; for Swift would strongly have disapproved of this latest contortion and if he had had some word of it he could hardly have failed to warn St. John. Harley was having secret meetings and correspondence with a few of the Whig leaders. He had always refused to see them as a solid phalanx; always he detested the very idea of party. Could not one or two of them—Lord Halifax, or Lord Somers, perhaps even their most able lieutenant, Robert Walpole—be detached from the Whig fanatics like Lord Wharton just as Shrewsbury, Newcastle and Somerset had been won over by Harley's seductions in the previous year? Might they not even at this eleventh hour join with him in keeping the administration wedded to moderate policies, thus freeing him from the pressures of the October Club and even perhaps from St. John himself? Not so many months before, Halifax and Somers in turn had had their own idea of detaching Harley from the Tories and thus making the breach which could bring them back to office and power. The whispers of the quarrel between Harley and St. John fed their hopes. Nervously and secretly the Tory leader and a few of the Whig Lords made approaches to one another. At the very least, from Harley's point of view, these overtures might mitigate the savagery of the Whig attack on the administration when Parliament met. On several occasions since he became Prime Minister Harley had started on this tortuous proceeding; always the project had faded to nothingness. Now when he learnt that seventeen of the Whig leaders, including some of his secret correspondents, had used the occasion of the autumn races at Newmarket to hold a grand council of war at the house of Lord Orford, he embarked on the manœuvre once more. 'Divide and rule' was his principle. Halifax and Somers nibbled at the bait, and Harley had fresh reason for regretting the impetuous St. John who had given such offence to the Duke of Somerset and others able to assist a scheme of infiltration among the Whigs.

In the middle of November a considerable victory encouraged Harley's hopes, although it was hardly gained by the methods which he had prescribed. Pensionary Buys had held out strongly for three or four weeks in his arguments with the English Ministers; then, in the face of St. John's intransigence, he began to wilt. The fear grew that, if the Dutch withheld the passports for the Peace Congress, all sympathy for the Dutch case in England might be forfeited. If, on the other hand, they made a concession, Holland might still retain favour and receive later satisfaction. Simultaneously heavy pressure was being applied to Heinsius at The Hague. It was an agonizing decision for the Dutch. Buys at last sent word back to The Hague favouring the concession. On the afternoon of November 10th the States-General debated for long hours behind locked doors. At last the painful choice was made. The Queen's demands would be met, Utrecht was named as the place where the Congress should meet, and the necessary passports were sent to Buys for presentation to the English Ministers. It was not the final word of Dutch blessing for the English Ministers' idea of a peace. Some room remained for further manœuvre. Dutch hopes from the assembly of the English Parliament were not abated. But for the Tories, amid all their other harassments, it was enough. 'God be thanked that the States have made such a friendly Resolution,' cried Mrs. Masham with tears of joy in her eyes, 'this will prolong the Queen's life.' St. John's diplomacy had provided Harley with a brilliant card for the enticement of any wayward Whigs, if such there might be, away from their rigid allegiance to the war party.

And yet the Tories were not granted much time for rejoicing. Even before the news of the States-General's decision was confirmed in England other events combined to push the intrigues of Harley and even the triumphs of St. John into the shadows. The Duke of Marlborough was on the way home. One year earlier, when the Tories were riding high after their electoral victory, the return of the Duke to the London scene had checked their plans for his own destruction and compelled the Tory Ministers to seek out new and unexpected courses. Now he was coming at a moment when his friends were immensely stronger and the issue more momentous. Something, too, had happened to him at The Hague. The weary victor of Bouchain, Mrs. Manley's victim, had suddenly recovered his vigour. And Sarah announced to an incredulous London that she intended to entertain her friends on a scale sparing no expense.

Some of the Dutch Deputies to the States-General claimed that they could not sleep at nights for the charge from their countrymen that, in approving the Queen's terms, they had played the part of traitors. Rumours circulated at The Hague of how French gold had been used to suborn the English Ministers. Doubtless the general mood of hostility to the peace terms affected Marlborough when he arrived there from Bouchain. Another spur to action may have cut more woundingly. For months past a Parliamentary committee stuffed with Tories had been inquiring into the alleged financial misdeameanours of the previous administration. Marlborough was obviously the chief quarry they were after. The story of his riches and his avarice was not only the favourite Tory count against him; it had a good foundation of truth, and was, moreover, intimately associated with the other gibe that he had a personal interest in perpetuating the war. In the course of their examination an unlooked-for plum fell into the laps of the Commissioners. Sir Solomon Medina, the principal Government contractor, gave evidence of large sums which he had provided to the Duke 'for his own use'. In fact, these monies had been used to sustain the vast intelligence service which had notably assisted his military campaigns. Marlborough explained the matter in a letter to the Commissioners and took the precaution of writing direct to Harley. 'Upon my arrival here,' he wrote, 'I had notice that my name was brought before the Commissioners of Accounts, possibly without any design to do me a prejudice.' Harley was then invited to read the Duke's report to the Commissioners and assist him in settling the matter in its true light. 'No one knows better than your lordship the great use and expense of intelligence.' Marlborough, it appeared, was not unduly alarmed by the episode. But in the later part of his letter to Harley there was some indication that he understood well enough the motives behind the inquiry. 'I do therefore boldly claim the benefit of your friendship . . .' he wrote. 'The endeavours of our enemies to destroy the friendship between us will double mine to continue and improve it.' How much faith Marlborough still reposed in Harley's good faith it is impossible to know. He may have considered a pose of equanimity the best protection against any attack which might follow. But, with or without Harley's friendship, he must brace himself to confront some ugly enemies on his return. And if he still had any doubts his mind was made up by another development at The Hague. Baron von Bothmar had arrived there from Hanover, also *en route* for London. He brought with him a memorial from the Elector for the Queen protesting against the proposed peace preliminaries in the most emphatic terms. The two men travelled on to London together. By the time they landed at Greenwich on November 17th the vital link in a new grand alliance had been formed.

November 17th was the anniversary of the great Queen Elizabeth's birthday and the occasion was often used by the London apprentices for a display of Protestant fervour. Effigies of the Pope and the Devil and any other topical opponent of the rights and religion of true Englishmen were accustomed to be consigned to the flames at Temple Bar. On this occasion—so the Tories believed or affected to believe—Lord Wharton and his friends of the Whig Kit-Kat Club had a plan to revive the ceremony on the most provocative scale. They intended a mighty demonstration against the Queen's Ministers and the peace to coincide with the Duke of Marlborough's home-coming. The Ministers were alarmed enough to take drastic action. At midnight before the great day an empty house in Drury Lane was raided by the Queen's messengers assisted by a detachment of foot guards. There they found the effigies of the Pope, the Pretender and the Devil (bearing a striking likeness to Harley) along with a vast assortment of pasteboard mockeries of Cardinals, Jesuit priests and friars. These were transferred to the Ministers' office at the Cockpit and the demonstration next day was effectively banned. For three days the trained bands patrolled the streets to prevent any further activities by the London mob.

But nothing could stop the uproar in Grub Street. The Whigs expressed their sense of outrage at this interference with the people's freedom: 'It appeared very strange that a popular Rejoicing, so grateful to this Protestant City and which was never attempted to be quash'd, but in the reign of James II, should at this time be suppressed.' On the other hand the *Postboy* made the charge that it was all 'a Conspiracy to raise a Mob to confront the best of Queens, and her Ministry, pull down the Homes of Several Honest, Worthy, Loyal, true English Gentlemen'. Money for the purpose had been collected from the Whig Lords ranging from Lord Wharton to the Duke of Somerset. Mrs. Manley, on Swift's prompting, was quick to elaborate the charge in a pamphlet. Never had a blacker design been formed, 'unless it were blowing up the Parliament House'. Among the effigies were to be those representing Harley, Mrs. Masham, Dr. Sacheverell and St. John, the last of these having actually been designed by the loving hands of Lady Mary Churchill, Duchess of Montagu and youngest daughter of the Duke of Marlborough. Sarah herself— the 'German Princess'—had been ready to subscribe in her new mood of careless generosity. Huge sums had been raised to ensure that the mobs were large enough and their equipment of flambeaux sufficient for the purpose. Stories were to be put

about that the Queen was dying or already dead. And amid these
wild scenes of arson and confusion, the Duke of Marlborough was
to make his entry through Aldgate amid cries of 'Victory, Bouchain, the lines, no peace, no peace'. The aim, hinted Mrs. Manley,
was to march him to St. James's Palace and crown him King.
Not even Mrs. Manley could really believe the tale she told. But
that the Ministers were truly frightened is clear. And the Whig
pamphleteers were unwilling to disown all the glory. Yes, they had
intended the most spectacular anti-Popish demonstration since the
days of Titus Oates and they were quite eager to admit that the
idea was highly topical. 'At the Temple, before the statue of that
illustrious lady whose anniversary was then celebrated, that queen
wearing a veil on which are drawn the picture of her present
majesty, and under it the battles of Blenheim, Ramillies, Oudenarde, and the passes of the lines in this present year of 1711, after
proper ditties were sung, the Pretender was to have been
committed to the flames, being first absolved by the Cardinal
GUALTIERI. After that, the said cardinal was to be absolved
by the pope, and burnt. And then the devil was to jump into the
flames with his holiness in his arms. And let all the people say,
Amen.'

The day after the abortive Whig demonstration, the Duke of
Marlborough presented himself at Hampton Court. He 'came to
me yesterday as soon as I had dined', wrote the Queen to Harley,
'made a great many of his usual professions of duty and affection
to me. He seemed dejected and very uneasy about this matter of
the publick accounts, stayed neare an hour and saw nobody heare
but myself'. How openly he broached the great issue of the peace
is not clear. All the political leaders in London waited anxiously for
a sign of the role he had marked out for himself in the drama
ahead. 'I hear', wrote St. John to Lord Strafford, 'that in his
conversation with the Queen, he has spoke against what we are
doing; in short, his fate hangs heavy upon him, and he has of late
pursued every council which was the worst for him.' It was true.
Marlborough opposed the peace, but it was still not revealed how
forcibly he intended to press his opinion. 'His Grace may take
what turn he pleases,' continued St. John, 'but I will venture to
assure your Excellency, that the bent of the nation is for peace; and
those who talk with the members, as they arrive from the several
counties, assure me, that they come up determined to support all

that we are doing; and that nothing is more popular, than that firmness and resolution which has been shown by the Queen's servants, in carrying on the great work, amidst so much opposition and so much clamour.' St. John was still confident, and his mood was shared by Swift who like the rest of London eagerly waited for authentic news of the Duke's intentions. 'The Duke', added Swift, 'is not so fond of me. What care I? I won seven shillings to-night at picquet.' The lack of affection was mutual, but with this difference: Marlborough cared deeply about Swift's attacks and Swift who was well aware of this weakness was preparing to make Marlborough smart as never before.

Yet even St. John's confidence was somewhat feigned. As the day for the meeting of Parliament came closer and as he and Harley were compelled to collaborate in preparing the Queen's speech, plentiful reports indicated that the real decision would not rest with members from the counties and that even they had not shed their disgruntlement with Harley's palsied methods. 'The House of Lords', wrote the Duke of Shrewsbury to Harley, 'is the place where our enemies have much hopes to prevail in, so I recommend you to take the requisite care that our friends come to town in time.' But even if they did arrive in time there was no guarantee of victory.

The truth was that, thanks to the quarrel between Harley and St. John, the administration had been robbed of its cohesion; it had lost the power to attract waverers by the magnet of leadership. Either Harley's or St. John's policy might have offered a chance of success; as it was, each tugged against the other. On the eve of Parliament's reassembly Harley's scheme for wheedling a majority by the appeasement of the moderates looked as if it had crumbled. Marlborough, for all the months of flattery and deception, had not retired to the country in lofty dudgeon; he had gone straight from his interview with the Queen to consort with the Whigs and the Hanoverian envoy. Somerset, insulted by St. John, spread the advantageous rumour, with all the authority of his Duchess to help win him credence, that the Queen herself might not look too unkindly on those who opposed the plans of her Ministers. Halifax and Somers were still ready to talk with Harley; but nothing concrete or practical emerged from their conversations. Most menacing of all were the reports about Nottingham; could it really be true that this most high-principled of the high-flying Tories was contemplating an association with his lifelong enemies, the Whigs? True, he had been excluded from office, but it was really impossible to suppose that the great defender of the English Church could ever meet amicably in the same room with that defiler of altars, Lord Wharton. One of Harley's most trusted intermediaries, Lord Poulett, was sent on an urgent errand to interview the great Tory Earl. 'I found him', reported Poulett, 'as sour and fiercely wild as you can imagine anything to be that has lived long in the desert.' Poulett's further animadversions on the general situation in the same letter amounted by implication to an indictment of Harley's conduct as leader. 'I am a great deal concerned,' he said, 'how your numbers may answer in the House, for I think the Queen's enemies at present generally understand one another much better than her friends and servants. The adversaries have been a long time prepared for a meeting which will decide the fate of Europe as well as Britain.'

No equivalent preparations for the great test had been made by Harley. Many of his supporters were disconsolate and spiritless. One portrait of him painted at this time by a leading high Tory explains how the chief architect of the Whigs' destruction a year before had failed to sustain his mastery once he achieved the position of Prime Minister. It appeared that 'his naturall temper and dexterity' lay rather 'in contriving snares to catch those he had a mind to undermine than in being the chief minister of state and prime favorite; for besides that he was too reserved and assumed too few into his secret designs, he did not shew that politeness and address so necessary in one of that high station to which he was now advanced, and seemed more to carry thorow his views by his cunning than by the influence, weight and authority of the Crown, and by supporting and encouraging the friends thereof; from whence it came to pass that he gained few friends and created personall enemys. He was indeed very civill to all who addressed him, but he generally either spoke so low in their ear or so misteriouslie that few knew what to make of his replys, and it would appear he took a secret pleasure in making people hing on and disappointing them'. This was also the criticism of St. John and Swift. No doubt Harley could have retorted that the abrupt methods of St. John ran the risk of driving every moderate into the Whig camp. But day by day that plea was losing its force. Only by the accident of Guiscard's attack had the earlier revolt of

the October Club been thwarted. Only by daring challenge had
the peace been brought so near. Many of the moderates had been
lost to the Tory cause in any case and no compensating advantage
had been gained in a rising vitality among the Tories. In short,
the hand of Harley had lost its cunning. On the very day before
Parliament was scheduled to meet, he received a warning which he
could not neglect. The Tory Speaker in the Commons, William
Bromley, told him that the October Club were on the war-path
once again. During the previous session they had been cheated of
their prey; this time they demanded ruthless action. Something
had been offered them in the report of the Commission on
Accounts, but more and much more would be required. If Harley
wished to remain leader of the Tories, he must lead. If not he
would have to make way for another. That was the inference; the
same thought had occurred with increasing frequency to St. John.
How he must have chafed to see the Tories summoned to the
battle with these feeble war-cries. Yet he was wise enough to
know that no distraction could be afforded when the Whig threat
had grown to such proportions. Immediately, it was necessary to
rescue his army from sudden ambush. On November 25th he told
Swift that the Parliament was to be prorogued once more for a few
days. 'The Whigs are too strong in the house of Lords,' wrote
Swift; 'other reasons are pretended, but that is the truth.' Next
day the decision was confirmed at a meeting of the Cabinet
Council. Parliament would meet on December 7th. 'This Prorogation, at so critical a Juncture, and so late in the Year', wrote
Abel Boyer, 'occasioned various Reasonings and Reflections; and
some People went so far, as to surmize, that the Parliament would
still be further prorogued from Time to Time, till the Peace was
concluded.'

Such no doubt would have been the solution of the dilemma
favoured by Charles I or Charles II. Queen Anne could not rule
without at least the connivance of her Parliament. Parliament too,
however much the Queen would have been horrified to admit it,
could not rule without paying heed to the insolent eruptions of the
printing press. While the Captain-General had spent his week in
London testing the resolution of the Whigs, the Vicar of Laracor
had put the finishing touches to his great labour of the previous
months. On November 27th was published *The Conduct of the
Allies and of the Late Ministry in Beginning and Carrying on the*

Present War. St. John had been the main source of Swift's inspiration in the work, yet by an extraordinary feat Harley's incomprehensible gropings for a national policy above the strife of faction now became articulate and persuasive. Here in words of glistening clarity was the leadership which the peace party craved. Here all their fiercest emotions paraded as arguments. The fire of St. John and the smooth oil of Harley were merged in perfect alchemy. While his friends were engaged in the most spectacular piece of treachery in English history and in defiance of the reputation and policy of the most successful of English soldiers, Swift so turned the tables that the Tory case now appeared in the guise of a more discriminating patriotism pitted against all the forces of avarice and pride.

CHAPTER ELEVEN

The Wonder-Working Pamphlet

(Publication date: November 27th, 1711)

'Use the point of your pen, not the
feather.'—SWIFT, *Literary Essays*

'A PERFORMANCE OF VERY LITTLE ABILITY,' said Dr.
Johnson in discussing *The Conduct of the Allies.* Some
members of his company demurred. 'Surely, Sir,' said one,
'you must allow it has strong facts.' 'Why, yes, Sir,' replied
Johnson; 'but what is that to the merit of the composition? In
the Sessions-paper of the Old Bailey there are strong facts. House-
breaking is a strong fact; robbery is a strong fact; and murder is a
mighty strong fact: but is great praise due to the historian of those
strong facts? No, Sir, Swift has told what he had to tell distinctly
enough, but that is all. He had to count ten, and he has counted it
right.' The verdict is reaffirmed in Johnson's *Life of Swift.*
'Surely whoever surveys this wonder-working pamphlet with cool
perusal,' he wrote, 'will confess that its efficacy was supplied by
the passions of its readers; that it operates by the mere weight of
facts, with very little assistance from the hand that produced them.'

The accusation—or the tribute—has a particle of validity.
Swift himself claimed that he would prove his case by the recital of
'plain matters of fact'. Yet any such judgement is as absurd as Dr.
Johnson's other curious belief that Swift was deficient in both
humour and wit; if the feat was counting to ten, no one else had
done it! Other critics have asserted, with more justice, that
the pamphlet contains only rare flashes of the irony which was
Swift's greatest talent. Yet the method he used was akin to irony.
Irony achieves its effect by taking a popular and accepted opinion
and turning it inside out; it is a conjuring trick with ideas both
contrived and concealed by the same patter of words. This ingred-
ient was certainly not lacking in *The Conduct of the Allies.* For
without once straining his voice or the credulity of his readers,
Swift managed to persuade them that the most shattering truth

about the age in which they lived could be unravelled only by the acceptance of the most startling of paradoxes.

The Duke of Marlborough, the hero whose glories were celebrated by sounding the tower guns and lighting the city bonfires, was in reality the chief cause of national misery and shame. Others before Swift, of course, and Swift himself before the publication of *The Conduct of the Allies*, had assailed the Duke, magnifying his foibles and probing for every weak joint in his armour. Swift's aim now was different. The Duke's vices—his avarice, his arrogance, his ambition—were no longer to be regarded as melancholy blots on his greatness. They were the engines which had shaped not only his policies but those of the Whigs and the nation. In short, Swift was not content to excite the party passions of his readers; the object was to turn them all against the Duke. This was to be achieved, moreover, without their knowing what spell had been cast upon them. The idea was to be instilled, at first at least, only by inference. But this was the aim and unless it is recognized *The Conduct of the Allies* is reduced to what Dr. Johnson thought it to be—an effective recapitulation of all the familiar Tory arguments against the war. In fact, the pamphlet was packed with the most daring novelties. It went far beyond the doctrine which either Harley or St. John had previously presented or which Swift himself had attempted in the *Examiner*. And, like every good pamphlet, it was designed to be swallowed in one gulp; every section, almost every sentence, adds to the potency. Only afterwards would the nation which drank it down so greedily realize the effect and be moved to the desired action. Marlborough must be destroyed! That was the supreme conclusion. It was not stated openly in so many words; like Mark Antony or Shakespeare, Swift knew that the response of his audience would be all the more effective if they were left to themselves to forge the last, inexorable link in the logic.

During the previous few months the emphasis in the Tory case had varied; in part at least it was an argument about dates. A peace had been possible in 1706 after Ramillies. A peace had been possible in 1709 or in 1710; only the intransigence of Marlborough, the Whigs or the Dutch had thrown it away. Now new terms had been offered by the French and a new opportunity had appeared. Thus different Tory spokesmen made differing claims. Considering that the Queen and her new Ministers had committed themselves to continue the war as recently as July 1711, all these pleas were open to separate objections; all might be made the subject of endless disputation; even the last was weakened if the others were shown to be unproven. Implied in them all was the view that the war itself had been necessary and justified—presumably for the very reasons that Marlborough and the Whigs affirmed: to prevent Louis XIV from becoming the master of Europe through the subjection of the Dutch and through the acquisition of Spain and the Spanish Indies by keeping his grandson on the Spanish throne. All these Tory claims thus acknowledged the debt to Marlborough; if the war had to be fought, it was better to fight it successfully.

Swift, in his pamphlet, denied the whole implication. The war from the very start had been a gigantic error. This was the unexpected premise from which he opened his attack. The point was made almost casually by lifting one corner of the curtain which shrouded the evil policies of the Marlborough family. 'It must be granted', he wrote, 'that the counsels of entering into the present war were violently opposed by the Church Party, who advised the late King to acknowledge the Duke of Anjou; and particularly, 'tis affirmed that the Earl of Godolphin, who was then in the Church-Interest, told the King in November, 1701, that since his Majesty was determined to engage in a war, so contrary to his private opinion, he could serve him no longer, and accordingly gave up his employment; though he happened afterwards to change his mind, when he was to be Lord Treasurer, and have the sole management of affairs at home; while those abroad were to be in the hands of *One*, whose advancement, by all sorts of ties, he was engaged to promote.' Among the reasons which persuaded the Church Party to oppose entry into the war—so Swift alleged—was a wise premonition of how any attempt to force a foreign King on the Spaniards would rouse their national pride and forge a much closer bond between King Louis and his grandson than would otherwise be natural. The most weighty arguments—so Swift implied—had been adduced by the far-seeing Tories. However the opposite opinion, 'or some private motives', prevailed; 'and so, without offering any other remedy, without taking time to consider the consequences, or to reflect on our own condition, we hastily engaged in a war which hath cost us sixty millions; and after repeated, as well as unexpected success in arms, hath put us

and our posterity in a worse condition, not only than any of our
allies, but even our conquered enemies themselves.'

Thus a new stage was set for the debate about the peace. The
nation had been tricked from the start and Swift proposed to show
how the trickery had been sustained by proving the three following
propositions.

'*First*, That against all manner of prudence or common reason, we
engaged in this war as principals, when we ought to have acted only as
auxiliaries.

'*Secondly*, That we spent all our vigour in pursuing that part of the
war, which could least answer the end we proposed by beginning of it;
and made no efforts at all where we could have most weakened the
common enemy, and at the same time enriched ourselves.

'*Lastly*, That we suffered each of our allies to break every article in
those treaties and agreements by which they were bound, and to lay the
burthen upon us'.

With these three themes Swift touched familiar chords. All had
figured in the Tory argument over the years. The first was the
doctrine which St. John had enunciated in his *Letter to the Examiner* a year before; the second was the favourite obsession of the
respected Tory leaders like Nottingham and Rochester; the third
rubbed and inflamed the natural irritation against allies to which
every war-weary nation is prone. But Swift was to weave these old
strands into a new pattern.

The first was the weakest of the three and Swift did not waste
much time in pressing it. The French King's actions which had
provided the occasion for the war threatened Dutch and Austrian
interests much more severely than England's. True, if the French
were left in control of Flanders and if the Duke of Anjou became a
French puppet, the consequences for England might be serious.
But England was bound by an ancient treaty to assist the Dutch
with ten thousand men if they were attacked by the French. If that
support and no more had been supplied and if the Dutch had thus
been compelled to exert themselves to the limit, they could have
defended their own frontiers. Even if they had been forced to make
peace, England could have afforded to watch and wait. Flanders
formed part of the Spanish dominions and if the French continued
to occupy them, 'hatred and jealousy' between the French King
and his grandson in Madrid might soon have broken out—'at that
time they had none of those endearments to each other which this

war hath created'. But instead of adopting this prudent course, a new war in which England was to assist with her whole strength was undertaken, 'upon the advice of those who, with their partisans and adherents, were to be the sole gainers by it'.

Much more attractive—from Swift's point of view—was the second proposition. Brilliant victories far exceeding anything which the original instigators of the war had thought conceivable had been won; yet now they asserted that a peace should not be considered or concluded. 'Ten glorious campaigns are passed, and now at last, like the sick man, we are just expiring with all sorts of good symptoms.' What could explain the mystery? Could it be that the war had been fought on the wrong strategy and in the wrong place; that the campaigns in Flanders offered no prospect of bringing France to terms, but only of taking a town a year for the Dutch at the cost of six millions of English pounds? 'I say not this, by any means, to detract from the army or its Leaders. Getting into the enemies' lines, passing rivers, and taking towns, may be actions attended with many glorious circumstances: but when all this brings no real solid advantage to us, when it hath no other end than to enlarge the territories of the Dutch, and increase the fame and wealth of our G——l, I conclude, however it comes about, that things are not as they should be; and that surely our forces and money might be better employed, both towards reducing our enemy, and working some benefit to ourselves?'

Here Swift was on shaky ground and he knew it. The old Tory cry had been that it was the war in Spain and against the Spaniards on the seas which should have been pursued much more vigorously. Indeed, when Lord Peterborough had won victories in Spain, the Tories had violently protested against his recall by the Whigs. The new Tory cry was that the attempt to conquer Spain had become hopeless. Swift had his answer to the dilemma. Either Peterborough should have been backed to the limit, or, when fortune turned against us in the Spanish theatre, we should have stayed on the defensive in Catalonia, and found other means of inflicting injury on the enemy. 'And what a field of honour and profit had we before us, wherein to employ the best of our strength, which against all the maxims of British policy, we suffered to lie wholly neglected? I have sometimes wondered how it came to pass, that the style of *Maritime Powers*, by which our Allies, in a sort of contemptuous manner, usually couple us with the Dutch, did never put us in mind of the sea; and while some politicians were shewing us the way to Spain, by Flanders, others by Savoy or Naples, that the West Indies should never come into our heads.' Both Spain and France could have been humbled in the seas of North and South America, whereas instead both had been allowed to draw their sorely-needed supplies of gold and other riches from this source. Why, then, had this prospect of victory and wealth been so wantonly neglected? 'Great events often turn upon very small circumstances,' wrote Swift. 'It was the Kingdom's misfortune, that the sea was not the D— of M——h's element, otherwise the whole force of war would infallibly have been bestowed there, infinitely to the advantage of his country, which would then have gone hand in hand with his own.' The idea was not so chimerical. Half a century later Chatham executed the maritime strategy prescribed in *The Conduct of the Allies*. St. John's expedition to Quebec—meanly denounced by the Dutch, according to Swift, because it offered some special commercial reward for England—had in it the seeds of a great national policy.

However, much nearer to the bosoms of his readers was the third of Swift's propositions—the charge that England's allies had broken faith and placed the principal burden of the war on English backs. Here indeed Swift relied on strong facts, many of them the commonplaces of Tory propaganda. Yet even these were enlivened by fresh revelations well calculated to stir the anti-Dutch or anti-Austrian sentiment never far beneath the surface. In October, 1709, the previous Ministry had signed the Barrier Treaty with the representatives of the States-General. The Treaty committed England to the Dutch much more tightly than the original terms of the Grand Alliance. The bargain had been made at the height of the Whig supremacy. Tremendous secrecy had always surrounded every circumstance connected with it. Only one of England's plentipotentiaries at The Hague at the time, Lord Townshend, had actually put his name to it. The other (and he was the Duke of Marlborough, although Swift did not specify him precisely) 'was heard to say, he would rather lose his right hand, than set it to such a treaty. Had he spoke those words in due season, and loud enough to be heard on this side of the water, considering the credit he had then at court, he might have saved much of his country's honour, and got as much for himself'. Now Swift revealed the reasons for all these clandestine precautions. Only two articles in the Barrier Treaty even purported to bring any direct advantage to England and these could easily be exposed as worthless. One comprised a Dutch pledge to help preserve the Protestant succession in England and the other engaged them not to treat with France until the French promised to acknowledge the Queen and the Hanoverian succession and to remove the Pretender from King Louis' dominions. But the Dutch were already bound in honour and interest to uphold the Protestant succession. 'What an impression of our Settlement must it give abroad, to see our Ministers offering such conditions to the Dutch, to prevail on them to be guarantees of our Acts of Parliament! As for the second article, it was a natural consequence that must attend any treaty of peace with France.' So the Dutch had given away nothing, and yet in return had received firm guarantees for their own trade and their barriers in Flanders and a promise they would share in any commercial advantage which might follow from the expulsion of the Duke of Anjou from Spain and the Indies. It was against this background that Swift recited the particular accusations that the Dutch had failed to supply the armed forces or the subsidies they had pledged; and all the while they had been whining that England, who had exceeded her original pledges, was not contributing more to the common cause. The same accusations—with much greater justification—were made against the Emperor and the Austrians. 'They computed easily, that it would cost them less to make large presents to one single person than to pay an army and turn to as good account.'

Detail was piled on detail until at last the crux of the pamphlet was reached. 'But if all this be true: if, according to what I have affirmed, we began this war contrary to reason: If, as the other party themselves, upon all occasions, acknowledge, the success we have had was more than we could reasonably expect: If, after all our success, we have not made that use of it, which in reason we ought to have done: If we have made weak and foolish bargains with our allies, suffered them tamely to break every article, even in those bargains to our disadvantage, and allowed them to treat us with insolence and contempt, at the very instant when we were gaining towns, provinces and kingdoms for them, at the price of our ruin, and without any prospect of interest to ourselves: If we have consumed all our strength in attacking the enemy on the strongest side, where (as the old Duke of Schomberg expressed it) *to engage with* France, *was to take a bull by the horns*; and left wholly unattempted, that part of the war, which could only enable us to continue or to end it; If all this, I say, be our case, it is a very obvious question to ask, by what motives, or what management, we are thus become the *Dupes and Bubbles of Europe?* Sure it cannot be owing to the stupidity arising from the coldness of our climate, since those among our allies, who have given us most reason to complain, are as far removed from the sun as ourselves.'

Only one solution could account for all the strange facets of the mystery. Already the hints had been given. Lord Godolphin had once been opposed to entering the war. But then the scene changed. 'His Lordship and the family with whom he was engaged by so complicated an alliance, were in the highest credit possible with the Q—n. The Treasurer's staff was ready for his Lordship, the Duke was to command the army and the Duchess by her employments, and the favour she was possessed of, to be always nearest her M——y's person; by which the whole power, at home and abroad, would be devolved upon that family. This was a prospect so very inviting, that, to confess the truth, it could not easily be withstood by any who have so keen an appetite for wealth and ambition. By an agreement subsequent to the Grand Alliance, we were to assist the Dutch with forty thousand men, all to be commanded by the D. of M. So that whether this war were prudently begun or not, it is plain, that the true spring or motive of it, was the aggrandising a particular family: and, in short, a War of the *General* and the *Ministry* and not of the *Prince* or *People*; since those very persons were against it when they knew the power, and consequently the profit, would be in other hands.'

Upon this foundation a conspiracy had been set on foot, one which embraced the whole politics of the nation. For the charge, be it noted, was not limited to the question of the General's 'unmeasurable love of wealth, which his best friends allow to be his predominant passion. I shall waive anything that is personal upon this subject. I shall say nothing of those great presents made by several princes, which the soldiers used to call winter foraging, and said it was better than that of summer; of two and a half per cent substracted out of all the subsidies we pay in those parts which amounts to no inconsiderable sum; and lastly, of the grand perquisites in a long successful war, which are so amicably adjusted between him and the States'. These were trifles. The truly serious matter was the far-reaching measures which the Marlborough family and their supporters were forced to embark upon to protect their usurpation of power in the state.

First, they made an alliance with the Monied Men whose 'perpetual harvest is war'. Next, they made a 'Solemn League and Covenant' with the discarded Whigs who were ready to return to office on any terms. Finally, the allies resolved to exploit the novel political situation in London for their own advantage, breaking their treaty obligations but engaging themselves more deeply to the political fortunes of the General and the Whigs. Proof of these machinations was abundant and well known. When at last the Queen sought to break loose from 'those ungrateful Servants who as they waxed fatter, did but kick the more, had not the Allies joined with the stockjobbers at home in seeking to prevent any change in her Ministers?' A common interest bound all the conspirators together. Only if the General and the Whigs retained power would such affronts and betrayals by the allies be tolerated; only if the allies rallied to the aid of the usurpers could the Tory attack be defeated or the Queen's resentment be overborne; only if the war continued could the union of all these evil forces be held together. The miracle was that the Queen had ever succeeded in breaking it. Some had sought to lessen the merit of this achievement by suggesting that the family had overreached themselves in their conduct towards the Queen. Had they not heaped 'rudeness, tyranny, oppression and ingratitude' upon her? Had she not been driven from Windsor Castle to take shelter in an adjoining cottage 'pursuant to the advice of *Solomon*, who tells us, *It is better to dwell in a corner of the housetop, than with a brawling woman in a wide house*?' Such excuses Swift would not accept. No; the truth was that the ambition of the Marlborough faction knew no bounds. Only in the nick of time had they been checked. In their own interests their onslaught on the Queen had been well advised. 'Their proceedings were right. For nothing is so apt to break even the bravest spirits, as a continual chain of oppressions: one injury is best defended by a second, and this by a third. By these steps, the old masters of the palace in France became masters of the kingdom; and by these steps a G——l *during pleasure*, might have grown into a G——l *for life*, and a G——l for life into a *King*. So that I still insist upon it as a wonder, how Her M——y, thus besieged on all sides, was able to extricate herself.'

Thus Swift fitted together the jig-saw puzzle of politics during the past decade. The popular conceptions, natural in the midst of a great war and up till recently bearing the stamp of the Queen's approval, were destroyed. Gone was the vision of a patriotic struggle waged against a foreign tyrant. Gone even was the other portrait which had become superimposed on the first of a people grown weary of such endless sacrifice and hardship. An entirely new picture emerged. Monied men who paraded their new wealth while the rest of the nation was weighed down by taxes; allies who broke their compacts with impunity; the Whigs who had actually rejected peace terms with France when they were offered; a Duchess who had lorded it over the Queen and ranted when a few of her privileges were stripped from her; a General who had amassed a tremendous fortune and had indeed applied to become General for life; all these were facts, verifiable by the public with their own eyes and from accepted hearsay. Adding them together it was not so outlandish to suggest there was 'a conspiracy on all sides to go on with those measures which must perpetuate the war'.

This was the blinding light which gave *The Conduct of the Allies* its power. No longer was the argument against the Marlboroughs confined to tittle-tattle about the Duchess and her tantrums, the Duke and his money-grabbing, the beautiful daughters and their tangled political and matrimonial alliances. No longer was the argument against the Whigs confined to their overbearing manners, their blasphemies and their corruption. No longer even was the argument about the war itself confined to the important but still secondary question as to precisely when a peace could have been most advantageously secured. All these considerations were now included in a much more extensive indictment. A fundamental clash of interest divided the Marlboroughs and their satellites from the nation. The whole war had been a grotesque deception practised by the one on the other.

Such if it could be believed—and clearly it was believed by many —was the message of *The Conduct of the Allies*. It is not so hard to realize that Swift's readers gasped with amazement as the veil was torn from their eyes. And, just to clinch the case before they could catch their breath, Swift imposed an even more spectacular change in the terms of the debate. The narrow argument on which so much turned that November was whether it was right and wise to abandon the aim of placing the Austrian Archduke on the Spanish

throne. This was the great point on which the Tory Ministers
had yielded in their recent negotiations with the French. This was
the point on which the Elector and the Emperor, if not the Dutch,
were most aggrieved and alarmed. This was certain to be the head
and front of the offence attacked by the Whigs at the meeting of the
Parliament. Yet by any reckoning the Whigs were not on strong
ground. The attempt to win in Spain did indeed appear vain and
unprofitable. Here at least Swift might have been expected not to
risk overstating his case. Instead he preferred to use the weak Whig
case about Spain to substantiate his main theme.

How was it possible that England became committed to the cry
of 'No peace without Spain'? It was, first, 'a new incident grafted
upon the original quarrel'. Nowhere in the clauses of the Grand
Alliance was there 'the least mention of demanding Spain for the
House of Austria, or of refusing any Peace without that condition;
the condition in this respect was that the same man should never
be king of both kingdoms and particularly that the French may
never be in possession of the Spanish West Indies'. But English,
or rather Whig, ambition had grown with Marlborough's victories.
A vote had been passed through both Houses of Parliament insisting that no peace should be tolerated until the Archduke's Kingdom had been conquered for him by English blood and treasure.
The Austrians naturally agreed; the Dutch who had little enough
interest in Spain were persuaded to agree by the Barrier Treaty;
and when the French pleaded for peace at Gertruydenburg in 1709
it was these heightened demands which ruined the chance of a
peace. The peace talks conducted by the Whigs had in fact been a
mockery. How was it possible that they had thrown away the fruits
of so many victories? 'Give me leave to suppose the continuance
of the war was the thing at heart, and then I can easily shew the
consistency of their proceedings; otherwise, they are wholly unaccountable or absurd.' Time and again Swift hammered on the same
nail. The pressure to continue the war was concerned not at all
with questions of national honour or national advantage; it derived
only from the personal and financial interest of the few who cheerfully piled fresh burdens and taxes on the many. Least of all should
anyone be persuaded by this trumpery excuse about Spain.
'What arts have been used to possess the people with a strong
delusion that Britain must infallibly be ruined without the recovery of Spain to the House of Austria? Making the safety of a great

and powerful Kingdom, as ours was then, to depend upon an event, which, even after a war of miraculous successes, proves impracticable. As if princes and great ministers could find no way of settling the public tranquillity without changing the possessions of kingdoms, and forcing sovereigns upon a people against their inclinations. Is there no security for the island of Britain unless a king of Spain be dethroned by the hands of his grandfather?' Frantically searching for a way to conceal their folly the advocates of war plunged into deeper follies. Now 'the common question is, if we must now surrender Spain, what have we been fighting for all this while?' So Swift returned to his original declaration. 'The answer is ready; we have been fighting for the ruin of the public interest, and the advancement of a private. We have been fighting to raise the wealth and grandeur of a particular family; to enrich usurers and stockjobbers; and to cultivate the pernicious designs of a faction, by destroying the Landed interest. The nation begins to think these blessings are not worth fighting for any longer, and therefore desires a peace.'

This was the style in which Swift counted ten! Dr. Johnson's verdict is peculiarly inapposite, since the obvious criticism is that Swift abandoned his fortress of strong facts to risk a much more adventurous battle. Most historians have agreed that it was legitimate and necessary to make the peace in 1711 and 1712 whatever strictures may be passed on the methods employed. Most historians have concurred in condemning the Whigs for their failure to conclude it in 1709. The weight of the argument on these two counts alone is overpowering. Why, then, was Swift, the great arguer, not content to prove a case so irrefragable? Why did he level his attack not solely against the continuance of the war, but against the war itself? Why did he lay himself open to the rejoinder from his Whig opponents that he had dismissed the whole Whig case against the exorbitant ambitions of Louis XIV and their menace to English interests in Flanders and elsewhere? The answer, of course, is that he was not writing for the benefit of the historians. His primary purpose was not even to put the general case for the peace, although naturally that case figured prominently in the pamphlet. His business was to change history, not to record it. Only by the means he chose could he isolate his victim. Only thus could he hurl at the head of his enemy a thunderbolt which might destroy him.

Neither Harley nor St. John could have appreciated fully the weapon they had helped to forge. Some critics have suggested that in his politics Swift was merely their servant or their dupe, that in *The Conduct of the Allies* his style was constricted, his natural bent twisted by the requirement to assist the Ministers' necessities. On the contrary, *The Conduct of the Allies* is the surest proof of Swift's independence and of his peculiar contribution to the policies of the triumvirate. Neither Harley nor St. John, either in their pronouncements before November 1711 or in their subsequent apologias, ever dared to make the case against the war or the Duke on the same massive scale. They could not if they wished; for both had once counted themselves among Marlborough's chief admirers and both had once been declared supporters of the war. In the autumn of 1711 they wanted Swift's aid to perform a particular service—to enable them to meet the Parliament with assurance and defeat the Marlborough-Whig alliance. Swift agreed to execute the assignment, but only after his own fashion. The Ministers, or at least St. John, supplied the facts (many of them inaccurate); Swift supplied the stroke of genius. For the Ministers the contest was personal, a matter of delicate political balance, a question of whether and when it might be advisable to risk a challenge to the Captain-General. This had also been Swift's view expressed in the *Examiner* earlier in the year. He had been restrained by the same calculations and also by a genuine respect for the Duke which he could never stifle entirely. But in *The Conduct of the Allies* his whole tone and purpose were changed. He saw that the grounds of the quarrel must be enlarged, that the war must be stripped of its nobility and exposed as the senseless thing he had always suspected it to be. Above all, if peace was to be secured, the weariness and anger of the nation must be concentrated against the man who more than any other could prevent it. The moment had come. Marlborough must be destroyed!

Harley, unlike St. John, had probably not yet made up his mind whether the climax might not still be avoided or postponed. Even on November 27th the chance remained that the Duke might abandon his intrigues with the Whigs and retire forlornly to his country estate. The chance, if indeed it existed, must have been considerably diminished by the appearance of Swift's pamphlet. Marlborough must have understood that the armistice between himself and the Ministers had always been a fraud. Meantime, on the behaviour of St. John during the previous months *The Conduct of the Allies* casts a glare of lurid illumination. He knew how perfectly the dagger was being sharpened. He had foreseen that the final trial of strength with Marlborough could not be averted; he had planned for it and he relished the prospect; week by week the work on which Swift was engaged occupied an ever larger place in his calculations. And all the while he fostered with the Duke such excellent relations that the Queen's courtiers suspected, as one of the counts against him, that he was up to the ears in a conspiracy of his own with Marlborough against his Cabinet colleagues. Deceit on such a scale has the quality of grandeur.

CHAPTER TWELVE

'The Queen is False'

(November 27th—December 8th, 1711)

'There was not, perhaps in all England, a person who understood more artificially how to disguise her passions than the late Queen.'—SWIFT, *Memoirs Relating to that Change in the Queen's Ministry*, 1710.

THE IMPACT OF *The Conduct of the Allies* was far-reaching and instantaneous. Within a few days everyone was reading it, Lords and Bishops, Members of Parliament and coffee-house politicians, Grub Street newsmongers and Oxford professors. On the day of publication—Tuesday, November 27th —Swift saw a copy on Harley's table and received congratulations and a few suggested changes from the Prime Minister. Next day he was able to report to Stella that 'it begins to make a noise'. Several people asked him whether he had seen the great work, urging him to read it, 'for it was something extraordinary'. On Thursday John Morphew, the publisher, called early in the morning; a thousand copies had been sold in two days and a second edition must be printed immediately. Work was to go ahead night and day to get it out by Saturday. On Sunday morning the publisher called again. The second edition had sold out in five hours and a third must be ready for Monday morning. Sunday or no Sunday, the printer's men worked on and the Vicar of Laracor was compelled to miss church to assist with the necessary corrections. That night Swift dined with St. John who told him that Willem Buys was planning a protest against the pamphlet's outrageous aspersions on the Dutch nation and its contribution to the war. Others, too, were smarting. On Monday Swift dined with John Morphew; they had business to discuss apart from the need for yet another edition. 'The Whigs are resolved to bring that pamphlet into the house of lords to have it condemned, *so I hear*,' reported Swift to Stella. 'But the printer will stand to it, and not own the author; he must say, he had it from the penny post.' Many were making guesses about the real criminal. Some believed it was Matthew Prior;

others accused St. John; but, among the rest, Swift was already named. The Whigs rushed out a number of replies. 'The pamphlet war grows fiercer than ever,' wrote Peter Wentworth to his brother, Lord Strafford, at The Hague, 'and if the Wisdom of the Legislature does not find out some remedy to moderate it, grave people think it may be of ill consequence.' *The Conduct of the Allies* had intensified this war to a pitch exceeding anything known even in the previous October; the stamp of authority which it bore made the Whig protests all the fiercer and kindled a new enthusiasm among the Tories. A don from Christchurch College, Oxford, who had long kept Harley's brother fed with the latest news from that centre of Tory fanaticism, was in ecstasy. A bare week after publication he rejoiced that the book 'takes as much as you could wish it. It will put the country gentlemen in the temper you desire; they are ready to battle it at home for peace abroad'. However, the verdict did not rest only with the country gentlemen. Others had been sharpening their weapons for the meeting of Parliament on December 7th. Indeed, during the week when edition after edition of *The Conduct of the Allies* was pouring from the printing press, a series of events crowded on one another, threatening to wreck both the Ministry and the peace. Had the rally of the Tories come too late?

On Tuesday, November 27th, Baron von Bothmar had an audience with the Queen. It is not known how forcibly he presented the objections of the Elector of Hanover to the proposed peace terms. Lord Rivers had brought back from the Hanoverian court letters which showed that the preliminaries were regarded there with distaste and suspicion. But these strictures were tempered by the polite language of official diplomacy. The likelihood is that Bothmar spoke more plainly to the Queen. Despite all the attempts of her Ministers to guard her from hearing the worst, she was beginning to learn how sharp was the resentment among all her allies. On the Wednesday Bothmar saw St. John; to him he spoke more plainly still and delivered a memorial which cogently argued how dangerous it was to put any trust in the word of King Louis and how disastrous it would be to leave his grandson on the throne of Spain. St. John listened impatiently and, when the Hanoverian envoy had gone, pushed aside the memorial without reading it, thinking it contained nothing more than a written recital of the doleful warnings he had just heard. St. John was not perturbed.

Clearly he had reckoned on some opposition from this quarter just as he had already had to meet it from the Dutch. But Dutch objections had been worn down; in the eyes of the Tory Ministers Willem Buys' conduct had now become 'irreproachable'. Might not Bothmar, too, be won over, especially if all went well when Parliament met? St. John in any case had his own thick skin of resolve and ambition to protect him against all complaints from disgruntled allies. But for the Queen it was different; for her the shock was severe. Bothmar spoke the same language which her own victorious General had used only a week before; he was even prepared to claim that the French defences were already pierced and that only one more fortress needed to be captured for the whole French Kingdom to be at the mercy of the allies. Plenty of others nearer home were eager to add their voices to the swelling tide of protest from the allied capitals; among them the Bishop of Salisbury, Gilbert Burnet. When the Queen expressed the hope that the Bishops would not be against peace, Bishop Burnet (according to his own account) replied with a torrent of Whig eloquence. A good peace was what the Bishops prayed for daily, but the preliminaries offered by France gave no such hope. 'I asked leave to speak my mind plainly; which she granted: I said, any treaty by which Spain and the West Indies were left to King Philip, must in a while deliver up all Europe into the hands of France; and, if any such peace should be made, she was betrayed, and we were all ruined; in less than three years time she would be murdered, and the fires would again be raised in Smithfield: I pursued this long, till I saw she grew uneasy; so I withdrew.'

Something must be allowed for the Bishop's own estimate of his powers of oratory; but undoubtedly whenever the Queen turned at that anxious moment to her old Whig advisers for a crumb of comfort, it was not forthcoming. Lord Somers, Lord Halifax and Lord Cowper would not allow a wedge to be driven between themselves and the Duke of Marlborough. And among all the famous Whig Lords one with a special access to the Queen was more diligent than all the others in seeking to undermine the influence of St. John and his control of the diplomatic machine. The Duke of Somerset was convinced that nothing but a drastic change in the administration could save the situation. On two previous occasions—in 1708 when Harley was removed from office and again in 1710 when Godolphin was overthrown—his voice had been influential in securing a fresh political combination. Now, with his credit restored among the Whigs he had previously deserted and with his Duchess still in good favour as the Queen's Mistress of the Stole, he was working tirelessly for the same purpose.

All these pressures together were bound to have some effect on the Queen although the countervailing influences were still immensely powerful. The Queen wanted peace. Marlborough alone would not have been able to make her waver. Apart from her deep-seated hatred of the Duchess, she had come near to accepting the Tory propaganda that the Duke wished to continue the war to suit his own interests. Mrs. Masham was still at her side, eager to counteract any whispered remonstrances from the Duchess of Somerset. Of all the Ministers who had ever served her, Harley was her prime favourite. During the previous weeks she had been more overflowing than ever in her inquiries about his health and her expressions of confidence in him. But no such affection could be aroused in her breast for St. John, despite all the efforts of Mrs. Masham to incite it, some of the Queen's entourage 'having infused an opinion into her, that he was not so regular in his life as he ought to be'. Above all, she detested all the talk of Whigs and Tories and their incessant bickering which interfered with her prerogative to choose the servants best suited to her mood and nature. Stubborn, harassed and gout-ridden, she hankered after the idea that the most amenable courtiers from both parties or none ought to be able to join together and give her peace at her own court as well as abroad. This vague dream was rudely affronted by the upsurge of antagonism against the peace terms, and for a moment she cried out pathetically for a release from the harsh choices thrust upon her. Harley understood her sentiments perfectly; in fact he shared them, and this was doubtless the true reason for his enduring claim upon her. If anyone could make her dream come true, he was the man to work the miracle. On Wednesday, November 28th, he visited the Duke of Somerset in a renewed effort to check his open intrigue against the measures of the court. The Queen's life might depend upon it, so Harley entreated. His own life, or at least the survival of his Ministry, might depend upon it too.

By Saturday of that week the situation, from the Tory point of view, had rapidly deteriorated. Daniel Defoe wrote to Harley to

'Let your Ldpp kno' your Enemyes and the Fury They Act with; The assurance They pretend to of Breaking all her Majties Measures abroad Makes Their Friends Perfectly Insolent, and The Feares Least They should, Terrifyes on the other hand'. The warning was superfluous; even the sluggish Harley had now been roused. Whether he had been roused in time was more doubtful. Replies were reaching him to the messages belatedly sent out a few days before summoning the Tories to London for the meeting of Parliament. Was the crisis really so serious? This from the Bishop of Exeter. He had not thought of coming to London until after Christmas, 'little business being usually done in Parliament before'; he was hardly in a fit state to travel; floods had made the roads wellnigh impassable. But if Harley told him positively— what he had already told him before—that the Queen's service imperatively demanded it, he would make the effort; of course, he could hardly be there by December 7th. Much the same woeful story came from the Bishop of Durham; he was 'brimful of loyalty and fidelity to the Queen', but 'old age and the depth of winter' made the journey extremely difficult. Others had less elaborate excuses. Far away from London and out of earshot of the Grub Street thunder, many Tories were slow to appreciate the scale of events. What had Harley done for them in the last Parliament when they clamoured for the heads of the Whigs? Let him stew in his own juice for a while. To the nerve-ridden agents of the Ministry London seemed stuffed with Whigs, 'but the Torys that think they have been neglected delay coming'.

Harley was by nature optimistic. Perhaps it was all a scare; when the day came every Tory up in arms against the war and the land taxes would be in his place. However, no one could disguise the gravity of other adverse developments. Somerset was as good as lost to the cause. Striking a rare note of near despondency Harley wrote a pressing letter to him 'from the bottom of my heart'. It was absolutely essential to escape from 'this ruinous war'. Those who raised such an outcry against the proposition were either opposed to any peace or angry that their political enemies might make such a good one. 'Your Grace's penetration easily sees this and much more that I can suggest.' But clearly His Grace's penetration saw nothing of the kind. The proud Duke could see no further than the exalted place in a new Ministry to which he alone felt himself entitled by his matchless talents. Harley, for all his goodwill and flattering humility, had nothing to offer. The smallest concession Somerset might be content to accept was St. John's head on a charger and that delicacy, however attractive, Harley could not supply without jeopardizing his own support and the peace itself. Much against his will Harley was forced to the conclusion which St. John had reached during the previous August. Somerset was no dependable associate. At worst, he might put himself at the head of the Whigs; at best, he would swim with the stream. And for several days the stream had been flowing strongly against the Tories. By the end of the week the 'irreproachable' Willem Buys of a few days before had become once more an obstinate Dutchman in league with the Queen's enemies. Increasingly he took refuge in the claim that he had no full powers to negotiate. 'My Lord, we are not deceived, we see through this slight veil,' wrote St. John to Strafford. The idea, Buys' idea, is 'to gain time, till they see what turn the parliament will take, and what is likely to be the effect of the cabals of their friends the Whigs'. Almost all the developments since the arrival of the Duke of Marlborough and Baron von Bothmar in London had combined to put fresh heart into Willem Buys.

Swift, despite all the excitement aroused by his pamphlet, was correspondingly depressed. 'The parliament will certainly meet on Friday next,' he wrote; 'the Whigs will have a great majority in the house of Lords; no care is taken to prevent it; there is too much neglect.' The Whigs, on the other hand had shown no such negligence. The story was that they had prepared 'some peevish address from the lords against a Peace'. 'Peevish' was no sufficient word to describe the look on the countenance of one of the Whig Lords whom Swift happened to meet on the night of that same Saturday of December 1st when the second edition of his pamphlet sold out in five hours. Calling at White's Chocolate House in St. James's Street he caught a glimpse of his old friend and enemy, Lord Wharton. Swift pretended to take no notice, but Wharton was not so churlish. 'He came through the crowd, called after me, and asked me how I did etc. This was pretty; and I believe he wished every word he spoke was a halter to hang me.' Lord Wharton had good reason for his high spirits. He had either just concluded or was about to conclude the most brilliant political stroke of his career.

Sometime over that week-end an extraordinary bargain was struck between the leading Whigs and the Earl of Nottingham.

Nottingham was deeply aggrieved at his exclusion from the Ministry. In the first days after the election he had recommended fierce measures against the Whigs; if he had his way, Wharton and Godolphin for a start would have been tried for high treason. But Harley rejected all such counsels. When in August the other great Tory leader, Lord Rochester, died, Nottingham felt his claims to succeed as Lord Privy Seal were overwhelming. But once again Harley demurred; at that time his hold on the Government seemed unchallengeable and he chose to appoint as his colleague a servant rather than a potential master. Nottingham had every personal motive for revenge, but who could believe that this gloomy, stiff-necked champion of high church principles could stoop to traffic with those blasphemous libertines, the Whigs? Harley discounted the peril up till the very last hour. Nottingham, like the members of the October Club, could chafe at the Prime Minister's moderation; always in the last resort they must sink their grievances to defeat a threat from the Whigs. But Nottingham's creed, to do him justice, was not confined to the one item of faith in his own qualifications for the highest office. He was a firm supporter of the Protestant succession; once he had moved a famous resolution proposing that the Elector of Hanover should be invited to take up residence in England immediately, a proposal which had greatly angered the Queen and possibly accounted for Harley's unwillingness to give him office. He was also a lifelong upholder of the maritime strategy of the Tories. Instead of squandering the nation's resources in arduous land campaigns, the war could have been fought much better and more cheaply at sea and in such theatres as Spain where English sea-power could be effectively exerted. Years before, Nottingham and the Tories had first raised the cry of 'No Peace without Spain'; they were using it then to bolster their charge that Marlborough was neglecting Spain to assist his own armies in Flanders. Now, to get the peace through, the Tories were willing to surrender Spain, while, to sustain the war, the Whigs had adopted Nottingham's old slogan. There, if he wanted it, was the bridge of consistency which could enable him to pass from the Tory to the Whig camp. But something more was needed to entice him over.

For nearly a generation the dream of the Tories had been to pass an Occasional Conformity Bill designed to stamp out the practice whereby dissenters circumvented the tyrannies of the Test Act.

Time and again in the early years of Anne's reign the Tories, led by Nottingham himself, had come near to making the Bill law; time and again they had been thwarted by the Whigs, led by Wharton. Now as a new session approached, when the Tory majority in the Commons would be thirsting for fresh measures to fulfil their high church programme, it was natural that a new attempt to push through an Occasional Conformity Bill should be considered. Nottingham obviously favoured the plan on its merits; others appreciated its value as a bargaining counter. It is not possible to judge from the cautious approaches made in so delicate a matter who made the first move. Some have supposed that Harley made an offer to Nottingham once he had discovered that the menace to the peace from that quarter was serious. Others deduce that an Occasional Conformity Bill was to form part of the bargain between Halifax and Somers on one side and Harley on the other; Halifax and Somers would concede the Bill in order to palliate for Harley his desertion of St. John and to help him bring more Tories into a moderate alliance with the Whigs. Whatever the truth about these murky transactions, it was Lord Wharton and his friends who clinched the deal. 'Honest Tom', the dissenters' champion, could beat all the others in cynical contrivance, even convincing his dissenting friends in the process that the operation was essential for their health. Nottingham could have his Bill to save the Church from the fiends of Hell if he would join the Whigs in fighting the peace and destroying the Tories. How many faithful Tories in the Lords would he bring with him on this sacred mission? It might be as many as twelve; it could hardly be less than three or four. At the Kit-Kat Club they brought out their bumpers to toast the Earl of Nottingham. Never before round those tables had prayers for the salvation of the Church been offered with such jubilant devotion. 'It is *Dismal* will save England at last,' said Lord Wharton.

Three times within a week the artifices of Harley had been exposed as worthless or too clever; that was the core of the matter. Somerset had been courted; but the only result was to sow confusion among the Tories. Nottingham might have been gained as a more reliable ally; but, like the October men, he had been scorned and insulted. And what had become of the intricate manœuvres with Halifax and Somers? They were parties to the Whig deal with Nottingham and had even been given the chance to make the

Queen nervous. How much time and ingenuity had been wasted on these subterfuges when the urgent need was to mobilize the Tory army! While they languished for lack of a lead, the Whig pygmies had grown to be giants, as Lord Peterborough had once prophesied they would. The Lord Treasurer, said Swift, 'stands too much on his own legs'. Never would he confide even in his own closest friends and now the trust which they had reposed in his superior statecraft had come near to collapse. Reluctantly Swift concluded that his hero was unfitted for the tests ahead. True, the mood varied from hour to hour with each new scrap of intelligence. One moment he could believe that Harley's 'good fortune' would carry them through; the next he was convinced again that 'this Ministry stand very unsteady'. But when his confidence revived for a moment, the credit was due to St. John, not Harley. St. John's resilience and the success of the pamphlet were the main props which sustained Swift's spirits. Indeed, as the great day approached, St. John made fresh efforts to stop the rot. All the foreign Ministers of the alliance were warned to pay no heed to the Whig cabals. Heinsius was informed that majorities of forty in the Lords and two hundred in the Commons were expected for the peace. Strafford at The Hague was instructed to take immediate action to ward off another peril; let him use his influence to prevent the Emperor from sending Prince Eugene to London. St. John itched to see the battle joined. 'Friday next'—so he wrote on Tuesday, December 4th—'the peace will be attacked in Parliament, indirectly; I am glad of it, for I hate a distant danger, which hovers over my head; we must receive their fire, and rout them once for all.'

But Wednesday brought another blow for the Tories; further proof, if such were needed, that the struggle ahead was to be waged without quarter. This was the day when the news of the Nottingham-Wharton alliance began to leak to the coffee-houses. Yet even these rumours were overshadowed. On Wednesday morning the Daily Courant published in full the Bothmar memorial which St. John had pushed on one side a few days before. Someone had taken the brave decision to bring out into the open, on the very eve of Parliament's reassembly, the quarrel between the Elector of Hanover and the Queen's Ministers. Not merely did the memorial present a potent case against the peace preliminaries. Not merely was a direct incitement offered to Members of Parliament to disrupt the negotiations. More serious still was the controversy about the succession to the throne stirred both by the disclosures themselves and the manner in which they had been made. Hitherto the Whigs had not been able to unearth much concrete evidence for their old charge that the Tories were secret Jacobites intent on bringing back the Pretender in place of the Elector as Queen Anne's successor. Now the Elector's bombshell showed that he too was alarmed by the Tory threat to his title. The Whigs were overjoyed. Thousands of copies of the *Courant* were sold in a few hours. Some were printed on large sheets so that they could be displayed in frames. Far and wide the story was spread that in fighting the peace the Whigs were upholding the cause of the Protestant succession and only a lame reply was available to the Tories. At first they stressed 'that it was highly impolitick in the Elector to intermeddle in our Affairs at this Juncture, and to seem to espouse a Party, which might lose him many friends'. Then they suggested that the whole document was a forgery. A variation on the same theme had the virtue of credibility and, perhaps, of truth. The memorial, they said, had 'more the Air of an Original than of a Translation'; probably it had been written, not in Hanover, but in London. The real authors, it was implied, were the Duke of Marlborough and the leading Whigs. Only they could have plotted so reckless a sensation at such an opportune moment.

Yet none of these explanations could destroy the effect of the document itself. It did its work in a quarter where even the most skilful among the Whig propagandists could scarcely have calculated the effect. The Duchess of Somerset read the printed memorial to the Queen who had never been allowed by her Ministers to see it before. Bothmar had made an impact at the English court sufficient to satisfy the Electress Sophia herself. No wonder—as Peter Wentworth reported to Strafford—'the Whigs were very upish'. One minor illustration of their growing arrogance was the call paid by a certain Dr. Garth on Lord Dartmouth, St. John's fellow Secretary of State. The doctor, a well-known Whig, announced gravely how sorry he was that he must go to law with the Minister for breaking into his house and stealing his goods. Asked to explain himself, Dr. Garth said that he had come to recover the images, in particular the one representing the devil, taken from his home on the night of November 16th. 'My Lord sayde he would return the Devel to him again. The Dr. said he designed to make a great funurel for the Devel and have a sarment preeched. My lord asked what the tex should be; he said it was, that his desyples came in the night and stoal him away.' The touch of Whiggish blasphemy was just another sign that the Junto and their backers could match St. John himself in eagerness for the fight.

Even Harley was somewhat downcast by the accumulation of misfortunes. Wednesday, December 5th, happened to be his birthday, but he was in no mood for celebration. During the day he felt obliged to deliver a stern warning to Willem Buys who many believed had acted in concert with Bothmar. If countenance was still given to 'the brigues of the general and the foreign minister', said Harley, the whole peace negotiations could be ruptured with most painful consequences for the Dutch. At night he dined soberly with Swift (fear that his rheumatism might return had made the Prime Minister forswear his favourite claret) and for the second time only in the year they had known one another Swift detected a weariness in Harley's imperturbable good temper. 'He was very pleasant as he always is; yet I fancied he was a little touched with the present posture of affairs.' Together they mulled over the Elector's 'violent memorial', the plans of the Whig Lords for Friday, the defection of Lord Nottingham, and the truculence of Lord Wharton. It could not have been a pleasant recital. And yet by the end of the evening some of Harley's geniality was restored. He insisted that Swift should read aloud to the company some scurrilous verses against himself just published under the title of the *English Catiline*. He also offered a constructive suggestion; could not Swift produce a ballad to celebrate Nottingham's apostasy?

Swift went to work at top speed on so agreeable a commission. Next morning he finished the ballad, 'two degrees above Grub Street', rushed it to the printers and went off to pick up the gossip from Mrs. Masham. Even so Grub Street had anticipated him on the same theme. On the morning of December 6th an advertisement appeared in the *Postboy*: 'Whereas a very Tall, Thin, Swarthy Complection'd Man, between Sixty and Seventy Years of Age, Wearing a brown Coat, with little Sleeves, and long Pockets, has lately withdrawn himself from his Friends, being seduced by wicked Persons to follow ill Courses: These are to give Notice,

That whoever shall discover him, shall have Ten shillings Reward;
or if he will voluntarily return, he shall be kindly receiv'd by his
Friends, who will not Reproach him for past Follies, provided he
give good Assurances, that, for the future, he will firmly adhere
to the Church of *England*, in which he was so carefully Educated
by his honest Parents.' A wistful hope mingled with the satire;
was it really true that Nottingham had deserted to the Whigs?
The Tories still could not believe it. None the less this was the
harsh fact which the Cabinet Council had to face when it met that
same evening. That the Whigs with Nottingham's backing would
make the challenge in one form or another was now certain. How it
would come and what reception it would receive no one could tell.
Some reports were a little more hopeful. Hour by hour the Tories
were arriving from the country. If Nottingham only carried two or
three with him, perhaps the Ministers could still win the critical
vote in the Lords. A few of them still argued in favour of another
prorogation, but after long debate the proposal was rejected. The
time had come 'to receive their fire and rout them once for all'.

Even at that last moment, however, Harley and his friends
scratched around for a release from the clash which must destroy
all hopes of a moderate policy and deliver the nation into the hands
of either the fanatical high Tories or the resurgent Whig Junto.
Lord Halifax, in particular, who had strayed so far from his old
rigid allegiance to his Junto colleagues, made a most ingenious
proposition. Day by day as the crisis mounted to its climax, he had
been searching for 'any expedient to prevent the straits we are
falling into'. Now he unfolded a scheme exactly designed to appeal
to Harley's temper. A majority in the Lords against the peace
terms was now certain; that was Halifax's calculation, whatever
might be Harley's. Why then should Harley continue to struggle
against the inevitable once the vote had been cast? Why not explain
that he had merely done his duty in presenting the terms offered by
France to the allies and the nation, but that if now the House of
Lords thought better terms could be secured, no one would wish
it more than he. 'If you thought it not improper to turn the debate
in this manner, you w'd remove the difficulties from yourself,
leave room for reasonable measures, and throw the blame of
extravagant ones on others.'

How seductive the idea must have appeared to the man who had
laboured so long to prevent the angry scenes likely to be enacted

in the days ahead! Halifax's solicitude for Harley's fate and the risks he ran to find an escape for him prove how close their association had become and how nearly Harley had moved in the previous weeks to a break with St. John and the high Tories. 'Burn this paper,' said Halifax to Harley with guilty precaution at the end of his letter. Next day the two men were to face each other across the gulf which divided Whig from Tory. Some modern historians, like the Harleys and Halifaxes, have tried to persuade themselves that the gulf was not really so deep and wide; party labels, we are told, did not mean much in those days. Queen Anne suffered from the same delusion. Lord Wharton and St. John had a better understanding of the new political world in which they lived. They and the men they enlisted to fight their campaigns in the pamphlet war were the real strategists who had drawn up the lines of battle.

No delusion about any rapprochement with the Whigs afflicted the Society of Brothers which Swift attended that same night. It was the largest meeting of the Society ever held. Now that the conflict was almost joined, this innermost clique among the supporters of the Ministers forgot or drowned in wine most of their anxieties of the previous week. The Tory squires riding in from the country all day spread an infectious enthusiasm. London was not so exclusively filled with Whigs after all. The Tory majority in the House of Commons at least was now assured. By midnight the Duke of Ormond and Lord Anglesey would have arrived from Ireland; two more precious votes in the House of Lords! A posse of Scotch peers had turned up just in time. Even the gouty Bishops had sent their proxies. Others besides Lord Halifax could make their calculations; Tory expectations were rising. So the Brothers kept up one another's courage. And the hero of the evening was Jonathan Swift. Not merely did his printer bring news of the plans for a fifth edition of *The Conduct of the Allies*. He also brought 'the ballad, which made them laugh very heartily a dozen times'.

> *An Orator* dismal *of* Nottinghamshire,
> *Who has forty Years let out his Conscience to hire,*
> *Out of Zeal for his Country, and want of a Place,*
> *Is come up,* vi & armis, *to break the Q——'s Peace.*
> *He has vamp't an old Speech, and the Court to their sorrow,*
> *Shall hear Him harangue against PRIOR to Morrow.*

When once he begins, he never will flinch,
But repeats the same Note a whole Day, like a Finch.
I have heard all the Speech repeated by Hoppy.
And, mistakes to prevent, *I* have obtain'd a Copy;

THE SPEECH

Whereas, Notwithstanding, *I am in Great Pain,*
To hear we are making a Peace without Spain;
But, most noble Senators, *'tis a great Shame*
There should be a Peace, while I'm Not in game.
The D— Shew'd me all his fine House; and the D—'s
From her Closet brought out a full Purse in her Clutches
I talk'd of a Peace, and they both gave a start,
His G— swore by —, and her G— let a F—t:
My long old-fashion'd Pocket, *was presently crammed:*
And sooner than Vote for a Peace I'll be d—nd.
But some will cry, Turn-Coat, *and rip up old Stories,*
How I always pretended to be for the Tories:
I answer; the Tories were in my good Graces,
Till all my Relations *were put into* places.
But still I'm in Principle ever the same,
And will quit my best Friends, while I'm Not in game.
When I and some others subscribed our Names
To a Plot for expelling my Master K. James;
I withdrew my subscription by help of a Blot,
And so might discover, or gain by the Plot:
I had my Advantage, and stood at Defiance,
For Daniel *was got from the Den of the Lions:*
I came in without Danger; and was I to blame?
For rather than hang, *I would be* Not in game.
I swore to the Q—— that the Pr—— of H——r
During Her Sacred Life, should never come over:
I made use of a Trope; *that an Heir to invite,*
Was like keeping her Monument always in sight.
But when I thought proper, I alter'd my Note;
And in Her own hearing I boldly did Vote,
That Her M—— stood in great need of a Tutor,
And must have an old, *or a* young Coadjutor:
For why; I would fain put all in a Flame,
Because, for some Reasons, I was Not in game.

Now my new Benefactors *have* brought me about,
And I'll Vote against Peace, with Spain, *or* without:
Tho' the Court *gives my* Nephews, *and* Brothers, *and* Cousins,
And all my whole Family, Places by Dozens;
Yet since I know where a full Purse *may be found,*
And hardly pay Eighteenpence Tax in the Pound:
Since the Tories *have thus disappointed my Hopes,*
And will neither regard my Figures *nor* Tropes;
I'll Speech *against* Peace *while* Dismal's *my Name,*
And be a true Whig, *while I am* Not in game.

Tomorrow, if he still dared, Dismal would face the House of Lords. Perhaps he could be laughed off the stage.

But, once the wine and wit had ceased to flow, Swift finished the day on a sober reflection. When he got home after all the excitement of the most thrilling week of his life he still wrote to Stella: 'To-morrow is the fatal day for the parliament meeting, and we are full of hopes and fears. We reckon we have a majority of ten on our side in the house of lords; yet I observed Mrs. Masham a little uneasy; she assures me the queen is stout. The duke of Marlborough has not seen the queen for some days past: Mrs. Masham is glad of it, because she says, he tells a hundred lies to his friends of what she says to him: he is one day humble, and the next on the high ropes.'

On Friday, December 7th, the Queen rode in state to the House of Lords to deliver her speech at the opening of the session. If Tory peers and commoners who packed the assembly to hear it were still alarmed, no trace of their mood appeared in the speech prepared by her Ministers. It was bold, polished and artful. No hint was given of weakness or retreat; yet with nimble assurance every advisable promise was offered to soothe the fears of the waverers. In particular, the aim was to prevent any moderate Tories (sometimes they were called Hanoverian Tories owing to their strong attachment to the Hanoverian succession; St. John dubbed them 'the whimsicals') from being tempted to join forces with the Duke of Marlborough and the Whigs. 'My Lords and Gentlemen,' said the Queen, 'I have called you together as soon as the public affairs would permit (the first lie!); and I am glad that I can now tell you that, notwithstanding the arts of those who delight in war, both place and time are appointed for opening the Treaty of

321

a general Peace.' The conference was to meet in a few weeks at Utrecht, but even this news confirmed by the Queen did not stir her audience so much as the direct reference to those 'who delight in war'. The Duke of Marlborough was in his place and the great company construed the words as a deliberate slight upon him. 'Our allies (especially the States General), whose interest I look upon as inseparable from our own,' continued the Queen, 'have, by their ready concurrence, expressed their entire confidence in me.' Willem Buys who was listening from the gallery could have told a different story, but his formal word had been secured and the Ministers were determined to exploit it to the limit. The next sentence was directed at Bothmar who sat beside him and, more urgently, at Nottingham and the whimsicals. 'My chief concern is, that the Protestant religion and the laws and liberties of these nations, may be continued to you, by securing the Succession to the crown, as it is limited by parliament, to the house of Hanover.' The 'dutiful and loyal' people of Britain were promised an enlargement of their commerce once the war was over. All the allies would receive 'reasonable satisfaction' at the conference table. To guard the peace, once secured, the Alliance would be sustained. And the best means to fulfil these aims was to vote the necessary supplies for the next year's war. The Queen's enemies would know that if a good peace could not be obtained, the war would be continued with vigour. 'As I have had your chearful assistance for the carrying on this long and changeable war; so I assure myself, that no true Protestant, or good subject, will envy Britain, or me, the glory and satisfaction of ending the same, by a just and honourable peace for us and all our allies.' The final appeal anticipated the Whig attack. 'I cannot conclude, without earnestly recommending to you all unanimity; and that you will carefully avoid everything which may give occasion to the enemy to think us a people divided among ourselves.' This was the best, the only way, to ensure that, 'being delivered from the hardships of war, you may become a happy and a flourishing people'.

Altogether, then, here was no wavering. How true could be the tales spread so sedulously by the Duke of Somerset that the Queen herself positively desired a vote against her Ministers? After the speech she appeared to confirm her resolution by breaking the normal custom. Often the Queen listened to the Lords' debates *incognito*, but not usually on the first day of the session. On this occasion she took off her royal robes in an adjoining room and returned to the special box prepared for her. The idea, thought some, was 'by her presence to moderate any heats that might arise'.

Two peers moved and seconded the motion returning thanks to Her Majesty for her most gracious speech. For a few hushed seconds it seemed that the debate was at an end. Then the silence was broken by the Earl of Nottingham. By some he was accounted one of the most eloquent orators of his age; others ridiculed his pomposity. No one dared mock on that day. Nottingham spoke for an hour or more. He 'set forth the insufficiency and captiousness of the late preliminaries; made a lively representation of the danger of treating upon so precarious a foundation; urged the express engagements, which Great Britain had entered into with her allies, to restore the entire monarchy of Spain to the house of Austria; and the necessity of carrying on the war with vigour till those engagements were made good'. Of course the war was expensive; of course it caused hardship. But he would rather contribute half his fortune to it than 'acquiesce in a Peace which he thought unsafe and dishonourable to his country and all Europe'. Then came the direct challenge; clearly the Nottingham-Wharton alliance was welded together by bonds of iron and the plot between them envisaged that the attack should be delivered without a moment's delay. For Nottingham proposed there and then that a clause should be inserted in the Address of thanks: 'To represent to Her Majesty, as the humble opinion and advice of the House, that no Peace could be safe or honourable to Great Britain, or Europe, if Spain and the West Indies were allotted to any branch of the House of Bourbon.'

In the Commons Harley had been considered the master of procedure. Revolt in the Lords was a disease beyond his practice. Confronted by the concerted plan of the Whigs he stuttered and stumbled. First he and his friends attempted to get the debate postponed. Floods had held up the arrival of some of the Scottish peers; no one knew how many votes Nottingham might carry with him; the wildest stories were circulating about bribes paid by the foreign Ministers to seduce members from their allegiance to the court. Harley played for time. But Lord Wharton scoffed and Lord Sunderland thundered. Where was the Order to stop the debate? 'The noble Lord', said Wharton, 'has, I fear, been too short a time in this house to be thoroughly conversant with its rules.' Was it really impossible, asked Sunderland, for the members of the

House of Lords to debate an issue which had been their principal concern for the previous ten years? Finally he breathed the fateful word. Impeachment! Peers had been impeached before now for their alleged surrender of English interests to the cause of France. Only ten years before in King William's time, when for a while the Tories held the upper hand, four leading members of the Whig Junto, including Sunderland himself, had been impeached. Harley needed no reminder: he had been a party to the proceedings. Wharton and Sunderland left little room for doubt how the Whig revenge would be executed once power was restored to their keeping.

Both the strength and the timing of the Whig fire reduced most of the Tories to silence. Only a few dared withstand it, and one brave spirit who did gave the cue for the most dramatic intervention of the whole debate. Peace could have been had after the battle of Ramillies, he insisted, if it had not been 'put off by some Persons, whose Interest it was to prolong the war'. At last the Tory gibe had been made to Marlborough's face. At last he rose to answer his traducers. The Duke was no orator; only on rare occasions did he address the House of Lords. Now he spoke with pathos and dignity. Bowing to the Queen as he spoke, he called upon her to witness that the charge against him was a slander. 'Knowing the integrity of my heart and the uprightness of my conduct, she will not fail to do me justice.' Had he not always informed the Queen and Her Ministers of all proposals for peace? Had he not always sought their instructions? Before the Queen, before his fellow-peers, before God he would swear that he had always striven to secure a safe and honourable peace. His age, the fatigues he had undergone, the honours and riches heaped upon him, all these made him want peace as ardently as any man. Yet it was not to plead with his enemies that Marlborough had spoken. After *The Conduct of the Allies* he must have known how vain such an entreaty would be with the Queen's Ministers, if not with the Queen herself. The humble Duke was soon on the high ropes. On the issue before the House he was blunt and unyielding. He agreed with the rest of the allies and with Lord Nottingham: the 'safety and liberties of Europe' would be in peril if these peace terms were accepted. In short, the Duke had put himself at the head of his army. Lord Cowper, Lord Halifax, Bishop Burnet pressed the advantage. No effective voice was raised against them. No man dared repeat the indictment against Marlborough.

The Whigs were sweeping all before them and only one resort was left to the 'officious courtiers' who took their lead from Harley. The debate was out of order; no vote should be taken that night. But again the Whigs treated these subterfuges with scorn. This was no petty affair to be settled by points of order. The eyes of all Europe marked their demeanour, the couriers were waiting in Palace Yard to carry the news to every allied capital. That night the deed must be done. So by a single vote it was agreed that Nottingham's clause should be put to the House; by 62 votes to 54 it was carried.

During that same day the debate on the same issue had taken place in the House of Commons. Walpole had moved the motion against the peace. St. John had replied and the Ministers had repelled this other Whig attack by 252 votes to 106. But no one seemed to care. The decision of the Lords could transform the whole political scene. And as the news of the voting spread round London another story followed hard on its heels to heighten the alarm. When the Queen left the House of Lords the Duke of Shrewsbury had asked whether he or the Great Chamberlain should accompany her out. 'Neither of you,' she replied sharply and gave her hand to the Duke of Somerset who, not content with casting his vote for Nottingham's resolution, had noisily encouraged others to follow his example. Was the Queen, after all, the prompter of Somerset's agitation? Had she sat at the debate all day with the express purpose of revealing her favour and consolidating the victory? In the London coffee-houses downcast Tories were ready to believe the worst. Swift had spent the afternoon in the city where his printer brought the company the latest information from Westminster. Amid their dejection, one feeble hope was born. Nottingham's resolution had been passed in committee; next day when it was reported to the House, the vote might be reversed. But Swift put little faith in such resorts. 'It is', he said 'a mighty blow and loss to lord treasurer, and may end in his ruin.' Harley himself gave way to a spasm of rage. He went straight from the Lords to upbraid Willem Buys, charging him directly with having conspired with Marlborough and the other foreign Ministers to attack the Queen and wrest the business of peacemaking from her hands. Very well; he would have to take the consequences. The Queen would make her own peace and the Dutch would be taught not to meddle in English affairs.

Next morning early Swift saw St. John; yes, there was a plan afoot to reverse the vote 'so the matter would go off, only with a little loss of reputation to lord treasurer'. Proxies for eight Scottish peers had now been delivered into the hands of the Duke of Hamilton, one of the Ministry's supporters; there was still a chance. Harley himself knew better and would not risk the further rebuff of being present when the second vote was taken. Amid scenes of dire confusion and tumult, the defeat of the leaderless Tories was turned to a rout. No room for doubt remained. 'Joy and vengeance sat visible on the countenance' of every Whig; the game was in their hands, and for a while it appeared the Tories would tear themselves to pieces in violent recrimination.

The arch-culprit, by his carelessness at least, was Harley; or could it be the Queen? That evening the panic-stricken Tories, Swift among them, gathered at Mrs. Masham's. 'It seems lord treasurer had been so negligent, that he was with the queen while the question was put in the house:' he wrote. 'I immediately told Mrs. Masham, that either she and lord treasurer had joined with the queen to betray us or that they two were betrayed by the queen.' Never had such a charge against his dearest friend entered his head before, but now the whole Tory scheme was in collapse about his ears. Mrs. Masham protested solemnly that neither she nor Harley had been guilty of such treachery, 'and I believed her, but she gave me some lights to suspect the queen is changed'. Swift had almost convinced himself: 'The Queen is false or at least very much wavering.' If it was really true, Harley had thrown away the most precious of his assets. Soon the Prime Minister himself arrived and the company resolved to berate him for his follies. How would the old magic prevail now that even Swift and Mrs. Masham saw the fatal weakness of his character, so long discerned by St. John, confirmed by catastrophe? He 'appeared in good humour as usual', said Swift, 'but I thought his countenance was much cast down. I rallied him, and desired him to give me his staff, which he did; I told him, if he would secure it me a week, I would set all right: he asked, How? I said, I would immediately turn lord Marlborough, his two daughters, the duke and duchess of Somerset, and Lord Cholmondeley out of all their employments; and I believe he had not a friend but was of my opinion'.

It was the old formula of the October Club—root out every Whig; cut their claws; bind them in chains; above all, destroy the Duke; pack him off to Blenheim or the Tower where he would be free to conspire no more. How the whole calamity might have been prevented if Harley had applied the remedy months before; how the waverers would have rallied to the Tory cause; how the Whig conspiracies would have been forestalled! Harley kept cool in face of the onslaught, but he had no answer. No answer, too, was forthcoming to the simple question put to him point-blank: how was it possible he had failed to secure his majority? Harley was cornered; 'he could not help it, if people would lie and forswear'. 'A poor answer for a great minister,' thought Swift. Yet even this was not the worst. Harley took refuge in his old mannerism of muttering beneath his breath, and 'there fell from him a scripture expression that *the hearts of kings are unsearchable*'. So it was true! The Queen was lost to the Tory cause. What else could he mean? No one could foretell how vast might be the consequences. For the moment Harley would say no more on the all-important topic. He did his skilful best to smooth the tempers of his friends, even offering them the hope that at last he would be ruthless. Together with St. John an hour or two later he drew up a list of all the placemen who had dared to vote against the court; at last Harley would choose between his friends and his enemies. But had not all these devices, even Swift's own grand recipe for the removal of the Duke and all his minions, come too late? How could the plan of proscription be executed if the terrible news was true; if indeed the Queen was false?

Both Harley and St. John knew—in St. John's words—that 'the crisis had come'. Late that night both sent their reports and instructions to Strafford at The Hague. St. John was certainly alarmed; but nothing could subdue his spirit. This was the challenge he had invited and he did not flinch. The thing had been done by a trick, by the cabals of the Whigs and the foreign Ministers; Bothmar's bribes and the Duke's call to battle had for a moment carried the day. But all could yet be saved. Let Strafford show 'great dryness' towards the Dutch; let him make it plain that the Queen would tolerate no tampering with her domestic affairs; let him, above all, redouble his efforts with the Emperor to prevent Eugene coming to London. 'It is high time', wrote St. John, 'to put a stop to this foreign influence on British councils; and we must either emancipate ourselves now, or be for ever slaves.' Only one real doubt persisted—'The whole turns on the Queen's resolution.' If she showed courage, the daring of the

Whigs could be made to recoil on their own heads. If not—well, in any case the Ministers would fight. Strafford should have no doubts; for 'you are joined to men who have acted honestly, and have, therefore, all the assurance and courage which become men conscious of merit: we are determined to stand or fall together'. Such was St. John with the enemy at the gates, the same St. John who had always felt that the fight must come. Subdued at that moment too was his hatred against his 'dear Master'. Necessity locked them together in the same cause and St. John understood that the reckoning must be postponed for another day. Harley's note to Strafford did not strike quite the same note of unshakeable defiance. Elaborate excuses and a whining resentment mingled with his resolution. Yet the facts spoke too plainly for any misconception. The Duke of Marlborough, fearful of the inquiries by the Commission of Accounts into his financial dealings—as Harley insisted with his unerring capacity to search out the most ignoble of his opponents' motives—had put himself at the head of the Whigs and the allies. Only one response was possible. 'This proceeding', he wrote, 'will oblige the Queen, without reserve, to use the gentlemen of England, and those who are for her prerogative.' Harley had adopted the programme of St. John.

Swift could not guess from his meeting with the Ministers at Mrs. Masham's that the choice had truly been made; even if he had known, he could hardly have dared to prophesy the outcome. 'This has been a day', he wrote to Stella, 'that may produce great alterations, and hazard the ruin of England. The Whigs are all in triumph; they foretold how all this would be, but we thought it boasting. Nay, they said parliament should be dissolved before Christmas, and perhaps it may: this is all your d——d duchess of Somerset's doings. I warned them of it nine months ago, and a hundred times since: the secretary always dreaded it. I told lord treasurer, I should have the advantage of him; for he would lose his head, and I should only be hanged, and so carry my body entire to the grave.'

The thought of these terrors was not entirely fanciful; it had occurred to some others. During the debate in the Lords Lord Wharton had made the point with his usual explicit good humour. Whenever any of the Ministers rose to speak, he smiled and put his hands to his neck 'by which he would have it understood that some heads were in danger'.

CHAPTER THIRTEEN

Climax in the Lords

(December 9th, 1711—January 2nd, 1712)

> 'He asked what methods were used to cultivate the
> minds and bodies of our young nobility, and in what
> kind of business they commonly spent the first and
> teachable part of their lives. What course was taken to
> supply that assembly when any noble family became
> extinct. What qualifications were necessary in those
> who are to be created new lords; whether the humour
> of the Prince, a sum of money to a court lady or a Prime
> Minister, or a design of strengthening a party opposite
> to the public interest, ever happened to be motives in
> those advancements. What share of knowledge these
> lords had in the laws of their country, and how they
> came by it, so as to enable them to decide the properties
> of their fellow-subjects in the last resort. Whether they
> were also so free from avarice, partialities, or want, that
> a bribe, or some other sinister view, could have no
> place among them.'—*Gulliver's Travels, A Voyage to
> Brobdingnag.*

S WIFT WITH A PEN IN HIS HAND, the masterful author
of *The Conduct of the Allies*, was a more intrepid figure than
the other Swift who rushed off to the court levees or the
coffee-houses to discuss with his friends the stunning defeat inflicted upon them in the House of Lords. For days afterwards no
one could console him. Indeed most of his friends were as downcast as himself. One of the gloomiest was Erasmus Lewis who
usually had his ear closer to the ground than any other gossip-
monger at Westminster. He believed that everything was settled
between the Queen and the Whigs, or at least so he told Swift.
Lord Somers was to be appointed Lord Treasurer, and the
Parliament was once more to be dissolved in order that a Whiggish
majority in the Commons could be secured to match their supremacy in the Lords. Lewis agreed with Swift in laying much of the
blame at the door of the Duchess of Somerset. The Queen was
determined to keep the Duchess at her side, and if the Ministers

objected they would have to go. Lewis himself thought it might be time to go too; he talked of retiring to one of his country estates in Wales. A similar idea occurred to Swift and he soon had fresh grounds for alarm. John Morphew, his publisher, was summoned before the Lord Chief Justice, Thomas Parker. Parker, a passionate Whig, was only too pleased to show that others besides St. John could play the game of suppressing their enemies in Grub Street. He displayed some papers and pamphlets, among them *The Conduct of the Allies*, demanded to know the authors, blustered for a while when he failed to get the answers, and bound over Morphew to appear when the courts reopened. 'He would not have the impudence to do this', wrote Swift, 'if he did not foresee what was coming at court.'

Many others read their misty crystal balls in the same sense. Willem Buys at last handed over the passports for the peace congress, but he was more than ever hopeful that the Whigs would soon be in a position to come to the rescue of his nation. Both the Duke of Buckingham and the Duke of Shrewsbury showed a characteristic reticence to rush to the aid of their tottering colleagues in the Ministry. Only two among the men in charge of affairs were not at all crushed by the blow. St. John never lost his *élan*, and Harley quickly recovered from the embarrassment he had failed to conceal at Mrs. Masham's on the night after the critical vote in the Lords. But neither had much success in comforting Swift. When he pressed the Secretary to consider providing him with some post abroad before the final catastrophe came—'I should hardly trust myself to the mercy of my enemies while their anger is fresh'—St. John laughed, put his hand round Swift's shoulder and promised all would yet be well. A day or two later St. John's equanimity was even more remarkable; yes, the Duke and the Duchess of Somerset would both be turned out, and if they were not, he himself would resign. Harley rebuked Swift for keeping bad company 'with such a fellow as Lewis, who has not the soul of a chicken, nor the heart of a mite', and asked jocularly whether he was afraid to walk home with such a marked man as the Lord Treasurer. But none of this blithe confidence which refused to come down to particulars could banish Swift's gnawing doubt. 'I could not forbear hinting, that he was not sure of the queen; and that those scoundrel, starving lords would never have dared to vote against the court, if Somerset had not assured them, that it would please the queen. He said, That was true, and Somerset did so.' How then was the disaster to be retrieved? To the direct question Harley offered nothing better than the most mysterious of hints and St. John his usual bravado. Swift knew them both too well to be convinced. 'The Queen is false'—on the morning after the night at Mrs. Masham's St. John in an unguarded moment had confirmed Swift's fear. Harley would make no direct denial. Most people believed that a new world had been opened by the Whig victory. All the most fervent and intimate admirers of the Prime Minister were as puzzled as Swift. 'It is very doubtful what to make of this business,' wrote Peter Wentworth, 'for people who know that my Lord Treasurer to be a very adroit and able man do say he cou'd not have been so out of his computation without some further fetch that we poor mortals can't dive into.' This was almost the same language which St. John had used to Swift. Harley, in his inscrutable wisdom, had invited defeat on purpose! Swift would not believe a word of it; as far as he could judge, the game was lost.

No visible sign from any quarter appeared in those first days of the session to confirm the optimism of Harley and St. John. Part of the game was being played in the Queen's palace. Hints and whispers were pieced together to unmask the role of the Duchess of Somerset. To some she was a red-headed witch plotting the downfall of the Queen's Ministers; to others she was the angel of deliverance who had outwitted the scheming Abigail. Everyone from the Duchess of Marlborough to the Vicar of Laracor paid tribute to her insinuating manners; no one was sure of the truth about her hold over Anne, not even St. John or Harley or Abigail herself. Meantime, the other and perhaps much the more important part of the game was being played in the arena where the Whigs had seized the initiative. Excited debates took place in both Houses of Parliament. Tory lords and country gentlemen showed how eloquently they could repeat large chunks from *The Conduct of the Allies*. Swift was greatly flattered, yet pride in his own influence, now at its zenith, could not kill the suspicion that Wharton and his friends were not overmuch worried by the startling apparition of Tory orators with a good argument on their lips. In the Commons St. John swept all before him; anything the Minister cared to demand, even land taxes and supplies for the army, were voted with enthusiasm. But it was the fight in the Lords that mattered. And there the Whig leaders unfolded their strategy

331

step by step with remorseless assurance. Wharton, Nottingham, Somerset and Marlborough made a formidable combination.

On Monday, December 10th—the first available opportunity after their vote on Nottingham's resolution—the Whigs made another move. A curious incident affecting the votes in the House of Lords during the previous week concerned the Duke of Hamilton, one of the sixteen peers from Scotland, who carried in his pocket the proxies of several of his colleagues. He was a supporter of the Ministry—indeed he was an avowed Jacobite—but pique had made him withhold his proxies in the first day's voting. A little while earlier he had been made a peer of Great Britain as the Duke of Brandon. Yet some of his fellow-peers had objected to his entry into their House under that title. According to the Act of Union sixteen Scotch peers had been admitted to the House of Lords. If now the principle was accepted that this total could be suddenly increased on the Queen's edict by the admission of any number of impecunious and mercenary Scotchmen, the constitution itself, not to mention the Whig majority, would be in danger. The Duke of Hamilton demanded of the Ministers that his status as Duke of Brandon should be regularized. The Whigs saw an opening. On that Monday a motion was moved to consider the grave constitutional issue. Graciously the Whig leaders agreed that the debate should be postponed until Wednesday; but the glint of battle was in their eyes. Once more they appeared to be challenging the actions of the Queen, and yet once more it seemed that they had the support of one of the Queen's most intimate servants, the Duke of Somerset.

Next day—on the Tuesday—there was fresh fuel to feed the doubt whether the Queen was firm in her allegiance to her leading Tory Ministers. The Lords waited on the Queen to present the fruits of the first Whig triumph—an address of thanks for the Queen's speech incorporating Nottingham's resolution with its demand for 'No peace without Spain'. 'I take the Thanks You give Me kindly,' replied the Queen, 'I should be Sorry anyone could think I would not do My Utmost to Recover Spain and the West Indies from the House of Bourbon.' The words were equivocal. They could be taken as evidence that the Queen *was* retreating from her earlier resolution to back the peace terms negotiated by her Ministers. The hope and the fear increased the excitement in the corridors at Westminster.

On the Wednesday when the Lords resumed their debate on the Duke of Hamilton some of the court Tories had recovered their voices. To debate the matter at all, they argued, was an attack on the royal prerogative. But once again they were defeated. By a majority of three it was decreed that, prerogative or no prerogative, the issue must be debated, and a day in the following week was set aside for the purpose. 'I designe to get to hear that debate,' reported Peter Wentworth, 'for there's a great deal to be said of both sides, and if ever any case was debated without party this will be so.' Lord Wharton did not approach the matter in quite the same objective spirit; it was necessary to sustain the momentum of the Whig attack, and if the Queen could be put in her place by the same stroke which discomforted the Tories he would like it all the better.

This, however, was only a skirmish; bigger things were to come. No time was to be lost by the Whigs in allowing the Earl of Nottingham to obtain the reward for his services; thereby he might be encouraged to bestow fresh favours in the future. He introduced his Occasional Conformity Bill, suitably disguised under another title to mitigate the offence which it must cause to the dissenters who had previously looked to the Whigs as their protectors. It was, said the rigmarole, 'An act for exempting her majesty's Protestant subjects, dissenting from the Church of England, from the penalties of certain laws, and *for supplying the defects thereof* . . .' It was in reality an Act for harrying from government employment any dissenter who dared to seek escape from the intolerance of the Test Act by receiving the sacrament once or twice a year in the orthodox churches. Tories jeered; Whig Bishops, like Burnet, squirmed; Daniel Defoe screamed his denunciations of the 'Party Juggle', incited his old dissenting friends to denounce the betrayal, and even had vain hopes that Harley would remember his Presbyterian ancestry and forbid the outrage. 'What Ridicule have I seen made at a certain Tall Man, *with nothing in him*, as they us'd to say of him? What a Jest have I seen some honest Gentlemen make of his Character, as an un-performing Cloud? What a doz'd and bewildered Character has been given of a certain Person! and what Lampoons was the Town full of, when he Encumbered the State! And now how Caress'd! How Embrac'd! and now to gratifie a Desire as pre-posterous as all the rest, how willing are some men to give up their Friends, as a Victim to this Convert, and to his mighty Interest!

nay, how do they abandon the Just and Righteous Interest they had before Espous'd, to oblige a Man of no Interest at all.' Angry protests against the double apostasy of Nottingham and the Whigs were natural enough but they could not stop the celebrations or stir a single conscience at the Kit-Kat Club.

On Saturday, December 15th, the Tall Man rose to bring in his Bill which the Whigs had thrown out on so many previous occasions. It was, said Peter Wentworth, 'so well cook't up that it met with noe opposition'. Lord Wharton would not let the delicious moment pass without giving his blessing in a speech oozing with piety. So tight was the Whig discipline in the Lords that not a voice was raised against him, not one stomach was turned. The Tories could do nothing but offer their grudging assent to a measure they approved but which yet set the seal on the biggest humiliation they had suffered since Dr. Sacheverell with his sermon had started them on the road to power. Swift had always been a strong supporter of any proposal for stamping out occasional conformity among the dissenters. But he had no doubt at all about the meaning of the scene in the Lords. 'Here', he wrote on that Saturday night, 'are the first steps towards the ruin of an excellent ministry; for I look upon them as certainly ruined: and God knows what may be the consequences.'

Over that week-end a flicker of hope for the Tories mingled with the general depression. Matthew Prior and Erasmus Lewis were as despondent as ever and Swift had made plans to clear out of London if the crisis broke; 'for they lay all things on me, even some I have never read.' But at Mrs. Masham's on the Saturday night the mood was better. Dr. Arbuthnot, the Queen's physician, was 'in good hopes that the Queen has not betrayed us; but only has been frightened and flattered'. Mr. and Mrs. Masham shared his opinion. Harley turned up more optimistic than ever. Next morning Swift himself put on his most cheerful countenance and went to the court levee. 'It was mightily crowded; both parties coming to observe each other's faces.' Some of the gossip was more cheerful too. For days one anxiety of the Tories had been that Prince Eugene would insist on coming to London to add his voice to the protests of Buys and Bothmar. Swift knew that Harley and St. John had been doing their best to stop him; the Whigs, on the other hand, had been preparing a great reception. Now Swift was told that Eugene was not coming at all; that was 'a good point gained'.

Much more hopefully titillating was the talk about the Duke and Duchess of Somerset. The Duke certainly, and possibly the Duchess, had left London the day before to spend Christmas at their country house. At once the Tories 'were full of news that he was turn'd out'. Perhaps at last the Ministers had plucked up their courage to persuade the Queen. Some were still doubtful. 'That's too tough a bite for them or anybody to meddle with,' thought Peter Wentworth. But soon another story was circulating to explain the mystery. Always the Queen had some excuse to save her favourite Duchess and the Duke from the Tory accusations against them. After his vote for Nottingham's resolution on the peace, complaints from the Tories about the conduct of her double-dealing servant became more clamant. But again she parried their importunate protests. Henceforth, she assured them, the Duke would reform and could be relied upon to vote according to the interest of the court. But that week his enemies had another count against him. On the matter of the Duke of Hamilton's peerage Somerset was known to object to the new title. Here surely was an issue directly touching the Queen's prerogative. 'If she cou'd not ingage him in that vote, 'twas plain he was more attach't to a party than to her.' For Somerset, the dilemma was awkward; either he must offend the Whigs or the Queen and, whichever choice he made, his delicate position as an official servant of the Queen consorting with her enemies would be jeopardized. But someone, perhaps the Duchess, had propounded an ingenious solution. When the Queen sent for him—so it was alleged—Somerset protested that he could not vote in person for the creation of more Scotch peers, but in order to show his compliance with the Queen's wishes he would depart for the country leaving behind his proxy vote to be cast in favour of the Duke of Hamilton. If the tale was true, the Duke of Somerset had once more slipped through the trap laid for him by the Tories. True or not, Swift learnt on the Monday that 'the duchess of Somerset is not gone to Petworth; only the duke; and that is a poor sacrifice'. Thus the bewildered Tories clutched at straws. 'We are still in a condition of suspense, and I think have little hopes,' wrote Swift on Monday. 'I believe the queen certainly designs to change the ministry; but perhaps may put it off till next session is over; and I think they had better give up now, if she will not deal openly.'

Tuesday brought news of a more directly personal interest.

Lord Nottingham solemnly protested in the House of Lords that a paper had been printed and published, contrary to a Standing Order of the House, purporting to describe the speech he had delivered against the peace. The report, said Nottingham with more truth than humour, was a travesty of the words he had actually used. Either the reference was to Swift's poem or to some pirated edition of it or conceivably to some similar product of another Grub Street craftsman. Promptly the Lords appointed a committee to discover the author, printer and publisher. The game was getting hot. Robert Walpole had named Swift as one of the culprits (or so Swift was told), vowing that he would pay for it. The threat put Swift on his mettle. On Wednesday he got home early 'to finish something I am doing' and quickly dispatched it to the printer 'to make a little mischief'. Pride in the power of his pen to wound such great men was restoring his courage. Yet the general situation looked gloomier than ever. 'Things do not mend at all. Lord Dartmouth despairs, and is for giving up: Lewis is of the same mind; but lord treasurer only says, Poh, poh, all will be well.' That Wednesday yet another Bill was introduced into the House of Lords for dealing with the menace which had baffled the statesmen of Queen Anne's reign, Whig and Tory alike, much more than all the Marshals of King Louis. Something must really be done about the scandalous licentiousness of the press. With their Lordships in their present mood Swift could not have supposed that their ire was directed against that French dog, Abel Boyer, or any of the other scoundrels who so richly deserved to be squeezed and swinged. The likelihood was that the author of *The Conduct of the Allies* would soon get the same treatment or worse. It was, after all, this same Lord Nottingham who had once been responsible for sending Daniel Defoe to Newgate prison.

During the last few days of that week when normally both peers and commoners would have left London to celebrate Christmas in their country homes, the parliamentary struggle mounted to a climax more hectic than anything known since the Revolution of 1688. The slender majority which the Whigs had wrested in the Lords confronted the Tory majority in the Commons with the Lords confident in their superior status and political acumen. Daily the gulf between the two Houses grew wider. On previous occasions when they had clashed, the impasse had usually been resolved by the shifting favour of the court. When the Queen and her Ministers threw their weight into the scales a sufficient number of peers could often be induced to waver in their chosen course or party allegiance. Elections for the Commons could be influenced, often decisively, by the same means; obstreperous country gentlemen, unlike the Lords, might be removable without resort to the extreme course of cutting off their heads. The obvious Whig strategy, therefore, was to capture the Queen, and the hope was that the Duchess of Somerset was gradually enticing her away from the embrace of Abigail and Harley. But the soul of the Queen, as Sarah had uncharitably discerned, could be moved by fear as much as flattery. If she saw more and more of the awe-inspiring grandees who wielded such authority in the state listing to the Whig side, might she not be compelled to withdraw her favour from lesser giants like Harley and St. John? This pressure had been the weapon whereby the first breach had been made in the Tory ramparts; if it was relaxed for fear of offending the Queen too sharply, all the gains of the past few weeks might be lost. It was a most tender calculation: how high a game ought the Whig managers to play?

This was the thought in the minds of many when on Thursday, December 20th, the Lords returned to the debate on the Duke of Hamilton's title. Theoretically party interests were supposed to play no part in the proceedings; the point to be settled was strictly legal and the debate was opened by counsel who put the case for the Duke. But all the protagonists in the great party struggle were there, eager to contest every inch of the ground. And there once again in her special box sat the Queen, listening to every word. Oratory must be directed to a proud and cynical aristocracy, then at the highest pitch of its authority, and at the same time to a sick and stubborn old woman, sensitive to every inflexion which might insult her dignity.

The Tory lawyers spoke bluntly. Of course the Queen could create any peers she wished, Scotchmen no less than Englishmen. The Crown could lose no prerogative that it had not given up by some express words in an Act of Parliament. No article in the Act of Union asserted that a Scotch peer could not be made a peer of Great Britain. Who would dare challenge so clear a ruling? At first it seemed that nobody would. But after a long pause Lord Guernsey, the brother of Lord Nottingham, rose to demur. With many dutiful expressions of loyalty to the Queen he still insisted on the letter of the Act of Union; there it was laid down that the nobility of Scotland should be represented in the Lords by sixteen of their number; great dangers would follow if that principle was abandoned. Let the Queen create what peers she wished; but let the Scotchmen ennobled by her enjoy all the privileges of the House except those of voting and trying their peers. Once Guernsey had shown the way, many others plucked up their courage. The debate continued longer than almost any other in living memory. Hairs were split with unerring deftness. Harley demanded that since the issue was one of law 'they were not to considere of the conveniance or inconveniance now, but whether by right his patent was good'; let them refer the matter to the judges.

This was the signal for the leaders of the Whig Junto to express their old anti-monarchical principles with something of their old disdainful flourish; none but the Lords themselves should settle an affair of such mighty consequence. With what distaste the Queen must have heard once more the accents of two among the five tyrannizing Whig Lords from whom Harley had once liberated her—with a third, Lord Halifax, appealing hopefully to Lord Nottingham to give his impartial voice to the same cause of Whiggish arrogance! Had Wharton and his friends pressed their claim too roughly? So some may have believed; when the time came for the division to be taken it was noted that the Duke of Marlborough and Lord Godolphin had left the chamber. But how could victories be won without risks? The Duke should know that. And, indeed, by the end of the day Wharton's brashness had gained another triumph. By a majority of twelve the Lords refused to refer the issue to the judges; by a majority of five they voted against the Duke of Hamilton despite all the Scotch threats that such an insult would wreck the Act of Union. Peter Wentworth who had heard the debate concluded that 'there did not seem to be much party in't', but it is hard to believe him. When the Society of Brothers met that night it is hard to suppose that fresh curses were not heaped on the head of Wharton and his new allies. When the apostasy of Nottingham went so far that he would cast a vote against the Queen's prerogative and when his brother was enlisted as the agent of these lordly republicans, it can be imagined how the still bewildered friends of the Tory Ministers trembled for the future.

Meantime, if the Duke of Marlborough ever supposed that his tactful withdrawal from the invidious vote in the Lords could soften party animosities, he was soon disillusioned. Next day the House of Commons showed its fighting spirit. Rumours had been current for some time about the sensational charges against the Duke which might be revealed when the Commission on the Public Accounts produced its report. Mr. Lockhart and Mr. Shippen, two strong Jacobites who sat on the Commission, had done their work with zest. Little encouragement was needed for the report to be presented at the first opportunity. 'Your Commissioners', said Mr. Lockhart, 'in the course of their examinations relating to the affairs of the army have already discovered some practices which they conceive highly detrimental to the public, and such as they are obliged to report to you.' Then he read the whole document, including, of course, the Commission's views on the depositions made by Sir Solomon Medina, the army contractor, who 'after expressing much uneasiness of the apprehensions he had of being thought an informer and of accusing a great man' had yet been persuaded to reveal what vast sums he had given to the Duke of Marlborough 'for his own use'. At once it was agreed that the report should be considered soon after Parliament reassembled and that the depositions of witnesses to the Commission should be made available to the House immediately.

It is not recorded that Members were shocked by these revelations. Charges of bribery and corruption were the normal weapons which politicians invoked against one another; a sense of outrage was not easily displayed when so many had been swilling in the same trough. But the political implications of the report helped to stir the most jaded conscience. Why had Lockhart acted at that particular moment? Everybody in the Commons believed he did so on the direct incitement of the Queen's Ministers. Something more might be in the wind than a mere sop for the October Club.

On Saturday, December 22nd, both Houses were roused to a last-minute frenzy in an effort to snatch the advantage from the other. In the Commons Mr. Shippen presented the depositions against the Duke. Every circumstance was contrived to ensure that they might be treated as documents of the gravest import. The clerk at the table was instructed to keep them under lock and key; only on the special request of Members of the House of Commons should copies be released. Thus the Members of the Commons would be enabled to proceed with the attack on the

Duke without intervention from any other quarter. The precaution was clearly directed against the press. What holes might not the Whig journalists pick in the documents if they once got them into their clutches! Might not this scare be lost in a bog of partisan controversy like the famous story of the stolen £35 millions earlier in the year?

Curiously, the malevolence of Grub Street was also the first item on the agenda of the House of Lords. The Duke of Devonshire made a report on behalf of the Committee set up three days earlier to search out the libellers of Lord Nottingham. The Duke's committee had no difficulty in pronouncing the offending poem both 'false and scandalous'. More baffling was the task of discovering the culprits, since the sheet had been 'printed by a sham name' and no one had been persuaded to offer information about the author. But the Duke's inquiries had not been entirely fruitless. A certain Andrew Hind, living at Peterborough Court, near Fleet Street, was, on the oath of an informer called Sarah Vickers, tracked down as the printer. Orders were at once given for his arrest by the officials of the House of Lords and Andrew Hind —innocent of this crime if not some others if, indeed, it was Swift's poem he was alleged to have printed—spent his Christmas in prison.

Curiously, too, on that afternoon Lords and Commons found themselves in unwitting agreement on another issue apart from the licentiousness of the press. When the Members of the Commons had completed the rest of their business—it included a motion to repeal an old Whig measure favouring Protestant refugees—they trooped along to the House of Lords at the summons of Black Rod to witness the royal assent being given to Lord Nottingham's Occasional Conformity measure. In a single week the Bill which had rent the nation for two decades was passed through all its stages, and now Whigs and Tories watched one another, wondering which had outmanœuvred the other. Then the Members of the Commons returned to their own Chamber and voted to adjourn until January 12th. For a moment it seemed that the battle must be suspended. But St. John and the Tory managers in the Commons had made their reckoning too soon. The last word lay with the Lords. Many of their number, thinking the business concluded, had also departed. But Lord Nottingham, in his new mood of rebellion, had stayed at his post. He introduced a new motion on the peace insisting that the Queen's plenipotentiaries should consult with the Dutch before the conference opened and demanding the most rigorous precautions to protect the Protestant succession. In a sparse House with the Tories hopelessly outvoted the Ministers and the court could not even risk a division. Finally, Lord Wharton produced his last-minute surprise. The House of Lords would adjourn, but it would meet again on January 2nd— ten days before the Commons. How much mischief could Wharton and his friends do in ten days while the gentlemen of England were recovering from their Christmas! Already since December 7th they had shaken the political fabric to its foundations.

'The lords made yesterday', wrote Swift, 'two or three votes about Peace, and Hanover, of a very angry kind, to vex the ministry, and they will meet sooner by a fortnight than the Commons; and they say, are preparing some knock-out addresses.' Wednesday, January 2nd, was to be the day for new alarms and convulsions. Once more the eyes of the political world were riveted on the prospect just as they had once looked forward with fear and hope to the fateful meeting of Parliament on December 7th. Few could doubt who had shown the greater skill in parliamentary manœuvre.

Christmas, 1711, was bitterly cold and the snow lay thick on the ground. The frost was too severe to allow the Vicar of Laracor to go to church either on the Sunday before or on Christmas day itself. Instead, except for one trip to the City to visit his printer, Swift stayed indoors, nursing his political dejection with his humour and his malice. The cure had seldom been known to fail, and on this occasion it produced, apart from a notable revival in his spirits, *The Windsor Prophecy*, a daring retaliation against the House of Lords for their insolence in classing him with the other denizens of Grub Street. Swift 'liked it mightily' and was certain everyone would guess it was his. On Christmas eve it was printed and on Boxing Day he took a copy proudly to Mrs. Masham, the heroine of the piece, who however at once took fright and urged him not to publish it 'for fear of angering the queen about the duchess of Somerset'. Swift made some efforts, although perhaps not too intently, to get the printer to stop it. On Thursday at the Society of Brothers the printer brought several copies for private circulation. ''Tis an admirable good one, and people are mad for it,' said the gleeful author. Orders were given to the printer not to part with any more copies, but already the town was full of it.

Talk about the Duchess of Somerset was on everyone's lips. The Duke, it seems, had played 'an imposition and a trick' on the Queen.

When he had offered to leave behind his proxy vote in favour of the Duke of Hamilton he had failed to mention that proxies would not be allowed on that occasion since the issue was classed as a legal one. The rumour was that the Duke had been dismissed by the Queen and that he in turn had insisted on taking his Duchess away from the court with him. No one knew the truth, but in the midst of all the gossip came Swift's onslaught on the Duchess, joyfully mocking her as the prime cause of England's danger and reviving, among other pleasantries, the old tale that she had murdered her second husband.

No great claim of literary merit can be made for *The Windsor Prophecy*; indeed the lines were purposely presented 'in a very Hobling kind of measure' in order to sustain the fiction that they had been unearthed from the rubbish in some ancient cave. But for sheer audacity it had no equal even in that age of scorching lampoons. For the exhortation which it contained was made to the Queen herself; the attack, apart from some scornful references to Nottingham and Marlborough thrown in as makeweight, was directed at the woman who was supposedly the Queen's first favourite; and the man who did it was the nightly companion of the Queen's own Ministers and was at that moment in danger of attention for other offences from the House of Lords or the Lord Chief Justice. Swift had written some terrible things before, but nothing quite so terrible as the concluding lines:

> *And dear Englond, if ought I understond,*
> *Beware of Carrots from Northumberlond.*
> *Carrots sown Thyn a deep root may get,*
> *If so be they are in Sommer set:*
> *Their Conyngs mark thou, for I have been told,*
> *They Assassine when young, and Poison when old.*
> *Root out these Carrots, O thou, whose Name*
> *Is backwards and forwards always the same;*
> *And keep close to Thee always that Name,*
> *Which backwards and forwards is allmost the same.*
> *And Englond wouldst thou be happy still,*
> *Bury those Carrots under a Hill.*

Why did he do it? No one knows to this day how true were the accusations that the Duchess was using her position to wield political influence; the charge rests primarily on the evidence contained in Swift's *Journal to Stella* and for him the Duchess had become an obsession. Personal motives may have mixed with his political suspicions; once the Duchess had criticized his conduct in dealing with Sir William Temple's *Memoirs*[1]. The case looks

[1] It has often been suggested that Swift's main motive in writing *The Windsor Prophecy* was to take his revenge for the part which the Duchess of Somerset, in company with the Archbishop of York, had played in persuading the Queen to deny him preferment. This suspicion makes the case against Swift look blacker still, and it has, therefore, been freely assumed to be justified. Swift's famous lines in his poem, *The Author on Himself*, seem to give colour to the suspicion.

> *By an old red-hair'd, murd'ring hag pursued,*
> *A crazy prelate, and a royal prude . . .*

Archbishop Sharp had been outraged by the tone of *The Tale of a Tub*. He saw the author as a dangerous free-thinker; such a man, he plausibly argued, should never be a Bishop, whatever supplications were made on his behalf by politicians of any party. That the Archbishop did intervene against Swift is fairly well authenticated, but insufficient attention has been paid to the question of when he did it. He may have known or suspected for some years that Swift was the author of *The Tale of a Tub*. When he used this information is another matter. In an article on 'Dean Swift and Ecclesiastical Preferment' published in *The Review of English Studies* (Vol. II, No. 5, January 1926) Professor C. H. Firth offers considerable evidence to show that Swift's earlier disappointments about preferment (for example in 1708) were not due to the Archbishop. He argues that 'Archbishop Sharp's intervention must have taken place between January and April 1713'—in other words a full year after the publication of *The Windsor Prophecy*. This belief is also borne out by the later lines in *The Author on Himself* written in 1714:

> *Now angry Somerset her vengeance vows*
> *On Swift's reproaches for her murdered spouse;*
> *From her red locks her mouth with venom fills;*
> *And thence into the royal ear instills.*

Thus Swift himself thought that the Duchess's attempt to rob him of a Bishopric came after he had attacked her and not before. Everything seems to suggest that this was the fact.

Mr. John Middleton Murry, in his life of Swift, offers a most ingenious argument to show that it was Swift's old quarrel with the Duchess about Sir William Temple's *Memoirs* which prompted him to make the savage reprisal. It may be, but there is really no necessity to discover an abstruse personal reason why he should have launched an invective against a political figure. His attacks on the Duke and Duchess of Marlborough—to mention only two names in the lengthy catalogue—are proof that he was quite capable of making his attacks sufficiently vindictive even in cases where he had no personal axe to grind. On that Christmas morning it is much more likely that he was inspired by the general political situation than by some ancient personal grudge which could have been paid off years before.

damning against Swift and his most consistent admirers have not attempted to palliate the offence. Possibly in pursuit of a personal vendetta he had cast aside his judgement along with any claims to taste or decency. And yet there *is* a defence, or at least an explanation, which can only be understood if we recall the exact moment when the poem was written.

On that bleak Sunday morning when he pondered the events of the day before in Parliament, Swift believed that everything he had fought for, including the friends he loved and admired, might soon be destroyed. The Duchess, so he believed, was a principal agent of their misfortune. Many were wavering in their devotion to the cause. Erasmus Lewis would soon be off to Wales; Swift himself had had thoughts of seeking sanctuary in Ireland. How he longed for a Bishopric! And how carelessly with a single lampoon dashed off one Sunday he cast away any further chance of getting it! After *The Windsor Prophecy*, no one surely should ever have been able to brand him—many have done so—as a time-server, a sycophant, a turncoat and a coward. At the height of the crisis Swift hurled himself into the conflict on what he thought to be the losing side with foolhardy loyalty, not caring even to take the usual precaution to disguise his handiwork. Once the idea was in his head and the pen was in his hand, nothing could check him. *The Windsor Prophecy* may have been a wicked libel; it was not the act of a mean spirit who would only stab in the dark. Meantime, whatever the judgement on Swift, one fact is sure. The Duchess of Somerset paid the penalty for her real or imaginary intrigues. 'A nickname', said William Hazlitt, 'is the heaviest stone the devil can throw at a man.' No nickname ever hit harder than Carrots of Northumberland. Others might be cowed by the blue blood of the Somersets, the royal favour in which they seemed to bask, the vast power they now wielded as the allies of Marlborough and the Whig aristocracy; but not the Vicar of Laracor who fought the battle for his friends and against the enemies of the peace with a courage to make even St. John gasp.

Christmas, even apart from Swift's sermon of goodwill, brought no respite in the political crisis. In the hands of every member of the House of Commons was a document denouncing the Duke of Marlborough as a man who had made a huge fortune by cheating his soldiers and pilfering from the public till. Once the news leaked out about the decisions of the Commons on that previous Saturday, he or the members of his entourage knew that no mercy was intended. The Duke's response was to do something he had always disdained. He stooped to find an ally in the printing press. On Thursday, December 27th, he allowed to be printed in the *Daily Courant* his reply to the Commissioners of Public Accounts which he had sent to the Commissioners and to Harley in November. The Ministers at once retaliated. On Friday they sent to the same journal the full report of the Commissioners and on Saturday the document was published. No one could possibly doubt now that when Parliament met the contest would be waged with unexampled ferocity.

Everything, it seemed, hinged on the meeting of the House of Lords arranged for the following week, and on that Saturday morning Swift had no idea what the outcome might be. The rumour was that the Queen had created one or two new peers, but Swift was still in doubts about the 'constancy' of the Queen. That morning he wrote both to Stella and to Archbishop King in Dublin. To the Archbishop he described the whole scene.

'In above twenty years', he wrote, 'that I have known something about courts, I have never observed so many odd, dark, unaccountable circumstances in any public affair. A majority against the Court, carried by five or six depending Lords, who owed the best of their bread to pensions from the Court, and who were told by the public enemy, that what they did would be pleasing to the Queen, though it was openly levelled against the first Minister's head: again, those whose purse-strings and heartstrings were the same, all on a sudden scattering their money to bribe votes'—[The Duke and Duchess of Marlborough, it was supposed, had disgorged vast sums from their fortune in a desperate effort to save the rest]—'a Lord, who had been so far always a Tory, as often to be thought in the Pretender's interest, giving his vote for the ruin of all his old friends, caressed by the Whigs who hated and abhorred him: the Whigs all chiming in with a Bill against Occasional Conformity; and the very Dissenting ministers agreeing to it, for reasons that nobody alive can tell; a resolution of breaking the treaty of peace, without any possible scheme for continuing the war: and all this owing to a doubtfulness and inconstancy in one certain quarter which, at this distance, I dare not describe; neither do I find any person, though deepest in affairs, who can tell what steps to take. On January 2nd, the House of Lords is to meet, and it is expected they will go on in their votes and addresses against a peace. On the other side, we are endeavouring to get a majority, and have called up two Earls' sons to the

345

House of Peers; and I thought six more would have been called and perhaps they may before Wednesday. We expect the Duke of Somerset and Lord Cholmondley will lose their places: but it is not yet done, and we wish for one more change at Court, which you may guess. To know upon what small consequences, and by what degrees, this change has been brought about, would require a great deal more than I can or dare write. There is not one which I did not give warning of, to those chiefly concerned, many months ago; and so did some others, for they were visible enough. This must infallibly end either in an entire change of measures and ministry, or in a firm establishment on our side. Delay, and tenderness to an inveterate party, have been very instrumental to this ill state of affairs. They tell me you in Ireland are furious against a peace; and it is a great jest to see people in Ireland furious for or against anything.'

With this last fling, Swift, even amid his other anxieties, could not resist a rebuke for his own Archbishop. He put the letters both to King and to Stella in his pocket, already sealed for the post, and went off to a coffee-house. There he learnt the tremendous news. The Queen had come to her senses. Everything was saved. Swift tore open the letters to add a triumphant postscript and then joined one of his favourite cronies to celebrate this glorious day of judgement in 'very good Irish wine'.

How the deed was done remains a considerable mystery. No remaining papers of St. John, still less of Harley, give more than a few clues to the story, and the most probable reason is that both were more cautious than ever in committing their thoughts to writing during those weeks of unprecedented tension. Both knew that if their plan failed they might pay for any indiscretions on the scaffold. The thought was certainly present in the mind of St. John. In the midst of the crisis he wrote to Strafford at The Hague recalling the fate of a greater Lord Strafford. The Queen must learn the moral. If she failed to shield the Ministers who had delivered her from bondage, her own throne might be at stake. Whether St. John ever believed that this threat was real, no one can tell. But the dangers for St. John and Harley were certainly not fanciful. If the Queen was persuaded to seek other advisers at that critical hour, if parleying with the French behind the backs of the allies suddenly came to be regarded as a treasonable offence, the evidence against St. John and Harley, despite all their precautions, was wellnigh conclusive. The great Strafford had gone to his death on a more slender indictment.

So when, on the night of December 7th, Harley and St. John saw Marlborough at the head of the victorious Whigs in the House of Lords, they resolved at all costs to strip him of his power. This was the logical culmination of St. John's manœuvres for months past; but now Harley was a convert to the same policy. Their resolution, so far as we know, was revealed to only one man. John Drummond, the old agent of the Tory Ministers at The Hague, was then in London. He was instructed to write to Heinsius informing him that the Duke would soon be removed from his post as commander of the army in Flanders, to be replaced by a devoted supporter of the Tories, the Duke of Ormond. Doubtless the calculation was that this intelligence would prevent the Dutch from embarking on any fresh *démarche* in London which might assist the Whigs. No one else was told, not even, it seems, the Duke of Ormond himself.

The rest of the plot required most intricate preparation. Even when they had made up their minds the Ministers were still nervous what consequences might follow from the overthrow of the victorious war leader. Plans must be set in train for the most opportune publication of the report of the Commissioners. More time was needed for *The Conduct of the Allies* to reap its full harvest. And the Queen must be persuaded. What arguments were deployed to convince her can only be surmised, but St. John's reports to Strafford give an indication of the central themes in his mind. First, the Queen had set her heart on making peace. Through all of St. John's duplicity his conviction that peace was inevitable shines forth. 'Those who oppose the Queen's measures', he wrote at the time in refuting the Whig argument, 'know, as well as we who pursue them, that the war is become impracticable; that the end which they pretend to aim at is chimerical; and that they ruin their country by driving on this vain, gaudy scheme which has so many years dazzled our eyes.' St. John contended further that the commotions in the House of Lords put the national will in an entirely false perspective. The power of the Whigs was built 'upon an adventitious strength'—'The true, real, genuine strength of Britain, belongs to other people'. This was the foundation on which St. John had sought to build for the previous three years, and the Queen's affection for the Church of England Party must have reinforced his appeal. For him, unlike Harley, the mood of the October Club represented much more than a sudden, swelling wave of popular emotion; it was the national tide moving forward inexorably. Was that not the reason why he had allied his fortune with it?

All these were arguments he could parade before Harley and the Queen. And now to them all was added another, presented, we must suppose, in a more peremptory tone. When the Duke of Marlborough returned from the battlefield to put himself at the head of the Whigs, when the Duchess re-emerged to flaunt her influence in London society on so lavish a scale, when the London mob had been checked only by the vigilance of the Ministers from lauding Marlborough through the streets as their national hero, what could it mean? The answer had already been given in *The Conduct of the Allies* and the meaning should be plain. The Duke, wrote Swift years later describing those days in retrospect, 'boldly fell, with his whole weight, into the design of ruining the ministry, at the expense of his duty to his sovereign, and the welfare of his country, after the mighty obligations he had received from both. WHIG and TORY were now no longer the dispute, but THE QUEEN or THE DUKE OF MARLBOROUGH'. Either the Queen must envisage getting rid of her present advisers, stopping the peace negotiations and dissolving Parliament, thus destroying the Tory majority in the Commons, or she must remove the Duke from his command and accept the further necessity of depriving the Duke and Duchess of Somerset of the power to influence votes in the House of Lords. Sometime in the middle of December the Queen half yielded. Marlborough would be dismissed; perhaps Somerset could be dismissed too; but must she really be driven to a breach with her beloved Duchess? On this count her Stuart stubbornness still prevailed.

Even with the Queen's assent to the most essential item of their programme, the Ministers had still not solved their immediate problem. The Whig majority in the Lords remained. Possibly the calculation was that with Somerset robbed of his authority as a friend of the Queen, half a dozen wavering votes in the Lords could be recovered for the court. But the risks were still too great. The Queen might still at the last moment jib at the removal of Somerset and, even if he went, a court majority was not guaranteed. Harley had indeed 'a further fetch' at his command. Either he made up his own mind that he could afford no more defeats in the Lords or he was presented with a lucky opening too tempting to resist. Possibly it was the Whig manœuvre over the Duke of Hamilton's title which turned the whole affair. For if the Queen could without question create English peers—as even the Whigs had been forced to admit when they were contesting her right to create Scottish peers—could she not create what number she chose and thus dictate her will to the recalcitrant Whig Lords?

Sometime over that Christmas recess, the brilliant notion occurred to Harley, and the decision was taken to create twelve new Lords, all of them obedient servants of the Queen's Ministers; three of them indeed were fellow-members of Swift's Society of Brothers. 'I was never so much surprised', wrote Lord Dartmouth, 'as when the queen drew a list of twelve lords out of her pocket, and ordered me to bring warrants for them; there not having been the least intimation before it was to be put into execution. I asked her, if she designed to have them all made at once. She asked me, if I had any exceptions to the legality of it. I said, No; but doubted very much of the expediency, for I feared it would have a very ill effect in the house of lords and no good one in the Kingdom.' Lord Dartmouth may be pardoned for his obtuseness. Everyone else was shocked, including Swift who deplored the 'strange, unhappy necessity' of such an unprecedented step which the Queen had 'drawn upon herself, by her confounded trimming and moderation'. One country gentleman, Sir Miles Wharton, refused his offer of a peerage on the grounds that it looked too much like 'serving a turn'; his place among the twelve was taken by the husband of Mrs. Masham who had no such scruple. Even the Queen was appalled by this last request; she had no desire to change a useful servant into 'a great lady'. Yet she consented. She and her great lords must accept the indignity of seeing Abigail ennobled since the terrible alternative might be to see Marlborough crowning himself as King, or at least re-establishing the tyranny of the Marlborough family and the Junto. To forestall the Duke, the House of Lords and the Constitution itself must be bent to the Queen's will.

This, then, was the great news which Swift had heard on the night of Saturday, December 29th, accompanied by the rumour that the Duke of Somerset had been turned out too. Next morning he attended the court levee and soon learnt that the rumour about the Duke of Somerset was false. A few weeks earlier renewed disappointment on this particular issue would have plunged him

349

back into despair. But now he sighed his regrets and waited expectantly. The Whigs dared not show their face; 'the queen is awaked and so is lord treasurer'. Everyone knew that a new day had dawned, and while Swift joined his rejoicing Tory friends the sight of one lonely figure confirmed that their dreams had come true. 'The Duke of Marlborough', he wrote, 'was at Court today, and nobody hardly took notice of him.'

How would the Whigs react to the trick played upon them? A storm might be expected, even if the twelve new peers ensured a majority for the court. Moreover, the Ministers had now received news that Prince Eugene, despite all their efforts to stop him, was on the way to London. Any day he might arrive in the capital to be greeted by crowds paid to demonstrate by the Whigs. Harley and St. John were leaving nothing to chance. They had, it appears, timed their successive strokes to fall in those few days when Parliament was adjourned for Christmas. The prospective arrival of Eugene and the decision of the Lords to meet on January 2nd, ten days before the Commons, speeded up the time-table. On Monday, December 31st, the culminating blow was struck in the form of a resolution passed at the Cabinet Council: 'That Her Majesty being informed, that as Information against the Duke of Marlborough was laid before the House of Commons by the Commissioners of Publick Accounts, Her Majesty thought fit to dismiss him from all Employments, that the Matter might take an Impartial Examination.' That night the Queen wrote in her own hand her note of dismissal to the Duke. He threw it in the fire and replied with a dignified protest against the manner in which he had been convicted before any charge had been proved against him. That night, too, Swift wrote to Stella: 'These are strong remedies: pray God the patient is able to bear them.' On Tuesday, the dismissal of Marlborough and the creation of the twelve peers were announced in the *Gazette*. On Wednesday the Lords met to face a demand from the Queen that they should adjourn until the day when the Commons was meeting too. Never before had such a demand been presented by a monarch to the House of Lords. The Whigs fought desperately in the last ditch. Only by the twelve votes of the new peers was the motion carried. 'If those twelve had not been enough,' jeered St. John when he got news of the vote, 'they would have been given another dozen,' and doubtless his taunt expressed the truth.

The great Whig rebellion against the peace had been broken, and no consolation was left to them but the wit of Lord Wharton. When the division was taken he asked whether the twelve would vote individually or by their foreman.

* * *

On the day that Marlborough fell, the Tories said 'this is something like'. If only action had been taken weeks before against him and the Duke of Somerset—so they argued with some justice—the agony of the past month could have been avoided. Others treated the event less light-heartedly; among them, strangely enough, Swift. Now that the terrible moment had come he shuddered, as the Ministers had so often shuddered before, at the thought of what might happen when the mightiest pillar of their world came crashing to the ground.

'If the ministry be not sure of Peace,' wrote Swift, 'I shall wonder at this step, and do not approve it at best. The queen and lord treasurer mortally hate the duke of Marlborough, and to that he owes his fall, more than to his other faults; unless he has been tampering too far with his party, of which I have not heard any particulars; however it be, the world abroad will blame us. I confess my belief, that he has not one good quality in the world besides that of general, and even that I have heard denied by several great soldiers. But we have had constant success in arms which he commanded. Opinion is a mighty matter in war, and I doubt but the French think it impossible to conquer an army he leads, and our soldiers think the same and how far even this step may encourage the French to play tricks with us, no man knows. I do not love to see personal resentment mix with public affairs.' This was Swift on January 1st while he still held his breath, waiting for the earthquake that must follow. The words have sometimes been cited as proof that Swift did not consider the removal of Marlborough as the primary measure required to secure the peace and the victory of his friends. But all his actions in the previous months make nonsense of the judgement. Only two weeks before at Mrs. Masham's he had been urging Harley to summon his courage and take this all-important step. One plausible explanation of the contradiction may be that Stella, who still kept Whig company in Ireland, had reproved him for the furious attacks on the Duke and that Swift was content in his letters to her to put the blame on other shoulders. Swift's anxiety, however, was natural enough. Unlike some others, he had never underrated his enemy.

As it happened, the crash sounded milder than all had expected. The heavens did not fall. The sun still kept its course. No sudden alarm swept the country. The coffee-houses, the country gentlemen, Members of the House of Commons, men of opinion everywhere had been prepared for the event. *The Conduct of the Allies*, the most deadly pamphlet in the English language, had done its work. Marlborough was no longer the nation's hero. He was, in the eyes of Swift's readers, the chief instigator of the war, the chief profiteer from it, the man who might still decree that the land taxes and the press-gang and the whole wearisome business should continue for ever. Years later Swift acknowledged how wise the Ministers had been in their own interests in screwing up their courage for the last challenge to the Duke, although he never lost his unwilling admiration for 'this lord who was beyond comparison the greatest subject in Christendom'. Two days after his first curious lament for the fallen idol he had sufficiently recovered his balance to dispatch to the printer a ballad called *The Widow and Her Cat* which put the fall of the giant in a more modest perspective.

A Widow kept a Favourite Cat,
*   At first a gentle Creature;*
But when he was grown Sleek and Fat,
With many a Mouse, and many a Rat,
*   He soon disclos'd his Nature.*

The Fox and He were Friends of old,
*   Nor cou'd they now be parted;*
They Nightly slunk to rob the Fold,
Devour'd the Lambs, the Fleeces sold,
*   And Puss grew Lion-hearted.*

He scratch'd her Maid, he stole the Cream,
*   He tore her best lac'd Pinner;*
Nor Chanticleer upon the Beam,
Nor Chick, nor Duckling 'scapes, when Grim
*   Invites the Fox to Dinner.*

The Dame full wisely did Decree,
  For fear He shou'd dispatch more,
That the false Wretch shou'd worry'd be:
But in a sawcy manner He
  Thus Speech'd it like a L—re.

' *Must I, against all Right and Law,*
  ' *Like Pole-Cat vile be treated?*
' *I! who so long with Tooth and Claw*
' *Have kept Domestick Mice in awe,*
  ' *And Foreign Foes defeated!*

' *Your Golden Pippins, and your Pies,*
  ' *How oft have I defended:*
' '*Tis true, the Pinner which you prize*
' *I tore in Frolick; to your Eyes*
  ' *I never Harm intended.*

' *I am a Cat of Honour,—Stay,*
  Quo' She, no longer parly;
Whate'er you did in Battle slay,
By Law of Arms became your Prey,
  I hope you won it fairly.

Of this, we'll grant you stand acquit,
  But not of your Outrages:
Tell me; Perfidious! Was it fit
To make my Cream a PERQUISITE,
  And Steal to mend your Wages?

So flagrant is Thy Insolence,
  So vile Thy Breach of Trust is;
That longer with Thee to Dispense,
Were want of Pow'r, or want of Sense:
  Here, Towzer!—*Do Him Justice.*

While Towzer—in other words, Parliament—went to work on the task, others in Grub Street produced more suitable epitaphs. One, for example, in the best ironical style, purported to have discovered a letter from the King of France to the Cardinal de Noailles, Archbishop of Paris.

'Cousin and Counsellor, We Greet you Well. This will let you understand that we have received the agreeable News of the surrender and demolishing of the strong, important Fortress of Mar—gh, hitherto thought impregnable, being so well fortified both by Nature and Art, and which, for Ten Years together, has baffled our Utmost efforts. And since immense sums promised could never corrupt the *Honesty*, numerous *Armies* terrify the *Bravery*, the *Conduct* of our most experienced Generals never surprise the *Vigilance* of the *Governor*; therefore we have been forced to pursue *other Measures*, and at length have had the Comfort of seeing the Disappointment of such as *delight in war*.

''Tis notorious to all the World how conformable it is to our innate goodness and Modesty not to assume to ourselves the Glory due to others; wherefore we must with all justice acknowledge this great Success to be owing, next under God, to our Trusty and Well-beloved Counsellors, the President *d'Harley* and Count *de St. John*. But as theirs is the Praise, so will the Benefit and Advantage accrue to Us and our People. For this reason we command you to cause TE DEUM to be sung in our Metropolitan Church of *Notre Dame*, in our good city of Paris, the 16th Day of this present January.'

The satire was close to the mark, for when King Louis heard the news from London he rejoiced that Marlborough's dismissal 'will do all we can desire'. King Louis, too, had received his copy of *The Conduct of the Allies*. He marvelled at the novel weapon which seemed to have achieved more than his greatest Generals had accomplished in the whole long struggle from Blenheim to Bouchain. It is not recorded whether he ever learnt that the author's name was Jonathan Swift. Since the Lord Chief Justice of England was interested in discovering the same information the secret was kept for some while longer. The Duke of Marlborough, however, had his suspicions. Not many days later St. John passed on the report to the Vicar of Laracor: 'The Duke of Marlborough says, there is nothing he now desires so much as to contrive some way to soften Dr. Swift.' Possibly St. John was telling a flattering lie and probably the Duke did not express himself in such moderate language. But at long last, it seems, the Captain-General had been forced to pay his tribute to Grub Street.

CHAPTER FOURTEEN

Epilogue

'Oh, when shall we have such another
Vicar of Laracor!'—WILLIAM HAZLITT.

AFTER HIS OVERTHROW in the great crisis of Christmas, 1711, the Duke of Marlborough lived on for another ten years, a few of them bitter beyond imagination and the rest offering no full recompense for the humiliation he had suffered. Never again was he to recover the resplendent power which Harley, St. John and Swift had stripped from him. For a while the world continued to marvel how quiet was the aftermath of so mighty an event. Later commentators have supposed that the Duke's authority had been drained from him months or years before, that the final act of his removal was no more than an inevitable incident in the drama of the peacemaking. Yet in November and December of 1711 Marlborough and the Whigs had come near to reversing the whole tide of Tory success. The deed which thwarted them was in truth decisive. Thereafter, the Grand Alliance was ground to pieces with an ever more reckless abandon; Harley and St. John were enabled to press ahead with their plans without further hesitancy; together or at loggerheads they plunged deep into a conspiracy against the Hanoverian Succession. Nowhere is the change in tempo better reflected than in Swift's Journal and correspondence. Never again did he play a leading part in so thrilling a victory; never again, at least in England, did politics absorb his whole mind and genius. When Marlborough left the scene some of his zest for the struggle subsided.

Immediately, the purpose of the Ministers was to drive home their advantage by securing the Duke's conviction on the charges of peculation. How nervous were some of the onlookers at the spectacle is best revealed in the twisted mind of Daniel Defoe. To Harley he wrote with his incorrigible sycophancy: 'God That Directs your Ldpp in all Things, has Moved you No doubt to Take This Most Necessary step of Deposeing The Idol Man, who Coveted to Set himself up as The head of a Party, and by whom

They pretended to Make Themselves Formidable. All wise men Own the Necessity, and Applaud the Wisdome of This step, and if it be Needfull for Majties Safety to go on, I believ no Man can Think Amiss That those who Eat her Majties Bread, should (when a Threatning behaviour Demands Such a Course) be left to kno' the want of it.' In his *Weekly Review*, however, where he was already under fire as a Tory time-server, Defoe had to be more circumspect. He would not join 'those who rejoyce at the Removing him upon Party Account, that are Personally piqu'd at him, and that desire his Fall, not only from his Command, but into all the Mischiefs of the Unfortunate. I abhor the Principle and can by no means join with the Men'. Defoe expatiated on the Duke's merits and denounced the attempt to convict him by popular clamour. Above all, he insisted that the Queen and her Government were determined to give him a fair trial. Mrs. Manley in the *Examiner* had better information and no such compunctions. Since 'the conversation of the Town rowls altogether upon what concerns the late General', she stabbed week by week without mercy, accusing him of every crime from cruelty practised on his own soldiers to a plot for seizing the crown.

Curiously Swift seemed to side more with Defoe than with his own protégée. He took credit for himself with Stella that he would not trample on the Duke when he was down. 'I am of your opinion', he wrote, 'that Lord Marlborough is used too hardly: I have often scratched out papers and pamphlets sent me before they were printed; because I thought them too severe. But, he is certainly a vile man, and has no sort of merit beside the military. The *Examiners* are good for little: I would fain have hindered the severity of the two or three last, but could not.' This, however, may have been no more than another disingenuous attempt to excuse his conduct to Stella. Within a few days—thanks partly perhaps to a widely current rumour that the Duke was to take a libel action against him for £20,000—Swift had broken his own vows of moderation. One Thursday the Brothers Society was regaled with a new poem—*The Fable of Midas*. It concluded with the lines:

> But *Gold* defiles with frequent Touch,
> There's nothing *fouls* the Hands so much:
> And Scholars give it for the Cause,
> Of *British Midas* dirty Paws:

Which while the *Senate* strove to scower,
They washt away with *Chymick* Power.
While He his utmost Strength apply'd,
To Swim against this *Pop'lar Tide*,
The *Golden* Spoils flew off apace,
Here fell a *Pension*, there a *Place*:
The *Torrent*, merciless, imbibes
Commissions, *Perquisites*, and *Bribes*,
By their own Weight sunk to the Bottom;
Much good may do 'em that have caught 'um.
And Midas now neglected stands,
With *asses Ears*, and *dirty Hands*.

This was Swift's method of treating the Duke gently. The contrast
with Defoe is instructive. Defoe applauded the Ministers unstint-
ingly in private, but was cautious in public. Swift saved his misgivings for his intimate circle, letting loose on the world the full
blast of his ferocity. These fresh *jeux d'esprit*, however, could add
nothing to what had already been achieved by *The Conduct of the
Allies*. After long debate the House of Commons declared by
265 votes to 155 that the huge payments made to Marlborough
over the years were 'unwarrantable and illegal'. On one count the
sum amounted to £60,000 and on the other to nearly a quarter of a
million. And the same Ministers who had pressed the charge
quickly arranged that the same unwarrantable and illegal perquisites should be made available to the Duke of Ormond,
Marlborough's successor in charge of the armies.

Throughout the year 1712, one disaster after another followed
for the Duke and the cause he had championed. Prince Eugene
had arrived in London, but too late to rally the disarrayed Whigs,
St. John was soon giving to the new Captain-General in Flanders
orders designed to assist his plan for a separate peace. They meant
that the British army was instructed to betray its allies in the field
and that the Generals of King Louis were enabled to gain their
first military victory in Flanders. No matter: St. John, soon created
Viscount Bolingbroke, was off to Versailles, there to drive through
the peace negotiations with ever more ruthless duplicity. In
September Lord Godolphin died—'the best man that ever lived,'
as Sarah called him. And Marlborough himself was sick in body as
well as mind. 'I hear', wrote Swift, 'Ld Marlbrow is growing ill

of his Diabetis, which if it be true, may soon carry him off; and then the Ministry will be something more at ease.' Month by month the political atmosphere grew more suffocating. Ugly rumours circulated that more extreme measures were intended. The Duke must be made to pay back the £250,000 he had allegedly stolen from the public coffers. He must be 'pursued to the blood'. A private message was sent to the Marquis of Torcy that the Ministers had a scheme to 'cut off the head' of their fallen enemy. No evidence exists that this project had been worked out in any detail, but the talk was widespread that an impeachment was to be the next resort. At last the Duke decided to leave the land of 'tigers and wolves'. Either he made the decision of his own accord or he did it in secret connivance with Harley who, it is also suggested, did not refrain from a blackmailing threat that Marlborough's old intrigues with the Jacobite Court of St. Germain's would be made public if he did not go quietly. 'Here is the duke of Marlborough', wrote Swift on October 28th, 'going out of England (Lord knows why), which causes many speculations. Some say he is conscious of guilt, and dare not stand it. Others think he has a mind to fling an odium on the government, as who should say, that one, who has done such great services to his country, cannot live quietly in it, by reason of the malice of his enemies.'

Two months later Sarah followed him to Flanders, and Swift sent her on her way with an even more graceless valediction. 'Duchess of Marlborough is leaving England to go to her Duke,' he wrote, 'and makes Presents of Rings to severall Friends, they say worth 200 ll a piece. I am sure she ought to give me one, Though the Duke pretended to think me his greatest Enemy, and got People to tell me so, and very mildly to let me know how gladly he would have me softned towards him. I bid a Lady of his Acquaintance and mine let him know, that I had hinderd many a bitter thing against him, not for his own sake, but because I thought it looked base; and I desired every thing should be left him except Power.'

Swift's capacity for self-deception must have been inordinate if he thought that anyone, even Stella, could be convinced by such an apologia; and yet there was one small grain of truth in the claim. Apart from the squibs and lampoons against the Duke and Duchess which he doubtless dashed off to amuse his friends, his political attack had been prompted by something other than personal malice. Indeed, the success of the campaign was due to the skilful discrimination introduced by him into the Tory propaganda. Had he not, in his first sustained assault in the early numbers of the *Examiner*, gradually changed his tone until Marlborough's qualities began to shine through amid all the invective? And was it not his love of peace and his detestation of military overlordship which had made *The Conduct of the Allies* so powerful a weapon in the hands of the Ministers?

No similar excuse can be made for the savagery with which he pursued Sarah. On the eve of her departure Swift talked over with Harley the contents of the coming Queen's speech. 'I sd, the Speech should begin thus. My Lds and Gentlemen; In Order to my own Quiet, and that of my Subjects I have thought fit to send the Duchess of Marlbr abroad after the Duke.' As she packed her bags the Duchess, it seems, had looked for means of expressing her natural feelings of disgust towards the Queen who had not cared to speak one syllable in defence of her old friends. Harley, reported Swift to Stella, 'shewd us a small Picture of enamell'd work, and sett in gold, worth about 20 ll, a Picture I mean of the Qu; which sh gave to Dutchess Marlbrough sett in Diamonds. When the Dutchess was leaving Engld, she took off all the Diamonds, and gave the Picture to one Mrs. Higgins, (an old intriguing woman whom everybody knows) bidding her to make the best of it she could. Ld Tr sent to Mrs. Higgins for this Picture, and gave her a hundred Pounds for it. Was ever such an ungratefull Beast as that Duchess? or did you ever hear such a Story. I suppose the Whigs will not believe it, pray try them: takes off the diamonds and gives away the Picture to an insignificant woman as a thing of no consequence, and gives it her to sell, like a piece of old fashion'd plate. Is she not a detestable Slut'. The story about Sarah, it must be confessed, rings true in every particular. But why should it have aroused anger in the breast of Swift? Sarah had excellent reasons for her loathing of the woman whom Swift, in his better moments, dismissed as 'the royal prude'.

The semi-voluntary exile of the Duke and Duchess lasted nearly two years. Together they toured through Flanders and the German states, receiving the veneration denied them in their native land. Comfort and repose could not have been altogether lacking since the Duke had transferred £50,000 from his immense fortune to The Hague. Yet even if he remained one of the richest men in

Europe and even if the applause which greeted him was unfeigned and overwhelming, nothing could hide the measure of his fall. Compared with the unexampled power he had wielded before, all his glories, conquests, triumphs, spoils had indeed shrunk to a little measure. The plenipotentiaries of the great powers met at Utrecht to make their peace. Marlborough regarded the terms agreed as a squalidly inadequate conclusion to his victorious war; he hated even more the dishonourable means by which they were secured. Yet throughout his exile he never cared or dared to raise his voice in criticism. Had he been bought? So the cynics have suggested and there are at least some grounds for the suspicion. Throughout those months he kept up a curious, guarded correspondence with Harley which culminated in January 1714 in the issue of a warrant of £10,000 by the Lord Treasurer for the resumption of work on Blenheim Palace. During those same months he revived his old relations with the Court of St. Germain's. 'A small sum' from his miser's hoard was dispatched to Queen Mary of Modena, the wife of James II, as a proof of his undying devotion, and the Jacobite courtiers were invited to perform for him a service in return. Could not the chivalrous King Louis XIV be persuaded to intercede on his behalf with Queen Anne to ensure that he was not robbed of all the gold and the estates which he had left behind him in England?

No hint of this traffic with Harley or with King Louis, it must be assumed, could be given to Sarah. If she had discovered the full truth of his reinsurance policies, even Swift's invective would have been outdone. To keep from her his secrets and at the same time to stay inactive in her presence while the diplomatic crisis mounted to its climax must have tested his patience to the limit. Somehow he did it; the man's face must have been made of marble. Never was the Duke more inscrutable than during those months of exile. Sarah herself quickly grew tired of the sights they saw on their journeyings, especially as these included the odious spectacle of fat priests battening on 'the poor, deluded People' of the cities where she and her husband were entertained. How she hated 'these dirty countries' of their banishment! How she longed for England and her English liberty and, above all, for action! 'I am confident', she asserted (and we can believe her), 'that I would have been the greatest hero that ever was known in the Parliament House, if I had been so happy as to have been a man.' As it was, even the husband she adored lost something of his lustre in her eyes; she accused him of being 'intolerably lazy'. But the charge was false. Even while he paid his court to the Pretender, much more precise and binding negotiations were conducted with the Elector of Hanover; even while he corresponded with Harley, his vigilant watch for other opportunities which might arise from the complexities of English politics never relaxed.

Queen Anne was dying. In the spring and summer of 1714 all else became subordinate to the great question of the succession to the throne. Harley and St. John played the double game of intrigue with the Courts of St. Germain's and Hanover less expertly than the Duke. And in the last days when the Queen lay on her death-bed the quarrel between the two Tory leaders, despite all Swift's efforts at reconciliation, ended in a furious clash. The Queen dismissed Harley on the ground that 'he neglected all business; that he was seldom to be understood; that when he did explain himself she could not depend upon the truth of what he said; that he never came to her at the time she appointed; that he often came drunk; lastly, to crown all, he had behaved himself towards her with bad manners, indecency and disrespect'. It is difficult to accept the whole indictment, even if some particulars on the charge sheet closely resemble those which St. John had drawn up years before. These were rather the excuses for the Queen's conduct elicited by Mrs. Masham who now betrayed Harley as she had once betrayed Sarah. Harley was overthrown by the same arts he had once employed against the Duke. For forty-eight hours St. John held the unfettered power he had fought for for so long. Then at the very last moment the Queen handed the Lord Treasurer's staff not to St. John but to the Duke of Shrewsbury who had joined with the Whig and Tory moderates to save the Protestant succession.

All these developments leading to the climax at the death-bed were watched by Marlborough's practised eye. Deep plans to make George I King had been laid with his support lest at the last moment the Queen surrendered to St. John and accepted the plot for a Jacobite restoration. In the event, these precautions were superfluous. The quarrel between Harley and St. John proved fatal to any effective Tory plan, and the Whigs were able to consummate the victory of which they had been robbed two years earlier. By the time the Duke and Duchess landed at Dover on the day after the Queen's death, nothing more remained for them to do. A few weeks later George I arrived. 'My lord Duke,' he said when the two men met, 'I hope your troubles are now all over.'

All the honours of which Marlborough had once been cheated were now restored. His fortune was saved, and Sarah was soon to add £100,000 to the splendid total by an inspired speculation on the South Sea Bubble. But the real drama of the Duke of Marlborough had ended during the crisis of Christmas, 1711. Other political figures and the overbearing follies of the Tory leaders, not the Duke himself, had been chiefly responsible for his return to favour. In 1715 he directed the campaign against the Jacobite invasion across the Scottish border from an arm-chair in London. For the rest, his day was over. As if to symbolize the end of the age, three of the leading figures—three out of five of the tyrannizing Whig Lords, Lord Wharton, Lord Halifax and Lord Somers—died in the first year of the new reign. A fourth among the jubilant Whigs, the Bishop of Salisbury, Gilbert Burnet, died in the same year, and Jonathan Swift, now safely but miserably installed as the Dean of St. Patrick's Cathedral in Dublin, celebrated the event with an epitaph. At least the poem is attributed to Swift and the internal evidence looks incontestable.

> *Here Sarum lyes*
> *Who was as wise*
> *And Learned as Tom Aquinas.*
> *Lawn Sleeves he wore*
> *Yet was no more*
> *A Christian than Socinus.*
>
> *Oaths pro and con*
> *He Swallow'd down*
> *Loved Gold like any Lay Man*
> *Wrote Preached and pray'd*
> *And yet betrayed*
> *God's Holy Church for Mammon.*
>
> *Of every Vice*
> *He had a Spice*
> *Altho' a learned Prelate*
> *And yet he dyed*
> *If not belyed*
> *A true Dissenting Zealote.*

If such a Soule
To Heaven has stole
And 'scaped old Satan's Clutches
We then assume
There may be a room
for M[arlboroug]h & his D[uche]ss.

Marlborough had seven years to wait for the release from decay and paralysis. When the end came he was given a funeral, the like that never was, costing, it was said, no less than £30,000. One incident which occurred during the preparations for that day might have pleased the Duke more than all the trumpeters and the gorgeous parade. The Tory journalists were not inclined to join the Whig carnival; among them Nathaniel Mist who had been released only a few weeks before from Newgate prison, where he was paying the penalty for his refusal to divulge the names of his contributors before the bar of the House of Commons. *Mist's Journal* recapitulated the magic story of the Captain-General in unsavoury detail, from the surrender of Marlborough's sister to the charms of James II way back in the old days to the Duke's demeanour on the battlefield where 'his conduct was not over-heated with too much personal courage'. A sequel was promised, but it never appeared, for the Whig Ministers of the day acted with a promptitude which the Duke would certainly have approved. Government agents raided Mist's printing house and took the printers off to prison. However, Nathaniel himself was still at large. A week later *Mist's Journal* was on the streets, greatly reduced in size, but not in spirit. 'We must beg our Readers' Pardon', it said, 'for not continuing, as we design'd, the CHARACTER begun in our Last; certain Gentlemen, with GREYHOUNDS at their Breasts, have seiz'd our Materials, desiring, as 'tis supposed, to have the first reading of our Memoirs.' Far away in Dublin Swift also did not let the moment pass. He pursued his vendetta to the grave, producing 'A Satirical Elegy on the Death of a late Famous General'.

His Grace! impossible! what dead!
Of old age too, and in his bed!
And could that Mighty Warrior fall?
And so inglorious after all!

Well, since he's gone, no matter how,
The last loud trump must wake him now:
And, trust me, as the noise grows stronger,
He'd wish to sleep a little longer.
And could he be indeed so old
As by the news-papers we're told:
Threescore, I think, is pretty high;
'Twas time in conscience he should die.
This world he cumber'd long enough;
He burnt his candle to the snuff;
And that's the reason, some folks think,
He left behind so great a s—k.
Behold his funeral appears,
Nor widow's sighs, nor orphan's tears,
Wont at such times each heart to pierce,
Attend the progress of his herse.
But what of that, his friends may say,
He had those honours in his day.
True to his profit and his pride,
He made them weep before he dy'd.

Come hither, all ye empty things,
Ye bubbles rais'd by breath of Kings;
Who float upon the tide of state,
Come hither, and behold your fate.
Let pride be taught by this rebuke,
How very mean a thing's a Duke;
From all his ill-got honours flung,
Turn'd to that dirt from whence he sprung.

*   *   *

To enable the Duke to rest in peace, to make his final victory un-qualified, it would have been necessary to keep Nathaniel Mist and all his villainous associates in Newgate permanently; in short, to make an end of Grub Street. Many others shared this wish, and the deed was almost done. To follow the fate of Grub Street it is necessary to return to the year 1712, after the Duke's removal from power. The Duke's enemies almost succeeded in making his dream come true. Queen Anne was insistent. While the Grand Alliance was strained to breaking-point, and while she must have been fully occupied in the hectic negotiations for the peace, she still required in a message to her Parliament in February 1712 that 'a remedy equal to the mischief' should be found for suppressing 'false and scandalous libels'.

Since Swift's Tory friends were then at the height of their authority, he must have known that the remedy, whatever precise measures it might include, would not be aimed at his own impersonal and objective discussions of public policy; the purpose was to crush the anti-Government libellers. Yet even he was somewhat shaken by the all-inclusive language of the Queen's instruction. He put in a soft word for leniency with the Ministers and reported to Stella without being quite able to suppress a glow of pride in his fellow-craftsmen: 'The Commons are very slow in bringing in their Bill to limit the Press, and the Pamphleteers make good use of their Time for there comes out 3 or 4 every day.' St. John had other cares, but, having discarded the idea that authors should be compelled by law to put their names to their works—perhaps the necessities of Dr. Swift extorted the concession—he still found time to fashion a more ingenious device. 'Grub Street has but ten days to live,' wrote Swift on July 19th, 1712, 'then an Act of Parlmt takes place, that ruins it, by taxing every half-sheet at a half-penny.' The Stamp Tax was intended to put the Whig libellers out of business while the Government still subsidized its own journals. Swift was leaving nothing to chance. In the last fortnight before the axe fell he 'plyed it pretty close and publisht at least 7 penny Papers of my own, besides some other Peoples'.

Then came the day for which Queen Anne had pleaded ever since in her first message to her first Parliament she had denounced the licentiousness of the press. 'This is the day', wrote Joseph Addison in the *Spectator*, 'on which many eminent Authors will probably publish their last words. I am afraid that few of our weekly historians, who are men that above all others delight in war, will be able to subsist under the weight of a stamp and an approaching peace.' Should he in 'this great crisis of the republic of letters' throw up his pen 'as an Author that is cashiered by Act of Parliament'? Addison himself did not dabble in the art of libel. He frowned on the terrible commotions and distortions perpetrated by his fellow-writers. 'Should a foreigner who knows nothing of our private factions, or one who is to act his part in the world, when our present heats and animosities are forgot, should, I say, such an one form to himself a notion of the greatest men of all sides in the *British* nation, who are now living, from the characters which are given them in some or other of those abominable writings which are daily published among us, what a nation of monsters must we appear!' No doubt the verdict was just, but Addison, among all the writers of the age, had the rare and not altogether enviable distinction of never once having offended the Lords, the Commons, the Lord Chief Justice or any other of the lynx-eyed censors who watched their opportunity for enforcing the Queen's will. Moreover, he had financial resources denied to the rest; how would they fare? 'Do you know', wrote Swift to Stella on August 7th, 'that Grub Street is dead and gone last week; No more Ghosts or Murders now for Love or Money . . . Every single half Sheet pays a half penny to the Qu—. The *Observator* is fallen, the *Medleys* are Jumbled together with the *Flying Post*, the *Examiner* is deadly sick, the *Spectator* keeps up, and doubles its price. I know not how long it will hold.' But his mourning was premature. In October 1712 Swift reported again: 'These devils of Grub Street rogues, that write the *Flying-Post* and *Medley* in one paper, will not be quiet. They are always mauling lord treasurer, lord Bolingbroke, and me. We have a dog under prosecution, but Bolingbroke is not active enough; but I hope to swinge him. He is a Scotch rogue, one Ridpath. They get out upon bail, and write on. We take them again, and get fresh bail; and so it goes round.'

Ridpath was eventually forced to flee the country. Robert Walpole, finding that no one would dare to print one of his pamphlets, had to set up a press in his own house. Many Whig writers were driven underground; the more intense the campaign against them, the more fiercely they lashed out. But Grub Street did not die. Nothing could kill it, not even the combined exertions of Tory Ministers who harried the Whigs and a Whig Lord Chief Justice who harried the Tories.

As her reign drew to its close poor Queen Anne was compelled to watch the licentiousness of the press successfully defying every form of censorship, new and old. Daniel Defoe resorted to his favourite method of irony which had first landed him in Newgate— and back he went to Newgate again. Like Swift himself, he was totally unaware of the intrigues with the Pretender conducted by

the masters he served. He wrote three pamphlets satirically exposing the charge that the Ministers were engaged in so devilish a
plot. At once the Whig Lord Chief Justice pounced—the same
Chief Justice Parker who had once tried to catch Swift—and
Defoe was only saved by the intervention of the Ministers. Free
but infuriated, he demanded action against Richard Steele who had
exposed the dangers to the Protestant Succession in his famous
pamphlet, *The Crisis*, published daringly under his own name.
Steele was expelled from the House of Commons. Swift pursued
him in his pamphlet *The Public Spirit of the Whigs*, whereupon the
House of Lords took Swift's publisher and printer into custody
and offered a reward of £300 for the discovery of the author. But,
thanks partly to Harley's assistance, Swift was protected.

Only a few more weeks remained of the age of Anne, the first
age of the printing press. How Swift would have survived if
Queen Anne had made him a Bishop and if he had lived on in
England in the years of the Whig hegemony no one can tell.
Within a few weeks of the Queen's death he was on the road back
to Dublin and Laracor. Neither Harley nor St. John had exerted
themselves (perhaps they thought the effort hopeless) to win for
him the preferment he desired. Swift had to be content with a
Deanery and was deeply disappointed, but never once did he
betray his friendship to either of the two Ministers he had served
so faithfully, even when at last they became mortal enemies.
There, in his land of exile, in the thirty years that followed, he
used the searing insight into the ways of politicians which he had
learnt in London to become the national hero of Ireland and to
write *Gulliver's Travels*. There he lived a life of frustration,
despite all the cheers which greeted him through the Dublin
streets; there at last he died—as he himself once prophesied he
would—like a 'poisoned rat in a hole'.

★   ★   ★

What happened to the others? St. John lost his nerve or his clarity
of purpose at the final test when the Queen was dying. He strutted
brashly in court society for a few months after King George's
Coronation and then, on a hint from Marlborough (perhaps
maliciously planted) that his life was in danger, fled to France into
the arms of the Pretender. Only after eight years was the Act of
Attainder against him lifted. Allowed back to England, but not to

his seat in the House of Lords, he survived until the middle of the century as a frustrated orator, a superficial philosopher and a brilliant journalist. Harley preferred to face the music. He went calmly as ever to the Tower, calmly faced his impeachment, watched most of his accusers, with the notable exception of Marlborough, abate their passion against him, and was permitted to die quietly, happy in the thought that he had used his own trial to turn the worst vindictiveness of his enemies against St. John.

Others in the cast ended their days in oblivion. Lord and Lady Masham made a speedy withdrawal to the country before George I arrived in London; neither was ever heard of again. Mrs. Manley, or whoever was in charge of the *Examiner*, closed the paper down with abrupt discretion before the heralds could raise the cry of 'Long live the King!' The Duchess of Somerset stayed at the Queen's side all through the years of Tory victory; in the last hour around the bedside her moment came. She was able to help guide the Lord Treasurer's White Staff into Shrewsbury's hands and thus perform her last service for the Hanoverian and Protestant cause. Swift, it seems, had been right after all in his fears about the witchcraft which might be wrought by Carrots of Northumberland. Her Duke was there too. Dismissed a few days after Marlborough, he returned to wreak his vengeance on St. John and Harley. He was not offered the highest office which he craved, but the proud Duke aspired to even greater things. Years later, when his own Duchess had died, he made his proposal of marriage to Sarah, to which she gave the superb reply: 'If I were young and handsome as I was, instead of old and faded as I am, and you could lay the empire of the world at my feet, you should never share the heart and hand that once belonged to John, Duke of Marlborough.'

Sarah lived on till the age of eighty-five. The story of her tantrums and her feuds with all who crossed her path has been told a hundred times. Swift had once summed up her character. 'Three Furies', he said, 'reigned in her breast, the most mortal enemies of all softer passions, which were sordid Avarice, disdainful Pride and ungovernable Rage.' Those last years seemed to confirm the stark analysis. But powerful minds are often made to look ridiculous when, instead of dealing with great affairs, they must spend all their energies on the most petty business of their families and their households. Sarah has suffered from the blaze of light which surrounds her long widowhood. She stands exposed as a rancorous old woman, while the proofs of her foresight as the leader of the Whigs in her greatest days are lost in obscurity. It was always, we are asked to believe, the same Sarah, cantankerous, meddling, disrupting by her spleen the requisite political combinations contrived by the Duke. Need we look further for the cause of his destruction? Did not Sarah by her quarrel with Anne open the backstairs to Abigail and Harley? This is the popular tale, but it is little better than a half-truth. Sarah quarrelled with Anne for political as well as personal reasons; Marlborough could have forestalled the catastrophe if he had been ready to adopt Sarah's remedy.

The real political battles of the reign were not fought in the palace; Parliament and the coffee-houses provided the arena where Whig and Tory were locked in deadly combat and, for all the corruption and motives of personal gain, large principles of national policy were the stake in the contest. Sarah recognized the truth. Even when Marlborough's friends had been expelled from office and the General Election had returned a Tory majority to the Commons, much might have been done to save the situation. But while Sarah respected the new force of public opinion and looked for means to direct it in her favour, the Duke despised the new engine of the printing press hardly less than Queen Anne herself. The Duke, despite his cultured demeanour, did not read books; Sarah did, and she developed a style of her own which would have made her a power in Grub Street as assuredly as she would have been a hero in the Parliament House.

During that wretched quarter of a century when she worked so tirelessly to revenge herself on her enemies, to multiply her wealth and to complete the parapets of Blenheim, one gleam of real pleasure may be seen to cross her countenance. It is the proof at once of the magnanimous streak in her character and of her understanding, wiser than the Duke's, of the politics of her age. For, in those last years, the Duchess paid her respects to Jonathan Swift.

Much earlier, in the days of strife, she had suspected him and had never underrated his powers. 'One great piece of art (undertaken by the Tory Ministers)', she wrote, 'was to spread the vilest calumnies and falsest stories of those who were to be attacked, all over the nation. For which purpose some underworkmen of prostituted consciences and hardened faces were necessary. They were not long seeking for such, when once the power of rewarding was seen to be in their hands, or to be certainly coming to them. The Rev. Mr. Swift and Mr. Prior quickly offered themselves to sale (besides a number of more ordinary scribblers); both men of wit and parts ready to prostitute all they had in the service of well-rewarded scandal, being both of a composition past the weakness of blushing or of a stumbling at anything for the interest of their new masters. The former of these had long ago turned all religion into a Tale of a Tub, and sold it for a jest. But he had taken it ill that the ministry had not promoted him in the Church for the great zeal he had shown for religion by his profane drollery; and so carried his atheism and his humour into the service of their enemies. They are now raising a great outcry against profaneness and deism and the like. And one of their first tools to be encouraged and promoted was a lewd libertine and an open ridiculer of all inspiration.'

This, however, was only the first, hasty judgement. In November, 1726, *Gulliver's Travels* was published. Within a few days the town knew that Sarah was 'in raptures at it'. John Gay and Alexander Pope reported eagerly to Swift: 'She says she can dream of nothing else since she read it; she declares that she has now found out, that her whole life has been lost in caressing the worst part of mankind, and treating the best as her foes; and that if she knew Gulliver, though he had been the worst enemy she ever had, she should give up her present acquaintance for his friendship.' How Swift received this tribute from 'the detested Slut' is unfortunately not recorded.

No one could say that the enthusiasm of the Duchess was transient. Ten years later she was telling Lord Stair that 'Swift gives the most exact account of Kings, ministers, bishops and courts of justice that is possible to be writ'. She was 'prodigiously fond of him'; she 'could easily forgive him all the slaps he has given me and the Duke of Marlborough'. This unique instance of Sarah's forgiving nature may be attributed to no more than the weakness of old age. But no sign of senile decay appears in the other judgement which she passed on her great adversary. Swift in his new disguise as the Drapier of Dublin had recently been engaged in a fight with the English Government over the issue of Wood's half-pence. He had won another victory by his pen only less spectacular than the one he helped secure for Harley and St. John. Sarah, normally so sparing in her compliments, was greatly impressed. 'He has certainly a vast wit,' she wrote, 'and since he could contribute so much to the pulling down the most honest and best-intentioned ministry that ever I knew, with the help only of Abigail and one or two more, and has certainly stopped the finishing stroke to ruin the Irish in the project of the half-pence, in spite of all the ministry could do, I could not help wishing that we had had his assistance in the opposition.'

No tribute to Swift as 'the prince of journalists' could be more conclusive. The thought of the stiff-jointed and indomitable old Duchess sitting up in bed and lamenting—'if only *he* had been on our side'—might have been enough, if the report had ever reached him, to achieve the miracle of softening Dr. Swift.

Whigs and Tories

I HAVE USED THE TERMS 'Whig' and 'Tory' to indicate the two main political parties in the state without raising in any detail the question of how these names should be applied.

Of course, the Whig and Tory parties of Queen Anne's time were not parties in the modern sense. They did not possess the paraphernalia of elected or nominated leaders, party conferences or national organizations. Yet, as I have occasionally suggested, many of the features of our present party system were being developed. A form of discipline prevailed within the two parties, both in the House of Lords and the House of Commons, in the sense that leading Ministers used the threat of resignation or the disruption of the administration to rally their followers. Harley used this implied threat to defeat the manœuvres of the October Club. Even in opposition, Lord Wharton and his Whig associates in the House of Lords were able—as a party manœuvre designed to unseat the Ministry—to engage all their followers to vote for an Occasional Conformity Bill which, on its merits, the Whigs traditionally detested. Considering how novel was the idea of party, the cohesion of the Whigs or the Tories strikes me as a more remarkable fact than their apparent lack of homogeneity compared with modern political parties.

When the Queen was choosing her Ministers their command of a party following in the Commons or the Lords entered into her calculations much less than today. The Cabinet Council was not a cohesive body, with its members bearing collective responsibility. Both the predominantly Whig Ministry of Lord Godolphin which was overthrown in the autumn of 1710 and the predominantly Tory Ministry which succeeded it were 'coalitions'. This term is an anachronism, but I have used it frequently as the most convenient to describe Ministries which contained minorities from the other party or persons whose party affiliation was much looser than that of their colleagues. 'Coalition' Ministries were obviously the rule, not the exception. Yet, even on this aspect of the matter, it is remarkable how strong was the pressure to make the Queen choose her servants in the main from one party. Witness the drive of the Whig Junto before 1709 to enforce their presence on the Queen, or the refusal of the Tories, notably St. John in 1711, to tolerate the continuance in office of a Whig Lord like the Duke of Somerset.

Of course, too, there were manifold shades of opinion within both parties and in between them a considerable number of Lords or Commoners who gave their allegiance to the court rather than to either party. The Tories ranged from the 'High Flyers', the 'Arbitrary' or 'Rigid' Tories, to the 'Moderates' or the 'Whimsicals', who rarely abandoned the idea of a combination with the Whigs, as a counterpoise to their own extremists. The Whigs, likewise, ranged from the 'Moderates' (or, as we have seen, to take one example, the Juntilla which for a period set itself up in opposition to the Whig Junto) to those whose opposition to passive obedience was so strong that they were almost Republicans. Such gradations of party enthusiasm are not altogether unknown in our day of the strict party machines.

Altogether, then, once the necessary qualifications have been made, I do not believe that the terms 'Whig' and 'Tory', used to describe political parties with continuing traditions, give a misleading impression. During the days of Queen Anne, whatever may have happened afterwards, the battle between recognizable parties—and not merely a tussle between powerful families and groups—governed the political scene. Many prominent persons—Marlborough and Harley, for example, hardly less than the Queen—detested this development but they could not thereby conjure it out of existence.

It is necessary to state that the whole of this conception has been challenged. Mr. Robert Walcott, an American historian, has spent twenty years of study in producing his book *English Politics in the Early Eighteenth Century* (Oxford University Press). He has analysed in detail the occupations of members of Parliament, their family connexions and the division lists, and has reached the conclusion that the terms 'Whig' and 'Tory' cannot be safely employed in the sense I have stated. His findings have not been swallowed whole by British historians, but equally they have not been violently repudiated. So great an expert, for example, as Mr. J. H. Plumb, the biographer of Sir Robert Walpole, gives his verdict thus: 'Certainly when analysed in terms of faction, the politics at Court and in Parliament gain in depth. To some extent, however, Professor Walcott overplays his thesis and relies too heavily on genealogical evidence. He underestimates, I think, the coherence of the Whigs and the power of party attachments, particularly in the constituencies, which he has not studied in detail. At times, as with the so-called Newcastle-Townshend-Walpole faction, he overvalues the force of family relationships. Nevertheless this is a book of real value for the eighteenth century historian.'

Mr. Plumb's criticism of Mr. Walcott's book, I believe, is insufficiently severe. Consider for a moment Mr. Walcott's general conclusion. 'The process by which the Godolphin ministry changed from a Court–Churchill–Harley–Rochester–Nottingham coalition into a Court–Churchill–Newcastle–Junto combination is a logical one, if one recognizes that the architects of governments and parliamentary majorities worked within a multi-party framework. This assumption often fits the facts far better than the two-party interpretation; but the party history of the period 1688–1714 has been explained so universally in terms of 'Whig and 'Tory' exclusively, that the many similarities between it and the later eighteenth century political structure have been commonly overlooked. The more one studies the party structure under William and Anne, the less it resembles the two-party system described by Trevelyan in his Romanes Lecture and the more it seems to have in common with the structure of politics in the Age of Newcastle as explained to us by Namier.'

One difficulty presented by this interpretation is that most of the leading figures of the time would have found it unrecognizable as a portrait of the political struggle in which they were engaged. Whether they liked the system or not, they never ceased to talk of 'the two parties'. Queen Anne prayed for liberation from 'the merciless men of both parties'. Marlborough wrote to Godolphin: 'There is nothing more certaine than what you say that either of the Partys wou'd be tyrants if they were left alone, and I am afraid it is as true that it will be very heard for the queen to prevent itt.' Harley said: 'I dread the thoughts of running from the extreme of one faction to another which is the natural consequence of party tyranny, and renders the government like a door which turns both ways upon its hinges to let in each party as it grows triumphant, and in truth this is the real parent and nurse of our factions here.'

That is an apposite, if jaundiced, account of what did actually occur. The metaphor describes the two-party system which Mr. Walcott comes near to dismissing as a figment. How much would Harley have preferred to see the facts fitting into the multi-party framework! After one election Lord Godolphin did not refrain from listing the results in a manner which would certainly stand condemned according to Mr. Walcott's scholarship. 'My computation runs thus,' he wrote to Harley. 'Of the 450 that chose the Speaker Tories 190, Whigs 160, Queen's servants 100'; the last two, he reckoned, could usually be counted upon to vote together. Never is Mr. Walcott so slipshod as Lord Godolphin; he would blench at the idea of referring indiscriminately to 160 plain, unconnected Whigs.

Politicians, even in those days, did not always testify to their principles in the voting lobbies. Personal interests and changing opinions often produced the severance of party allegiances. However, here we can adduce the exception to prove the rule. The most spectacular apostasy of the reign was Lord Nottingham's desertion of the Tories in December 1711. But he did not carry the whole of his family 'connexion' with him in the act of desertion and the event was marked in all quarters as one of the greatest magnitude and denounced by the Tories as an offence worthy of the strongest rebuke. If apostasies had been so common and the ties of party so weak, it is hard to believe that the indignation of the Tories would have been so marked.

A further flaw in Mr. Walcott's thesis is that it makes the writings of many of the journalists of the time wellnigh incomprehensible. Jonathan Swift hated, or affected to hate, the party system; he spent much of his time elaborately explaining that the modern Tories inherited the best of the old Whiggery. If the distinction in men's minds at the time even between such a 'moderate' Whig as Lord Halifax and such a 'moderate' Tory as Harley had not been fairly clear, Swift's explanations would have been superfluous. Daniel Defoe advanced a more paradoxical theory. He argued over a period of months that the Tories, despite all their extremist propaganda, would be compelled to behave like Whigs once they assumed office. If the divergent conceptions of 'Whig' and 'Tory' had not been well established in the public mind, the point would not have been worth making. As it happens, both Swift and Defoe were erstwhile Whigs who turned to serve the Tories. They were cursed for their waywardness by their fellow-craftsmen who showed a stronger sense of party loyalty. All the journalists were ceaselessly engaged in defining and re-defining the doctrines which distinguished Whigs from Tories. They thought the two-party battle was real. Certainly they would have been surprised by Mr. Walcott's discovery that they were mere tools in a contest decided by the manœuvre of family con-nexions.

When men like Godolphin and Swift spoke so frequently of a two-party system, it may be pardonable for us to do the same. Mr. Walcott's warning against the misuse of these terms may have no greater significance than Mark Twain's theory about Homer. The Iliad, he concluded, after long study, was not written by Homer but by another person of the same name.

Notes on Sources

THE NUMBER OF BOOKS about Swift, Marlborough and the reign of Queen Anne generally is huge. In this selected list I have attempted to refer only to those books, ancient and modern, from which most assistance has been derived. If I have omitted any of major importance I must apologize.

I owe a special word of gratitude to the authors or editors of about a dozen books on which anyone who writes about Swift or Marlborough must chiefly rely. Of course, they are not responsible for my opinions and many of them might wish to disown the conclusions I have reached. But no doubt is possible about the scale of my indebtedness.

On Jonathan Swift, there are six major works on which I have been dependent both for the text of Swift's writings and the editorial notes. At the head of the list stand the two princely works by Harold Williams—his edition of Swift's *Journal to Stella* (Clarendon Press) and *The Poems of Jonathan Swift* (Clarendon Press). All my quotations from the journal and the poems are taken from these editions. Three other editions have proved hardly less valuable—*The Prose Works of Jonathan Swift*, edited by Temple Scott (George Bell & Sons); *The Correspondence of Jonathan Swift*, edited by F. Elrington Ball (George Bell & Sons); and *The Letters of Jonathan Swift to Charles Ford*, edited by David Nichol Smith (Clarendon Press). Most of my quotations from Swift's prose writings (apart from the *Journal*) are taken from the Temple Scott edition. I have on occasion, however, used the text of the actual copies of the *Examiner* or individual pamphlets which are in my possession. The Shakespeare Head edition of *The Prose Works of Jonathan Swift*, edited by Herbert Davis (Basil Blackwell) was appearing while I was reading for this book. It is, of course, a wonderful production, but I have preferred for the most part to use the Temple Scott edition with which I was more familiar.

Of the innumerable lives of Swift I have found the most valuable to be *Jonathan Swift*, by John Middleton Murry (Jonathan

Cape); *The Life of Jonathan Swift*, by Henry Craik (John Murray); *The Mind and Art of Jonathan Swift*, by Ricardo Quintana (Methuen); *Jonathan Swift*, by Bertram Newman (Allen & Unwin); and *The Life of Jonathan Swift*, by John Forster (Harper & Brothers, New York).

On the Duke of Marlborough, my principal debt is due to Winston Churchill's *Marlborough, His Life and Times* (Harrap & Co.). No other book on the subject deserves to be mentioned in the same breath. Except for one quotation on the title page, I have not quoted Sir Winston directly, but several quotations have come from Sir Winston's selection of the Duke's letters. The rest come from the still valuable *Memoirs of John, Duke of Marlborough*, by Archdeacon Coxe (Bohn's Library) or from various volumes of the Historical Manuscripts Commission (listed below).

On the Duchess of Marlborough, I owe most to her own *Account of the Conduct of the Dowager Duchess of Marlborough*, reprinted in *Memoirs of the Duchess of Marlborough* (Routledge) and her *Private Correspondence* (Henry Colburn). She speaks for herself much better than anyone else.

Apart from the newspapers, periodicals and pamphlets of the time, which are to be found in the British Museum or the London Library, and some of which I have collected myself over the years, I feel that the writings of two of Swift's contemporaries should be specially mentioned.

The first is Abel Boyer, the Huguenot journalist to whom I have often referred in the text. His three works—*The History of the Reign of Queen Anne Digested into Annals*, *The Political State of Great Britain* and *The History of the Life and Reign of Queen Anne*—not only contain a wealth of information about the politics and journalism of the time; they deserve also, in my opinion, to rank high both for the quality of their writing and their political judgments. Abel Boyer is a name much less well known than that of Daniel Defoe. But as a journalist he is surely Defoe's equal and as an historian he stands much higher. However, my debt to Daniel Defoe's *Review* (Facsimile Text Society, Columbia University Press) is also immense.

The other books chiefly consulted are as follows:

ACWORTH, BERNARD: *Swift* (Eyre & Spottiswoode).

CASE, ARTHUR E.: *Four Essays on Gulliver's Travels* (Princeton University Press).

COLLINS, JOHN CHURTON: *Jonathan Swift: a biographical and critical Study* (Chatto & Windus).

DELANY, PATRICK: *Observations upon Lord Orrery's Remarks on the life and writings of Dr. Jonathan Swift.*

DILKE, CHARLES WENTWORTH: 'Swift, etc." in his *Papers of a Critic* (John Murray).

EWALD, WILLIAM B.: *The Masks of Jonathan Swift* (Basil Blackwell).

FIRTH, C. H.: 'Dean Swift and ecclesiastical preferment', in *Review of English Studies*, II (1928).
The Political Significance of Gulliver's Travels (Proceedings of the British Academy 1919–1920).

HAY, JAMES: *Swift: the mystery of his life and love* (Chapman & Hall).

HILL, GEORGE BIRKBECK: *Unpublished Letters of Dean Swift* (Fisher Unwin).

JACKSON, ROBERT WYSE: *Jonathan Swift: Dean and Pastor* (London Society for Promoting Christian Knowledge).

JOHNSON, SAMUEL: 'Swift' in his *Lives of the English Poets* (Everyman).

LESLIE, SHANE: *The Skull of Swift* (Chatto & Windus).

LEYBURN, ELLEN D.: 'Swift's view of the Dutch' in *Publications of the Modern Language Association* LXVI (1951).

ORRERY, 5TH EARL OF, JOHN BOYLE: *Remarks on the life and writings of Dr. Jonathan Swift.*

PAUL, HERBERT: 'The Prince of Journalists' in his *Men and Letters.*

QUINTANA, RICARDO: *Swift: an introduction* (Oxford University Press).

ROSSI, MARIO M. and JOSEPH M. HONE: *Swift or The Egotist* (Gollancz).

SCOTT, SIR WALTER: *The Works of Jonathan Swift* (Edinburgh, 1824).

SHERIDAN, THOMAS: *The Life of Rev. Dr. Jonathan Swift.*

TAYLOR, WILLIAM D.: *Jonathan Swift* (Peter Davies).

THACKERAY, W. M.: 'Swift' in his *English Humorists of the Eighteenth Century.*

THOMAS, JOSEPH M.: 'Swift and the Stamp Act of 1712' in the *Publications of the Modern Language Association*, XXXI (1916).

WHIBLEY, CHARLES: *Jonathan Swift* (Cambridge University Press).

FOR THE DUKE OF MARLBOROUGH

ASHLEY, MAURICE: *Marlborough* (Duckworth).

LEDIARD, THOMAS: *Life of John, Duke of Marlborough.*

MURRAY, SIR GEORGE: *Letters and Dispatches of John Churchill, Duke of Marlborough* (John Murray).

REID, STUART J.: *John and Sarah, Duke and Duchess of Marlborough* (John Murray).

ROWSE, A. L.: *The Early Churchills* (Macmillan).

FOR THE DUCHESS OF MARLBOROUGH

CAMPBELL, KATHLEEN: *Sarah, Duchess of Marlborough* (Thornton Butterworth).

CHANCELLOR, FRANK: *Sarah Churchill* (Philip Allan).

DOBRÉE, BONAMY: *Sarah Churchill* (Gerald Howe).

FIELDING, HENRY: *A Full Vindication of the Dowager Duchess of Marlborough.*

MANLEY, MRS.: *The Secret History of Queen Zarah.*

THOMSON, A. T.: *Memoirs of the Duchess of Marlborough* (Henry Colburn).

FOR HENRY ST. JOHN

COLLINS, J. CHURTON: *Bolingbroke* (John Murray).

FIELDHOUSE, H. N.: 'Bolingbroke and the D'Iberville Correspondence' *English Historical Review*, Vol. LII.

HASSALL, ARTHUR: *Life of Viscount Bolingbroke* (Basil Blackwell).

MACKNIGHT, THOMAS: *Life of Viscount Bolingbroke* (Chapman & Hall).

PARKE, G.: *Letters and Correspondence of Henry St. John, Viscount Bolingbroke.*

PETRIE, SIR CHARLES: *Bolingbroke* (Collins).

SICHEL, WALTER: *Bolingbroke and His Times* (Nisbet & Co.).

STEBBING, WILLIAM: *Some Verdicts of History Reviewed* (John Murray).

FOR ROBERT HARLEY

MILLER, O. B.: *Robert Harley* (Basil Blackwell).

ROSCOE, E. S.: *Robert Harley, Earl of Oxford* (Methuen).

HISTORICAL MANUSCRIPTS COMMISSION: *Portland Papers and Papers of the Marquess of Bath at Longleat.*

FOR DANIEL DEFOE

DEFOE'S *Review* (Facsimile Text Society).

DEFOE: 'The Poor Man's Plea' (1708).

'Reasons Why This Nation ought to put a speedy END to this Expensive War.'

'The Secret History of the White Staff.'

'A Tour through England and Wales' (*Everyman*).

FITZGERALD, BRIAN: *Daniel Defoe* (Secker & Warburg).

FREEMAN, WILLIAM: *The Incredible Defoe* (Herbert Jenkins).

HEALEY, G. H.: *The Letters of Daniel Defoe* (Oxford University Press).

MOORE, J. R.: *Defoe in the Pillory.*

SUTHERLAND, JAMES: *Defoe* (Methuen).

FOR NEWSPAPERS (*particularly Chapter III*)

BALJAME, ALEXANDRE: *Men and letters and the English Public in the Eighteenth Century.* Edited with an introduction and notes by Bonamy Dobrée (Kegan Paul).

BOURNE, H. R. FOX: *English Newspapers* (Chatto & Windus).

DUNTON, JOHN: *Life and Errors of John Dunton.*

GRANT, JAMES: *The Newspaper Press* (Tinsley Brothers).

HANSON, LAURENCE: *Government and the Press.*

HUNT, E. H.: *The Fourth Estate* (David Bogue).

GENERAL

AITKEN, G. A.: *Life and Works of John Arbuthnot* (Oxford).

ALLEN, R. J.: *The Clubs of Augustan London.*

ASHTON, J.: *Social Life in the Reign of Queen Anne* (Chatto & Windus).

BAKER, COLLIN and MURIEL: *The Life and Circumstances of James Brydges, First Duke of Chandos* (Oxford).

BERWICK, DUKE OF: *Memoirs*.

BICKLEY, FRANCIS: *Life of Mathew Prior* (Pitman).

BLANCHARD, RAE: *The Correspondence of Richard Steele* (Oxford).

BURNET, GILBERT: *History of His Own Time* (Oxford).

CAMPBELL, LORD: *Lives of the Chancellors* (John Murray).

CARSWELL, JOHN: *The Old Cause* (Cresset Press).

CHAMBERLAYNE, J.: *Angliae Notitia or the Present State of England*.

CHANDLER, RICHARD: *The History of the Proceedings of the House of Commons from the Restoration to the Present Time*.

CLARK, G. N.: *The Later Stuarts* (Oxford).

COBBETT, WILLIAM (editor): *Parliamentary History of England*, Vol. VII.

CONNELL, NEVILLE: *Anne, The Last Stuart Monarch* (Thornton Butterworth).

CONNELLY, WILLIAM: *Sir Richard Steele* (Jonathan Cape).

CROKER AND ELWIN: *The Works of Alexander Pope* (John Murray)

COWPER, EARL: *Private Diary* (Roxburgh Club).

COXE, W. C.: *Life and Administration of Sir Robert Walpole*.

COXE, W.: *Private and Original Correspondence of Charles Talbot, Duke of Shrewsbury*.

CUNNINGHAM, A.: *The History of Great Britain from the Revolution of 1688 to the Accession of George I.*

CURTIS BROWN, B.: *Anne Stuart, Queen of England* (Geoffrey Bles). *The Letters of Queen Anne* (Cassell).

ELLIOT, H.: *Sidney, Earl of Godolphin* (Longmans).

EWALD, WILLIAM B.: *The Newsmen of Queen Anne* (Basil Blackwell).

FEILING, KEITH: *A History of the Tory Party (1640–1714)*, (Oxford).

GEIKIE, R. and I. MONTGOMERY: *The Dutch Barrier (1705–19)*, (Cambridge University Press).

HANMER, SIR THOMAS: *Correspondence* (ed. Sir H. Bunbury).

HEARNE, THOMAS: *Collections* (edited C. E. Doble).

KLOPP, ONNO: *Der Fall des Hauses Stuart*.

KRONENBERGER, LOUIS: *Kings and Desperate Men* (Gollancz).

LAPRADE, W. T.: *Public Opinion and Politics in Eighteenth-century England.*

LEADHAM, I. S.: *Political History of England* 1702–60 (Longmans & Co.).

LEGG, WICKHAM: *Mathew Prior* (Cambridge).

LECKY, W. E. H.: *History of England in the Eighteenth Century*, Vol. I (Longmans).

LEVER TRESHAM: *Godolphin, His Life and Times* (John Murray).

LOCKHART, GEORGE: *The Lockhart Papers* (William Anderson)

LUTTRELL, NARCISSUS: *A Brief Historical Relation of State Affairs.*

MACAULAY, LORD: *The History of England*, edited by Sir Charles Firth (Macmillan).

MACKY, JOHN: *Memoirs of the Secret Service.*

MACPHERSON, JAMES: *Original Papers containing the Secret History of Great Britain.*

MELVILLE, LEWIS: *In the Days of Queen Anne* (Hutchinson).

MERZ, TERESA: *The Junto* (Andrew Reid).

MORGAN, W. T.: 'The General Election of 1710' in *Political Science Quarterly*, Vol. XIV.
English Political Parties and Leaders in the Reign of Queen Anne (Yale Press).

NICHOLLS, JOHN: *Illustrations of the Literary History of the Eighteenth Century.*
Literary Anecdotes of the Eighteenth Century.

NICHOLSON, T. C. and A. S. TURBERVILLE: *Charles Talbot, Duke of Shrewsbury* (Cambridge University Press.)

OLDMIXON: *Life and Works of Arthur Maynwaring.*

OLIVER, F. S.: *The Endless Adventure* (Macmillan & Co.).

PAUL, HERBERT: *Queen Anne* (Hodder & Stoughton).

PLUMB, J. H.: *Sir Robert Walpole* (Cresset Press).

SCOTT, WALTER (editor): *Somers Tracts.*

SOMERVILLE, T.: *History of Great Britain during the Reign of Queen Anne.*

STANHOPE, EARL: *History of the Reign of Queen Anne* (John Murray).

STRICKLAND, AGNES: *Lives of the Queens of England.*

SUTHERLAND, JAMES: *Background for Queen Anne* (Methuen).

SMITHERS, PETER: *Life of Joseph Addison* (Clarendon Press).

THOMSON, MARK A.: *The Secretary of State, 1681–1708* (Oxford).

THORNTON, P. M.: 'The Hanover Papers' (1695–1719) *English Historical Review,* Vol. I.

TINDAL, N.: *Continuation of Rapin's History.*

TORCY, MARQUIS DE: *Memoires.*

TREVELYAN, G. M.: *England under Queen Anne* (Longmans).
'The Jersey Period of the Utrecht Negotiations,' *English Historical Review,* Vol. XLIX.

TURBERVILLE, A. S.: *The House of Lords in the XVIIIth Century* (Oxford).

UFFENBACH, Z. C.: *London in 1710.*

VON RANKE, LEOPOLD: *History of England.*

WENTWORTH, THOMAS: *The Wentworth Papers* (edited J. J. Cartwright).

WILLIAMS, BASIL: *Stanhope* (Clarendon Press).

WYON, F. W.: *History of Great Britain during the Reign of Anne* (Chapman & Hall).

Dictionary of National Biography.

HISTORICAL MANUSCRIPTS COMMISSION REPORTS:
'Bath Papers,' Vols. I, III (1904) (Harley, Shrewsbury, St. John and Marlborough correspondence).
'Dartmouth Papers' (1889).
'Downshire Papers' (1924). (Queen's death).
'Hare Papers' (1895). (Francis Hare, Chaplain-General.)
'Mar Papers' (1904). (Jacobite correspondence.)
'Marlborough Papers' (1881).
'Portland Papers,' Vols. II, IV, V, VII (1897). (Harley correspondence.)
'Round Papers' (1895). (Petkum correspondence.)
'Russell-Frankland-Astley Papers' (1900).
'Seafield Papers' (1894). (Godolphin letters.)
'Stuart Papers,' Vol. I. (1902). (Jacobite correspondence).
'Townshend Papers' (1887).

Index